THE PEOPLE'S WAR IN NEPAL
Left Perspectives

The views expressed in the chapters of this book are those of authors and do not, however, necessarily reflect the opinions of those of editors and publisher of the book.

THE PEOPLE'S WAR IN NEPAL
Left Perspectives

by

Arjun Karki
David Seddon

ADROIT PUBLISHERS
DELHI-110 002

Published by
ADROIT PUBLISHERS
4675/21, Ganpati Bhawan, Ansari Road,
Daryaganj, New Delhi-110 002
Phones : 23266030, 23242552

Distributors
AKHIL BOOK DISTRIBUTORS
e-mail: akhilbooks@yahoo.com
akhilbooks@hotmail.com

All rights reserved

© Editors, 2003

No part of this publication may be reproduced or transmitted
in any form or by any means, electronic or mechanical,
including photocopying, recording, or any information
storage and retrieval system, without permission
in writing from the publisher.

Requests for permission to make copies of
any part of the work should be mailed to:
Copyrights & Permissions Department
ADROIT PUBLISHERS

ISBN : 81-87392-38-X

Layout
Sudhir Vatsa

Laser Typeset by
Nidhi Laser Point
e-mail: nidhi_vatsa@hotmail.com

Printed in India on behalf of M/s Adroit Publishers by
Arpit Printographers, B-7, Saraswati Complex,
Subhash Chowk, Laxmi Nagar, Delhi-110 092

Contents

Introduction —*Arjun Karki & David Seddon*	*vii*
Short Introduction to the Contributors	*xxiii*

PART ONE
OVERVIEW

1. The People's War in Historical Context —*Arjun Karki & David Seddon*	3
2. Introduction to 'The People's War' and Its Implicatons —*Mukunda Kattel*	49

PART TWO
MAOIST PERSPECTIVES

3. Inside the Revolution in Nepal —*Puspa Kamal Dahal* (Prachanda)	75
4. The Political Economy of the People's War —*Babu Ram Bhattarai*	117
5. Women's Participation in the People's War —*Comrade Parvati*	165
6. Maoist Statements & Documents 6.1. The Maoists' 40-Point Demands	183

6.2. March Along the Path of People's War to Smash the Reactionary State and Establish a New Democratic State!
6.3. Review of the Historic Initiation (Launch) of the People's War and Future Strategy of the Party
6.4. One Year of the People's War in Nepal
6.5. Two Momentous Years of Revolutionary Transformation
6.6. Experiences of the People's War and Some Important Questions
6.7. The Third Turbulent Year of the People's War
6.8. The Second National Conference
6.9. A Great Achievement: Prachanda Path
6.10. However Tortuous the Road, the Victory of World Proletarian Revolution is Certain
6.11. A Rejoinder on Some Current Issues
6.12. The Furious One Speaks

PART THREE
LEFT PERSPECTIVES

7. The Maoist Movement in Nepal: A Class Perspective — *Govinda Neupane* — 291

8. The Royal Palace Massacre and the Maoists' Pro-King Political Line — *Mohan Bikram Singh* — 315

9. The Maoist Movement in Nepal: An Analysis from the Women's Perspective — *Sujita Shakya* — 375

10. The Maoist Movement and Its Impact in Nepal — *Pradip Nepal* — 405

11. A Radical Reform Agenda for Conflict Resolution in Nepal — *Arjun Karki* — 438

References and Bibliography — 477

Index — 483

Introduction

In February 1996, the Communist Party of Nepal (Maoist), operating as the United People's Front of Nepal, declared the start of a 'People's War' in Nepal. Pointing to the failure of the new regime instituted following the People's Movement (*Jana Andolan*) and of successive governments since 1990 to bring genuine democracy and broad-based development to the people of Nepal, they argued that only a revolutionary armed struggle could create the basis for the overthrow and replacement of the corrupt and inadequate ruling classes by a popular democratic republic representing the workers and peasants of Nepal. They had prepared for this struggle during the previous 2 years and now launched a programme that drew its inspiration from the many revolutionary rural movements that have taken similar initiatives in Africa, Asia and Latin America during the twentieth century, basing themselves in the remote and isolated hill districts of the mid-west of the country, while aiming to expand throughout the country and create a revolution in Nepal.

The People's War, as the Maoists refer to their revolutionary struggle, is now in its seventh year. Despite the efforts of the state to re-establish control, notably through two notorious police operations, Operation Romeo and Operation Kilo Sierra-II, the rebellion gained considerable support during the first 4 years and progressively, in a well-defined phased programme, extended its activities and its scale across the country, from its 'heartlands' in the hills of the mid-west of Nepal. In the last 3 years, the success of the Maoists and the increasing effect on Nepali economy and society, not to say politics, of the ongoing struggle has become a matter of central concern and debate, both within Nepal and abroad. Intellectuals, journalists and politicians alike have grappled in public—just as many across the country have done in private—with the theoretical and practical issues involved, approaching the subject, however, from many different ideological and political perspectives, with different preoccupations and concerns, and for different audiences and readerships.

In Chapter 1 of this collection, we provide a historical overview of these 6–7 years, as well as of the previous decades leading up to the launching of the armed struggle. Chapter 2 is also an attempt to provide a general introduction to the People's War from a 'sociological' perspective. Many of the other contributors also provide accounts, from differing perspectives, of the course of the War, attempting often at the same time to develop their own analysis of the dynamics of the Maoist movement, the class, caste, ethnic and gender relations that characterise Nepali society and the historical development and underdevelopment of the political economy of Nepal.

This book was conceived and planned over a year ago, before the events of late 2001 (the attack on Washington and New York on 11 September, the breaking off of talks between the Maoists and the government on 23 November and the declaration of a State of Emergency on 26 November). It was—and still is—intended to provide a commentary on the Peoples' War, and on the political, economic and social issues associated with the development of the insurgency, from a variety of perspectives on the 'left' of the political spectrum—on the roots of the conflict, on the evolution of the conflict over the last half decade and on the implications for the future of Nepal and its people. In the long tradition of Marxist analysis (within which this collection is situated), it is intended not only to try to *understand* the complexities of the armed struggle and its wider political economic context, but also to make an intervention whose purpose is to bring closer the time when social justice and the welfare of the people of Nepal are guaranteed by a popular and democratic government, that is, *to contribute positively to the process of change.*

Some of the contributions in the section (Part Two) devoted to the statements and commentaries of the Maoist leadership were written several years ago, and provide vivid, if partisan, accounts and analyses of the early years of the People's War. Most, however, are more recent, and the majority of the contributions in the section on 'left perspectives' (Part Three) were written especially for this collection within the last year or so; at least one has an explicit 'postscript'. But the situation is extremely fast-moving now, and even since some of the contributions were written, there have been significant developments on the ground. Today, as we write this Introduction, in October 2002, more than six and a half years after the initiation of the People's War, and immediately after the Hindu religious festival of Dasain, the king has intervened directly (and controversially) in the political process and formed his own government, the major political parties (Nepali Congress and UML) are in disarray, the country lacks any form of elected government (at national, district and local level) and the United States and United Kingdom are providing increased assistance to the government for 'counter-terrorism'. The Maoist insurgency is now a key issue in the politics of Nepal, and the events of the coming months could affect the future of Nepal for many years to come.

The last year has been a turning point in the People's War. The events of 2001—the massacre of the Nepali royal family in June, the attack on Washington and New York in September, which gave rise to a U.S.-led, international 'war on terrorism' and the breakdown of talks between the Maoists and the government followed immediately by attacks on army installations by the Maoists and a declaration of a State of Emergency by the government—combined to change the political context of the People's War. No longer could the conflict be considered a local matter of law and order to be dealt with by the Nepali police force. The political implications for Nepal—even for the future of multi-party democracy under the present constitution—were evidently becoming extremely serious; the consequences for the lives and livelihoods of the Nepali people were becoming a matter of urgent concern, as were the issues of human rights abuses by both parties to the conflict (the Maoists and the state); the wider implications for the economy and for 'development' in Nepal were now an issue not only for Nepalis, but also for the multitude of foreign so-called development agencies (bilateral and multilateral) and non-government organisations, whose projects in the field and programmes across the country were being increasingly threatened and compromised by the conflict and finally, the wider political implications of instability and insurgency in Nepal were an issue for other states whose governments felt they had a stake in Nepal—the United States, the United Kingdom and India in particular.

During the summer of 2002, as the military conflict in Nepal abated somewhat through the monsoon months, there were major political developments within Nepal and abroad. In June, a meeting was held in London, with representatives from a wide range of states, including Nepal, to develop a more coherent, international perspective and position on the conflict in Nepal, and on the action that might be taken, both by the government of Nepal and other interested parties. Background papers were prepared, one of which—that by Arjun Karki—is reproduced as the final contribution to this collection. Views expressed were diverse and the statements made by different participants in the London Meeting varied considerably as to whether they emphasised the 'security' aspects of the issue, the issue of 'good governance' or the 'development' dimension.

In Nepal, meanwhile, in mid-July, the term of office of elected local government officials (at district and village level) had come to an end, and had not been extended. There were by now many areas of the country where the elected local government had been replaced by Maoist structures, but the failure to extend the term of office of those who remained in place meant that there was now no properly elected local government in Nepal. At the national level, increasing divisions within the ruling Nepali Congress party led the prime minister to dissolve the House of Representatives in August and call for mid-term elections in November. In September, after much wrangling between the parties as to how to proceed, and it had been proposed that the elections be postponed for a year, the King eventually stepped in to dismiss Prime Minister Sher Bahadur Deuba. There was now no elected national government in Nepal; indeed, there was now no elected representation at any level. In October, the King, having effectively taken power, nominated his own cabinet. Nepal now faced a new political crisis.*

It could be argued that by emphasising the military aspects of the current conflict, the People's *War*, there is a danger of ignoring the fact that the armed struggle is a political movement first and foremost—an extension of politics by other means, based on the belief that, ultimately, power grows from the barrel of a gun—and that root causes are political. It could also be argued that by emphasising the political aspects of the insurgency there is a danger of ignoring the economic and the social dimensions of what the Maoists at least see as a revolutionary struggle to transform the political economy of Nepal and that by emphasising the immediate, short-term issues, there is a danger of ignoring the longer-term and structural problems facing Nepal.

It is certainly our view that the current 'crisis' is multi-dimensional and that the underlying causes are structural and historical. For this reason, we have been at pains, in this collection of essays to combine contributions that address shorter-term and immediate issues with contributions that take a longer perspective. We would wish to emphasise as editors that although we have tried to ensure a degree of coherence we have in no way, other than by our choice of contributions, attempted to edit the views and perspectives of the various authors represented here. We have also tried to maintain a light touch as regards matters of writing style, while ensuring clarity and comprehensibility.

Most of the contributors are well known in Nepal, as political theorists as well as activists, and most have already written on the subject in a variety of places. But the majority of the contributions, particularly in Parts One and Three, are original, in the sense that they were commissioned for the book and that this is the first time they have been published. The analyses, statements and declarations of the Maoist leadership, presented in Part Two, include some documents that have had some

---

* We are reminded of Martin Hoftun's prescient comment at the end of his analysis of the 1990 'revolution': '...there is still a long way to go to create strong democratic institutions and traditions. Until that goal is reached, the movement which started in the spring of 1990 might develop in any direction, including a political come-back by the palace.'

previous circulation, but in many cases these too will be new at least to the English-language readership of this collection. Here, for the first time, they find their place alongside the contribution of other left political analysts and activists. The collection can be seen, perhaps, as an attempt to bring the analysis of the Maoists back into the mainstream of Nepali theoretical and political discourse, and ultimately to make a collective argument, albeit filtered through diverse left perspectives, for radical reform—political, social and economic in Nepal.

The contributions in Part One provide an introduction and an overview, from a historical and from a sociological perspective. As far as the first is concerned, the authors here include the two editors of this collection, **Arjun Karki and David Seddon**. The historical overview is an attempt to put the People's War in perspective, both as part of the history (ideological as well as political) of the communist movement in Nepal and also as part of the political history of Nepal. It has no pretensions to 'a history of the People's War', still less 'a history of the Maoist movement in Nepal'—that would require a more protracted effort—but merely attempts to provide an introduction and a distinctive perspective in which the 'demands' of the Maoists, and the objectives of their struggle as well as the chosen form of their struggle to achieve these objectives, are situated within a longer, broader history of such demands and such struggles—for popular democracy and for social justice. It ends with the dramatic intervention in the political process by the king and his nomination of a new government in October 2002.

Mukunda Kattel's contribution provides a valuable counterpoint to the political historical perspective, emphasising above all the social context and social character of the People's War. His contribution, as he claims, provides a 'face value analysis' of the People's War based largely on the events and issues that occurred between February 1995 and October 2001. Charting the evolution of the People's War over this period, Kattel makes a central claim that People's War does not justify the entirely negative comments familiar from the what is presented often as the 'mainstream' discourse, although he is all too aware—as a human rights activists and former Director of INSEC—of the real human cost as well as the social costs of the armed struggle, and condemns the abuses of human rights that have increasingly accompanied the insurgency. One of the major contributions of the People's War is the radicalisation of Nepali society—a necessity, Kattel emphasizes, if the social and political stagnation of Nepal is to be overcome and a living, vital civil society is to emerge. Another possible contribution may prove to be the creation of an opportunity to sort out differences, to weed out wrong habits or beliefs developed through recent history and to forge new synergies, which, if effectively pursued, may bring about a progressive transformation in Nepal. But, this (Kattel warns) requires all concerned—Maoists, Congress, Palace and other forces—to abandon their narrow, selfish and short-term interests in favour of a genuine commitment to human development in Nepal.

The contributions to the second Part of the collection provide an insight first into the outlook and analysis of the Maoist leadership, not only of the two best known figures in the movement but also of the leadership of the women's movement within the Communist Party of Nepal (Maoist). These three chapters are followed by a number of shorter documents and public 'statements'. This collection of documents presenting what might be termed 'Maoist perspectives'—on the origins and evolution of the People's War, on strategy and tactics, on the political economy of Nepal, on the class struggle and the struggle against imperialism, on the role of gender analysis and the position of women within the movement and the People's War, and on the possible future(s) of Nepal—provides the starting point, as it were, for the other contributions, which constitute Part Three of the book. This section presents a range of perspectives, on the People's War, on the Maoist movement itself, on the class, gender, caste and ethnic characteristics of Nepali society and on the underlying dynamics of the political economy of Nepal.

We do not attempt to provide a conclusion to the collection, for the story continues and whatever we as editors (and contributors) may have to say about the political economy of Nepal, the class struggle and the Peoples' War ourselves, in this context at least, will be included in this introduction, and in our own individual contributions.

It would be invidious to label the contributors in advance in terms of their perspective or position or the left in terms of their party or other affiliation in such a way as to imply that they were presenting some kind of 'party line', but it might help to situate their contributions within the overall spectrum of commentaries and analysis, as they tend to represent particular perspectives and positions vis-à-vis the Peoples' War associated with particular movements, groups or parties in Nepal and internationally. Short biographies are included at the end of the book, by way of further clarification as to the intellectual as well as the political history of the contributors to this book. But let us briefly outline the main thrust of the contributions to this collection on the People's War.

The major statement by Puspa Kamal Dahal (**Prachanda**), at that time Secretary General and currently Chairman of the CPN (Maoist), given in the course of an interview to a sympathetic journalist (which opens this Part of the collection), is clearly a key document, produced by the main leader of the movement, at a significant juncture in the armed struggle. In this interview, Prachanda explains why he and his party think it is possible to successfully wage a protracted People's War, to organise the masses through armed struggle, why this is the correct strategy given the situation in Nepal and what the Party feels is possible to achieve with this strategy. He also considers the general socio-economic, political, cultural, gender, caste and class structure of Nepali society and explains how the CPN (Maoist) is mobilising support not only from within Nepal but also from international groups and communities in South Asia and elsewhere that are sympathetic to the peoples' war in Nepal.

It is a comprehensive statement, issued at a point in the People's War when it was possible to look back at several years of struggle and achievement, and look forward at the same time with confidence. It is revealing to compare the views expressed here with those expressed by Prachanda in earlier annual reviews of the progress of the People's War, which we present later in the same section.

The contribution of **Dr. Babu Ram Bhattarai** is, by contrast, more of a 'political economy'—an attempt to delineate the objective and subjective conditions within which the armed struggle is developing, an understanding of which, he suggests in effect, is essential if all efforts to bring about a revolutionary transformation will be condemned to a blind and essentially ad hoc struggle. Bhattarai is well known as one of the leading intellectuals and ideologues of the Maoist movement and his publications on 'the political economy of Nepal' (as well as his PhD thesis from JNU in India) reveal him to be a serious analyst. Here he develops, in outline, a comprehensive vision of the historical and contemporary realities of Nepal and provides a foundation, in his analysis of economic and social relations, for the political and ideological struggle of which the People's War is an integral part. Bhattarai's contribution, not only here but more widely, is of major importance. There have been all too few attempts to provide a class analysis of the political economy of Nepal that adequately take into consideration the distinctive political and cultural specificities of Nepali society and that are soundly based on empirical research and analysis. This essay should provide a valuable introduction to the fuller analysis developed in his *Rajanitic Arthasastra ko Aankhijhyal Bata*, which remains to be translated into English.

The third major contribution from the Maoists is provided by **Comrade Parvati**, of the All Nepal Women's Association (Revolutionary)–ANWA(R). The piece makes a contribution from the distinctive perspective of the women's wing of the Party and reflects the importance attributed by the Maoists to gender analysis and the position of women in the context of class struggle and the People's War. Women are involved directly in the CPN(M) through the organisational or military wing, and thus participate directly in the People's War in a military or in a political capacity. However, they can also become involved through ANWA(R), which is the women's wing of the Maoists, as well as through the All Nepal National Independent Students Union (Revolutionary), the various ethnic liberation fronts and People's Cultural Forums. From these front organisations they undertake propaganda and mobilise political support, and, more specifically, care for the wounded and provide shelter and other logistical support.

The Maoists have been very clear, from the outset, about the importance of women in the struggle and regarding the objectives of the movement as a whole as regards gender relations and women's emancipation. This has been recognised by many commentators outside the movement. An earlier article by Parvati (in 1999) stressed the anti-feudal nature of the New Democratic Revolution and described how the revolution will eventually liberate women from their feudal bonds.* In February 2000, Prachanda elaborated further the position of the Maoists on gender relations and 'the question of women.'† For many women, the current struggle is emancipatory, both in the immediate and potentially in the longer term, for it is linked with a recognition of the fact that class struggle need not inhibit—indeed may encourage and promote—other forms of struggle against exploitation and oppression.

In this case, the focus is on gender relations and the position of women, but Comrade Parvati, like Bhattarai and Prachanda, recognises the importance of the struggle against caste and ethnic hierarchy and for the recognition of 'national' identities, as well as against patriarchy and gender oppression for the emancipation of women. Indeed, one of the important themes that constitutes an integral part of the Maoists' strategy is to link the class struggle to other struggles against exploitation, oppression and social discrimination in Nepal. This has been particularly the case with respect to the struggle of ethnic minorities (so-called *jana jati*) against the dominant religious/political ideology, which has enabled 'Nepal' to be constituted as a Hindu monarchy both at the ideological and at the very concrete political levels over a lengthy period, from 'unification' in the mid to late eighteenth century under Prithivi Narayan Shah to the present day, under King Gyanendra.

The other articles and statements, published as clarification of the evolving public analysis by the Maoist leadership in the context of the People's War, constitute a mixture of commentaries on the immediate situation as regards the progress of the People's War, statements on the position of the CPN (Maoist) as regards their 'negotiations' with the government and on their tactical and strategic aims and analyses of the overall 'balance of forces' in the class struggle of which the People's War is an integral part. This set of documents— which is organised in chronological order and starts with the 40 demands made on the eve of the launching of the People's War— provides, we believe, a useful complement to the lengthier analyses by the Maoist leadership presented earlier in the same section.

---

* Women's Participation in People's War in Nepal, *The Worker*, Issue 5, October 1999.
† *Revolutionary Worker*, Issue 1043, February 20, 2000.

The set of texts, as a whole, emphasises the distinction between tactics and strategy in the analysis of the balance of forces, and the central belief of the Maoists that immediate and short-term considerations and the analysis of 'the moment' (the present conjuncture), though sometimes of critical importance, must be situated within the longer-term and broader strategic considerations and fundamental analysis of the overall balance of class forces. The last two texts are very recent contributions by Bhattarai and Prachanda respectively, the last of these following the king's intervention in the political process in October 2002. This corpus of statements and documents provides a starting point, as it were, for our other contributors, in Part Three of the collection, who provide a critical counterpoint and lay out alternative perspectives, not only on the current conflict but also on strategies for development and democracy in the future.

The first of these, by **Govinda Neupane**, is essentially a commentary by someone who might be termed a 'fellow traveller'. Close to the position of the Maoists, he was an early and founder member of the CPN (ML), but has had a political career that took him for some while out of the mainstream of Nepali left politics. His contribution falls into a number of related parts. In the first, he is concerned to examine more closely the structure and dynamic of class relations in Nepal, with a view to assessing the extent of its 'underdevelopment' and the potential for progressive change. He sees Nepal as 'transitional' in terms of its political economy and class dynamics; the contradictions inherent in this transitional political economy and the implications of these for class struggle are explored further in the second and third sections of his chapter. To a greater extent and in greater depth than the contributions of Prachanda, Parvati or even Bhattarai, Neupane examines the contemporary dynamics of capitalist development in Nepal and explores the implications for the emergence and development of the working class and the 'middle classes'. After a brief discussion of the Maoist movement he turns to a consideration of the People's War as a political phenomenon, examining in particular the notion of the united front. Finally, he develops a number of criticisms of the Maoist movement as a whole, the most trenchant of which is the weakness, in his view, of its class analysis and its failure to recognise the extent and the significance of the working classes in Nepal.

The second critical contribution from 'the far left' is by one of the best known theorists and political activists on the left of Nepali politics. Mohand Bikram Singh was closely involved with the Maoists in the Unity Centre, prior to the split that led to the establishment of the CPN (Mashal) and the CPN (Maoist). Currently, he is the secretary general of CPN (Mashal-Unity Centre) formed after the unification of CPN (Mashal) and CPN (Unity Centre). His essay on the 'pro-king' line of the Maoists grapples with the relationship between the revolutionaries currently waging a protracted People's War and the monarchy. The pertinence of this topic has become even greater since October 2002, with the king's intervention, which has, in effect, marginalised the major parties and created an interim government.

From the earliest days of the communist movement in Nepal, the objective of a democratic republic has been part of the central political vision of the 'far left' and even the democratic socialists and social democrats in the Nepali Congress Party had anticipated progress towards a constitutional monarchy of the European kind, in which the role of parliament was pre-eminent. Successive monarchs have compromised that vision, but the relationship between the Maoists and the monarchy is, from Mohan Bikram's perspective, the most bizarre: fundamentally antagonistic to the monarchy and committed to a 'new democracy', they also claim to have had a special relationship with the late King Birendra and, despite their overt antagonism towards the monarchy and particularly towards the recent intervention by the king, some claim that Maoists and monarch have certain fundamentals in common. Mohan Bikram Singh's fear is that both the Maoists on the far left and the Palace itself on the right represent a threat to parliamentary democracy and thus to the room for manoeuvre and class struggle that even a rudimentary 'bourgeois democracy' affords the forces of the left. His analysis, which is brought up to date in an 'after-thought' or Post-script, provides the kind of detailed description, debate, analysis and invective that only an intimate knowledge of left politics in Nepal over the last half-century could generate.

Pradip Nepal is a spokesperson of the CPN (UML). The Communist Party of Nepal United Marxist–Leninist (UML) is a grouping of several pre-existing communist parties, which embraced parliamentary politics in the early 1990s, while retaining a willingness to be involved in extra-parliamentary activities, including *bandhs*, demonstrations, marches etc. as a form of 'pressure' on the government of the day. Briefly in government during the mid-1990s, it was able to implement a few progressive policies, but has presented itself more as a day-to-day opposition to the Nepali Congress ruling party than as a strategic alternative with a programme for revolutionary transformation. Seeing itself as the most powerful of the leftist organisations, it has been critical of those espousing armed struggle. The divisions between UML activists and the Maoist cadres and supporters at the local level have resulted in numerous clashes and a number of killings. His contribution provides a sweeping critique of the Maoists, from the UML perspective, first through a discussion of the various factors giving rise to the armed struggle and then through a critique of the basic premises and the actual practice of the Maoists. He ends with an attempt to outline some of the basic requirements for a progressive, long-term strategy for the left in Nepal, recognising implicitly the importance of the distinction between the insurrectionist tradition (of Leninism and Maoism) and the 'social revolutionary' perspective of more recent Marxist theoreticians and activists (e.g. Gramsci).

The chapter by **Sujita Shakya** presents an analysis from the perspective of the UML's All Nepal Women's Association (ANWA). Like the contribution of Comrade Parvati, the position of women—and their struggle against the repressive economic, social and religious–cultural structures of Nepali society—is emphasised, and the long history and strength of the women's movement in Nepal is underlined. This is a significant contribution to the history of the women's movement in Nepal—which badly needs to be written—and establishes the basis for an understanding of some of the ideological and political divisions within the movement. Like the contribution of Pradip Nepal, this discussion emphasises the importance, in the UML perspective and strategy, of 'social revolution'.

The ANWA, as Shakya shows, adopts a position that is perhaps best termed 'pragmatic' in that, while struggling actively for significant change, it recognises that a revolution cannot take place over night and that a long process may be required before women's full emancipation is achieved. From the perspective of the Maoist ANWA(R), of course, such a position will be regarded as 'reformist'. But one cannot help but be impressed by the attention to detail given by Shakya in her description and analysis of the historical and contemporary struggles of the women's movement as a whole and the section of the movement represented by her Association in particular. She is critical of the Maoist tendency to 'sectarianism' and sees it as marginal to the mainstream of the democratic progressive women's movement. She defends the ANWA from the accusation that it is 'reactionary' and in turn accuses the Maoist women of being 'opportunist'; in a telling phrase, she argues that 'the injustice, tyranny, exploitation and oppression faced by women cannot be overcome just by beating someone with 50–100 bamboo sticks and breaking pots of local wine'— a reference to the anti-alcohol campaign in which ANWA(R) has been very active.

Her account of the Maoist People's War and its impact (which takes up nearly half of the chapter) is very detailed and complements that of Pradip Nepal. It provides an assessment in which an attempt is made to be balanced—listing the positive and negative points successively—but that eventually is negative both in terms of the impact of the war on women and children, family life and rural economy and society generally and in terms of the armed struggle as a form of class struggle. After this, the discussion finally turns back to the women's movement as a whole and provides a vision of 'what is to be done', by the mainstream left parties and the women's movement combined, to achieve real progress in terms of women's emancipation (the freedom of women), the strengthening of ethnic groups and other minorities and the lives and livelihoods of working people in Nepal.

Arjun Karki, one of the editors of this collection, is a former student activist, who continues to be involved politically in the human rights movement, in rural development and, most recently, also in efforts to promote debates on the current conflict. President of a well-known NGO, Rural Reconstruction Nepal, Karki is also a prominent intellectual (his PhD thesis from the University of East Anglia, on the politics of poverty and movements from below in Nepal, included a detailed analysis of the *kamaiya* bonded labourers, of the land rights movements and of the Maoist insurgency). His contribution to this collection—indeed, the final contribution—is based on a paper that he prepared, on request, as background for the London Meeting in June 2002. It is based on the belief that progress towards a solution of the current crisis will be made only on the basis of a firm and clear commitment on the part of the government of Nepal (and all other major players) to an agreed framework for radical reform in Nepal to meet the real needs of the Nepali people.

Short Introduction to the Contributors

Dr. Babu Ram Bhattarai was educated at JNU in India. He is well known as one of the leading ideologues of the Maoist movement and his publications on 'the political economy of Nepal' are extensive. He is the Coordinator of the Sanyukta Krantikari Jana Parishad (United Revolutionary People's Council—the underground 'government' formed by the Maoist). His book by the name *Rajanitic Arthasastra ko Aankhijhyal Bata* is well known among the Nepalese political thinkers. His dissertation for the degree of Doctor of Philosophy on 'The nature of underdevelopment and the regional structure of Nepal (Jawarlal University, India) is considered as a noteworthy critique in relation to Nepal's development. He has been in the influential left political scene since long.

Puspa Kamal Dahal, who is known as **Prachanda**, was born in the hills but brought up in Chitwan in the *terai*. After agricultural college he became a teacher, until he became involved in left politics and went underground in the mid-1980s. Formerly Secretary-General of the CPN (Maoist), he is now Chairman of CPN (Maoist) and the Supreme Commander of People's Liberation Army (underground military wing of the Maoist). He is a well known figure in the Nepalese left political arena. He is considered one of the top strategists of his underground party. He has written several articles in different papers.

Parvati (an assumed name) is a member of the leadership of the Maoist movement. She is also associated with the All Nepal Women's Association (Revolutionary). She and her other women colleagues are strongly committed to the emancipation of Nepalese women. She is currently 'underground'.

Govinda Neupane is one of the founding members of the CPN (Marxist–Leninist). There are a number of thought provoking books and articles on leftist movements in Nepal to his credit. Aside from being an influential political thinker of the far left, he has considerable experience in the development field. He has had a political career that took him for some while out of the mainstream of Nepali left politics.

Mohan Bikram Singh is the General Secretary of CPN (Masal–Unity Centre), formed by the merger of the CPN (Masal) and the CPN (Unity

Centre). He is one of the best known senior theorists and political leaders on the left of Nepali politics. He was closely involved with the Maoists in the Unity Centre, prior to the split that led to the separate establishment of the CPN (Masal) and the CPN (Maoist). There are several articles critically analysing the far leftist movement in Nepal to his credit.

Pradip Nepal is the spokesperson and a standing committee member of CPN (United Marxist–Leninist). He is one of the best known literary writers on the left in Nepal. His literary works and thoughtprovoking articles are published in different print media in Nepal. There are several books and articles to his credit. He is one of the founders of the Marxist study centre. He was also the central committee member of Nepal Communist Revolutionaries Coordination Committee. Mr. Nepal had also served as the Member of Parliament and as a cabinet minister in the past.

Sujita Shakya is a central committee member and chief of the department of foreign affairs of All Nepal Women's Association (one of the sister organisations of CPN (UML)). She is also a women activist involved in different activities to liberate the Nepalese women from the age-old social and economic discriminatory practices in Nepal.

Mukunda Kattel is the former Director of Informal Sector Service Centre (INSEC, an established human rights organisation), a human rights activist and is currently working with Child Workers in Asia, based in Bangkok, Thailand. He has an MA in Sociology. His academic and research interests are in the field of socio-cultural aspects of poverty, violence and slavery/bonded labour. This article draws much from his MA dissertation on *Sociology of the People's War in Nepal: The Genesis, Development and Aftermath.* He can be contacted at kattelmr@yahoo.com

Dr. David Seddon is Professor of Development Studies and former Managing Director of the Overseas Development Group (ODG) at the University of East Anglia (UK). He is a member of the Socialist Alliance, a new political grouping on the left in Britain. He has worked in Nepal for more than 25 years as a rural/social development researcher and as consultant to numerous projects. He is author (or co-author) of several books on Nepal, including 'The Struggle for Basic Needs in Nepal', 'Peasants and Workers in Nepal', 'Nepal in Crisis', 'Nepal—A State of Poverty', and, recently, 'Pokhara: The Biography of a Town' and 'The New Lahures: Foreign Labour Migration and the Remittance Economy of Nepal', as well as many articles in academic and professional journals.

Dr. Arjun Karki is a former student activist. Deeply involved politically as an activist and as the President of a well-known NGO, Rural Reconstruction Nepal (RRN), Dr. Karki is also a prominent intellectual. His PhD thesis (awarded in summer 2002 by the School of Development Studies at the University of East Anglia), on "Politics of poverty and movements from below in Nepal", included a detailed analysis of the *kamaiya* bonded labourers, of the land rights movements and of the Maoist insurgency. He has been active in the human rights movement and in efforts to promote debates on the current conflict.

Part One
OVERVIEW

Chapter 1

The People's War in Historical Context

Arjun Karki and David Seddon

The history of rebellion in Nepal

Although many commentators, both within as well as outside Nepal, have expressed their surprise and indeed 'shock' that a protracted People's War—an armed struggle to overthrow the existing regime and lay the foundations for the transformation of the economy and society—should have been initiated in Nepal, there are precedents under broadly similar circumstances elsewhere in south Asia as well as in Nepal itself. As Liz Philipson has pointed out, 'democracy was achieved in Nepal after a long struggle which included illegal underground parties and armed insurrections and so the country is no stranger to either clandestine politics or armed struggles'.[1] The same point is made in this collection by Pradip Nepal (Chapter 9). Furthermore, the demands of the Maoists (expressed during their talks with the government during 2001)—for a constituent assembly, a new, more democratic constitution and the establishment of a popular democratic republic in Nepal—are not without precedent. Indeed these were, from the very early days of the Communist Party of Nepal, central concerns and major objectives.

There is a long but largely undocumented history of popular uprisings and revolts against the autocratic rulers of Nepal, calling for social justice and a change of regime. While there are scattered references in the historical literature[2] to rebellions against the

Gorkhali regime, often led by local rulers or rural landowners, and to the brutal punishment meted out to rebels, one of the earliest examples of popular or populist revolt of which we know anything much was a revolt against Jung Bahadur Rana among the Tamu (Gurungs) of Lamjung and Gorkha. Initiated by Jamadar Sripati Gurung of Lamjung, during a military parade at the Tundikhel in Kathmandu, it was led after Sripati Gurung's death by his associate Sukadev Gurung who mobilised the Gurungs of Lamjung and Gorkha against the government. The insurgency was suppressed and Sukadev was imprisoned for life, accused of trying to become the King of the Buddhists. He died in prison in 1875.[3]

In 1876, Lakhan Thapa Magar also led a revolt against Jung Bahadur Rana from the central hill region of Gorkha. A poem by Gyan Dildas, who supported the revolt, spoke out against the way in which the regime had strengthened the position of the rich and failed to provide justice (*Adam Bajyo Dhaniko Firyo Jaga Janha, Ghusyaha Bichari Nishaf Herchha Kaha*). The uprising involved hundreds of people. The leaders—Lakhan Thapa Magar, Aja Singh Thapa and Achhami Magar—were eventually executed by hanging in Gorkha; others were jailed or sent into exile.[4]

In the early twentieth century, a movement led by a young widow, Yog Maya, from the eastern hill region of Bhojpur, against caste discrimination and oppression, and against the many and various forms of state discrimination, lasted from the first decade of the century until the 1930s. This movement was articulated or expressed as a campaign for justice and truth (*Satya Dharma Bhichha*) and was essentially non-violent, but it mobilised several thousand people. Again the struggle was against poverty, discrimination and injustice and for *Dharma Rajya*. Yog Maya's analysis was, like that of Gyan Dildas, reflected in a poem— '*Maharaj Chhan Darbarma Herna Aaundainan; Dukhi Janle Niya Nishaf Sidha Paudainan*'—which criticized the rulers for their lack of compassion for the suffering of the poor and for the lack of justice. (She was jailed in Dhankuta in 1939, but released within a year or so. After her release from prison she led a mass suicide when she, along with 59 of her followers, drowned themselves in the Arun River, in 1942.)

Many other satirical poems, pamphlets and books were

published during the late 1920s and the 1930s, implicitly criticising the Rana regime. Dharanidhar Koirala wrote a poem—*Jaga, Jaga, Aba Jaga* (Awake, Awake, Now Awake)—which called on the Nepali elite to rouse themselves from their comfortable way of life and intellectual slumber and work for the progress of their country. Koirala was not alone in his criticism of the ruling classes. Around 1920, a controversial little book, *Makai ko Kheti* (The Cultivation of Maize), was published under the name of Krishna Lal Adhikari (or Subba Krishana Lal). A satire on life under the Ranas—particularly under Chandra Shumsher Rana—the book called for social and economic reform, including land reform and the introduction of new techniques in the cultivation of maize.[5] Almost all copies of the book were seized and more than nine people, including Krishna Lal, were arrested. Krishna Lal remained for 3 years in prison, during which time he was treated brutally. He died in prison.[6] The significance of this text and of the 'Corn Scandal' *(makai parba)* it aroused continues, although the original work seems to have literally disappeared.

Other Nepalis, both at home and abroad, were now expressing opposition to the regime, and it was not long before those opposed to the regime began to take matters into their own hands. In 1932, a group of young Nepalis calling themselves Prachanda Gorkha, planned to bomb all the senior Ranas ruler. They were arrested before they could undertake their plan; some were exiled, others were jailed. Shortly after this, in 1935, the Praja Parishad was formed. The goals of the party were democracy and a constitutional monarchy, on the British model. The party distributed leaflets in Kathmandu during 1940. In October of that year those involved were arrested and charged with plotting the assassination of the Rana family. Four were sentenced to death and others to long jail sentences. Overt political activity was dampened for a while, but dissent continued, with protest often taking a literary form.

The first 'nationalist' rebellion

Major changes were to take place, however, after Indian independence. The Communist Party of Nepal (CPN) was established in Calcutta in 1947 under the leadership of Pushpa Lal Shrestha and the communist movement in Nepal began to take shape after the publication of the Nepali edition of the

Communist Manifesto in April 1949. The espousal of armed struggle as an element in the strategy of the Nepali communist movement was clear from the start: the first leaflet produced by the Communist Party of Nepal published in April 1949, declared that Nepal should establish a 'new democracy' as in China—if necessary through armed struggle—so as to create a People's Republic. The establishment of the CPN and the formation in April 1950 of the Nepali Congress—with the merging of the Nepali National Congress (formed in 1947) and the Nepal Democratic Congress (formed in 1948)—were of critical importance in establishing the basis for left politics in Nepal.

Significantly, at its inaugural meeting, the new Nepali Congress Party put aside the principles of non-violence, which the Nepali National Congress had previously adopted, and agreed that only armed struggle would lead to the overthrow of the Rana regime in Nepal. The new party elected the Nepali National Congress's M.P. Koirala as its president and planned an armed revolt. Their initial plans for a coup or uprising were thwarted, but preparations were renewed at a conference at Bairgania in Bihar towards the end of the year. At this meeting, M.P. Koirala was appointed to the post of military supreme, and the main leaders of the party were allocated military responsibility for the different regions of Nepal.*

The initiative of King Mahendra in seeking refuge in the Indian Embassy in Kathmandu in November, 1950 followed by his flight to India, coincided with the crossing of the Indian–Nepali border by Nepali Congress rebel forces and their attack on the district headquarters at Birgunj. The government garrison there was quickly compelled to surrender to the *Mukti Sena* (Liberation Army), as the armed volunteers of the Nepali Congress styled themselves. A large proportion of the rebel army, the *Mukti Sena*, was ex-Gurkha servicemen dissatisfied with the ruling regime.

---

* According to Gobar Dhan Maskey, B.P. Koirala went to Biratnagar, Subarna to Birgunj and Mahendra Bikram Shah to Nepalgunj together with Gobar Dhan Maskey and Rajeshwar Devkota who were responsible for the far west. Parmanand, however, suggests that Subarna was in overall command, with B.P. Koirala and Mahendra Bikram Shah in charge of the eastern and western fronts respectively (cf. Hoftun, Raeper, & Whelpton 1999, p. 18, fn. 66).

The nucleus of this force had been formed by the Nepal Democratic Congress before the 1950 merger with B.P. Koirala's party. They had recruited a number of officers who had served in the British Indian army but subsequently joined Subash Chandra Bose's Indian National Army (INA) to fight against the British. A report by the district governor of Birgunj described the Congress force, which took the town and subdued the garrison, as 'mostly mercenaries', and there was other evidence (e.g. reports that 50–60 Sikhs were members of the Congress forces at Taplejung) of this kind. But there is little doubt that the majority were Nepalis, and that many of the officers were indeed former members of the INA.[7]

Throughout the next month or so the armed insurrection developed and spread, involving for the most part the actions of the *Mukti Sena*, launched initially from bases in India and equipped with weapons purchased in Burma, picking up support from within the country—notably the defection of the Palpa garrison to the rebels in early January 1951—and accompanied by civil unrest in Kathmandu, several towns in the *terai* and among the Limbus of the eastern hills. Small bands of armed Congress volunteers were able to drive out small and generally ill-trained army garrisons from various hill towns, but though there were anti-Rana demonstrations in some places outside the Kathmandu Valley and the towns of the *terai*, large numbers were generally not involved. Nevertheless, the combination of armed insurrection, the fleeing of King Tribhuvan to India and the pressure exerted by the Indian government on the Rana regime, proved decisive.

Indian 'imperialism' and the 'national' consensus in Nepal

Talks were held in New Delhi in mid-January and a ceasefire agreed. Significantly, not only was the Nepali Congress Party excluded from these talks, they apparently hardly knew of their existence. As Gobar Dhan Maskey remarked, of Indian involvement during 1950–51, 'India only supported our movement from behind. They never came into the country. There was never one Indian soldier in Nepal during the revolution".[8] But there is considerable evidence to suggest that, behind an official position of non-involvement during the revolt, the Indian government was actively supporting both King Tribhuvan and the Nepali Congress Party—even if their support was apparently sometimes less than wholehearted. It is even probable that undercover Indian agents were involved in promoting internal civil disturbances in Kathmandu and elsewhere.[9] There can be little doubt that Indian intervention during 1950–51 proved decisive. In retrospect, this may be seen as an early manifestation of Indian imperialism in the determination of the direction and construction of Nepali politics by the government of India. If so, it proved willing at this point to support the progressive forces moving against the Ranas, *albeit only to a certain extent*, and to extend its power to achieve a more stable and broadly acceptable regime in Nepal on its northern borders.

Nehru was very clear about the need to seize 'the tide in the affairs of men'. In March 1950, before the Nepali movement had begun, he declared in the Lok Sabha that 'in the inner context of Nepal it is desirable to pay attention to the forces that are moving in the world—the democratic forces, the forces of freedom—and to put oneself in line with them, because not to do so is not only wrong according to modern ideas but unwise according to what is happening in the world today'.[10] Of course, he had in mind not only the issue of democracy in Nepal, but the importance of stability in that country, in the context of a potential threat to India from China to the north of the Himalayas following the invasion of Tibet. The specific foreign policy of the government of India towards Nepal was to prove equally dependent on its vision of India's wider strategic interests, in the region as a whole and in the wider world throughout the next half-century.

A party manifesto written by B. P. Koirala in 1950 and a leaflet dropped by the Nepali Congress from the air over Kathmandu at the very beginning of the revolt (10 November 1950) both promised radical social reforms and loyalty to the king; apart from a brief reference to constitutional monarchy and to democracy 'as in the West', hardly anything was mentioned about the party's political ideology and long-term political goals for Nepal after 'the revolution'. In the event, the immediate outcome of the talks in New Delhi was an agreement between the Rana government, King Tribhuvan, the Nepali Congress and the Indian government, and the establishment of a Rana–Congress coalition government. India effectively ensured that the Nepali Congress settled for less than the total overthrow of the old regime that had formerly been their proclaimed goal. The king agreed—under a tripartite agreement popularly known as the Delhi compromise—to play the role of a constitutional monarch under a new democratic constitution to be framed by a constituent assembly elected by the people. This agreement was never honoured (and remains a key demand of the Maoists today); an interim government was formed in February 1951 to carry out the task, but the king refused to allow the framing of a new democratic constitution. King Mahendra, who succeeded Tribhuvan in 1955, also failed to honour the Royal Proclamation of 1951.

From multipartyism to the royal coup

The CPN committed itself at its first conference in September–October 1951 to struggle for an all-party conference, an interim government and an elected constituent assembly. It was unable to press effectively for this, however, for lack of an organisational base. It reiterated its demands and objectives at the First Congress of the Party in January 1954, and again at its Second Congress in 28 May -6 June 1957. There were, even at this time, however, divisions within the CPN regarding the role of the monarchy; the more conciliatory wing succeeded in electing Keshar Jung Rayamaji as secretary general of the Party, replacing Man Mohan Adhikari.

In 1959, instead of a constituent assembly, a new constitution was drafted and promulgated by the king. Under the new constitution, the king retained the power to dissolve parliament and the cabinet without consulting the Prime Minister. The political parties did not venture to contest the new constitution, and eventually agreed to participate (under the 1959 constitution) in parliamentary elections. The Nepali Congress Party emerged as the dominant political force, with a more than two-thirds majority (74 out of 109 seats). The CPN, partly as a result of its internal divisions, won only four seats. In terms of votes cast, the top seven 'most communist' constituencies were in the urban areas of Kathmandu and Lalitpur, in Rautahat, Saptari and Siraha (in the east) and Palpa (in the west).

In 1960, King Mahendra, with the support of the military, took power (using the emergency powers vested in him by the 1959 constitution) dismissing and dissolving the cabinet and parliament. Two years later, in 1962, he promulgated a new constitution, with provision for a partyless electoral system, under which all political parties were banned. Many of the senior political figures of the Nepali Congress Party and the CPN were encouraged to join the Panchayat System and to take positions in the government; this, by and large, they did. On the other hand, some sections of the Nepali Congress Party made several attempts to reverse King Mahendra's intervention, notably a bomb attack attempted in Janakpur in January 1962.

The royal coup also caused a split in the CPN. CPN's general secretary, Keshar Jung Rayamajhi, and his followers backed the Panchayat System, and Rayamajhi himself was appointed to the Raj Sabha, the royal advisory group. They were expelled from the Party and Tulsi Lal Amatya was elected general secretary at the Third Congress, in April 1962. The Congress approved support for a 'powerful and sovereign parliament' (implying *either* a republic *or* a constitutional monarchy) and again demanded the election of a constituent assembly. From this point onwards, CPN began to experience significant divisions, not only as a result of different orientations towards popular struggle and revolution within Nepal, but also as a result of the Sino–Soviet split and its international repercussions.

The rise of Maoism

In 1971, under the influence of both the teachings of Mao Tse-Tung and the experience of Charu Mazumdar, architect of the Naxalite uprising in India, young Party activists in Jhapa, in the eastern *terai*, formed the Koshi Regional Committee of the CPN, later known as the All Nepal Revolutionary Coordination Committee (ML). These young activists launched an underground guerrilla movement (popularly known as the Jhapa Uprising), in line with the concept of 'the protracted People's War'. The Jhapa Uprising was the first attempt by Nepali communists to undertake armed struggle as a central component of their revolutionary strategy. The movement actually started from Jymirgadi village in Jhapa on 16 May 1971 and attracted the attention and support of many young political activists across the country. The movement was brought to a swift end by a brutal counter-insurgency campaign by the police, which led to the deaths of many of the cadres.

The failure of the Jhapa Movement caused the leadership of the All Nepal Revolutionary Coordination Committee (ML) to review both strategy and tactics. This faction re-emerged in 1978 as the Nepal Communist Party (Marxist–Leninist). As a result of their 're-appraisal', the ML rejected the simple application of imported political dogma and recognised 'the need to analyse and understand the objective conditions of Nepal'. The ML emphasised that a distinctive revolutionary 'Nepali road to socialism' would be based on an understanding of economic and social conditions in Nepal.[11] As Mikesell records, 'it changed its name to the Communist Party Marxist-Leninist, taking the Nepali acronym "Ma–Le" and abandoned the people's war for underground educating and organizing in village, town, school and campus in order to build a mass movement. This marked the first emergence in Nepal of a large, cadre-based and ideologically coherent party with a strong organizational base among the masses. Although the Ma–Le continued to draw its leadership almost completely from the same national propertied classes that had been vying for state power, the party represented itself in terms of a radical programme along the ideological lines of the Chinese cultural revolution, and for the first time Nepali Communist Party members lived and worked among the rural and urban working classes on a relatively large scale".[12]

In the meanwhile, the initiation of the Cultural Revolution in China under the leadership of Mao Tse-Tung led to debates within the CPN as a whole about 'fighting revisionism' and the role of armed struggle. Pushpa Lal Shrestha argued, in the Gorakhpur Conference, that it would be impossible to establish a new democratic system in Nepal without waging a protracted war.[13] Others, including Mohan Bikram Singh and Nirmal Lama, agreed. But, while Pushpa Lal maintained the need for the communists to unite with all forces (including the Nepali Congress Party) in the fight against absolute monarchy, the more radical leaders disagreed. Another difference was that the radicals wanted an election to a constituent assembly to prepare a constitution, as opposed to Pushpa Lal who merely called for restoration of the parliament dismantled by King Mahendra. This 'radical' faction, which also tended towards 'Maoism', began to break with the decidedly pro-Soviet CPN (Marxist) tendency.

In 1971, Mohan Bikram Singh and others formed the 'Central

Nucleus', which, following a Fourth Party Congress (or Convention), held in September 1974, became known as the CPN (Fourth Congress or Fourth Convention). This new group was led by Mohan Bikram Singh and Nirmal Lama. Its strategy was to launch a people's movement that could at the opportune moment be converted into an armed revolt. As Deepak Thapa observes, 'the top leadership of today's Maoists comes from this school',[14] even if the divisions that subsequently developed within the group became of critical significance, as may be seen from the contribution by Mohan Bikram Singh to this collection.

While the communists struggled to come to terms with the Jhapa experience and with the implications of Maoism, some sections of the Nepali Congress Party continued to struggle actively against the Panchayat regime, and against the king. There were bombings in Haripur, in Saptrai District, in August 1972, and in Biratnagar and Malangawa in December 1973; there was a passenger plane hijacking in June 1973; a failed attempt to assassinate King Birendra by a bomb attack in Biratnagar in March 1974; another bomb attack against Prayagraj Singh Suwal in May 1974 and an armed insurgency in Timburbote in Solukhumbu District in December 1974. These violent incidents were invariably condemned as 'terrorist', 'anti-national', 'anti-constitutional' and 'anti-King' by the regime and the government press.[15]

The death of Chairman Mao and the overthrow of the "Gang of Four" in China in 1976, led to intense ideological struggle within the communist movement, perhaps particularly among the 'Maoists'. The Ma–Le had not entirely rejected armed struggle, and 'later in 1979, a proposal for training guerrillas, proletarianising party cadres, creating separate base areas, taking action against local cheats, and initiating an agrarian uprising was adopted'.[16] The Ma–Le also launched a student movement in 1979. In the CPN (Fourth Congress), Nirmal Lama recognised the new Chinese leadership, but Mohan Bikram Singh denounced Chinese revisionism and labelled the Chinese leadership under Deng Hsiao Ping, 'counter-revolutionary'. He (and his supporters) pledged allegiance to orthodox Maoism and the Cultural Revolution. The faction led by Nirmal Lama broke its formal relationship with Mohan Bikram Singh's faction in 1983–84 but continued to operate, albeit now as a separate party, under the name of the CPN (Fourth Congress). Some of the 'Maoists', including Mohan Baidya (who is now underground and goes by the nom de guerre Kiran) together with Mohan Bikram Singh and his faction formed the CPN (Masal).

This divided 2 years later into two—confusingly,* the CPN (Masal) and the CPN (Mashal)—the former led by Mohan Bikram Singh and Babu Ram Bhattarai (one of the leaders of the current Maoist movement). It was in the Mashal party (the Mohan Baidya group) that Pushpa Kamal Dahal—now known better as 'Prachanda' and chairman of the CPN (Maoist)—emerged as one of the leaders, to become its general secretary in 1989. In 1990, all parties, except for the MB-led group i.e. CPN (Masal), split from the CPN (Fourth Congress) united as the CPN (Unity Centre) under the leadership of Prachanda in 1990.

From the People's Movement to the People's War: 1985–95

In May 1985, the Nepali Congress Party launched a campaign of *satyagraha* (civil disobedience) to protest the continuation of the partyless Panchayat System, starting with a general strike, and the various communist parties initiated a 'fill the jails' campaign. This movement appeared to be gaining ground when a series of bombings took place, in June 1986, in Pokhara and in Kathmandu, initiated, it was claimed, by the *Nepal Janabadi Morcha* (People's Front), a group based in India, led by Ram Raja Prasad Singh, who stated that they had planted the bombs to proclaim the start of a campaign to topple the monarchy, install a democratic republic and abolish private property in Nepal. Some suggested that the bombs were planted 'by the palace itself' to create a 'national emergency' that could be used to disrupt the upsurge of opposition. In any case, there were mass arrests as the state security services cracked down hard, and the Destructive Crimes (Special Control and Punishment) Act was rushed through parliament. The civil disobedience campaign was called off. But from the elections of 1986 onwards, pressure began to grow for political change.

During the late 1980s, all of the various communist parties were involved in the growing mobilisation of various sections of Nepali society in opposition to the political status quo and the

---

* both mean 'torch' in Nepali.

Panchayat System. Finally, in 1989, the Ma–Le leadership considered the time ripe to launch another movement, leading them to call the Fourth Convention of the Communist Party Ma–Le. Under extremely tight security,[17] 90 delegates from all the regional committees across the country met in August in the forest of Udayapur near Siraha. The party leadership decided to call upon all the 11 communist factions and groupings, and the Congress Party, to unite to bring an end to the Panchayat System. By early 1990, an alliance of seven communist parties had been created, as a United Left Front, to constitute—with the Nepali Congress Party—a broader Movement for the Restoration of Multi-Party Democracy—a 'united front' to bring about the end of the partyless Panchayat System. During February and March, support for the 'democracy movement' or the National People's Movement (*Jana Andolan*) grew to the point where it could no longer be ignored. In April 1990, the Panchayat System effectively came to an end.

Liz Philipson has pointed out that 'after the introduction of democracy there were ideological struggles within the Maoist party as to whether they should opt for constitutional politics or remain committed to classic Maoist armed struggle. Since then Maoist parties have split and re-amalgamated over questions of ideology, tactics, power and personalities in a bewildering and never-ending fashion".[18] They however agreed on some things. The two Masal/Mashal groups and the Revolutionary Workers Party continued to maintain a commitment to the 'people's war' and united to support but not formally participate in the National People's Movement. They formed the *Samyukta Rastriya Janaandolan* (United National People's Movement–UNPM) and joined in the street protests in April 1990 once the People's Movement had gained momentum.

Many have described the extraordinary events leading up to the agreement in early April 1990 on the part of the king to suspend the article in the constitution banning political parties and to form an interim government consisting of representatives from the Nepali Congress, the Left Front and the Palace and we shall not repeat them here. Suffice it to say that the mass movement, initiated and supported by the underground communist party groups, which had brought about the political crisis, which led to the events of April 1990, was henceforward progressively marginalised. Even the Left Front found itself in a distinct minority in the interim government that was formed in May 1990, and its demands for the constituent assembly originally promised in 1951 were avoided. The UNPM, which also called for the formation of a constituent assembly to draft the national constitution, was equally sidelined. A drafting committee framed a new multi-party constitution based on a Westminster-type parliamentary model, while the king produced his own version. Faced with mass demonstrations organised by all of the left forces, however, he was forced to compromise and, after a final review, the new constitution was promulgated at the beginning of November.

The UNPM rejected the new constitution, and initially agreed to boycott the general election scheduled for May 1991. The same month (November), the Communist Party of Nepal (Unity Centre–*Ekata Kendra*) was established, with Pushpa Kamal Dahal (Prachanda) as General Secretary. Shortly afterwards, in January 1991, the United People's Front of Nepal (UPFN) was formed, with the objective of fighting elections, if required. The Unity Centre was to be the revolutionary front; the UPFN, the political front of the same party. The Unity Centre brought together several Maoist communist parties: the CPN (Mashal), under Prachanda; the CPN (Fourth Congress), under Nirmal Lama; the Proletariat Workers' Organisation, under Ruplal Bishwakarma and a splinter group of the CPN (Masal) led by Dr. Babu Ram Bhattarai (which had broken away from the main CPN (Masal), still under Mohan Bikram Singh). The CPN Unity Centre rejected the November 1990 Constitution promulgated by the king, considering it an inadequate basis for a genuine democracy, and continued to demand a constituent assembly, with a view to drawing up a new democratic Constitution and, eventually, the formation of a People's Republic.

The two major communist parties—the CPN (Marxist), the remnants of Pushpa Lal's original party, and the CPN (Marxist–Leninist or ML), founded by the leaders of the Jhapa movement and the largest left organisation at this time—joined together, with some smaller groupings on the left, to form the Nepal Communist Party (United Marxist–Leninist) in 1991. The CPN (UML) participated in the first general election of 1991 and established itself not only as the mainstream communist party but, together with the Nepali Congress Party, as one of the two major parties in Nepal (winning 2,051,269 votes and 69 seats as compared with the 2,749,844 votes and 110 seats gained by the Nepali Congress Party).

The CPN (Unity Centre) also fought the 1991 general election as the United Peoples' Front of Nepal (UPFN) with Babu Ram Bhattarai as co-ordinator and won nine seats. In this general election, UPFN won only 352,129 votes, but gained seats in Siraha and Ramechhap in the east, in Lalitpur in the Kathmandu Valley and in Kavrepalanchowk in the central hills, in Chitwan in the west-central *terai*, in Rolpa (two MPs) in the mid-western hills and in Humla in the far northwest. This made it the third largest party in Parliament. However, '...despite its status as a legitimate party, it had underground groups working within the party, as it continued to espouse the cause of revolutionary struggle in order to capture state power through armed struggle...'.[19] As a political force it was weakened by splits, even within the first few months of its existence. Formed in January 1991, it was initially composed of the splinter group of Masal under Bhattarai, the Fourth Congress under Nirmal Lama, the CPN-Marxist under Sahana Pradhan, the CPN Marxist–Leninist–Maoist (MLM) under Krishna Das, and the Nepal Workers and Peasants Party under Narayan Man Bijukchhe (Rohit). The Rohit group left the UPFN, however, even before the 1991 general elections, and the MLM withdrew afterwards. Others also gradually withdrew.

As the CPN-UML emerged as a major political force within the new parliamentary system, the Nepali Congress government began to demonstrate its hostility towards the more radical leftist parties. Some of the smaller communist parties became even more sceptical of the possibilities of a 'parliamentary road to socialism' for Nepal. The CPN (Unity Centre) held its first congress in December 1991 and decided to adopt 'Marxism–Leninism–Maoism' as the ideological 'direction' of the Party and the path of 'protracted People's War' through the initiation of open class struggle in the rural areas on the classic Chinese model, rather than the 'mass uprising' line proposed by Nirmal Lama, as the appropriate revolutionary strategy for Nepal.[20] The CPN (Unity Centre) dismissed the new parliamentary politics as incapable of leading to progressive change.[21] According to Prachanda,[22] the 'parliamentary road to socialism' had been undermined by the Constitution and the limited form of 'politics' being adopted by what were evidently no more than fractions of the political elite and acceptance of the doctrine of economic liberalisation and collaboration in parliamentary politics risked the party's revolutionary goals.

It was decided that the Unity Centre would go underground although, in practice, it remained semi-underground, but the UPFN was to remain active and 'in the open'. The UPFN fared badly in the 1992 elections, but in April–May 1992, a UPFN-led general strike plunged the country into nationwide violence.[23] There followed a period (1993–94) of intense debate and considerable disagreement within the CPN (Unity Centre) regarding tactics, timing and other aspects of a programme of armed struggle. Similar disagreements developed within the UPFN, and Bhattarai expelled several members of the Nirmal Lama group from the UPFN. In 1994, the CPN (Unity Centre) divided into two parties, the CPN (Unity Centre) and the CPN (Maoist). The former, under Mohan Bikram Singh and Nirmal Lama, participated in the mid-term elections in November 1994 (through the 'recognised' wing of the UPFN under Niranjan Govinda Vaidya, see below) while the latter— the Maoist Party, headed by Prachanda—boycotted the elections. The UPFN also split, with a group led by Babu Ram Bhattarai supporting Prachanda and a group led by Niranjan Govinda Vaidya supporting Mohan Bikram Singh and Nirmal Lama. The Electoral Commission refused to recognise the UPFN faction led by Bhattarai and recognised that of Vaidya. While the CPN (Unity Centre) continued to work within the framework of parliamentary politics, the CPN (Unity Centre) now abandoned all political work within the existing legal framework and started preparing for a People's War.

The outcome of the 1994 mid-term elections was that the CPN (UML) became the largest party in parliament, with 88 seats (as against the 83 of the Nepali Congress Party). The CPN (UML) formed a minority government, which lasted 9 months. It was replaced by a coalition of the Nepali Congress and Rastriya Prajatantrik Party (RPP), before this in turn was replaced by a wholly Nepali Congress Party government. The UPFN group under Babu Ram Bhattarai, having been marginalised by the decision of the Electoral Commission 'boycotted' the 1994 parliamentary mid-term elections, now used the opportunity to criticise the parliamentary democratic system and to prepare cadres to bring 'radical change' through the armed struggle. Some years later, the courts ruled that Bhattarai's faction of the UPFN was the legitimate party, but by then it was too late.

The scene was set for the People's War. During this critical period, the CPN (Maoist) was able to strengthen its party base. In March 1995, at the Third Plenum of the Central Committee, it foreswore elections, changed its name to the Communist Party of Nepal (Maoist) and adopted 'The Strategy and Tactics of Armed Struggle in Nepal'. This document states that 'the conscious peasant class struggle developed in the western hill districts, particularly in Rolpa and Rukum, represents the high level of anti-feudal and anti-imperialist revolutionary struggle. That struggle has given birth to some new tendencies in the Nepali Communist Movement which have inspired us to be more serious about the business of armed struggle'.[24] By now, the CPN (Maoist) was also a member of the Revolutionary Internationalist Movement (RIM), which provided moral support and encouragement.

In their 'Plan for the Historical Initiation of the People's War', adopted by the CPN (Maoist) central committee in September 1995, the Maoists stated that 'on the occasion of the formulation of the plan for the initiation of the process that will unfold as a protracted People's War, based on the strategy of encircling the city from the countryside according to the specificities of our country, the Party once again reiterates its eternal commitment to the theory of People's War developed by Mao as the universal and invincible theory of war'.[25] The theory of the People's War sets out three stages as the balance of forces changes in favour of the revolutionaries: the strategic-defensive stage, the equilibrium or stalemate stage and the strategic-offensive stage. There are four phases in the initial stage: the preparatory phase, the initiation phase, the continuity phase and the base area formation phase. The period 1994–995 could be said to represent the first 'preparatory' phase of the People's War in Nepal.

Arguably, it was only during this period that the Party began to consider launching the armed struggle from the mid-western hills. There were, however, good reasons for adopting this area as the platform for the launch of the People's War—the physical environment was suitable for the launching of a guerrilla war, the economy and society of the region was particularly isolated and remote from urban centres and heavily dependent on small-scale predominantly rain-fed farming, the people were hardy and self-reliant but deeply aware of their own poverty and marginalisation from the mainstream of Nepal's political economy, local inequalities and class divisions, although less marked than in some areas (notably in the *terai*), were sharp and social discrimination intense both within the Brahmin-Chetri-dalit caste communities (against 'untouchables'/dalits and women) and between the Brahmin-Chetris and the distinctive ethnic Magars of the region. The region had also been affected by the long-term involvement of U.S. 'development aid' in the form of the Rapti project, which had offered considerable hopes for the development of the region, poured in resources and had entirely failed to transform the lives of the ordinary people as promised. This 'failed development' may also have played its part.

But there were also specific political reasons why Rolpa and Rukum became the launching ground for the People's War. These two districts had been a stronghold for revolutionary communist activists since the late 1950s and throughout the Panchayat years. As far back as 1980, during the national referendum when people were asked by the king to choose between a reformed Panchayat system and a multi-party regime, the army had to be put on alert in Rolpa since the Fourth Congress had called for a boycott of the vote. The large village of Thawang, which had voted overwhelmingly communist in the first parliamentary elections of 1959, at a time when the Nepali Congress Party achieved a landslide victory across the country as a whole, not only boycotted the elections but, later, apparently, replaced the portraits of the king and queen in government offices with those of Marx and Lenin.

Increasingly, after 1991, and particularly after 1993–94, political activists of the UPFN and other leftist parties in Rolpa and Rukum (where they were particularly strong—the UPFN/CPN (Unity Centre) had two elected MPs from Rolpa and one of the two from Rukum in 1991) were harassed by district government representatives and the local authorities as well as by activists from the Nepali Congress Party. Thapa[26] suggests that each side gave as good as it got, but Karki found, in the course of his fieldwork in Rolpa and Salyan during March 2001, that there was a good deal of evidence from a variety of sources to support the Maoists' claim that they and their supporters had experienced severe harassment during the first part of the decade, and particularly during 1994–95, after their rejection of parliamentary politics. In Rolpa and Rukum districts, for example, some 500 individual criminal charges were filed against UPFN party workers (Karki, 2001, p. 169) and most of those accused—who were local, grass-roots workers for the Party—were obliged to flee their homes and even their home districts as they could find no one prepared to defend them against the charges brought by the authorities.

The Human Rights Yearbook for 1992 produced by the Kathmandu-based organisation INSEC reports on the repression directed mainly against UPFN supporters in the region by the Nepali Congress Party, local authorities and police. Widespread arrests and ill-treatment, and some use of torture while in detention, were reported. The Human Rights Yearbook for 1993 also reports on continuing repression and brutality directed against the UPFN. Even as the abuse of state power continued, through 1994 and 1995, the Maoists (and Babu Ram's UPFN) began what has been called the 'Sija Campaign', after Sisne and Jaljala, two prominent mountain peaks in Rukum and Rolpa respectively, to propagate Maoist ideology through focused training-action programmes whose aim was 'to arouse the masses and heighten political consciousness. These teams of leaders worked with the masses building roads and bridges, and farming', according to one of the participants.[27]

The response of the government to this increase in political activity and continuing fighting between UPFN and Nepali Congress (and also UML) supporters was a police operation codenamed R for Romeo (Rolpa), ostensibly to win the hearts and minds of the people and to demonstrate once and for all to the UPFN and the Maoists who was in control. The ruthlessness of this Operation Romeo became a notorious subject of discussion at the time and some have seen it as the crucial precipitating factor behind the Maoists' eventual commitment to the launching of a People's War. In a newspaper interview in

December 1995, Babu Ram Bhattarai stated that 'around 1,500 policemen, including a specially trained commando force sent from Kathmandu, have been deployed to let loose a reign of terror against the poor peasants...there has been indiscriminate ransacking and looting of properties of common people by the ruling party hoodlums under the protection of the police force. More than 10,000 rural youth, out of a population of 200,000 for the whole district, have been forced to flee their homes and take shelter in the remote jungles'.[28]

The Human Rights Yearbook for 1995 reported that 'The government initiated.. suppressive operations to a degree of state terror. Especially, the workers of the UFPN were brutally suppressed. Under the direct leadership of ruling party workers of the locality, police searched, tortured and arrested, without arrest warrants, in 11 villages of the district. Nearly 6,000 locals had left the villages due to the police operation. One hundred and thirty two people were arrested without serving any warrants. The arrested included elderly people above 75 years. All the detained were subjected to torture'.[29]

This official repression culminated in actions taken by the government-appointed Chief District Officers (CDOs) of Rolpa and Rukum, which were the subject of a statement by the UPFN accusing the authorities of 'barbaric oppression'.[30] Babu Ram Bhattarai, the leader of the UPFN, condemned the 'barbaric repression of the people of Rolpa and Rukum by the Nepali Congress government' and submitted a strongly worded memorandum on 4 February 1996 in which he demanded the dismissal of the CDO of Rolpa, the cancellation of all false criminal charges/cases and the release of all those detained and implicated. He requested an end to administrative repression and state terrorism, and called for an independent investigation.[31] A team of all-party parliamentarians was constituted and its report substantiated many of the claims and accusations made by the UPFN.

In the same month as Babu Ram Bhattarai submitted his memorandum on administrative repression (or by other accounts in January 1996), the United People's Front of Nepal (UPFN) presented a 40-point demand on behalf of the CPN (Maoist) to the Nepali Congress government led by Sher Bahadur Deuba (see Part Two, Chapter 6.1 of this collection). This document focused on a number of issues that had become increasingly pressing in the mid-western hills and particularly in Rolpa and Rukum, but it also made more general demands. As Thapa (2002, p. 82) observes, these demands were not much different from the points outlined in the 1991 election manifesto of the above-ground and till then united UPFN.[32] The UPFN insisted that if no progress was made towards fulfilment of the demands by 17 February 1996, they would have no choice but to resort to armed struggle against the existing state. The government, far from responding positively, cracked down further.

The 'People's War': 1996–2001

On 13 February 1996 (four days before expiry of their deadline), the Communist Party of Nepal (Maoist) declared a People's War in Nepal, issuing a leaflet that called on the people of Nepal to 'March Along the Path of the People's War to Smash the Reactionary State and Establish a New Democratic State' (see Part Two, Chapter 6.2 of this collection). The stated objectives were to overthrow the bureaucratic–capitalist class and state system, to uproot semi-feudalism and to drive out imperialism, in order to establish a new democratic republic with a view to building a new socialist society. To achieve these objectives, CPN (Maoist) adopted the strategy and tactics of a 'protracted People's War', with the aim or purpose of establishing base areas in the rural and remote areas, so as, eventually, to surround urban areas and seize state power. The 'Maoist strategy' divided the People's War into three strategic stages: defensive, equilibrium or stalemate, and strategic offence. Each strategic stage is further divided into sub-stages or phases. Within each of these, tactical action plans are developed and employed to achieve the strategic plan.

The 'People's War' was actually launched in six districts— Rukum, Rolpa, Jajarkot, Salyan and Gorkha in mid-western and western Nepal, and in Sindhuli in the centre-east of Nepal. The first four of these districts were in the mid-west and came to constitute the 'core' areas of Maoist support and to provide 'their temporary base areas'. On the first day, the people's militia and commandos of CPN (Maoist) captured police stations, including Athbiskot police post in Rukum District and Holeri police post in Rolpa District. The same day, 'people's commandos' in Gorkha District captured the Small Farmers' Development Project office, seized the land ownership documents kept as collateral by the Agriculture Development Bank (ADB), distributed them to their owners and destroyed the official loan documents and records kept by the bank.[33] During the first month, it is estimated that more than 6,000 'people's actions' were carried out, which were classified by the Maoists as primarily 'publicity' (80 per cent), but also 'destruction' (15 per cent) and 'other activities' (5 per cent). This was said to launch the 'initiation' phase of the People's War under the first plan (see Part Two of this collection).

The declaration of Peoples War in 1996 received remarkably little attention. The police was despatched to deal with what was perceived as a law and order question for several years. During Operation Romeo and the later Operation Kilo Sierra (see below), however, the police was particularly violent and even barbaric in operations in the mid western hills. They treated everyone as a potential Maoist and many innocent people were arrested, ill-treated, tortured and killed almost randomly. The police actions resulted in a substantial proportion of the local population making common cause with the Maoists and the mid west was effectively confirmed as a Maoist heartland. This was not immediately obvious and the government must have been convinced at the time that the insurgency was a matter that could be kept under control by strong policing.

The second plan, which is said to have lasted from March 1996 to June 1997, was 'to develop the people's war in an organised way', and included the 'elimination of selected enemies'. During this period the Maoists were very successful in capturing weapons and developing guerrilla zones on a small scale (see Part Two, 6.3 and 6.4). The third plan was said to have lasted a year, from June 1997. During this period of around 2 years, the guerrilla war was further developed and extended, a programme to boycott the local elections and subsequently to force the elected officials to resign from their posts was undertaken with a fair degree of success, despite a massive police deployment to protect the process, and in a couple of districts the Maoists filled the vacuum created in local government by their operations with 'people's committees' (see Part Two, 6.5 and 6.6).

In February 1998, they declared the existence of a Central Military Commission; they also organised a rally in Delhi under the banner 'Solidarity Forum to Support the People's War in

Nepal' with the support of six local Indian organisations. Looking back over the first 2 years of the People's War, considerable progress appeared to have been made. But as the Maoists intensified and extended their activities, however, the government launched a major repressive police operation, Kilo Sierra 2. Starting in 1998, this operation led to a massive increase in confrontations and clashes between the police and the Maoists, and also to an extraordinary rise in the injuries and deaths resulting from the conflict. While under the Surya Bahadur Thapa government from October 1997 to April 1998 (6 months), the total number of deaths officially recorded was 34 (18 by the police), under the Koirala government, which succeeded it, from April 1998 to May 1999 (14 months), the number of deaths was 596 (457 of them the result of police action).[34]

As with the earlier Operation Romeo, it was recognised after the event that this second police operation proved another contribution to the intensification of the People's War—as the English language *Nepali Times* stated in an editorial in October 2000, 'it is now clear that it was state terrorism unleashed by the police in 1997–98 in Rukum, Rolpa and Jajarkot that lit the spark for an expanding insurgency".[35] At the time, it seems it was not so clear. If Operation Romeo had concentrated pretty much exclusively on the mid west, where the Maoists were active, Operation Kilo Sierra 2 was much more comprehensive, even if it too focused on the mid west. In principle it was intended to crush the insurgency across all 'the Maoist-affected areas'. The police carried out the operation over a period of more than a year in 18 districts across the country.

Writing in 1998, prior to the unleashing of the police operation Kilo Sierra 2, Stephen Mikesell argued that 'the problem is that this self-described People's War feeds on real, pervasive dissatisfaction and suffering in the countryside and, especially among the youth, frustration and anger. The recent democratic constitutional transformation has aggravated and deepened the exploitation and inequality always at the basis of the state. Consequently, repression of the Maoists, whomever or whatever they are, must take the form of a war against the countryside which by necessity would escalate to the scale of Suharto's massacre of one-half to a million of Indonesia's populace in 1964'.[36] He guessed that, "although many of Nepal's leaders might have it in them to do this.. the conditions are not ready for such a "solution"...no government could dare mount a full-scale war and survive, until the position of a wide array of the ruling class becomes desperate".[37] He did, however, note that 'at the time of this writing in 1988, the parliament is considering Draconian anti-terrorist legislation. It was unable to muster the necessary political support under Surya Bahadur Thapa's weak ministry, though it might pass under the historically hardline Girija Koirala, who announced a "priority to end the Maoist insurgency" in his swearing in as prime minister on 15 April'.

The attempt to introduce a 'black law' against terrorism failed, in the face of widespread protests from the Nepalese intelligentsia and human rights organisations, and from abroad, but later, in 1998, the CPN (ML), which had split from the CPN (UML), joined the Nepali Congress government as a junior partner barely 2 months after the police operation 'Kilo Sierra 2' had been launched. In fact, the Nepali Congress government under Girija Prasad Koirala was actually being propped up from the outside by the CPN (ML) when Kilo Sierra began. In fact, from mid-1998 onwards, the killing of Maoists and their supporters, as well as civilians caught in the cross-fire or indistinguishable to the security forces from the Maoists, escalated to reach the highest point ever in the 5 years between the launching of the People's War in February 1996 and the declaration of the State of Emergency in November 2001. The Lokendra Bahadur Chand RPP government set up the Dhami Commission to find ways of resolving the crisis, but he was ousted shortly afterwards, and the report was, it seems, never produced or published.

Although the Operation, its character and its extent have been denied, it undoubtedly took place and had a dramatic impact wherever it was implemented, even if the response was arguably the direct opposite of what was intended. The major response by the Maoists to Operation Kilo Sierra 2 was the initiation of their fourth plan, which began on 27 October 1998, with unprecedented attacks across the country and adopted the slogan 'Let us embark on the great path of creating base areas'. The fifth plan, which is said to have begun in August 1999, was also related to the creation of base areas. There is constant reference in the Nepali Maoist literature and in the statements of the CPN (Maoist) at this time to 'temporary base areas'. This implies that although there is undoubtedly a geographical 'core' to the movement, in the relatively remote mid-western hills, these do not as yet constitute 'base areas'. Maoist sources suggest that there were four phases within the first strategic-defensive stage: a preparatory phase, an initiation phase, a continuity phase and a phase of base area formation. By 1998–99, the struggle was considered by the Maoist leadership to have completed the initial three phases and to have entered the fourth, 'base area formation phase', of the stage of 'strategic defence'.

In February 1999, 3 years after the launch of the People's War, the formation of a regular People's Army was announced, as was the formation of a Central Military Commission. The military activities of the Maoist movement now began to increase both in scale and scope, and in frequency. From perhaps 8–10 districts, the 'reach' of the Maoists now began to increase to involve some 20 or more. The Nepali Congress Party under Krishna Prasad Bhattarai won the elections and appointed Sher Bahadur Deuba to explore possible negotiations with the Maoists. During May and June 1999 Deuba held informal talks with representatives of the Maoists and two top Maoist leaders, Deb Gurung and Suresh Ale Magar, were freed as a result. Later in the year, however, the killing of CPN (Maoist) alternative politburo member Suresh Wagle by the police in Gorkha was followed by simultaneous attacks by the Maoists in 25 districts during the night of 22 September 1999 and the organisation of a Nepal *bandh* (shut-down) on 7 October.

By February 2000, the Maoists claimed that there were only 9 (out of a total of 75) districts that had not come 'under their direct influence'.[38] More conservative estimates suggested that Maoist activities had spread to over 45 districts.[39] The capacity of the Maoists to wage their People's War across a significant area of the countryside was now becoming increasingly evident. As one observer has commented: 'whereas the Maoists and those suspected of sympathising with them were initially at the receiving end, after 2000, the tables turned. Official figures for the number of those killed during the conflict reveal that during the two years between April 1998 when Koirala took power and March 2000 when Bhattarai gave way to Koirala once again, the total number of deaths was 1,016—596 under the Koirala government and 420 under the Bhattarai government. But whereas in the first period (14 months), over three-quarters (457 out of 596) were the result of police action and one quarter (139) the result of Maoist action, in the second period (10 months), two-thirds (279 out of 420) were the result of police action and one-third (141) the result of Maoist action. In other words, although the bulk of the killing was done by the police in both periods, the balance shifted significantly between the two periods.[40]

In March 2000, K.P. Bhattarai was ousted by Girija Prasad Koirala, who accused the party leader of failing to maintain law and order. Koirala now took over, with a promise to use all possible means including the army to combat the Maoists. There was much discussion at the time, as to who controlled the army—the government or the king. The army was not called out, but the embattled police began consolidating thinly spread out posts into relatively more secure strongholds. But, as events in September 2000 and April 2001—when Maoists overran major police strongholds—were to demonstrate, such a strategy evidently did not work".[41]

But the People's War has always been more than a simple military insurgency. The consolidation of the political strategy of the movement kept pace, more or less, with the military expansion and consolidation. As early as February 2000— around the time that Prachanda gave his interview to Li Onesto for the *Revolutionary Worker* (see Part Two, Chapter 3)—the Maoist leadership had been in contact with government representatives and Prachanda had indicated a willingness to enter into talks, provided certain conditions were met. These included (1) revealing the whereabouts of a central committee member along with others who had 'disappeared', (2) initiating moves to release arrested workers and sympathisers and (3) ending state terrorism and beginning the process of investigating an incident of arson and killing in Rukum district, providing compensation and taking action against the guilty. 'Should these minimum conditions be fulfilled, we are ready to send our representatives for high-level negotiations and we would like to inform you that we will cease all operations during the period of talks', wrote Prachanda.[42] However, despite repeated calls from both sides indicating a willingness to talk, nothing substantial took place.

At the fourth extended meeting of the Party, held in April

2000, it was agreed to move towards the establishment of a United Revolutionary People's Council (URPC) of patriotic, leftist and progressive forces, instead of organising through UPFN. It was subsequently announced that UPFN was to be dissolved—according to Dr. Babu Ram Bhattarai, it was to be re-organised as the Revolutionary United Front of the Maoist Party.[43] However, a year passed and still the CPN (Maoist) had not declared a Revolutionary United Front.[44] UPFN was in fact not eventually dissolved until February 2001, almost a year later. Maoist leaders began talks with various ethnic, regional and political forces for the formation of URPC and they also established an ethnic department at the central level. The linking of the regional question to the 'national question' (relating to the role of ethnic and caste minorities or *jana jati* in the case of Nepal) is very explicit—and has been much debated outside the Maoist movement by those concerned with the role of ethnic minorities in Nepal.

Between the period of the fourth extended meeting and the dissolution of UPFN, a number of front organisations were formed, including the following: Magarant (Magar) National Liberational Front, Tamang National Liberational Front, Tamuwan (Gurung) National Liberation Front, Limbuwan Liberation National Front, Nepal Dalit Liberation Front, Tharuwan National Liberation Front, Madheshi Liberation Front, Karnali Regional Liberation Front, Thami Liberation Front, Majhi National Liberation Front and Newa Khala. URPC has a 75-point policy and programme with a special chapter on the "Ethnic and Regional Question", which includes the right of autonomous areas and the right to keep or modify traditional religions and custom. It is led by Babu Ram Bhattarai and has an organisational structure based on central, regional, district and village/town levels. Regional or ethnic fronts have been given the work of running the autonomous regions until the 'People's Republic' is fully established. The Maoists plan extensive devolution of power to the regions and this is all detailed in the URPC constitution. The regions proposed are as follows:

> Seti-Mahakali Autonomous Region—Hill area of Seti and Mahakali Zone
>
> Bheri-Karnali Autonomous Region—Hill area of Bheri and Karnali Zone

Tharuwan Autonomous Region—Western terai area of Rapti to Mahakali Zone

Magarat Autonomous Region—From Kali Gandaki region to the hill area of Dhaulagiri, Rapti and Lumbini Zone

Tamuwan Autonomous Region Gandak Region

Tamang Saling Autonomous Region—Hill area of Bagmati, Narayani and Janakpur Zone except Kathmandu valley

Newar Autonomous Region—Kathmandu valley

Kirat Autonomous Region—Hill area of Mechi, Koshi and Sagarmatha Zone

Madhesh Autonomous Region—Awadh area of the mid terai and Bhojpuri and Mithila Pradesh of the eastern terai

The process of devolution envisaged and the work with the ethnic fronts will be a formidable challenge for the Maoists. They have already experienced some difficulties with military discipline in the East with the Kirat front, who at one stage dissolved their alliance with the Maoists.*

The sixth plan, which was said to have begun in July 2000 and to have ended with the Second National Conference in February 2001, adopted the slogan 'raise to new heights the guerrilla war and the people's resistance struggle'. It was during this period, in September 2000, that a major assault on Dunai, the capital of Dolpa District, was carried out by the Maoist forces (about 1,000 Maoist guerrillas were involved). Koirala wished to send the army in hot pursuit but was inhibited from doing so, apparently at the highest level. The Home Minister, Govinda Raj Joshi, resigned in protest 4 days later. After this major incident, the Royal Nepalese Army was deployed in the capitals of 16 districts. At the same time, in October, Deputy Prime Minister, Ram Chandra Poudel, met Maoist central committee member, Rabindra Shrestha, in the first-ever one-to-one between the government and the Maoists. Shortly thereafter, in November, the government released several high-level Maoists, including Dinesh Sharma, who denounced the insurgency, only to retract

---

* The whole issue of the relationship between the Maoist People's War and what might be called 'the national question' is a matter of much debate and disagreement. For one, radical but certainly non-Maoist perspective see Bhattachan (2000, 135–62).

their statements immediately. There is little doubt that, throughout the first 4 years of the War, popular support for the Maoists was considerable. Stephen Mikesell argued in October 2000, 'there is widespread support for the Maoists in the countryside and great sympathy for them in the cities. There is satisfaction in many circles that corrupt officials, who have gone so long unpunished, are now getting their comeuppance. There is a general consensus in the press that the problem is a political one and that the solution will also be political'.[45] There is evidence to indicate that the Maoists were still interested in the possibility of talks. At the same time, they remained clearly committed to the armed struggle and to supporting open dissent in the urban areas, including riots towards the end of December.

In January 2001, Koirala obtained royal approval for the establishment of a new para-military force and the appointment of regional administrators, but the bill was not ratified by parliament. At their Second National Conference in February 2001, for reasons that are not entirely clear, but perhaps as a result of their broad success to date in expanding the war and building support, the Maoists began to redefine their policies and plans beyond the confines of the People's War. Prachanda was elevated from secretary general of the Party to chairman and the Conference adopted as their guiding principle, the 'Prachanda Path'. What was hailed as 'the Prachanda Path' emerged as a 'new' strategy for a revolution, that would involve a fusion of the Maoist model of protracted people's war (expand from villages to towns) with a Leninist model of general armed insurrection. One aim of the Prachanda Path was to use the People's War in order to expand their base areas in villages and use that as the foundation for a people's revolt at the centre in order to overthrow the government. This strategy recognised both the risks involved in taking on the Royal Army in the rural areas and the importance of building the base for a popular revolt at the centre, in Kathmandu.

To this end, the Maoists once again began to raise the political issues of a constituent assembly, a new constitution, a republic and national sovereignty, and sought to embark on talks with the government, through intermediaries. Thapa notes that an earlier scheduled meeting between the two sides was called off only when the Maoists indicated their preference for a public statement at the Second National Conference. In addition to its emphasis on 'a continuous struggle against wrong tendencies', the statement issued after the Conference called for a dialogue with 'all concerned sections' as a step towards a conference of 'all political parties, organisations and representatives of mass organisations in the country, election of an interim government by such a conference with the guarantee of a people's constitution under the leadership of the interim government'.

This appeared to some at least as 'a climb-down'. Thapa argues that 'considering that the Maoists's September 1995 Central Committee document was clear that they would "never allow this struggle to become a mere instrument for introducing partial reforms in the condition of the people, or terminating in a simple compromise by exerting pressure on the reactionary classes", and that one of the main hurdles during possible talks would have been their demand for a constituent assembly, this was a climb-down from their earlier uncompromising stance'.[46] But, if they showing themselves willing to talk, the Maoist were also totally committed to the continuation of the People's War and their long-term strategy. Wrongly reading Prachanda Path to mean that the Maoists were softening, the government met a long-standing demand as a pre-condition for dialogue and anounced the whereabouts of those Maoists in custody. A major assault by the Maoists in April on two police strongholds, resulting in the deaths of 70 policemen demonstrated their commitment clearly as did the fact that by June they had declared District People's Governments in Rukum, Jajarkot and Salyan, in addition to numerous Village Peoples' Government at VDC level throughout these three districts and Rolpa. Police chief, Pradeep Shumshere Rana, admitted that the police were finding it hard to fight the Maoists, and ordinances for setting up a para-military force and appointing regional administrators were promulgated once again. The opposition UML party stepped up street protests against Koirala, and Deuba stepped up a growing campaign from within the Nepali Congress party to unseat him.

The massacre in June 2001 of the Royal Family, by a member of the Royal Family, was entirely unforeseen and certainly affected the Maoists' plans and tactics, if not their overall strategy. The apparent opportunism with which the Maoists responded to the massacre—claiming it as an imperialist and reactionary plot involving the new king, Gyanendra, and India—and proposing the immediate formation of an interim government, a new constitution and the establishment of a republic—did not arouse much support, even from the left (despite the fact that these were long-standing claims). Hopes that the government of China might provide support proved misplaced, and attempts to claim the previous King Birendra as an ally aroused a storm of controversy regarding the relationship between the Palace and the Maoists (see the contribution by Mohan Bikram Singh in Part Three, Chapter 8, of this collection). The Maoists infiltrated street demonstrations following the massacre and also continued to keep up the military pressure. The Maoist women's organisation, ANWA (Revolutionary), declared Chitwan a dry area, and the student wing of the Maoists stepped up attacks on private schools.

The government issued Public Security Regulations amidst widespread protest from the left parties and human rights organisations. In July, the Maoists killed 41 policemen in attacks on police posts in Lamjung, Nuwakot, Ramechhap, Gulmi and Dailekh—on the occasion of the new King Gyanandra's birthday—and attacked a police post at Holeri in Rolpa, taking 69 policemen hostage. The Koirala government sent in the army, but after brief clashes, the army was called back. When the soldiers failed to engage the Maoists, Koirala resigned, privately citing disagreement with the king. It was around this time that the Maoists formed a regional alliance with other Maoist parties in the sub-continent, - the Confederation of Communist and Maoist Parties of South Asia (CCOMPOSA).

The Holeri incident—where the Maoists found themselves inadvertently on the verge of a confrontation with the Army—combined with a change of government (as Prime Minister Girija Prasad Koirala resigned to be replaced on 19 July by Sher Bahadur Deuba, who became prime minister for the second time) led to a ceasefire on 23 July (after a Maoist attack on a police post in Bajura) and the initiation of a programme of talks between the Maoists and the government. Moves towards talks had in fact begun during the first quarter of 2001 with prisoner releases. Immediately after taking office, Sher Bahadur Deuba made a public statement on 24 July giving priority to a dialogue with the Maoists. The Maoist response was positive and a ceasefire was agreed. With a truce in place, the Maoists surfaced and held open rallies all over the country. Gatherings were also held in Kathmandu. There were three rounds of talks on 30 August, 13–15 September and 13 November. The Maoists demanded not only a continuation of the ceasefire and return of prisoners, but the establishment of a constituent assembly as the first stage in the democratic construction of a new republican constitution.

Prior to the talks and after the second round, Prime Minister Deuba held all-party meetings. These meetings fully supported the dialogue with the Maoists and endorsed the government's position of refusing to yield on the Maoist political demands—especially the demand for institutionalisation of a republican state. Prachanda called a meeting of the various Nepalese left and Communist parties in Nepal in Silguri (India) on 21 August. After this, Madhav Kumar Nepal, general secretary of the CPN-UML, informed an emergency meeting of the UML central committee that he had rejected outright Prachanda's proposal for the left parties to work together for a constituent assembly and republican state. The first round of talks was held at Godavari. They involved three Maoists and five government negotiators. The talks were facilitated by two respected intermediaries, Daman Nath Dhungana (a lawyer who contributed to the drafting of the 1990 constitution) and Padma Ratna Tuladhar (a former UML Member of Parliament and now an independent leftist with some Maoist sympathies).

The talks appeared to begin well. The second round of talks was held in mid-September, and the Maoists again tabled their three core political demands: for an interim government, a constituent assembly and a new constitution, looking forward to the establishment of a republic. The third round of talks was held, after some delays on 13 November. Just before the talks, the government scrapped the Public Security Regulations and freed 68 political prisoners as a gesture of goodwill. The Maoists abandoned their demands for a republic, but stuck to the need for a constituent assembly. All of the mainstream parties involved rejected this proposal. On 21 November, Prachanda declared that he saw little point in continuing the talks and, even as the government was preparing for a fourth round of talks the Maoists broke off discussions.

Virtually 4 months to the day after the ceasefire was

announced, the Maoists declared the formation of the United (or Joint) Revolutionary People's Council of Nepal (described by them as 'an embryonic Central People's Government Organising Committee') to be led by Babu Ram Bhattaai, and on 23 November re-launched their military activities, with an assault on the army base at Ghorahi in Dang district in western Nepal (killing 14 soldiers) and attacks in other parts of the country, in Dang, Surkhet, Syangjya and elsewhere. There were also attacks on police posts, resulting in 23 deaths among the police. Banks were raided and some Rs 225 million looted over the week. They attacked the army again at Salleri, Solukhumbu district, killing four soldiers, 27 policemen and a Chief District Officer. But their casualties were said to be high (over 60 killed in official reports).

There has been much speculation as to why the talks 'failed'. After all, the first meeting was described as 'a meeting of all friends who have not seen each other for a long time, after all one of the Maoists was earlier in Parliament with us.' However, by the second round, 'the Maoists seemed tougher and more theoretical. They began to give us lectures and try to teach us Marxism. We got irritated and asked them not to lecture us'.[47] The talks were unsuccessful for a number of reasons.

Some have argued that the government was unprepared. Narahari Achharya, a government negotiator, recently stated that 'the government did not have any concrete agenda and vision while holding the peace talks with the Maoists'.[48] He felt that the government was not fully prepared and had no view of the final destination of the talks. Others talk of lack of negotiating skills on both sides. One of the facilitators was quite self critical after the event. He said, 'I felt very uneasy afterwards about our failure. We had no experience of conflict resolution and we do not have the technical skills. We wanted a peaceful dialogue and tried to use our experience to create it. At the time of the talks I thought both sides were serious. Now I think the government side were not serious. The problem was created by a lack of seriousness in all the political parties".[49] The other facilitator felt that both parties were unprepared but blamed the government more for this. He felt that in both camps pro-military groups had prevailed. The government and the Maoists had both been using the time of the negotiations to consolidate their position and prepare for war. This was to a certain extent confirmed by one of the government negotiators who stated that the problem for the government had been the collapse of the security infrastructure without a space to recreate it. With that collapse, security information had also dried up, although they had begun to recreate this by inaugurating the armed police. On the other hand, by November 2001 there were District Level People's Governments in 21 districts (out of 72)—all hill districts.*

Another explanation relates to the relationship between tactics and strategy in the Maoists 'protracted People's War'. The call for an early move to a republic in Nepal, following the June massacre, attracted little support, and they played this down over the next few months, emphasising instead the long-standing demands of the left for a constituent assembly and ultimately a revised 'democratic' constitution. The negotiations themselves may well have been, some argued, simply a tactic to provide a chance to re-group militarily and politically, to test the water as regards public opinion and support in the urban areas and among 'the parliamentary left' in general. When they felt they had a better grasp on the situation, they simply broke off the talks and resumed the armed struggle 'as usual'. Support for this view would come from the fact that almost immediately they broke off talks they launched a wide-ranging assault on the army and the police in several places across the country—this would have taken some time to prepare and must have been planned well before they broke off talks.

The official Maoist position was that the government was unwilling to take seriously any of the demands or proposals put forward by the Maoists and that there was no point in pursuing the talks further. *Maoist Information Bulletin 1* reported that the government rejected everything they proposed and offered nothing themselves; so 'what was the point in continuing with endless rounds of talks with no political solution in sight'?[50]

Others suggest that the talks themselves created major divisions within the Party, in part because of a fear on the part of

---

* Rolpa, Rukum, Salyan, Jajarkot, Dailekh, Kalikot-Accham-Bajura, Jumla-Kalikot, Dolakha, Dhading, Gorkha, Tanahun, Parbat, Palpa, Lamjung, Sankhuwasabha, Ramechhap, Sindhuli, Sindhupal chowk, Gulmi, Nuwakot-Rasuwa and Terathum, (according to Sharma, 2001, p. 12).

some cadres in the field that they might lead to proper negotiations and some form of 'settlement', and in part because the talks focused on some issues rather than others. The Maoists put forward a set of political demands and a set of other demands (which included socio-economic issues) to the government negotiating team. The socio-economic and other demands received no attention; the focus was totally on the political demands. It could have seemed that the talks were more about the political possibilities for the leadership while the broader aims of the revolutionary war were sidelined. Or it could have represented a certain tension between the political and the military tendencies within the Maoist camp. Certainly lots of posters appeared in support of Badal in the Mid-West around that time,* which may have reflected a concerted effort to rally around Badal and exert pressure to end the negotiations. The significance of this is denied by the Maoists themselves.

One set of factors, however, must have been the changes brought about by the June massacre and the accession of King Gyanendra to the throne, and the events of 11 September in the United States. President George W. Bush's declaration of the 'war against terrorism' and the shifting international balance of forces (as the United States and its allies went to war against Al Qaida and the Taliban regime in Afghanistan, and India struggled to find an appropriate foreign policy stance, given the massive Western support to the Pakistan regime), undoubtedly encouraged the new king, Gyanendra, and the government to adopt a somewhat harder line than hitherto. One indication of this is that the Maoists had planned a mass meeting in Kathmandu for 21 September with hundreds of thousands expected to participate, but in the light of '11/9', the government was able to prevent this from taking place. For whatever reasons, the new king, Gyanendra, certainly appeared prepared in principle to adopt a much stronger line with respect to the Maoists than the previous king, Birendra, and other hardliners in the government were emboldened by the worldwide concern with 'terrorism' after 11 September and determined to take advantage of this to strengthen their position. The deployment of the army

---

* Confirmed during conversations with staff from various projects in the Mid West with the author January and April 2002.

to various locations in the hill areas and plans to establish an Integrated Internal Security and Development Programme (IISDP) indicated a greater willingness on the part of Gyanendra to listen to the army chiefs and entertain a military solution.

In any case, on 23 November, the Maoists broke off the talks and breached the ceasefire, launching a series of attacks on various targets, both military and civilian, in Surkhet, Dang, Syangja and other parts of the country. In all, they undertook 48 simultaneous attacks in 30 districts and struck a devastating blow at the credibility of the army: for the first time the guerrillas attacked the Royal Nepal Army, killing 14 soldiers at the Ghorahi base in Dang District. They used 'waves' of cadres and militia, not all of them armed, against their other selected targets. They looted an estimated Rs. 225 million from banks in 1 week. It is estimated that 250 people (Maoists and government forces) were killed in the 3 days between 23 November 2001 and the government's declaration of a State of Emergency on 26 November alone.

A State of Emergency: 2001–02

On 26 November 2001, after talks between the government of Nepal and the Maoists broke down, and the latter had launched attacks on police and army posts, a State of Emergency was declared, the army was called out and the Terrorist and Disruptive Activities (Control and Punishment) Ordinance (TADO) was promulgated, granting wide powers to the security forces to arrest people involved in 'terrorist' activities. CPN (Maoist) was declared a 'terrorist organisation' under the Ordinance. The declaration of the State of Emergency was accompanied by the suspension of sub-clauses a), b) and d) of Article 12, clause 1) of Article 13 and Articles 15, 16, 17, 22 and 23 of the Constitution of Nepal. The rights contained in these clauses—the rights to freedom of thought and expression, assembly and movement, the right not to be held in preventive detention without sufficient ground, and the rights to information, property, privacy and constitutional remedy—were suspended throughout the whole country.

Prime Minister Deuba was clearly very upset at the ending of the negotiations by the Maoists; speaking to Indian journalists in early December, he announced, "They betrayed me, my government and the whole people of Nepal. Now there is nothing for us to do but wipe them out".[51] Until this point, the conflict had been, largely, a low intensity conflict—it was estimated in October 2001 that around 1,800 people had been killed up to that point in the conflict over a period of five and a half years, with hundreds reported missing, and thousands displaced.[52] After the break-up of the talks, the resumption of the conflict and the declaration of the State of Emergency, the intensity and the scale of the conflict increased significantly. During the first month of the Emergency, the Nepali human rights organisation INSEC reported 606 people killed by the state security forces and a further 153 killed by the Maoists. The Maoists claimed that, in the first 3 months of the Emergency, they had killed some 600 Royal Nepalese Army personnel.

Thapa suggests that 'the Maoists seemed buoyed by their initial successes against the army, but there also seems to have been some doubt about their ultimate victory by military tactics alone'.[53] The government introduced a "surrender scheme" when the emergency was imposed on 26 November and invited Maoists to surrender. For the next few months there were reports of hundreds of Maoists surrendering throughout the country. On 19 December 2001 it was reported that 1,689 Maoists had surrendered since the declaration of the state of emergency, including 364 people who had served in Maoist 'People's Governments'.

Deuba had rapidly moved the country onto a full military footing and now began to enlist international help for this. In early December, the Maoists also sent a statement to members of the international community asking them not to interfere in Nepal's internal affairs and promising to keep them informed of its policy commitments as 'an embryonic new state'. They also stated that they had shown maximum flexibility in the negotiations until they had been forced to withdraw. They said, 'We are still open to this proposal [elected constituent assembly] and prepared to suspend all armed activities and resume the broken talks if the other side makes a matching gesture'.[54] In the press statement issued by Prachanda on the sixth anniversary of the launching of the People's War, he appealed 'to all parties within parliament and outside and pro-people forces to come together against the military dictatorship of the near-dead feudal autocracy. In this historic moment we are ready to be involved in talks, dialogue, fronts, or show any kind of flexibility...We have never closed the door for talks to find a political solution and we will never do so in the future either'.[55]

After this, however, the conflict intensified further, with the Maoists launching several further major attacks on army positions, police posts, infrastructure and other targets (including one on the Coca Cola bottling plant in Kathmandu), and the police and army responding; even tourist areas (including Lukla, the main entry point for trekkers in the Solukhumbu/Everest region) were now directly affected by the conflict for the first time in the 6-year war. On 13 February 2002, 6 years almost to the day after the declaration of a People's War by the Communist Party of Nepal (Maoist), and at about the same time as Prachanda's appeal for unity and dialogue, Maoist rebels killed at least 130 policemen, soldiers and civilians in one of the largest attacks on government security forces since the conflict began. Earlier in February, the rebels had set off two bombs in government tax offices in the capital.

On Saturday 16 February 2002, more than 100 people were killed when rebels attacked government offices and police posts in Mangalsen, the district headquaters of Achham district 200 miles to the west of Kathmandu. In a separate strike hours later, another 30 or so policemen were killed at nearby airport. As an indication of the impact of such attacks on the work of development agencies, the international U.S.-funded CARE Nepal was obliged to make an immediate re-assessment of its work in Accham and was eventually obliged to withdraw. This action was followed by a call for a nation-wide general strike later in the week to mark the sixth anniversary of the start of the People's War. The planned strike (or *bandh*) was in fact called off (ostensibly to enable students across the country to sit their SLC examinations), and proposed for a week in the latter part of April. On 21 February 2002 parliament extended the state of emergency by 3 months. In the meanwhile, the war continued. According to reports in the international media, 62 Maoist guerrillas were killed by the Nepalese army in March; 48 policemen and 6 civilians were killed by Maoist guerrillas in Dang District in early April 2002 and 35 policemen and 8 Maoists were killed in subsequent related confrontations, with 13 policemen killed in Lamahi (*The Guardian*,

13 April). These were only the major clashes.

Throughout April, human rights activists in Kathmandu received faxes and letters from the Maoists, asking them to help facilitate a dialogue with the Government. A flurry of articles speculating about peace initiatives appeared in the press, one citing an unofficial meeting between the parties as about to take place in Bhairahawa. The demand for dialogue on the part of the Maoists appeared to be strong and continuing. A former Maoist commander, Puskar Gautam, interviewed by Liz Philipson, explained the Maoist tactics: 'They now need to try and restore their political credentials. This could be why the Maoists are being forced by public opinion to resort to more democratic means of protest such as *bandhs* and dialogue.' 'Now they are under pressure to strike a better balance between legitimate political protest and armed struggle'. 'That all three rebel tactics—the talks, continued fighting and *bandhs*—are all being used together could be hints (if hints are still needed) that the Maoists understand that the heavy death toll of soldiers in Mangalsen has little meaning unless they are able to show their presence in the streets of Kathmandu'.[56] So, in other words, the Maoists apparently remain concerned to developing a political debate and encourage political mobilisation, particularly in the urban areas and among the 'middle classes', as well as seeking talks and maintaining the armed struggle—all at the same time. The similarities with the tactics adopted over the years by the Irish Republican Army in Northern Ireland are striking.

The government, however, was not impressed by these overtures and on 23 April they underscored their hard line policy by placing a price on the heads of the top Maoist leaders.[57] During April, the conflict intensified. As the Maoist rebels multiplied their attacks in strategically important remote districts, even after the re-imposition of state of emergency, security was tightened still further in response, bringing about increasing concern from international human rights organisations. Amnesty International, for example, reported that month that, according to official sources, more than 3,300 people had been arrested since 26 November; that many had been held in army camps without access to a lawyer or a doctor, or their families and few of those arrested had been brought to court.[58] During April and May, the government deployed the Royal Nepalese Army to an increasing degree, denounced the Maoists continually as 'terrorists' and effectively curtailed civil rights and press freedoms.

The report by Amnesty International[59] called upon armed groups to observe the minimum human standards in all situations where law enforcement personnel and an entity opposing them undertake military-style activities on a regular and consistent basis. These principles are contained primarily in Article 3, common to four Geneva Conventions of 1949, and should be upheld by the police, army and members of the CPN (Maoist). The report provides a useful summary of the background to the current situation and then documents in some detail the human rights violations perpetrated by the state security forces, and by the Maoists. It also criticises the government for permitting human rights violations 'in the field', but also for not having taken more decisive action regarding arbitrary detention, 'disappearances', deaths in custody and unfair trials. It criticises the Maoists for deliberate and unlawful killings, hostage taking, the use of child soldiers and human rights abuses by 'people's courts'. The report concludes with a set of recommendations, primarily for the government and state security forces, but it also calls on the leadership of the Maoists to uphold minimum humane standards applicable to the situation in Nepal, including those contained in Article 3 common to the four Geneva Conventions of 1949. At the beginning of June 2002, the National Human Rights Commission (NHRC) constituted 2 years ago—produced a report on human rights in Nepal after the team had completed an on-the-spot investigation of the situation in Rolpa, Rukum, Salyan and Jajarkot since the declaration of the State of Emergency. The Commission blamed both the government of Nepal and its security forces and the Maoist rebels for 'naked human rights violations'.*

Increasingly, also, the conflict was being reported in the international press, and foreign governments and international agencies were becoming increasingly alarmed at the intensification of the conflict. Observers estimated in April that up to 4,800 people had died in the conflict, more than half of them since November

---

* On 23 April 2002 the government announced a cash prize ranging from NRs 100,000 to 5,000,000 (U.S. $13,000–64,000) for those bringing in the Maoists' top figures whether alive or dead (*Kathmandu Post*, 12 April 2002.

2001. There was now growing concern abroad, and particularly on the part of those states who felt they had a stake in Nepal's political struggle, and had 'signed up' after 11 September 2001 to the international 'war against terrorism', at the escalating violence and the apparent failure of the constitutional political actors, even with a significant deployment of the security forces, to deal with the insurgency. At the end of April, at least a dozen specialist personnel from U.S. Pacific Command spent several weeks with the Royal Nepalese Army touring western districts where fighting has been most intense. A Pentagon spokesman went on the record to state that the mission's purpose was to assess how best to spend U.S. funds to help the government of Nepal fight the insurgents. In May, Prime Minister Deuba was in Washington trying to secure further assistance from the United States. The U.S. government appeared prepared to consider an allocation of $20 million for military assistance and to double the development aid allocation to $38 million for 2003. Deuba's trip to the United States followed a visit to Kathmandu earlier in the year by U.S. Secretary of State Colin Powell.

Towards the end of the month, amid deepening political crisis as the Prime Minister decided to dissolve parliament and hold elections in November, the British Chief of Defence Staff, General Michael Boyee, visited Nepal on a 4-day official visit at the invitation of Royal Nepalese Army Chief General Prajwalla SJB Rana. His schedule included not only meetings with army personnel, and with the King, but also flying visits to the western and eastern regions to inspect RNA's bases. Nepal also called on China and Russia for assistance; the former responded in positive fashion, denying the 'Maoists' any recognition. Until late 2001, the Government of India had effectively turned a blind eye to the fact that such links with Indian armed movements existed and to the use, by the Maoist leadership, of safe houses and other locations in India for meetings and for organisational purposes. After 11 September, however, the Indian government had explicitly condemned the Maoist movement in Nepal, referring to it as a 'terrorist' movement, and moved some of its own troops closer to the borders. Over the next 6 months, as tension in respect of Kashmir and India's relationship with Pakistan increased, the Government of India has made clear its support for the Government of Nepal in its efforts to contain and suppress the

Maoist movement. It has provided truckloads of military hardware to Nepal and carried out surveillance operations with a view to cracking down on Indian revolutionary groups providing support to the Nepali Maoists.

Foreign development agencies (and their constituent programmes and projects), increasingly aware of the risk to their own field staff—from both the Maoists and the security services—were now beginning to draft their own responses to conflict, and to consider the extent to which they would be able to operate in the field, under the present circumstances. Some had been discussing this since early in the year, but there was a sense of increasing concern, as not only the security situation but also the political situation deteriorated rapidly over the summer months. The increasing tendency of the Maoist forces to target rural transport, communications and power infrastructures, already apparent earlier in the year, was now becoming of major significance to government and non-government programmes and projects in those areas in particular, while the threats to the lives and livelihoods of rural people generally associated with the conflict, and particularly the restrictions on gatherings and on physical movement by the security forces (and the Maoists), was now visibly affecting rural economy and society to an increasing extent. A growing concern now permeated the various 'development agencies' as their operations on the ground appeared increasingly threatened and even compromised, and as their field personnel were increasingly obliged to negotiate on a regular basis with the Maoists and were increasingly coming under scrutiny.

By May 2002, the Maoists were officially considered to be in effective control of about 25 per cent of the country, and to have a significant influence over much of the rest. The Maoists themselves now claimed an active presence and support in virtually every district in the country. Newspaper reports tended to confirm their claims. At the very beginning of May, the army launched a 2-day offensive near the Maoist stronghold of Rolpa. The army apparently encircled a rebel training camp and killed a significant number of guerrillas from the air, using helicopter gunships.* The Maoists

---

* '50 Maoists killed by government forces in Rolpa on 3 May', according to BBC Radio, May 3.

immediately took revenge, storming the army garrison in the village of Gam, Rolpa and killing 130 men. After a week of major clashes with government forces, in which as many as 500 people were reported killed, the Maoists proposed a 1-month ceasefire. They warned, however, that they would launch 'an even more deadly war' if the government offensive continued. Their proposal was rejected by Prime Minister Deuba who, later in the month, decided to dissolve parliament and to call fresh elections in November. His decision created confusion and dissent among the members of the government, but was welcomed by the opposition. This initiated a period of several months of extreme uncertainty with regard to the future of democratic politics in Nepal. In June, the State of Emergency was extended until 27 August 2002.

In the meanwhile, the British government had hosted an international meeting (19–20 June), in which almost all of those states and some non-government organisations with a stake in the situation in Nepal, including a delegation from Nepal, participated with a view to developing a more concerted and coherent approach to the issue. A number of 'background papers' were commissioned (including one by Arjun Karki, which is the last of the contributions to this collection, and another, by Liz Philipson, an independent conflict analyst) and a wide range of views and positions were presented and discussed. A statement by the Chair after the London Meeting implied that a general position had been taken with respect to supporting a combined 'twin-track approach' that would address both the security issues and the issues of governance and development considered by many to be the underlying causes of the Maoist movement.

But even two of the British ministers present chose to make statements with very different implications. The Minister for International Development, Clare Short, emphasised the development aspect—accepting that 'Nepal is in crisis, and we fully support the struggle against the Maoist insurgency' but arguing that 'it is important that developmental and military assistance packages are considered as part of an overall framework of support for the country', and noting in particular that 'radical reform is needed to prioritise delivery of services to poor people' and that 'there is also an urgent need to address the underlying issues of corruption, discrimination and weak governance that have allowed the crisis to develop'. The Under

Secretary of State for the Foreign and Commonwealth Office (FCO), Mike O'Brien, made it clear that in his view, and that of the British government, 'Maoist terrorists are conducting a savage campaign of intimidation in Nepal to further their own political aims... It is imperative that we help the government of Nepal in its struggle against terrorism. We cannot allow the terrorists to win. Nepal must not be allowed to become a failed state'. He also announced a package of assistance to Nepal, which included nearly GBP 7 million for military assistance. Meanwhile, the new British Ambassador to Nepal—a former head of counter-terrorism—had taken up his post, fully briefed by the FCO on the situation in Nepal and on his own government's position and priorities.

In Nepal, in mid-July, as the current elected represen-tatives in local government at district and village level came to the end of their term of office, the possibility of their extending their period of office was ruled out and they were obliged to leave their posts. The District Development Committees and the Village Development Committees were formally dissolved, with the responsibilities for local government at the district level being taken over by the Chief District Officer (CDO) and the Local Development Officer (LDO)—appointed by and answerable to the Ministries of Home Affairs and Local Development respectively—supported by five representatives of the government line agencies, and at the village level being taken over by a single appointed village Secretary. There was now no elected government in Nepal, at any level—national, district or village.

The Maoists continued to gain ground, although fighting was somewhat reduced during the rainy monsoon months of July and August. Even so, in the first 9 months after the declaration of the first state of emergency, 2,481 Maoists had been reported killed by state security forces and 259 police and 166 military personnel had been killed by the Maoists; at least 296 ordinary civilians had also been killed. Human rights activists, who were by now routinely monitoring casualties and the conflict more generally, argued that the real number of the people who had lost their lives was greater than the officially reported figures. It was remarked that the difficulty faced by the security forces in determining who is or is not a Maoist in the rural areas may well have inflated the figures for the number of Maoists killed and underestimated the number of ordinary civilians who had died or been injured.

Just 12 days after the extended state of emergency expired, on 8 September 2002, at least 49 policemen were killed and 22 wounded as Maoist rebels made a fresh strike on a police post in the Bhiman area of Sindhuli district in eastern Nepal. The rebels were also successful in snatching arms and explosives from the Bhiman police station. The Maoist guerrillas launched another 'successful' assault on a large scale within 24 hours (on 9 September 2002), killing 65 security personnel (including 17 Royal Nepal Army soldiers, 31 members of the Nepal Police and 9 others belonging to the Armed Police Force) in Sandhikharka, the district headquarters of Arghakhanchi in western Nepal. The state of emergency was not officially extended, although it was evident that the armed conflict was becoming more intense, and the capacity of the rebel forces to mount major assaults on military as well as police positions.

During September, there was increasing uncertainty regarding the realism of the proposed November national elections. Various alternative possibilities were canvassed and formally announced, including a phased process lasting from November through December into January, postponement for 6 months and postponement for a year. As the debate and uncertainty grew, the Maoists increased their attacks not only against the army and the police but also against the sympathisers of Nepali Congress and CPN (UML) in remote villages. The security forces responded and casualties continued to rise.

On 4 October 2002, the king intervened, sacking Prime Minister Sher Bahadur Deuba and taking over all executive powers 'until alternative arrangements can be made'. In the meanwhile, British Foreign Office minister, Mike O'Brien, had visited Nepal to convene a meting of the International Contact Group, as a follow up to the June London Meeting, and had declared that 'terrorists' would 'not be allowed to succeed in Nepal'. A few days later, on 11 October, after the leaders of the main political parties had revealed their almost total lack of principle or direction, apart from complaining belatedly (having first offered to put themselves forward) that the king's action was unconstitutional (which it probably was), he announced the appointment of a new interim government, under the leader of the RPP and former Prime Minister Lokendra Bahadur Chand. Nepal then entered the annual hiatus of Dasain and Tihar, even more uncertain than ever of the future of its fragile democracy.

At this point, we are reminded of Martin Hoftun's prescient remarks at the end of his analysis of the 1990 'revolution' (which we noted in our Introduction): '...there is still a long way to go to create strong democratic institutions and traditions. Until that goal is reached the movement which started in the spring of 1990 might develop in any direction, including a political comeback by the palace'.[60]

NOTES

1. Philipson, 2002; see also Bhattachan 2000, pp. 140–41.
2. e.g. Regmi (1999: pp. 13, 118);
3. Bhattachan, 2000, pp. 140–41.
4. Bhattachan, 2000, p. 140; Karki, 2001, p. 3.
5. cf. Uprety, 1992, 25–28, for a discussion of this work.
6. Neupane, 2001, 2–3.
7. cf. Hoftun, Raeper, & Whelpton, 1999, p. 19.
8. cited in Hoftun, Raeper, & Whelpton, 1999, p. 20.
9. cf. Hoftun, Raeper, & Whelpton, 1999, 16–25, esp. 20, fn. 79.
10. Hoftun, Raeper, & Whelpton, 1999, 23.
11. Rawal, 1991, pp. 80–87.
12. Mikesell, 1999, p. 100.
13. CPN-Maoist, 1995, 4.
14. Thapa, 2002, p. 79.
15. Bhattachan, 2000, p. 141.
16. Thapa, 2001.
17. according to Mikesell, 1999, p. 100.
18. Philipson, 2002.
19. Khatri, undated, cited by Philipson, 2002.
20. Neupane, 2001, pp. 100–09; Thapa, 2002, p. 81
21. *The Worker*, 1997, p. 5.
22. *The Revolutionary Worker*, no. 1043, 20 February 2000.
23. see Khatri, undated, p. 31.
24. CPN Maoist, 1995.
25. cited in Karki, 2001, p. 174.
26. Thapa, 2002, p. 83.
27. cited in Thapa, 2002, p. 84.
28. cited in Thapa, 2002, pp. 84–85.
29. according to Thapa, 2002.

30. *Mulprabaha,* 2000, p. 8.
31. Bhandari, 1999, p. 12.
32. Bhandari, 1999, p. 12.
33. Neupane, 2000, p. 3.
34. Maharjan, 2000, p. 172.
35. cited in Thapa, 2002, p. 90.
36. Mikesell, 1999, p. 111.
37. Mikesell, 1999, p. 111.
38. *Mulprabaha,* 14 February 2000.
39. Karki, 2001, p. 185.
40. Maharjan, 2000, p. 172.
41. Thapa, 2002, pp. 90-91.
42. Thapa, 2002, p. 91.
43. *Janadesh,* 2 May 2000.
44. Karki, 2001, p. 183.
45. Mikesell, 2001, p. 21.
46. Thapa, 2002, p. 92.
47. Conversation with government negotiator April 2000, cited in Philipson, 2002.
48. Kathmandu Post, 29 April 2002.
49. Conversation with Philipson, January 2002, cited in Philipson, 2002.
50. cited in Philipson, 2002.
51. *Indian Express,* 2 December 2001.
52. Manandhar, 2001. The Human Rights Yearbook, September 2000 records 1,312 deaths, 883 killed by the police and 429 by the Maoists.
53. Thapa, 2002, 95.
54. *Times of India,* 8 December 2001.
55. cited in Thapa, 2002, p. 95.
56. 'Dead end deadline', *Nepali Times* 22–28 March 2002.
57. *Kathmandu Post,* 24 April 2002.
58. Amnesty International, 2002.
59. Nepal—A Human Rights Crisis.
60. Hoftun, 2001, p. 27.

Chapter 2

Introduction to 'The People's War' and Its Implications

Mukunda Kattel

Science is a bit like the joke about the drunk who is looking under a lamppost for a key that he has lost on the other side of the street, because that is where the light is. It has no other choice.

—**Noam Chomsky**

'Is the People's War genuine?' asked my supervisor as I was defending my MA thesis on the *Sociology of the People's War in Nepal*.* I was perplexed for a minute and then answered hesitatingly: 'It is certainly genuine in principle and methodology if the present Cuban State, for example, is genuine. The Maoists are adopting the methodology of guerrilla warfare as the Cubans did to form their present State'. My supervisor did not ask me any further, but I am not satisfied with my answer. I still ask myself: How genuine is the War? And how might we assess its 'genuineness'? This contribution is a synthesis of what I found in my research as a student of sociology, and also of what I have seen and gone through as a civilian caught between the parties perpetrating the

---

* This article draws on the work of author's master degree unpublished thesis on the *Sociology of People's war in Nepal*, 2001, Tribhuvan University, Nepal.

War. With the above-mentioned question still in mind, this is an 'at face-value' analysis of the War, in the light of the facts available—a reconnaissance for the truth that is hidden in the shadow of rhetoric and apparent realities.

Background

In the evening of 13 February 1996, members of the fledgling Communist Party of Nepal (Maoist) descended from the mountain areas in the mid-western hills of Nepal to attack police outposts in Rukum, Rolpa and Jajarkot of Rapti Zone. Armed with stones, *khukuris* and petrol bombs, the insurgents had declared a 'People's War' on the Nepalese State, 'with the proclaimed aim of establishing a New Democratic socio-economic system and state'.[1] The State replied to it with bullets, with the explicit aim of containing the 'terrorists within 5 or 6 days'.[2] Ever since, the insurgents and the security forces (mainly the police) have been fighting to promote their respective goals on a regular basis. More than 6 years have elapsed, not just 6 days, 6 weeks or even 6 months. But the government has blatantly failed to check the violence of what it names 'terrorists'.

Much blood-clotted water has flown down the Rapti River, hundreds of corpses, honoured as 'martyrs' and demeaned as 'terrorists' or 'spies', have been cremated along its bank. Yet, the fighting continues* the State is fighting 'terrorists', which means killing those suspected to be Maoists; the Maoists are fighting the 'imperialist-serving State',† which means killing civilians considered to be 'enemies of the people', 'spies' against their activities and policemen in outposts at mid-night attacks.

---

* For two and a half months in the summer of 2001, a 'cease-fire' was observed, as the Maoists and the State security forces temporarily suspended 'physical actions' in response to Prime Minister Sher Bahadur Deuba's public appeal (of July 23) to resolve the problem through dialogue. But the violence was not over—talks broke down, the government declared a State of Emergency and the conflict was resumed more intensively than ever.

† Communist Party of Nepal (Maoist) Chairman Prachanda explains in detail the philosophy, strategy and tactics of his party in a long interview published in *Revolutionary Worker*, #1043, 20 February 2000. Internet version is available at www.rwor.org/home-e.htm. It is reproduced here in this collection as Chapter 3.

Five and a half years after the conflict started, amidst claims of justifications and counter-justifications, over 1,695 people, including 422 police personnel, had been killed,[3] and properties worth 237.4 million rupees (Rs. 102.8 million from ordinary people and Rs. 134.6 million from banks) had been looted or destroyed by Maoists.[4] The law and order situation had visibly deteriorated, and the personal and socio-economic security of the people is at risk.

Already marred with poverty, unemployment, low level of literacy, social discrimination and unequal distribution of wealth and power, the Nepali State faces a new challenge. After only 5 years of multi-party democracy (from 1990 to 1995)—which followed a century of the closed oligarchy of the Rana family, a decade of unorganised and intermittent democracy, and a three-decade-long partyless system of governance directly headed by the king—the War was declared 'to overthrow the existing State'.[5] In other words, it was a call to do away with the new 'democratic' State, only just healing from the wounds of dictatorship and despotism.

Painful though it is, the War has expanded geometrically, even exponentially. Every year, the roots have gone deeper into the soil of Nepal. Every year, the War has reached out to a new group of people, attracting new fighters and supporters, and attaching new justifications to its inevitability. There is no one, as an individual or as a group, now unaffected by the War. And the effects, although in many ways a matter of concern, are not all entirely negative and despicable.

What should be highlighted here, is that the People's War feeds on a diet of political, social and economic deprivation and discrimination in Nepal. It is wrong to see the War solely as an imposition by some careerist politicians on the misled rank and file of the Maoist Party. It is a response to the real concerns and demands of many Nepalese young people who were left to languish in despair and violence between 1990 and 1995, due to the failure of the State in the delivery of justice.

Implications

Bringing not only a message of despair and anger, directed by 'terrorists', the People's War has also hinted at enormous revolutionary possibilities and opportunities. However, as in all wars, the People's War records more wrongs than rights, and more despair than hope. The sections below enumerates some of them in a good-to-bad order.

The Empowerment of Women

The People's War has embarked on a radical agenda in its actions in respect to some aspects of Nepalese lives. One of its major contributions lies in the high level of mobilisation of women in all levels of Party structures and actions. Through the 'women in 3-in-1' principle, women do participate in a wide range of Maoist activities, as Party members, as members of the people's army and as constituents of mass organisations.[6] In the areas where the Maoists have their strongholds, widows, unmarried women and those neglected as co-wives have had land and property restored by what the Maoists call People's Courts. Domestic and social violence against women has been conspicuously reduced in the Maoist strongholds. Six women guerrillas set a historic record when on 31 March 2001, they broke out of a jail in Gorkha, a district categorised by the government as one of 'the most affected'. In this particular case, Prachanda's observation is valid: '...the heroic women prisoners showed the great power of oppressed people by making a tunnel under the prison wall, and escaped'.[7] At a certain level, the Maoist movement has inculcated in women a sense of self-respect and empowerment.

Introduction to Land Reform

'Land to the tiller' is a catchy economic slogan in Nepal: governments utter it; legal oppositions cry it aloud in mass rallies and print the slogan in official documents. However, it is the Maoists who have put the slogan into practice, albeit through the use of force. The denial and/or failure of the State to discharge its role as the major legitimate force in those areas where it is required, leaves room for other forces to take its place. The Maoists have done this; they have exploited their military and political strength to handle one of the most crucial of issues in an agrarian economy and society. This use of force can be likened to the use of 'forceps' by 'a doctor attending childbirth', as Guevara (1969) explains. The doctor or the midwife know when it is illegitimate *not* to use the force, and the cost of *not* using it.

Agrarian revolution is central to the People's War. 'Land to the tiller' and 'women's equal right to property' are maxims repeatedly pronounced by the Maoists at all levels. These are very fundamental tasks and are at the heart of agrarian relationships in Nepal. Unlike other parties, who have used these slogans just to cheat the people for too long, the Maoists have been trying them in actions. Only in the first week of July 2001, Maoists reportedly captured almost 30 *bighas* of land and planted paddy in various villages of Kailali, a far-western *terai* (plains) district—an action highly supported by former bonded labourers (*kamaiyas*) now living a desperate life without resources, and having 'no other option than to support the Maoist campaign'.[8] The vast majority of the rural population support the land-reform agenda of the Maoists.

As the Maoists pushed through their agenda, the government was forced to break its previous indifference. On 16 August 2001, in a dramatic move, the Deuba cabinet of the Nepali Congress government announced new land reform programmes. Initially, the announcement drew much support from the communist parties, including the main opposition UML. But, the leftist forces fell into disagreement over the land ceiling to be imposed (the communists wanted to keep it down) and the definition of those people constituting 'a family', for the purpose of 'family holdings'.[9]

Although the government-proposed reform measures will move slowly, if they move at all, the Maoists actually forced the Nepali Congress Party, hitherto seemingly resistant to land reform, to bring it into and up their political agenda. Alliances are now being forged for and against it: the Nepal Sadvawana Party and the Rastriya Prajantra Party—parties representing large numbers of landowners—are vehemently opposed. So are some of Nepali Congress Party members, including MP Surendra Chaudhari. The leftist parties have already taken over this agenda and claimed it for their own. The Maoist actions have undoubtedly given a strong impetus to land reform in Nepal.

Resistance Against Social Ills

In their strongholds, the Maoists have banned the production and consumption of alcohol, largely through the mobilisation of women. Increasing socio-familial tensions and health hazards are attributed to the excessive consumption of alcohol in rural villages. This is apparently true. In Dhola and Maidi VDCs of Dhading, a district adjacent to Kathmandu, around thousand litres of liquor was destroyed in one 'action' by local women.[10] Similarly, Maoists took action against many people in Deukhuri, Dang, as they did not stop the transaction of alcohol.[11] Other Maoist targets in the villages include those who sexually assault women, deny maintenance to widows and other helpless people and those who swindle the common people.

Maoists have been successful in regulating other walks of lives as well. 'In the Maoist strongholds, schoolteachers are regular; health workers regularly attend their duties. Private schools cannot charge fees indiscriminately, they should follow the standards set by the Maoists', observed Krishna Subedi, West-Regional Programme Coordinator of INSEC. Even District Education Officers (DEOs) commend the contribution the Maoists have made to regulating the educational activities in villages. 'Those taking salaries without attending their duty properly have become dutiful', one DEO observed.[12] It is seen and felt that thugs and goons at all levels have been warned by the Maoist People's War. Such actions are widely hailed by the victims of these local criminals, the ordinary people, the commoners.

Decentralisation and Justice

Yet another attraction of the Maoists is their mobile court system. Their People's Courts hear complaints at the grassroots and give verdicts instantaneously. 'Cases are immediately settled in the people's courts, unlike in regular courts, which are time-consuming as well as costly. This is the reason why people are being attracted to the Maoist justice system', commented advocate Saroj Upreti of Dolakha.[13] The rate of case registration reportedly decreased in district courts following the Maoist announcement of handling cases through their people's courts. Space Time Daily has quoted a Maoist source as saying that the People's Court in Dolakha settled a case that had been pending for 14 years, within a day. It was a land case and the victim was poor and disabled.[14] For the victims, tired of the slow pace of regular courts, Maoist mobile courts give a sense of relief, and People's Courts are the only judicial forums available for the poor, who cannot access the expensive judicial forums provided under the rubric of the regular court system.

Forging of Synergies and Alliances

The Maoist People's War has radicalised Nepalese society. It has helped intensify what conflict transformation theorists identify as 'latent conflict',[15] which, if accepted positively and addressed effectively, provides an opportunity to create a synergy for conflict transformation, a comprehensive process that addresses existing social and political sources promoting and sustaining discrimination and seeks to transform the energy being invested in war into positive social and political change.

The War has obliged the depressed, exploited and neglected to rise up to fight complacency, and the state that has institutionalised their oppression and exploitation. If the words of Jean Dreze and Amartya Sen[16] carry any merit, social order undergoes swift changes once the neglected and deprived rise in fury about illiteracy, hunger, illness or economic insecurity. Following Paulo Freire it is the oppressed who must 'wage struggle for a fuller humanity'.[17] The oppressors cannot lead such struggles as they are already 'dehumanised', morally corrupt and crippled by exploiting others. The deprived and oppressed in Nepal have risen in fury over longstanding exploitation and poverty, oppression and lack of social justice, thanks to the People's War. In the last 6 years, the oppressors have paid a high cost for their actions (sins?). They also wish for restitution. This may create a fresh opportunity to establish a broad alliance to fight institutions that maintain discrimination and deprivation in the society.

The opportunity is seemingly very much in order following the departure of the longest serving Prime Minister Girija Prasad Koirala, who is known as a troublemaker in the country, from Singha Durbar, the prime minister's office. Sher Bahadur Deuba, who was in office as Prime Minister when the first flare of the People's War was lit, succeeded Koirala, vowing to resolve the Maoist problem. He made an appeal to the Maoists, before being sworn in as prime minister: 'come for negotiations', and declared 'a government ceasefire.' In response, Chairman Prachanda asked his guerrillas to ' "postpone" all their pre-planned offensive actions' and remain alert to let the 'ceasefire offer of the prime minister'[18] work. For a while, dialogue came to the centre of the political discussion, which might have established a new culture in the political discourse of Nepal. The talks broke down, and the conflict was resumed. Despite this, Prachanda has repeatedly spoken of the need for dialogue to help resolve the problem, and the Maoists' commitment to 'leading the process to a logical conclusion by respecting the sentiments and aspirations of the general public'.[19]

Looking back, this period offered an opportunity for Prime Minister Sher Bahadur Deuba to take reconciliatory initiatives. As Prime Minister in 1996, it was Deuba who received the 40-point demands from Maoists on 25 January 1996. He was warned of 'terrible consequences' if he failed to respond to the demands.[20] He did not heed the warning; he did not spend a single hour to think of the consequences. In the summer of 2001, Deuba was back in place as Prime Minister, after 6 years. Now, he put the Maoist issue on top of his agenda. For 3 months, following Deuba's public appeal for ceasefire, several rounds of 'dialogue' took place. One of the substantive outcomes of the dialogue was the process of release of Maoists arrested by the government, and of police and public held captive by Maoists.[21] Hopes for a peaceful resolution, however, were broken when talks were broken off in November; the Maoists launched a series of new attacks on the state security forces, and the government declared a State of Emergency.

Since November 2001, the conflict has undoubtedly intensified, but both sides have, at various times during the past year, expressed a willingness to hold talks, under the right conditions. It is to be hoped that this willingness—as well as the increasing cost to all concerned in terms of loss of life and restriction of human rights—will eventually lead to another ceasefire and further talks.

Left Unity in the Making

The history of leftist forces in Nepal is that of splits, paranoia and narcissism. One extreme is the Maoists in the jungle. The other extreme, however, can be seen in the factions and blocks that struggle for any small political advantage at the expense of the others, in parliament and outside. As violence sweeps through Nepal nationwide, the various political forces and parties are increasingly polarised for and against it, from differing ideological perspectives and specific political positions. Interestingly, almost all of the left parties, except the Maoists themselves, have formed a loose alliance to fight the violence arising from the People's War. This is a unity against violence created by the People's War itself. This leftist unity matters a lot, if sustained, and has the capacity to right the wrongs and excesses committed by Maoists as well as other forces. The power base of the legal left parties is nationwide, equally effective in urban and rural areas. Together, they can perhaps break through the socio-political stagnation and inertia that has long bedevilled Nepal. This unity must surely exert pressure on the Maoists to rethink their strategy, as it is impossible for the Maoists to operate for long without the overt or covert help of other left forces. Left unity, non-violence and the crusading spirit of the Maoists is badly needed for the transformation of Nepalese society, and it is possible that it will be established eventually, thanks in part to the People's War.

Destruction and Decimation

The other aspect of the People's War, however, is very horrible. It has been a term that has, from the start, implied violence, against property and against people.

The catalogue of killing stands as the first indicator to show the level of violence and destruction wrought by conflict arising from the People's War. Krishna Bahadur Budha, aged 50, of Korja Mahat VDC in Rukum was possibly the first casualty of the People's War. He was chopped dead by Maoists on 25 February 1996, 12 days after the announcement of the People's War. The next day, police shot dead a student of Surya Jyoti High School, Dil Bahadur Ramtel, aged 14, of Pandrung VDC Gorkha. His only fault was to resist the arrest of his headmaster, Bir Bahadur Gurung, on school premises by the police. The Maoists and police thus sowed the seed of killings in the beautiful hills of west Nepal.

In the first 2 years of the People's War, the level of violence remained relatively low (see Fig. 1). But through 1998 and 1999, a police reign of terror was unleashed, which reduced in intensity and ferocity only at the beginning of March 1999. During this period, as can be seen from the figure, the police killed a very large number of people. Police 'suspicion' of being a Maoist would lead to butchery, and the state-control media would

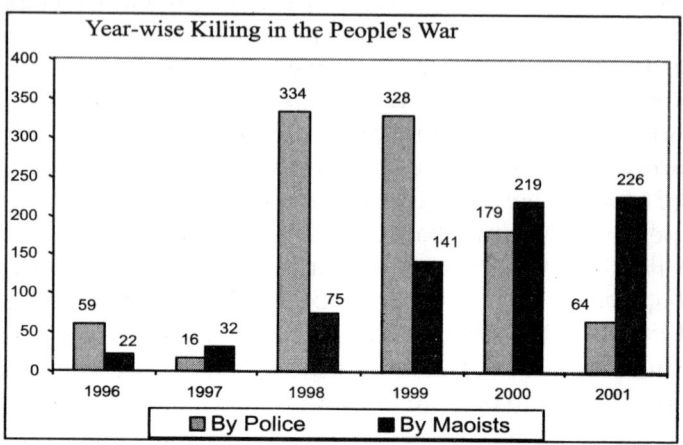

immediately justify it as an 'encounter killing'. But if the number of 'Maoists' killed might well exaggerate the real numbers, and underestimate the number of innocent civilians killed 'on suspicion', the official figures for those killed by the Maoists might well also be an underestimate. Police officers rarely reported casualties, and in fact repeatedly refused to return the bodies of their dead colleagues to their relatives. This was a trick to cover up the reality—which was the increasing response of the Maoists to this state terrorism and the steadily growing numbers of policemen injured and killed.[22]

During this period—that of the notorious Operation Romeo—Nepali Congressmen played the role of local guides to help police hunt for their prey. The police, sent to rural villages assured of promotion and additional allowances for killing Maoists, would act in a manner best illustrated by the case that follows:

> Kotgaon VDC Vice Chairman Tikaram Budha, aged 38, was arrested from his house at 21:00 hrs on 11 April 1996. He was brought to Madichaur, being beaten all along the way. Nepali Congressmen, accompanying the police, pressured him to oppose the People's War and join the Nepali Congress Party. As he refused, the policemen cut off his nose and ears and shot him dead. His hands and legs were then cut from his body.[23]

On 3 March 1999, the Maoists descended on the police post in Shantinagar in Dang district, killing 7 policemen en masse. It was the first 'successful action' of the Maoists against a police post since the initiation of the People's War. Earlier, they were usually only able to attack 'spies', 'thugs' and the local 'enemies of the people', including political cadres of the Nepali Congress Party and others not in agreement with their activities. Figure 1 shows the stark picture of police killing in 1998 and 1999, and the steadily rising toll of Maoist killings thereafter. In the year 2001 alone, of the total 226 persons killed, policemen accounted for some three quarters, and a number 4.5 times higher than all the civilian killed by the Maoists combined.[24] The security forces became the major targets of the Maoists as the armed struggle expanded and intensified during 1999–2001. In the 9 months up to the end of July 2001, when Prime Minister Deuba appealed for a ceasefire, approximately two policemen were killed every 3 days. Lacking their own security, policemen have also failed to guarantee the security of the people.

In Fig. 2 we can see illustrated the fact that around 30 per cent of those killed by the Maoists have been members of the rural population (farmers) caught in the crossfire between police and Maoists. Relatively few of these have been large

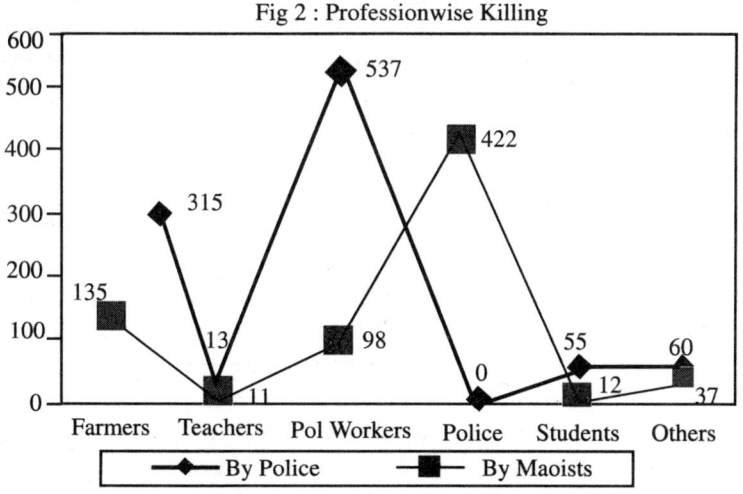

landowners and moneylenders—the enemies of the people in class terms—most have little to do with politics; most have been killed by the police as 'suspected Maoists' or by mistake. Although major sufferers, they are seemingly divided so far. If the War continues the way it is today, there is a strong possibility that the ordinary rural population, increasingly harassed and brutalised by the security forces who cannot distinguish a Maoist from an ordinary member of the local community, will respond to their suffering in a more unified fashion. If the government of the day is now far away from the people and has completely failed to maintain any positive relations with the mass of the rural people, the people will obviously be closer to the Maoists who are around them, for better or for worse, and familiar with their needs and demands. Many will prefer to join the Maoists rather than risk being caught in between.

The morale of the police is low, largely due to the combination of their losses at the hands of the Maoists and their abuse by the government and other political parties who have tended to use the police as a buffer against the Maoists, maintaining their narrow vision of national politics without trying too hard to face the People's War itself directly and strategically as a political issue. They gained and lost ground, they won and lost elections, became ministers or fell out of favour, and earned as much as they could. In the meanwhile, the police lost the public's trust as an independent law-enforcing agency. The public image of the police now is that they are the allies of corrupt politicians. Besides, sycophancy, nepotism and favouritism have influenced the promotion and transfer of police officials. All this has resulted in 'a kind of revolt' of police officials, and in an anger that was expressed at the funeral of Police Inspector Dhruba Kumar Dulal, who was killed by Maoists on 6 April 2001 in Naumule, Dailekh, when 'policemen and officers demanded the resignation of Home Minister and Prime Minister'.[25]

Both the opposing parties to the conflict have used the harshest possible methods to kill and terrorise their enemies. People have been killed while eating, dragged out of their houses into the courtyard and killed in the presence of the family members, thrown off cliffs, killed after rape, tied to trees, hacked and shot in various parts of bodies to let them die of utmost pain. Both the Maoists and the security forces have increasingly failed to observe any code of decency in their activities. Once Baburam Bhattarai, leading politburo member of the CPN (Maoist), lamented, '[i]t is obvious that people are killed in wars, people from both parties in war. However, all wars have certain rules and norms, whether declared or not. Our present concern is only that the war-norms and rules should be followed'.²⁶ He was referring to the killing of Suresh Wagle, the alternate politburo member of the CPN (Maoist), the highest such figure to have been killed by police. He felt that the government should not kill such a high-ranking person.

It is all the more shameful that the Maoist leadership, which includes Dr. Bhattarai himself, does not appear to observe any 'war-norms and rules' in its actions. The killing of Yadu Gautam, UML National Council Member and candidate for the House of Representatives, on 5 March 2000, is one unpleasant example. Maoist atrocities are reported in other arenas of day-to-day life. They appear to come down violently upon those, irrespective of class position and interests, who do not accept their orders or cannot do so for various reasons. In a recent case, Nim Lal Rokka, a UML member, of Jhenam in Rolpa, was beaten dead by Maoists simply on the basis that Rokka could not or would not provide the Maoists with food and shelter. This incident happened while the government and Maoist dialogue was going on during the summer of 2001.

As regards 'the use of indiscriminate force', the police have been responsible for more than 'four dozens of mass killings' whereas Maoists have been responsible for around two dozens of such events.²⁷

Rape and Sexual Harassment Against Women

In every war, women and children are the prime targets and first victims. The People's War in Nepal is no exception. Nepalese women and girls have paid dearly in the wake of the People's War. The police have used rape as a systematic weapon in their counterattack on 'terrorism'. Women have suffered sexual harassment even in detention centres. On 27 February 1996, after a mass killing of six people at Pipal VDC, Rukum, the police caught two minors and a young woman, Khal Kumari Khatri Chhetri, aged 14, Tirtha Khatri Chhetri, aged 17, and Deosari Khatri Chhetri, aged 18, and gangraped them right in front of the dead bodies of their loved ones.²⁸ According to Amnesty International, a 19-year-old woman arrested in March 1996 from Kapilakot, Sindhuli, on suspicion of involvement in a robbery of grain attributed to the Maoists, alleged that the DSP took her into his residence without anybody else present, kissed her and touched her private parts.²⁹ Two girls and a young woman, aged 15, 16 and 19, arrested on 13 July 1998 from a house in Lalitpur reported to an AI investigation team that they were stripped naked, threatened to have sexual intercourse or be ready to die. One of the three alleged she was repeatedly raped.³⁰ Kamala Bhatta, then Secretary of the Gorkha Revolutionary Women's Association (ANWA–Revolutionary) and a teacher, was found dead on 20 October 1997 on the banks of the Daraundi river in Gorkha.³¹ It was alleged that commando police raped her after she was arrested from a programme organised by ANWA-R, killed her and threw her body in the stream.³² These are only a few examples.

Although it can generally be observed that regard for women is high among the Maoist rank and file, Maoists have also sometimes been found involved in incest and rape cases. In one of the recent and most publicised cases, Kaila Giri, aged 25, of Haldekali, Nuwakot raped a 12-year old minor of the same VDC on 9 September 2001. Giri was a member of the Maoist Village People's Government in Haldekali. The Maoists identified the crime and took action against the culprit 'by breaking his limbs in public'.³³ Maoist involvement in the abuse of women allegedly increased following the ceasefire in 2001.

Displacement/Migration

In the last 6 years, many people have been rendered homeless and displaced by the People's War. Those who have permanently left their villages have done so mainly for three reasons: in fear of being trapped in the crossfire, in fear of being targeted by Maoists as they do not support the Maoists and in fear of police persecution as they are seen by police as being closer to Maoists. In any case, those displaced as well as those vulnerable to displacement are often farmers who eke out their living out of hard labour. Public attention to displacement was drawn back in August 1999 when some 85 people left their villages in Jajarkot for Surkhet, fearing Maoist reprisals. The Surkhet District Administration did not allow them to stay there, and they were sent further to Dang.³⁴

In June 2000, a group of people, who identified themselves as the victims of Maoist assaults, came to Kathmandu and organised a series of demonstrations demanding that the government recognise them as internal refugees and allow them to settle on government land. But the government dismissed their demands, alleging that they were simply trying to take advantage of the Maoist People's War.[35] Whether or not the government accepts it, displacement is a fact and it poses long-term implications, relating to social cohesion and stability. Those who have money, fly to Kathmandu and other urban centres. In just over a year, Kathmandu has grown significantly as a result, and this has a cumulative effect on the price of daily goods and construction equipment, pollution, leakages, vandalism and corruption. Yet another alarming factor is the increase in the youth brain/labour drain. One can find young men queuing everyday in embassies or in manpower agencies in Kathmandu for work contracts and visa interviews. One can find youths requesting NGOs for short-term internship certificates, as often required by Western universities. One can hear intellectual (and wealthy) parents speak of opportunities available overseas for their children. If all this continues for the next 10 years, Nepal will be the land of stale minds, brokers, corrupt bureaucrats and impotent politicians.

Membes of Parliament from the Maoist affected districts have a heavy burden to bear. MP Tirtha Gautam from Rukum reported that her constituents 'moved away from their homes fearing clashes between the Maoists and the police'. Displaced persons even come to Kathmandu and expect her to help arrange passports so that they can go to the Gulf for employment. Govinda Bikram Shah, another parliamentarian from Jajarkot tells a similar story. He is worried to see that the seasonal workers who go to India to find works in the 'off' season (which is a common practice for a long time) have stopped returning home due to the fear of harassment.[36]

'Unrealistic' Security Expenses on the Rise

The governments of Nepal have tried to finish off the Maoists through bullets because they are 'terrorists.'* As the civil police

---

* Whether Maoists are *terrorists* or *political beings* was resolved in political circles until after 11 September 2001. When in opposition, almost all parties have given them some political recognition. While in power, they tend to refer to the Maoists as terrorists. A few days before quitting as Deputy Prime Minister and Home Minister, Ram Chandra Poudel again called them 'terrorists' in a BBC (Nepali Service) interview, dated 11 July 2001.

institutions have failed, another armed police institution has been set up. This adds an additional burden on the taxpayers, and cuts the amount that would otherwise be allocated for development programmes. Former Finance Minister and opposition leader Bharat Mohan Adhikari was not satisfied with the budget allocation for security in 2001–02. He termed the allocation 'unrealistic', arguing that 'a poor country like Nepal cannot afford to allocate and spend around 25 per cent of the revenue on security'.* Another former Finance Minister Dr. Prakash Chandra Lohani was perplexed to see the amount allocated for the agriculture sector, which was hardly 20 per cent. The allocation contradicts with 'the Ninth Development Plan', which allocates "33 per cent of the budget to the agricultural sector'.† The budget allocated for army and police (Rs. 10315.8 million) was more or less equivalent to the money allocated for education sector, illiteracy eradication, health and health sector development, rural and special area development programme, basic primary education programme and welfare allowances for the old, weak and disabled combined together (Rs. 10797.9 million).[37]

Similarly, a highly placed source was quoted in the media as saying that the cabinet meeting held on 12 July 2001 decided to purchase two 'night-vision' helicopters to operate at night, as the Maoists tend to launch their actions at night. For this, 250 million rupees were allocated.[38] This shift of focus from development to security is not a good sign.

Corruption, Pillage, and Obstruction in Development Works

The People's War has been a pretext to justify crimes by the State as well as by the Maoists. For ministers, police officers in Kathmandu and concerned bureaucrats, the War stands as a means of justifying any misdeeds. Everything, including corruption, is to 'check violence' created by 'terrorists', to 'maintain law and order' and to 'protect the lives and properties

---

* Opposition leader Bharat Mohan Adhikari's budget reactions in The Kathmandu Post, 12 July 2001.

† Opposition leader Bharat Mohan Adhikari's budget reactions in The Kathmandu Post, 12 July 2001.

of people'. For the Maoists, everything is just, as they are fighting a 'just War'. The looting of banks, setting vehicles on fire, placing bombs in public places (such as the one placed in a cinema hall in the Madhyapur Thimi Municipality area on 6 July 2001[39]), terrorising schoolchildren, levying unbearable taxes on wage workers, breaking telephone booths and destroying telecommunications systems, and so on are all just. All they do is take responsibility for the actions and congratulate the militias involved as these activities are targeted against the 'fascist government'.

As the 'victims of Maoist attack', Nepali Congress Party cadres are regularly reported to be receiving money from the government treasury. Most of them are well off, staying in district headquarters and receiving what I call the allowance for fear—the fear created by Maoists for the good of the oppressed. The real victims of such incidents—such as the one that happened in Panchkatiya—get nothing. On 8 June 2001, five members of a family were killed and their houses were completely burned to ashes as Maoists attacked a police post in Panchkatiya village. The police post was kept inside the village despite repeated complaints and request by the villagers to remove it, for fear of Maoist attack. The government used these people in effect as 'human shields' against the Maoists, by placing the police post in the middle of private houses. For 'heroic' Maoists fighting the 'fascist' regime and 'imperial forces', the human consideration did not stop them from throwing bombs. They killed 12 policemen and 7 civilians, including a 3-year-old baby. Those who survived, lost everything, their belongings and their beloved ones. However, they got nothing in reparation, from the government or from the Maoists, who have a huge underground economy underground.

It is palpable that the majority of the so-called victims of the conflict are considered unworthy: they are not ministers, may not even be Nepali Congress members, and hence do not qualify for State assistance. The party cadres are waiting in headquarters for allowances in the name of these deceased. For the Maoists, such events are 'normal'. After all, they are fighting for 'New Democracy', in which, 'you will enjoy more democratic rights than you are enjoying today'.[40] The oppressed die now; compensation will be paid when Maoists establish 'New Democracy'.

Maoist hostility towards International NGOs and other development agencies has created obstacles to many 'development' programmes and projects. As Maoists see it, however, these agencies are 'foreign imperialistic spy agencies' being run largely—despite what they proclaim—to provide jobs 'to the relatives of Nepali Congress, the UML and other influential people', to quote the words of the Maoist commander who ordered his comrades to set on fire a vehicle bearing registration plate No. 72030 (blue plate).[41] The vehicle belonged to the Gulmi-Arghakhanchi Rural Development Project (GARDEP), being run under the joint management of His Majesty's Government and the European Union under the grant assistance of the European Union.

The project vehicle was set ablaze while the staff were on the way to the project site to monitor project activities, which included soil conservation, forest nursery, small hydroelectric plants and school construction. Despite repeated requests and warnings by the project staff that the project would be cancelled if they burned the vehicle, the Maoists did not stop, as it was their Party decision to cancel the project.[42] Following this, GARDEP has decided to suspend its projects. The fear, the incident, has generated has pushed two promising water-supply schemes—the Nuwakot Khilji Asurkot Project and the Bangla-Sandhikharka Project—which were supposed to set up 200 taps and 100 taps respectively benefiting about 12,000 households, into the doldrums.[43]

'Deep Rooted Conflict' on the Rise

The Maoists have promoted ethnic/national fronts, such as the Tharu Liberation Front, Limbu Liberation Front, etc., with parallel demands for the right to self-determination and regional/local autonomy in terms of governance, which, in common parlance, refers to regionalism based on ethnicity and a governance system based on kinship and ethnicity. These Fronts have been mobilising people with hopes that they would some day be able to grasp 'state power' and would be able to replace it with kinship-based rule. Rather than political education and training, they have had kinship concerns as a driving force. Ethnicity-based insurgency is in the making and growing racial conflict is very likely.

There is a real risk, given the feeling that exists around the issue of *jana jati*, that if sincere efforts are not initiated from all quarters to transform the existing anger and resentments, Nepal will be driven into 'deep-rooted conflict',[44] a costly internal conflict, which results in 'ethnic expulsion and annihilation',[45] in which women, children, the old, poor and weak are deliberate targets, and which 'militarises the entire society' in such a manner where 'violence becomes accepted, civilian casualties multiply, rape and starvation become organised weapons of war...'[46] Negotiating internal conflicts, once they have been fuelled, is one of the most difficult jobs, and, as experiences show, about two-thirds of them have ended in the surrender and effective subsequent elimination of one of the parties in conflict (Zartman, 1995, p. 3). Nepalese experts have already warned the rulers of dire consequences if they fail to be considerate, mindful and accommodative in these arenas.[47]

Maoist actions resulting in cultural hatred is already being expressed in villages in the interior. In the name of cultural rights, news of the killings of cows is being reported from Ramechhap and Dolakha under the guidance of Maoists.[48] In Hindu religion, the killing of cows is prohibited, as cows symbolise the goddess Laxmi. There are some communities for whom eating beef is culturally acceptable, but they do not kill cows. If this continues, there is a danger that hostile cultural groupings will form at the grassroots, and social belief systems and norms will break down paving way for a bloody religious strife.

Local Resistance to the Maoists

There are indications that political resistance to Maoist activities is now developing at the grassroots. People took up arms against Maoists, for example, in a dozen VDCS in Parsa District on 7 and 8 September 2001. Maoist Resistance Committees have been formed in some areas at the grassroots to fight them in an organised way.[49] How far this resistance is spontaneous and popular, and how far it is generated by political forces from outside, is not entirely clear.

Certainly, the CPN (UML) announced that it will fight tough with Maoists ideologically. 'The UML alone is capable to make Maoists bite the dust', K.P. Oli, an influential UML leader, has been quoted as saying in media.[50] The UML pronouncement of strong resistance came at a time when the Maoists were forcing elected representatives, majority of whom were UML supporters, to resign from their posts in favour of what the Maoists called their Village/District People's Governments. The UML officially declared that it was launching an 'Ideological Campaign' nationwide to 'correct, resist and fight ultra-leftist ideology and path' which 'badly cripples the Communist movement'.[51]

Similarly, the Nepali Congress, which was the major target of the Maoists initially, has also avowedly prepared to resist the Maoists through its Party structures. Bal Krishna Khand, Chairman of the Tarun Dal, a youth wing of Nepali Congress Party asked the government either to 'seize weapons from the Maoists or to allow [the Dal] to purchase weapons' to fight Maoists. Mr. Khand claimed, 'if weapons are made available, Tarun Dal is able to crush Maoists'.[52] If Maoists do not reform their tactics at least, it is possible that they will face growing resistance, possibly including armed resistance, from local militias and vigilante groups, promoted by other parties. If this materialises to any significant extent, the risk to a democracy in transition will be great.

Conclusion

The People's War in Nepal is rooted in the socio-economic conditions of the country. It offers a radical recipe: *break the old to make new*. The recipe, although it underlies violence, is not senseless for many—including the growing numbers of unemployed youth and those hit hard as UPFN supporters by the governments of 1991–95 just because of their political ideology. Resolving the crisis will require the politicians to break out of their narrow self-serving conception of party politics, and other non-elected political and social forces (including the Palace and the forces of civil society) to apply pressure for far-reaching change, political and economic as well as socio-cultural, to restore hopes and possibilities. There must now be a determined move towards radical reform: opportunity creation calls for actions to give motion and dynamic to the stagnant politico-economic lives of the country.

While the violent activities of the Maoists cannot be supported, the issues they have raised are right in the heart of every Nepali. Socio-economic equalities, equal political opportunities, border regulations, regional and local autonomy, respect for languages and cultures of all communities, promotion of national industries, etc. are very much legitimate issues. Unless they are addressed comprehensively, with the participation of all concerned, the current crisis does not end. In case it disappeared in the name of the People's War now, it will reappear in other names.

Radical programmes *per se* do not pose a threat to peace and stability. They provide an opportunity to eradicate long sitting social problems. In our case, radical actions are required for structural transformation of agrarian relations. We need structural reforms in the education system, justice delivery and community policing. Fighting social mores that justify caste systems, degrade certain groups of people and women needs radical efforts. The People's War has hinted that all this is possible. Only we need the lasting sacrifice: the giving up of our vested interests. The People's War surely poses a threat to those, individuals and institutions, who hold on to vested interests.

Closely watching the political life in the nineties finds an inverse trend of social transformation in Nepal. Political parties and other institutions that advocate for plurality, transparency and progressive social transformation have in practice been traditional. The Nepali Congress Party, which has ruled the nation for 120 months (88%)* of 137-month life of Nepalese democracy, indulged more in criminal and indecent activities than it did any good for the people, hence widening the chasm between the people and the Party. The proportionate share of wrongs goes to the UML, the contending force, which was in power for 17 months (12%), although the UML initiated a few noted public empowerment and development programmes. On the contrary, the monarchy, the oldest institution in Nepal, has evidently undergone rapid reforms in the 1990s, thereby coming closer to the hearts of people. In the aftermath of the death of King Birendra and his family members on June 1, the closeness was very manifest. People throughout Nepal paid heartily genuine tributes, even the Maoists fighting for a republican state,[53] to the deceased king, the major reformer of the royal institution, whereas the prime minister in office—Girija Prasad Koirla, considered being a hardliner, chauvinist and the person

---

* The period is calculated from April 1990 to July 2001, from the interim government to the present Sher Bahadur Deuba-headed governments. Coalition governments have been counted on the basis of the support of the major parties, not on the basis of who headed the government.

responsible for the upsurge of the People's War—was stoned by the people while he was at the funeral of the deceased royal family. Why a prime minister is attacked in such a tragic time by the people who elected him explains that the person is the most unwanted and hatred figure. What if such an unwanted figure remains in post by all means?

'War and mass violence usually result from deliberate political decisions, and ...that these decisions can be affected so that mass violence does not result'.[54] Narrow-mindedness and chauvinism prevailing in Nepalese leadership are a major threat to peace, progress and stability. Substantial reform is a must in political leadership of the day. The reform process in the royal institution should continue. If the society and the people do not want, nothing lives long; not even the People's War.

NOTES

1. Bhattarai, 1998, p. 2.
2. NINO, 1997, pp. 96–97.
3. Data made available by INSEC Human Rights and Documentation Centre covering the period to the end of September 2001. Most recent data suggest well over 4,000 by mid-2002.
4. 'Toll So Far', *Nepali Times*, #54, 3–9 August 2001. It covers the period from the start of the War to 26 July 2001, the day prime minister Sher Bahadur Deuba took office.
5. Bhattarai, 1998, p. 2.
6. The Revolutionary Worker, #1033, December 5, 1999. Dispatches: Report from the People's War, Part 15. [www.rwor.org/a/v21/1030-039/1033/nepal15.htm] 10 July 2001.
7. *The Kathmandu Post*, 2 April 2001.
8. *The Kathmandu Post*, 6 July 2001.
9. See, the commentary carried by the Kathmandu Post, 11 October 2001.
10. Rajdhani Nepali National Daily, 12 July 2001, p. 6.
11. *Rajdhani* Nepali National Daily, 25 July 2001.
12. Arjun Khadka's commentary entitled 'Maoist Activity has Become Positive to the Education Sector', *Rajdhani* Nepali National Daily, Wednesday 1 August 2001.
13. From the news commentary entitled 'legal professionals in search of an alternative' by Rajendra Manandhar, *Space Time Daily* (Nepali), 22 November 2000, p. 1.

14. From the news commentary entitled 'legal professionals in search of an alternative' by Rajendra Manandhar, *Space Time Daily* (Nepali), 22 November 2000, p. 1.
15. Fisher, et al., 2000
16. Sen and Dreze, 1996.
17. Freire, 1996, p. 29.
18. *The Kathmandu Post*, 24 July 2000.
19. The Rising Nepal, 29 July 2001 (Prachanda's press release)
20. NINO, 1997, pp. 19–22.
21. The Kathmandu Post, 12 October 2001.
22. Also, refer to AI, 1997, 1999, p. 8.
23. Kattel, 2000.
24. Data made available by Human Rights Year Book Centre, INSEC.
25. Kantipur Daily, Tuesday, April 10, 2001, editorial article.
26. See, Dr. Bhattarai's article 'Issues Raised by Ghankhu Event' in Kantipur Daily, 5 October 2000, p. 6.
27. *Budhabar Weekly* (Nepali), 15 August 2001. This article is based on the findings of a UML Task Force formed under the chairmanship of Jhalanath Khanal on 11 September 2000 aimed at investigating the People's War.
28. INSEC, 1996, p. 434 (Nepali version)
29. AI, 1997, p. 11.
30. AI, 1999, p. 6.
31. INSEC, 1997, p. 305 (Nepali version).
32. Also see *Janadesh*, a weekly close to the Maoists, 16 May 2000, p. 4.
33. *Spacetime Daily*, 26 September 2001, carries news of this kind of punishment, quoting Bharat Dhungel—who recently resigned as District Development Committee Chairman to support the Maoist movement.
34. Maharjan, 2000.
35. Home Minister Govinda Raj Joshi was quoted as saying so by state-owned newspaper *Gorkhapatra Daily*, 17 June 2000.
36. 'People Moved by People's War', Hemlata Rai's article in *Nepal Times*, 4–10 May 2001.
37. Opposition leader Bharat Mohan Adhikari's budget reactions in The *Kathmandu Post*, 12 July 2001. Calculated from 'Abstract of budget estimate for fiscal year 2001/02', p. 5.
38. *Kantipur Daily*, 13 July 2001. A year later the purchase was still 'on-going'.
39. The Kathmandu Post, 7 July 2001.
40. Nepali Times, 13–19 July 2001 (Baburam Bhattaria's interview).
41. The Kathmandu Post, 13 May 2001, p. 3.
42. The Kathmandu Post, 13 May 2001, p. 3.

43. *The Kathmandu Post*, June 20, 2001.
44. Harris and Reilly, 1998.
45. Carnegie Commission, 1997, p. xvii.
46. Harris and Reilly, 1998, p. 11.
47. Bhattachan, 2000.
48. *Spacetime Daily*, 14 September 2001.
49. For detailed description, see Spacetime Daily, 9 October 2001.
50. Rajdhani Daily, 8 October 2001.
51. Nabayug (UML's bimonthly news paper) No. 22, October 2001.
52. Kantipur, 11 September 2001.
53. See, Dr. Bhattarai's much publicised and controversial article published in Kantipur on 6 June 2001.
54. Carnegie Commission, 1997, p. xvii.

Part Two
MAOIST PERSPECTIVES

Chapter 3

Inside the Revolution in Nepal
An Interview* with Comrade Prachanda

RW reporter Li Onesto interviews Comrade Prachanda, General Secretary of the Communist Party of Nepal (Maoist)†

*In the **Revolutionary Worker** #1043, February 20, 2000*

> *We are fully conscious that this war to break the shackles of thousands of years of slavery and to establish a New Democratic state will be quite uphill, full of twists and turns and of a protracted nature. But this and this alone is the path of people's liberation and a great and bright future.*
>
> From the leaflet distributed by the CPN (Maoist),
> in hundreds of thousands of copies, all over Nepal
> on February 13, 1996

Introduction

On February 13, 1996, a People's War was initiated in Nepal under the leadership of the Communist Party of Nepal (Maoist). In the first 2 weeks, almost 5,000 actions were carried out throughout the country—including armed assaults on police stations in rural districts, the confiscation of property from oppressive landlords

---

* Red Flag Flying on the Roof of the World. http://www.mcs.net/~rwor/a/v21/1040-049/1043/interv.htm

† This interview is also posted in English and Spanish on Revolutionary Worker Online
http://www.mcs.net/~rw available at, or Write to Box 3486, Merchandise Mart, Chicago, IL 60654;
Phone: 773-227-4066 Fax: 773-227-4497
(RW Online does not currently communicate via e-mail.)

and punishment of local tyrants. This was truly an inspiring and significant development in the world and for the international proletariat. As in other Third World countries, the revolutionaries in Nepal must confront 'three mountains' to achieve liberation: Their goals are to overthrow the bureaucrat–capitalist class and state system, which are dependent on and serve imperialism; uproot semi-feudalism and drive out imperialism.

To do this, the CPN (Maoist) is applying Mao's strategy of a protracted people's war—establishing base areas in the countryside and aiming to surround the cities, seize nationwide power and establish a new democratic republic as a step toward building a new socialist society. Their struggle is part of the world proletarian revolution. For the last (6) years, the government of Nepal has carried out vicious counter-revolutionary campaigns against the People's War— over 1,000 people have already been killed and many more have been arrested, jailed and tortured. But in the face of this, the revolution has continued to advance and grow. The People's War in Nepal has advanced from the level of primitive fighter groups to that of disciplined and trained squads and platoons. The People's Army has established guerrilla zones and is sinking deep roots among the people. Women continue to play a major role as fighters in the people's army. And in areas where the People's War is the strongest—like the Rolpa and Rukum districts in the West—local reactionaries have run away and the police stay away, afraid to patrol. Elected in May 1999, the government of Krishna Prasad Bhattarai has been unstable and fraught with infighting over how to deal with the insurgency.

In the spring of 1999, Revolutionary Worker reporter Li Onesto traveled throughout Nepal with the people's army— meeting and talking with party leaders, guerrillas and activists in mass organisations and villagers. At that time, the CPN (Maoist) was in the process of leading the people to carry out their fourth military plan, aimed at establishing base areas and exercising new people's power. Military actions by the guerrillas were becoming larger and more sophisticated.

The following interview with Comrade Prachanda, the General Secretary of the Communist Party of Nepal (Maoist), was conducted during Li Onesto's visit to Nepal, in 1999.

Li Onesto (Revolutionary Worker): There are revolu-tionaries all over the world who want to hear about the People's War in Nepal. So it would be of great interest if you could give a basic picture of the objective situation and the material basis in Nepal for initiating the People's War. Why does the party think it is possible to successfully wage a protracted People's War, to organise the masses through armed struggle? Why is this the correct strategy, given the situation in Nepal? And why does the party feel it is possible to win with this strategy?

Comrade Prachanda: First of all, I want to respond to this question in ideological terms. Nepal is a semi-feudal and semi-colonial country, and MLM (Marxism–Leninism–Maoism) suggests that in oppressed countries like this—semi-feudal and semi-colonial countries, in general—an objective revolutionary situation prevails. This is the ideological basis from which we started to study the concrete situation, because the main thing is ideological clarity, and through the course of class struggle, mass movements, mass struggle and mainly ideological struggle inside the communist movement, we came to the conclusion that a situation prevails in Nepal for initiating the People's War.

We see that Nepal is a small and poor country. More than 85 per cent of the population lives in the rural areas, and the people are very poor—they are very oppressed. Feudal relations—the feudal forms of exploitation and oppression—are very severe in the rural areas. Industrial development is very limited, and the kind of industrial base that does exist is in the hands of a comprador bourgeois class—mainly the Indian expansionist bourgeoisie. Therefore, there are sharp class distinctions, and people have been struggling for reforms, for independence, and for basic livelihoods, for a long time. There has been continuous mass struggle, but due to the lack of revolutionary leadership, due to revisionism in the communist movement and due to a crisis of leadership, every time there has been mass struggle, this leadership has been able to confuse the masses, to make compromises with the ruling classes and to obtain some concessions for this revisionist group.

I want to remind you that in 1815 there was a big struggle with British India. The Nepali people fought heroically against British India but ultimately they did not succeed—they failed.

This was armed struggle, this war with British India, and people participated in this war in different ways—different kinds of guerrilla warfare were used. In that war, the British ruling class saw that the Nepali people were very heroic and brave, and that they fought heroically against British India. For more than 1 year they fought and fought, and in many places they actually defeated the British army. Hundreds and hundreds of ordinary people, including women and old men, fought in that war. But the Nepali ruling class, mainly the monarchy, the king, surrendered to India.

There was a negotiation in Sugauli, and they made a compromise. After that, more Nepali territory was taken by India. Before this, geographically, Nepal was more or less three times larger. But all this land was taken by India with the Sugauli Treaty. From that point onwards, Nepal became a semi-colonial country. After Sugauli came the Rana government clique. The great Karl Marx called Jang Bahadur Rana a British puppet and dog. People suffered very much from different kinds of oppression and exploitation, and Nepal evolved into a semi-feudal country. When the British left India, Nepal became a semi-colony of Indian expansionism. But in 1949, when the Nepalese Communist Party was established, it was a great and far-reaching historical event. The party was established at the time that the great Chinese revolution had been won and socialism was developing in the USSR.

RW: Was the victory of the Chinese revolution a big factor in the establishment of the Communist Party of Nepal?

Prachanda: Yes, a very big factor. And there was also, at the time, a very substantial armed struggle among the peasants in India. This was the wider revolutionary situation at the time when the Communist Party in Nepal was established. The party started to work among the peasant masses, and for 3 or 4 years there was a significant peasant movement—a kind of revolutionary upsurge. But, at the same time, the leadership of the party changed and took a revisionist stand. The leadership of the movement, the general secretary at the time, appealed to the king, saying we will do all our work peacefully, therefore please regard our party in this way, and the party leadership totally went revisionist. After that there were so many mass struggles, mass movements. But every time, this revisionist clique confused people, made compromises with the ruling class and betrayed the masses. Every time they betrayed the masses, and at the same time there was also an ideological struggle going on inside the movement.

Then, when the Great Proletarian Cultural Revolution was initiated in China, under the leadership of great comrade Mao, it directly impacted on the revolution in Nepal. There were so many materials from the Chinese Cultural Revolution that came to Nepal. This Cultural Revolution inspired mainly the younger generation of communists and the masses. And at the same time young people in the communist movement were also inspired by the Naxalite Movement in India. This specifically inspired young people in Jhapa district and provoked a kind of rebellion against the revisionist leadership, and there followed a process of reconstitution of the party. At the same time the Fourth Party Congress was held, and it also put the question of armed struggle on the agenda. But there was still no clear or fully developed political line on how to reorganise a new kind of party and explain to the masses the need to rebel. There was a big ideological and political debate for 10 years after the Great Proletarian Cultural Revolution, and all our leadership team today is a product of that ideological struggle.

And at the same time, inside our party, there was a big two-line struggle, first with the Lama clique, because there was a rightist tendency there. We fought vigorously with that line. Later on we fought with 'Dumdum' M.B. Singh's line, because it involved eclecticism and rightism and was very muddle-headed. Individually, M.B. Singh was an established leader, but his line was totally revisionist, and it was so confusing, clouded with eclectic phrases. We fought with that line, and when we fought with that line, we developed the correct line, which is that now leading the people and the People's War. We came to an understanding from that struggle with Dumdum (M.B. Singh), and we defined our ideology as Marxism–Leninism–Maoism.

RW: What year is this now you're talking about?

Prachanda: It was 1986, I think, when we finalised Marxism–Leninism–Maoism as our ideology. At the time, only the Communist Party of Peru had developed in the same way, and we made use of some documents from the PCP. But on the questions—Why Mao Tse Tung thought? Why not Maoism?

—there had been this discussion for 4–5 years. That kind of discussion had been going on inside our party. We debated for a year about changing the terminology and then the whole party adopted Marxism–Leninism–Maoism as our ideology. It was not only a change of terminology, but it was also our understanding of Mao's contribution. We also defined the People's War and our military line, our political line. And this is our ideological, political, subjective basis. At the same time, class struggle was developing, and, in the circumstances of that class struggle and the two-line struggle, we were able to see the objective and subjective situation in which to initiate the People's War.

On your question about the relationship between objective and subjective factors, I want to say that in oppressed countries, according to Marxism–Leninism–Maoism, an objective revolutionary situation generally prevails in one or another part of the country. The development of such countries as Nepal is uneven. Therefore, in any part of the country there is the possibility of initiating armed struggle and then of sustaining and developing the struggle. In general, as a whole, you can say that an objective revolutionary situation prevails. In oppressed countries, the question is the subjective preparation—the main question, the principal factor is subjective. And subjective means the communist party, the revolutionary communist party, armed with Marxism–Leninism–Maoism. We can also say, in this way, that the main question in this type of country is how to fight against revisionism and build a new type of party armed with MLM. This is the principal question in these countries.

In imperialist countries this is not the case. In the imperialist countries, the principal question is not the subjective factor. The principal factor deciding tactics and line is objective. Objectively, the imperialist countries suck the blood of the oppressed countries and control them. Therefore, the main question for revolutionaries in those imperialist countries is to continuously expose the whole system and build the party and make continuous preparation and consciously try to make the objective situation a revolutionary one—and when an objective revolutionary situation develops, at that time, to deal a big blow. We think this kind of line should be applied there.

But the strategy is different in semi-feudal, semi-colonial countries like Nepal, where more than 80–85 per cent of the population live in the rural areas, whose development is uneven, and where modern workers, proletarian workers, are very limited in number. Some people say that an objective revolutionary situation does not prevail in these types of countries. Just as in our country, the revisionists always say that the objective situation is not there, and they also say the subjective situation is not there to initiate the armed struggle. They always say this, and we condemn this line. This is not a matter of fact. In these types of countries the question is subjective preparation. It was in this way that we looked at the conditions for initiating People's War.

And at the time of initiation, we tried to figure out the whole history and contemporary reality of Nepal. What is the cultural standard, the cultural level of the masses, what are the economic conditions, what are the social relations, what are the forces, what is the class analysis? We did all these things before the last final preparation. And at that time we found some specific characteristics of the situation in Nepal. Although Nepal is a small country, we think, that, in another sense, it is not a small country. Geographically, when you consider the whole country, you can travel in 1 or 2 days to every part and corner of India. But in Nepal you have to walk up and down for many days—I know you understand this. It is more remote than America.

RW: Yes, I have some direct experience of this!

Prachanda: Therefore, while Nepal is a small country, the mountainous region is very favorable for guerrilla warfare, for a People's War. And we also realised that because there has been a centralised reactionary government for more than 200 years there has also been a historical tendency for the masses to resist throughout all of Nepal. The centralised government has its guns and control everywhere—controlled from Kathmandu. And in the long process of resistance and struggle, the Nepalese masses have developed a kind of situation where—from east to west, from north to south— everywhere there is mass, class struggle. So we saw a situation in which if we called for a programme of resistance, of mass movement, then all of Nepal would engage in that movement.

We also looked at the fact that we are surrounded on three sides by the vast Indian presence. To the east, the west, the south, there is India. But to the north, there is China. To the north it is very difficult to come and go. The Himalayan Range is there. There are some places where people can go to and from Tibet, but in general it is not like it is with India. We also analysed this situation.

We also recognised that Nepal is a 'big' country because there are so many nationalities. The population is only 20 million, but there are more or less between 20 and 25 different oppressed nationalities. There are many different languages, and there are several different religions. This also is a particularity of the situation of Nepal. We studied all these questions and how to solve the nationality question. We fundamentally depart here from all the revisionist and bourgeois parties: we uphold the right of self-determination for the oppressed nationalities, and, for now, in our concrete situation, we say that autonomy should be part of the programme. We express this and explain this as a specific situation in our movement.

In the *terai* region—again you can say Nepal is 'big' because you can see that in the southern part from east to west there are the plains—the *terai*—which is little more than 300 metres above sea level. It is a big area, a big agrarian area, with big forests. There is also the mountainous region, where there are big mountains—this is where you traveled, so you know exactly about this. And the majority of the population live in these mountainous areas and the big Himalayan Range, which is very cold. In this way you can also say Nepal is a 'big' country, not a small country. We studied these geographical conditions.

We also studied our subjective organisational situation. We were in the Eastern Region, we were in the Central and Middle Region and we were also in the Western Region. The West is historically, geographically and culturally the core of the revolution. It is the main starting point for the revolution—the people here are more oppressed by the ruling classes, and the government in Kathmandu is very far from here.

RW: What is the material basis for the revolution being more advanced in the West? Is the question of the oppressed nationalities a big factor?

Prachanda: Yes, and one thing is that economically the ruling class always neglects the development of the West.

RW: Why?

Prachanda: Because they think that to invest there will not be profitable. This is one factor we can identify. Another is that there are mainly oppressed nationalities in the West and the ruling class there is particularly hegemonistic and chauvinistic—upper caste chauvinistic. Therefore they neglect and oppress these nationalities. And the other thing is that, in the time of making this country, before 1800, in the last part of the eighteenth century, at that time, this part of the country was not totally captured by the central government. There was a kind of compromise. With the Gorkha empire, this part of the country was captured later on. First they annexed the east, later on they expanded to the west side. The main point here, though, is not whether it was first or later; the main point is that those areas were not totally captured. The local authorities had some power and the central authorities had some power. In this way these areas had some kind of autonomy even at that time.

So the masses of the Western Region were not so much under the control of the ruling government, and they did not care what the government did and did not do. This is another historical fact about the West. And in Western Nepal there are the Mongoloid ethnic groups—you saw how all our comrades there look Chinese. These nationalities are so sincere and such brave fighters—historically they have had this kind of culture. Upper caste chauvinism and feudal ties do not prevail among these nationalities.

RW: You're saying feudal traditions are weaker among these oppressed nationalities?

Prachanda: Yes, weaker. Really. When you went to the Middle Region or the Eastern Region you saw that feudal traditions are very strong.

RW: When I was in Rolpa and Rukum I didn't see any temples.

Prachanda: Yes, in Rolpa and Rukum there are not too many temples, and in the cultural traditions of these nationalities, there is a kind of democracy, a primitive democracy. Even male domination in these places is weaker - it is not like it is among the dominating castes. And at the same time, our party has a long history of working in these areas, like in Thabang and Rolpa.

RW: And the revisionists in these areas are weaker?

Prachanda: Very weak. There has been a continuity of consistent revolutionary leadership there. The revisionist influence in that area has always been weak, and the revolutionary tendency has prevailed. There are all these factors. Geographically, there are no transportation facilities, there is no electricity and communication is also very weak for the ruling classes. All these factors led us to the conclusion that the West is the key region for the People's War. But we also recognised that we cannot wage the People's War only in the western part, because the ruling class is very powerful. They have a powerful army, powerful communications systems and all these things. Therefore, if we initiated armed struggle only in the Western part, then the government would centralise all their forces and crush us.

Subjectively we also saw a favourable situation for developing mass movements all over the country. And we had organisation throughout the whole country. Therefore, we concluded that we should initiate People's War from different parts of the country. We should focus mainly on three areas—the East, the Middle and the West—and the capital. Cities should also be another focus, not so much for armed clashes, but for propaganda and such things. And one other area where we should concentrate work is in India, because more than 7 million Nepalis live in India. Therefore, India should be the other point where we should make efforts to resist the ruling classes. In this way we made our plans. These are the specificities we saw in Nepal. We did not see the exact same situation and plan for initiating the armed struggle as in the Philippines, Peru, Turkey and other countries where there is some kind of People's War. There are perhaps more similarities with the struggle of the Communist Party of Peru (PCP), but not exactly. They started from one election booth, they initially attacked one election booth. But we began from different parts of the country—with thousands of actions in the first plan. When we studied in detail the historical, geographical and cultural situation in Nepal, we came to the conclusion that we should initiate the People's War in this way.

More than 72 per cent of the Nepalese people live below the poverty line. This is a grave situation. We have always explained to the people that nothing can be achieved from this multi-party system—that it is fake, it is imperialist, it is feudal. Therefore after 3, 4 years, the masses saw that, 'Yes, what the Maoists have been saying is really correct.' These kinds of sentiments prevailed. Just before the launching of the War we organised so many big mass demonstrations and mass meetings. Thousands and thousands of masses participated. We had already declared that we were going to initiate the People's War, but the ruling class didn't believe it and thought, 'these people are talking, only talking.'

RW: In some of your writings you have talked about how the party had to make a big break or rupture—ideologically, politically and militarily—in order to initiate the People's War. This is a very big question for parties around the world, and it is a dividing line between revisionism and MLM—the question of actually carrying out the necessary ideological, political and organisational changes in the party, to initiate the armed struggle. So could you talk about the kind of ruptures your party had to make to initiate the People's War?

Prachanda: These are very serious, important questions you have raised. The question of rupture is a question of making a breakthrough. First of all there is the question of understanding our ideology, which means Marxism–Leninism–Maoism. How does Maoism explain or define this rupture, this developing process? Some people see a process of evolution, a process of continuous development, an evolutionary process. But Marxism–Leninism–Maoism teaches that this is not the case, this is not the scientific case, in scientific analysis. The real process of development is breaking with continuation and making a rupture. Everything in nature, in human history and society, in human thinking—the very process of development—is the process of breaking with continuation and continuity. We came to grasp this question very seriously before the launch of the War.

RW: You're talking about making a leap.

Prachanda: Yes, making a leap. At one point in our party, for every comrade, on the lip of every comrade was the question of leap, leap—we have to make a leap. We made this question of making a leap very sharp, that we *had* to make the leap. The revisionist parties and revisionist leaders always teach the people reform, reform, reform. And reform is reformism, is revisionism. But making leaps is revolutionary.

We condemn all the revisionist cliques as vulgar evolutionarism. We are revolutionary, and revolution means breaking with continuation and making leaps. Before the launch, we had a big debate on these questions. When we changed our terminology from 'Marxism–Leninism–Mao Thought' to 'Marxism–Leninism–Maoism,' at that point, we had a big debate inside the party on this question of leap. And we came to an understanding. Mao said that the theory of knowledge is a two-stage theory—there is the stage of sense or perception and the stage of logical conclusion. We tried to educate the whole party in Mao's theory of knowledge, this two-stage theory. And this gave us a new understanding of MLM. Before that, there was some kind of thinking that MLM meant different kinds of reforms and gradualism. But when we defined things in this new way, then new feelings, a new confidence, a new situation developed inside the party. There was a struggle with rightist tendencies at that time, and we fought, mainly with rightists, revisionism.

Then, when the plan for launching the War was drawn up, there was another debate over questions of how to initiate People's War. Our party was so much influenced by rightist tendencies. At the same time, we had indirectly participated in the national elections, and we had 11 members of parliament, nine in the lower house and two in the upper house. That had a big influence inside our party circles—the rightist influence was there. That was a big challenge for our party, *how* to make a leap. The party was so encircled by rightist revisionism, by petty bourgeois tendencies, all these things. And many people were at that time working openly, although I want to mention and stress the fact that our main leadership team was not working openly at that time. There were our MPs (members in the parliament) who were public. But our main PBMs (politbureau members) and comrades, the main regional leaders and main district leaders, were not in the open, they were underground. There was parliamentary work, but the main party organisational mechanism was underground at that time—you should note this.

So in making the plan for the launch, there was great debate over how to embark on the armed struggle because many people were influenced by 'peaceful' struggle, work in the parliament, rightist and petty bourgeois feelings, and a long tradition of the reformist movement. Then we said that the only process must be a big push, a big leap. Not gradual change. There was some thinking from some people in the party that we should first act without declaring the People's War, and then see what happened. We discussed this: is this the process? And we said no, this is not revolutionary, this also is reformism. It is a conspiratorial approach, and armed struggle is not a conspiracy. The People's War is not a conspiracy—it is open, politically open and openly declared. This conspiracy theory will not work, and it is also not revolutionary. Doing one action then saying, 'OK, let's see what will happen', then doing another action... No, nothing will work like this.

There was also some suggestion that we could start the armed struggle in different parts of the country but not say we had initiated the war and then, later on, when we saw how the situation developed, we could declare the People's War. This kind of logic was also debated. Some wanted to initiate the war but at the same time to participate in the parliamentary system in an independent way. They argued that some people should still be in the parliament, that it would 'help'. Later, some of these people did not exactly degenerate but retreated politically after the launch of the War. They followed the logic that, 'OK, we will initiate People's War, but in the main region, in Rolpa, Rukum, four MPs should be in parliament because we can win there and this will give strength to the People's War'. And we condemned this logic and said, no, this is not Marxism–Leninism–Maoism.

RW: This period you're talking about is 1995, the year of preparation before the launch of the War?

Prachanda: Yes, mainly 1995. We condemned all this logic, saying this is not Marxism–Leninism–Maoism, this is not according to the objective and subjective situation of Nepal. Our view was that we should declare freely and frankly that we have initiated the People's War and that this is the only alternative left for the people, for their emancipation, for their independence from the brutal imperialists. We should distribute leaflets all over the country. We should put posters up all over the country. We should carry out actions all over the country. And we should launch a great debate all over the country. There was some doubt about this line, some thinking that it may be 'ultra left' or 'adventuristic'. That kind of doubt was there. Such people did not openly voice that line, but only doubted. When there was a discussion they unanimously agreed, but there were these tendencies all the same.

Only 1 month after the initiation there was a big national debate about the question of People's War. Every newspaper, every radio, everybody in the country was asking: what is this People's War, what is this Maoist party? In one push, the party was established in a big and national way and it was in the center of debate—after only 1 month. We had a politbureau meeting, and we synthesised the experience of this first month. It was a big transformation process for the whole party—for the whole of our mass organisation—because it was not a gradual change. It was a big question of life-and-death struggle and everything was shaken up. We concluded that this process of initiation had been correct, that the party's first plan of initiation had proven to be correct and had really shaken the country. Then the enemy started to massacre the people. Arresting, raping, killing, looting—they started all these things. Then we drew up the Second Plan, immediately, 1 month after initiation.

RW: Before you go on to talk about the Second Plan, in terms of the ideological struggle that went on during the period of preparation, what role did the international communist movement play?

Prachanda: Yes, really, I have to mention this. In the whole process of this final preparation, there was consistent international involvement. First and foremost, there was the RIM (Revolutionary Internationalist Movement) Committee. There was an important ideological and political exchange. From the RIM Committee, we gained the experience of the PCP (Communist Party of Peru) and of the two-line struggle there, and also we shared the experience in Turkey, in Iran and in the Philippines. We learned from the experience in Bangladesh and from some of the experience in Sri Lanka. There was a South Asian conference in which we participated. At the same time we were also having direct and continuous debate with the Indian communists, mainly the People's War (PW) and Maoist Communist Centre (MCC) groups. And all of this helped in one way or another; it helped us to understand the whole process of People's War.

Therefore, one of the specific things about our People's War, the initiation of our People's War, is that there was international involvement right from the beginning. Right from the time of preparation, up to the time of initiation, and after the initiation, there was international involvement: help, debate and discussion. It was a big benefit for us; it was a big help for the Nepali masses. Theoretically we are clear, and every time we insist, that the Nepali revolution is part of the world revolution and the Nepali people's army is a detachment of the whole international proletarian army. This is clear. But during preparation for the initiation and after the initiation we came to understand this, not only in a theoretical sense, but came to see the practical implications of this proletarian internationalism, what practical role it played. We made the point to the RIM Committee that when the People's War in Nepal faces setbacks, then it will not only be a question for the CPN (Maoist), but will be a direct question for the RIM as a whole.

People's War, Maoist Communist Centre and others in the revolutionary struggle in India have been seriously involved in this process in one way or another. We understood right from the beginning that we should try to involve more and more sections of revolutionary masses in the process of our initiation. Therefore, beforehand, we made some investigation of the situation in Bihar in India. We went to Andhra Pradesh to look at the struggle there and we tried to understand the practical situation and the practical problems of armed struggle.

Generally, the debate and discussion within the RIM was very helpful. And after the initiation, with this debate, this big result: thousands and thousands of Indian masses came to understand the People's War in Nepal. And our People's War also helped the whole international movement—because there had been a big setback with the People's War in Peru [with the capture of the PCP's leader, Chairman Gonzalo, and the emergence of a right opportunist line]. At a South Asian conference, I told other parties that, in this situation, helping Peru was not only a matter of giving the revolutionaries support, but of initiating People's Wars in our own countries. That would be a *big help*. And after the initiation of the People's War in Nepal it has been shown to be true—we helped the PCP, we helped the RIM as a whole, we helped the whole revolutionary masses, and we in turn received help from all over the world.

Yesterday I saw a note in your journal from your trip, and, really, I am very impressed. You noted there that, in Nepal, after only 3 years of People's War, there have been very big advances.

You saw this yourself and noted it there. But you also observed that a very crucial period is coming up. Right now things are at a crucial point. The enemy's involvement against the People's War is going to get much greater, and this will be a big challenge. We were really impressed that you came to this conclusion. You understand the kind of situation that is developing and the challenge that this presents. You also emphasised in your notes that the whole international community should be alert to this situation and should play a role in talking about and helping to develop the People's War and opposing the government's reactionary moves.

From this point of view we also think international relations and the importance of the People's War in Nepal has been developed. We think that your tour itself is also a vital moment in this. It is not merely a case of 'you came here and left'. It has historical implications, and it is a very big and good initiative. Your trip in Nepal, your project in Nepal, will be a very big initiative for proletarian revolution—for opposing the reactionary ruling classes and for helping the masses of Nepal. It will be a very significant initiative. It is not completed—there should be a continuous process taking it forward from here and now.

From your experiences we have come to understand more deeply that these kinds of projects should be done in a continuous and planned and organised way, and now the RIM will learn from your experience in Nepal after the success of your trip. There have been so many physical hardships you've fought, but you've succeeded. And therefore, internationally, we also want to mention this project and this whole trip.

RW: In a number of places I met comrades who talked about how before the initiation of the War the party was composed mainly of intellectuals. They told me how there was a lot of ideological struggle among intellectuals to make the necessary rupture, to make the necessary sacrifices, to go underground, leave their jobs and so on—how there was a lot of turmoil among some party members over the sacrifices that needed to be made. Some people fell away, some people came forward; particularly, new people came forward from among the masses. Could you talk some about this process of the rupture and the change in the composition of the party—with the initiation of the War and over the last 3 years of the People's War?

Prachanda: This is also a very important question. Yes, there has been a big change in the party, really. We realised, even before the initiation, that after the process of initiation there would be a big process of transformation inside the party. We thought that, possibly more than 50 per cent of our party members could fall away but were confident that other new comrades and new people would come and join the party. We thought this would happen. We considered this question beforehand and we prepared mentally for this to happen—because there were so many petty bourgeois tendencies, so much intellectualism. We mentally prepared for dealing with the question of how to sustain the People's War after this big leap. We discussed this question again and again in the Central Committee and in regional bureaux and in important district committees—that this could happen and we have to be prepared. We said that a very big problem may arise if we do not prepare ourselves, but if we are prepared mentally, then it will not shake us. That was one point.

In the plan for initiation we had a military plan to attack the police force, the landlords, the local goons in the rural areas. But we did not have a big plan for sabotage in the capital city because, at that time, we did not want to create a situation where, at one stroke, the intellectuals would turn away from us. We wanted to maintain their support; we did not want to make the intellectuals in the capital city or other cities run away and stop working with the party.

But what happened was that, after 1 month, we saw a big change in the rural areas. Big changes started in the rural areas: some people fled, some new people came forward. Thousands and thousands of people went underground. In Rolpa, in 1 month, thousands of people went underground. Not only party members but also masses went underground—in Rukum, in Jarjarkot, in Salyan, in Kalikot. That kind of situation developed. So the process of transformation was very big in those rural areas. But in the cities, where there are more intellectuals, the process of transformation was very, very limited, and we can say generally unsatisfactory. We were not satisfied with the petty bourgeois reactions. One example is what happened just after the initiation of People's War, in the capital city, in Kathmandu. There was government repression everywhere. Artists, journalists, professors, lecturers—everywhere, those who had sympathy with us—were arrested. And at that time, what happened in the city? Wherever we went people said, 'You should not stay here, the police will come.' There was so much terror among the different sections of intellectuals. For a long time they had been with us, but at that point, they were so afraid, they had so much terror, that even for us, they did not dare to fight—or even to give us shelter. So for 3 weeks we had to move about continuously in the city.

But when we got a report from Rolpa, Rukum, Gorkha, Sindhuli, Kabre, the rural areas, there was confidence among the masses and the revolutionary cadres. The sentiment there was, 'Yes, we have done a big job. Now new life has started'. There was new mass support and mass upsurge in the rural areas. In the city, though, the intellectuals were vacillating so much, they were so terrorised, and we saw that this was a question of class. Which class thinks that now we are taking destiny into our hands? This was the situation, and so we had to wage ideological struggle in the cities.

RW: What about the proletarian forces in the city?

Prachanda: The proletarians were in a better position. During this tough time they were the forces in the city—labourers, workers—who helped the party, indeed saved the party. Workers from our All Nepal Trade Labour Organization helped us very much. They were not so terrorised. Their feeling was, 'OK, this is a new thing'. Another important section was that of women—this is very, very important. Women in Kathmandu were the other force who, in that time of terror, boldly supported us and gave us shelter and helped us move around. The women helped us at that time. There was also help from students, because we had good organisation among the students all over the country, and at that time the students were also not so afraid. They felt enlightened, that this was a new thing for Nepal that our party had done. So it was mainly labourers, women and students who helped us. But the intellectuals, who had good knowledge of revolutionary philosophy, theories etc., these people were wavering so much they could not help very much.

And after 1 year, we saw further big transformations in the rural areas. Thousands and thousands of mass organisations were built up, and the party's influence spread in new areas and new organisations developed. Some petty bourgeois revolutionaries, due to terror, fled to India, to the Arab countries and elsewhere. Others stayed strong. And at the same time, in the rural areas, there was a mass upsurge of women, and thousands of full-time cadres came forward. People who we did not know beforehand became heroes, really. Just 1 year after the initiation of the War, I was in Rolpa, Rukum, Jarjarkot and Salyan for a month, and I saw, and our party saw, that a new thing had developed. The people were not only fighting with the police or reactionary, feudal agents, but they were also breaking the feudal chains of exploitation and oppression and a whole cultural revolution was going on among the people. Questions of marriage, questions of love, questions of family, questions of relations between people—all of these things were being turned upside down and changed in the rural areas.

We came to understand Mao's vision that the backward rural areas will be the core of the revolution—the real base of the revolution. We saw in Rolpa, Rukum, Gorkha, Sindhuli and Kabre, the seeds of the new society, the examples to inspire people. Everywhere in the country, in the revolution, the masses feel proud of their Rolpa and Rukum. And we see, at the ground level, on the mass level, that the transformation process is not only in the party and mass organisations, but among the masses as a whole. The chains of feudal oppression, mainly feudal relations, are breaking.

RW: Yes, especially between men and women.

Prachanda: Yes, between men and women, really. And our party has tried to develop the leadership of women comrades. There have been problems in doing this, but now we are, step by step, working to solve this problem. Masses of women have come forward as revolutionary fighters. And we had a plan right from the beginning that the women and the men comrades should be in the same squad, the same platoon and that all things should be done in this way. We have worked to make new relations between men and women—new relations, new society, new things.

In the Western Region, right from the beginning, we did not have any big problems and setbacks in this process of transformation, because thousands and thousands of ordinary people were seeing that here was another life. But in the Middle Region and in the Eastern Region that was not the situation. There were more intellectuals there inside the party. When the party would go on the offensive and be victorious these forces would go, 'Oh yeah, we should do this'. But when there was some kind of setback and repression then they would say, 'Oh, no, this will not do'. There was this kind of thing in the Middle Region. Here many of the people in the party were petty bourgeois intellectuals, from petty bourgeois class backgrounds. And there is also there a more well-to-do economic situation—pretty much every family has some land, some electricity, roads, educational facilities. All these things are there and many party members are from this class, so there are wavering tendencies.

But in this 3-year process we have also seen a transformation in this Middle Region—a cultural transformation, an ideological transformation. And some of the very best leaders and cadres are now developing from this region. This is an important thing we are seeing: new things coming up, old things going down—some of the older and petty bourgeois people are going downward, and the new masses are coming forward. New cadres are coming forward, and we are trying our best to give responsibility to these new comrades. That is our party's policy. We have to try to do this, not only on the regional and district level, but even at the Central Committee level. Just in the last Fourth Plenum, in the fourth historical plenum, we brought onto the Central Committee seven new younger comrades from the regional level who are really fighting on the ground. You know the comrade who you met in Rolpa in charge of the Task Force?

RW: Yes, he's a very good comrade!

Prachanda: That comrade, just in the last Fourth Plenum became a central committee member. There are so many comrades like this. If we do not do this, some of the old comrades have the problem of lagging behind. In a quickly developing situation with challenging questions, there are comrades who cannot change their whole thinking; they think just like before, and that is a problem. So our party is trying to give responsibility to those comrades who have been steeled in the process of 3 years of People's War, and this helps the party to stay on the correct path. Leadership should not be in the hands of any kind of opportunistic tendencies. We are very serious about developing new leadership, and the forces we are developing are very enthusiastic, very good. We see that there have been more than 700 martyrs. But thousands have stepped forward. This process does not harm us, it helps us.

When the ruling class started their repressive Kilo Sierra 2 operation, we thought it would be a very big thing for our party, that there may be vacillation among the ranks. But ultimately the objective results were that there was not so much vacillation. In some regions there was some vacillation, but in the Western Region there was no vacillation. Instead there was more confidence, more determination, more confidence to fight. On the mass level, there is no vacillation, therefore we are proud of the masses in our party ranks. In the Middle Region there is some vacillation, there are some vacillating tendencies there; and in the capital city, as you already know, there is vacillation among some intellectuals. But there are also good comrades among the labourers, women and students. Very good comrades, with commitment and determination.

During these last 3 years of the People's War, there have also been other kinds of changes. Peoples of the oppressed nationalities—the Mongoloid peoples, the *terai* peoples and the far western peoples—have been very supportive of the People's War. They feel it is the only alternative for them. And this is also a big victory for the People's War and a big defeat for the reactionary ruling class. So many new organisations among the oppressed nationalities developed after the initiation, like the Magar National Liberation Front.

RW: Yes, I met one of the leaders of that organisation.

Prachanda: There is also the Tharu National Liberation Front in the *terai* region and the Terai National Liberation Front and the Rai and Limbu and Tamang. And in the capital city there is Newa Khala, the mass organisation of that nationality which has had so many programmes—like the recent successful Kathmandu *bandh* (shutdown). This new organisation, generated by the party, is carrying out the plan of the party. This process is a new thing that has been born. The reactionary ruling class feels that if these forces grow and develop it will be very dangerous for their whole system. Therefore, they try to manipulate the people. They try to make some concessions to the oppressed nationalities and say they will do all kinds of things for them. And they say about the Maoists: "They want to divide the country. 'They want to divide the Mongoloid peoples. They want to divide the Rai and Limbu, and the *terai*. Everywhere they want to divide the people. These are separatists and they will break up the country. Don't follow them'. This is the kind of propaganda they try to spread. But people don't believe them. The people know that we are taking the national question seriously and, from a political point of view, and a national and historical point of view, this is the only solution for the oppressed nationalities. Nobody, not even the ruling class people of oppressed nationalities, dare to oppose our policy. They are forced to say that this policy of the Maoists is correct. There are so many members of parliament who say, 'Yeah, the policy of Maoists is correct for oppressed nationalities'.

There are also certainly some problems because we have not been able to develop a big wave of struggle of the oppressed nationalities. But new things have been born among the oppressed nationalities, and this is a very big force to sustain the People's War and to make the People's War victorious.

RW: The People's War is about the destruction of the enemy. But it is also about construction. One of the biggest achievements of the 3 years of the People's War is how the masses are beginning to exercise people's power. One important contribution of Mao is that he showed us that the process of protracted people's war is also a process of training the masses to run society in a new way, to train the masses ideologically and politically in MLM and to begin transforming themselves and society—even before the seizure of nationwide power and the building of a new socialist society. Could you talk about the importance of exercising people's power at this stage of the revolution?

Prachanda: We mentioned in our initiation document that embarking on the People's War means not only crushing the enemy—it means also changing ourselves, changing the masses. The great Karl Marx stated that the working class would have to go through 15, 20 even 50 years of civil war, not only to crush the enemy but also to transform itself, to make itself fit to exercise new power. We quoted this, and we quoted Lenin, about how the process of civil war will come with an extremely complex situation, and by facing this situation, the party will be able to exercise power. We also quoted comrade Mao about how the process of People's War is not only to crush the enemy, but also to cleanse our own dirtiness and all our bad habits—bad things we have had for a long time. To clean all these things, that is also the aim of the People's War. Right from the beginning, we tried to give the masses this message, and we tried to train the whole party in this direction. And in our country where the proletarian class is very weak numerically, the labourers who work in factories in Kathmandu and other cities have also not totally broken with bad habits.

Therefore, in this type of country, protracted People's War is also part of forming a new type of revolutionary party. This is a lesson of history. Without this kind of revolutionary struggle, a revolutionary communist party is not possible in these types of countries. We train the people in this thinking. We have said that, ultimately, the process of destruction is not only a process of destruction, it is also a process of construction. Without destruction there will not be construction, as Mao and other great leaders have said. But which is principal? After the initiation of the War we said, for us, destruction is principal, construction is secondary. And when we reach the point of seizing and exercising real power, at that point, questions of construction will be the main point. But even then, it will be the case that without destruction there will not be any construction. Like Mao said, people usually think that war is very destructive, war is very bad, it kills people, all these things. But people do not understand that war is a great process of construction. War has a very big cleansing effect. We also try to teach the people and train the cadres to understand this.

And we must also learn war by waging war. The intellectuals' instinctive tendency is that we have to learn all these things, we should read everything, we have to do all these things, first, and *then* we can make war. These kinds of tendencies were there, right from the beginning. But we said, no, this is not Maoism. This is not Marxism. This is not dialectical materialism. This is not according to the scientific theory of knowledge. The issue is that of learning war through war itself. Comrade Mao said, 'We had nothing at first. We had only millet. We ate millet. We had some rifles, and we fought, and we captured all these things. We were not clear at that time what to hit and what not to hit'. We went to hit and we learned how to hit. We also try to do things in this way.

You asked about the question of people's power. In the Western Region, in some districts, there was a kind of power vacuum just after 1 year. But at that point, we were not in a position to exercise power in an organised form. We had not defeated the police enough. This was the kind of situation there.

RW: You mean like the government Village Development Committee (VDC) chairmen were gone, but the police were still strong?

Prachanda: Yes, the police were strong. There were no VDC chairmen working there, but the police post was still there. This was the particular kind of situation there 1 year after the initiation. And after 2 years, the question of power became a burning question. It was coming onto the agenda, and we started to study the question of exercising power. We discussed at what level we could organise the process of exercising people's power. And after 2 years, 2½ years, we saw that, in our core region, mainly in the Western Region, the local police were mainly defeated. They stopped going into the villages in the rural areas. They were so afraid that they did not go into the villages. They stayed in their offices, at their posts. And even then, sometimes the police would sleep outside the post. They would put a candle or lantern inside the post, and when the Maoists came to attack the post, then they would be outside in the forest. This kind of thing happened. This was the kind of situation at hundreds and hundreds of police posts. Our squads succeeded in carrying out some important ambushes and some important raids and that terrorised the police. They suffered a kind of defeat. And at that point in the villages there were not any Village Development Committees and there were not any police.

But at first, our exercising of power was not well planned, it was not well defined. It was not well done. In the process of 2 years of People's War, in the core region, a power vacuum developed, and our comrades should have begun exercising power. They did not understand what they were doing, that we needed to exercise power. But they had to do everything. The masses were demanding this. Among the masses there were some issues that needed to be settled; there were the questions of marriage, education and land—mainly land questions—that needed to be settled. All these things. At one point, when we studied what was going on in the field, we found that the squad commander was becoming the political leader. Power was in the hands of the squad commander, not in the hands of the the party DCS (district committee secretary) or area secretary. People saw the squad commander as their political leader. The squad commander would give speeches and attack the rural agents. And everything he did—well, he was in uniform; so then the people thought, he is our leader. Power was in the hands of the squad commander.

At one point, for 3–4 months, that was the situation. And we said, this is not a good thing. The guns should be led by the party; the guns should not lead the party. This is the Maoist view. This was not a mistake on the part of the squad commanders. It was not well planned, it was not well discussed. It was spontaneous. Then the party centre discussed all these questions, and the questions of united front and the questions of power were defined.

RW: This was 2 years after the initiation?

Prachanda: Two and a half years. The spontaneous exercise of power started after just 2 years. For 4 months, not only in the Western Region, but in some areas in the Eastern Region and some rural areas in the Middle Region, there was a power vacuum, and in fact power was administered by the people themselves, by the people's army, by the squads. That was the situation.

RW: So the party's organised plan and strategy for exercising people's power is fairly new?

Prachanda: Really we can say this started after the Fourth Plenum, when we said, 'now we are going forward on the path of creating base areas'. Then we had a well-defined plan of exercising people's power.

RW: So this was at the end of 1998?

Prachanda: Yes. But before then, a general vision was there— that we should have a united front, that we have to exercise power. A general vision was there, but a complete plan was not. And before our plan was completed, real power was in our hands. You have already heard how our comrades tax the local businessmen, how there are people's courts, land distribution, and collective farming, divorce, marriage—all these things the people do. We saw this new people's power develop. At first, we did not teach the masses—they taught us how to begin exercising power. It cannot be dictated from above. The masses themselves, through the process of the People's War, through the process of struggle, gave birth to the forms of new people's power. They started to do all these things.

Just after starting this whole process, we completed plans to make a united front, organise mass gatherings and have the masses elect leaders to exercise people's power. We said we should follow the three-in-one principle [forming leadership groups which combine the party, the army and united front masses]. We saw that we needed to study more and more the process of making revolutionary committees, as it happened in the Great Proletarian Cultural Revolution in China—that we should learn from how they formed revolutionary committees and applied the three-in-one principle. We are now in a preliminary process; it is not yet refined. But we are seeing big things happen. And now, what people think, when they see this whole process, is that they have power and they feel proud. The masses feel, 'we have power now; we can distribute land, we have collective farming, we can divorce, we can make arrangements, we can break all the chains, we can tax the businessmen, we can manage the forests, we can do all these things by ourselves—no VDC, no police. Our united front is here, our squad is here'. The people really feel this. And this great feeling is the basis for the success of the People's War. This is the base the enemy can never crush.

This great feeling among the masses is mainly in the Western Region. In the Eastern and Middle Region this feeling is also developing, but the situation for the enemy in these regions is very favorable. The government can go everywhere and crush the people. Therefore, there are problems. But even in these areas people are gradually understanding the importance of power. In the Middle Region, many hectares of land have been captured, and thousands and thousands of quintals of grain have been captured and distributed to the masses. And this process makes the people feel like, 'Yes, this is ours'.

RW: In terms of exercising people's power, one of the areas that is less developed is that of land reform and more collective forms of production among the peasants. For revolutions in oppressed countries, the land question and production relations in the countryside are crucial in terms of revolutionising society. What is the party's vision of this process of revolutionising production relations in the countryside, as part of the process of construction in the People's War?

Prachanda: We say that this new democratic revolution is an agrarian revolution. Basically, the character of this revolution is agrarian. But the situation in Nepal is not classical, not traditional. In the *terai* region we find landlords with estates, and we have to seize the land and distribute it among the poor peasants. But in the mountainous regions, that is not the case; there are small holdings, and there are not big landlords. Therefore our main plan in those areas is to develop collective farming and revolutionise production relations. How to develop production? How to raise production? These are the main problems here. The small pieces of land mean the peasants have low productivity. With collective farming it will be more scientific and things can be done to raise production. But we cannot do this collective farming instantly. In terms of land ownership, it will be private ownership by the peasant. But the production process will be collective. We are trying to do this in our regions. And, mainly in our developed regions, collective farming has already been established.

RW: Can you explain this more, how that is happening?

Prachanda: In the developed areas we have already made a plan and started, in some areas of Rolpa and some areas of Rukum and some areas of Jarjarkot and some in Salyan—less in Salyan, mainly in Rolpa, Rukum and Jarjarkot. First we seized some land from landlords who live in Kathmandu, and from usurers and such people. We seized that land, but we did not distribute that land to the peasants. Because to distribute that land piece by piece to peasants will not work, will not help to develop their livelihood, their economic level. So, first there is the kind of land seized from landlords and usurers. Then there are other kinds of land, like public land which can be cultivated. And thirdly, there is land owned by peasants. These are the three types of lands. When we seize the land from landlords, that land will become collectively owned—there will be collective mass ownership; that land will be the land of the masses, and all the peasants will work on that land, and the earnings from that land will be the property of that locality.

RW: How is the grain from that land distributed? Does it become a collective fund?

Prachanda: Yes. The returns from that land will constitute the collective fund of the masses, used for the needs of the masses of that locality. Up to this point we have done it like this. And the fallow land, or public land which can be cultivated—we are trying to cultivate this land collectively and distribute the return to the masses collectively. Collective distribution means according to what per cent of the work has been done, according to the number of hours worked. How many work hours a particular family did on that land—the return will be in that proportion.

RW: So there is some system of accounting where the peasants work and they get so much credit for hours worked and grains are distributed accordingly.

Prachanda: Yes, exactly that. Where our mass base is strong and the masses are in the process of struggle, we are starting to have collective farming. Private ownership, but farming collectively. This has already shown itself effective in the process of production.

RW: So this would be like, five farmers who own five separate plots of land, but they all work on the land together. Will they collectivise the tools, implements, animals?

Prachanda: Animals, tools, land—according to the land, tools they use and working hours—according to the percentage of the work done—they divide the production. In this way we can raise the quantity of production. This is what we are doing in the developed areas. But in less developed areas, in the Eastern Region and the Middle Region, we are trying a kind of system that is rather like an exchange of labour power. So, during the rainy season, if you have less manpower or your own labour power is not sufficient and you cannot manage cultivation easily, then other peasant families are there to help. My family will help you, and your family will help me, and we will help him. This kind of tradition is there in peasant families.

RW: This kind of tradition already existed?

Prachanda: These kinds of traditions were there, and now we are developing this tradition in an organised way. We are also starting to develop, in a more organised way, different kinds of collective farming—and measures that lead to collective farming. We are trying to organise this system of farming, to enable the peasants to achieve a kind of unity among themselves. They are doing all these things to break the chains of feudalism, and it is a real school of cultural transformation. When all our families work together, eat together, sing together, dance together—then it is more communal.

In the *terai*, up to this time, we have not had a strong mass base. There is not a strong struggle. There is guerrilla action going on in the *terai*, in the plains. There are big landlords, there is the king's land, the queen's land—so many big bourgeois lands are there. Up to now, what we have done is seize the grain of landlords. We are not yet able, in the *terai*, to seize the land, but we are able to seize stored grain. This enables the masses to understand the importance of the People's War, the importance of the revolution. Gradually they are coming to see, 'Yes, this is ours'. And so we are also developing a mass base in the *terai*.

RW: One very important question I wanted to ask relates to the party's Fourth Strategic Plan of developing base areas. Could you speak about where that process is now and what needs to be achieved in this next period to carry out that plan.

Prachanda: This is also a very important question. Our Fourth Plenum has sketched out, figured out, the questions of building base areas. To make this plan of developing base areas, first of all we tried to clarify the theoretical conception of base areas, because in South Asia there is a tendency of armed economism—a kind of reformism, armed reformism.

RW: Armed struggle with no vision?

Prachanda: No vision—exactly. This line exists in India. Some groups say guerrilla zone, guerrilla zone, guerrilla zone. For 25 years they say guerrilla zone, but there is no real perspective. And we knew this question of guerrilla zone and base area was going to be a very serious issue. We tried to clear up these questions because the question of base areas is a strategic question for protracted people's war. Without the aim of securing base areas there is no real people's war. Without a strategic view of base areas there is no question of protracted people's war.

The question of guerrilla zones is not a strategic question. It is a transitional question—from unarmed masses to armed masses and from the masses without power to the masses with power. To go through this process, the guerrilla zone is only transitional. It is not a strategic question. Therefore, we should not confuse the terms guerrilla zone and base area. Our main strategy is to seize, to capture, base areas, and to build up base areas. First we clarified this in our plan.

Second, in our concrete situation we are not, right now, going to establish base areas. We are not in that position. We are not going to establish base areas in this Fourth Plan. We are concentrating all our efforts on building base areas. Our political, ideological, military efforts are all concentrated on forming base areas, but now we are not establishing base areas. We are in the *process of* building base areas. We need to understand this.

RW: What is the distinction between permanent and temporary base areas?

Prachanda: Not exactly. We are not using the terms temporary and permanent. We are in the *process of* building base areas. We are not saying 'temporary base area'. It may be temporary or permanent. It depends on the force of the people's power—which means our military capacity.

RW: What will distinguish a base area? Right now you say you are in the process of forming base areas. But what will be the criteria to say: now we have established a base area?

Prachanda: The criteria for having a base area, from the military point of view, is that we have defeated the military capacity of the enemy at that point. Until and unless we defeat a section of the military sent against us, the enemy's armed forces, we cannot say we have a stable base area. We can exercise a kind of preliminary form of base area. But we cannot say it is stable.

We see that Mao did not use the term permanent or temporary. He referred to stable base area, unstable base area, and base area in preliminary form. Mao experienced and synthesised these three types of area. To have a stable base area we have to crush the enemy's armed force. But before this we can form unstable base areas. We fight with the armed forces, and, for the time being, they do not come; therefore, we have in effect a base area. But when they come, then they will fight, and it will be unstable—and for the time being, it may be just like a guerrilla zone. Then again, we capture it, we defeat the enemy and then it will be stable. This kind of stable and unstable process will be there. We see it like this.

And you asked about the preconditions for a base area. First, is a strong party organisation. There should be strong, consistent leadership. Second, is a good mass base, just like Mao said; a good base of struggling masses—and having a good mass base means having not only sympathisers, but masses who themselves are trained in the war. That is the meaning of a good mass base. Third, you need a strong people's army. Up to this point, we have not said, 'People's Army', or 'People's Liberation Army'—we have used guerrilla squad, guerrilla platoon.

RW: So you do not use the term 'people's army'?

Prachanda: In the theoretical sense we use the term *people's army*. But as a formal name of the army, we are not saying, 'This is our PLA, People's Liberation Army'. We have a people's army, but we have not called this form of organisation the 'People's Liberation Army'. Now we have the goal of forming companies. We are organised now, up to the platoon. And you saw the Special Task Force—this is a step, moving towards forming companies. When we sustain a company formation, when there are two, three, four companies, and, at the same time, there are platoons elsewhere, then we will say this is a strong army. Our vision is that when we have companies, then we will have the strong army needed to have a base area. That is also a critical factor.

Finally, to establish base areas, a particular national situation and international situation is necessary. This means there are big contradictions among the ruling classes—they are fighting among each other—and there is also an unstable situation with regard to India. Because for us, ultimately, we will have to fight with the Indian army. That is the reality of the situation. Therefore, we have to take into account the Indian army. When the Indian army comes in with thousands and thousands of soldiers, it will be a very big thing. But we are not afraid of the Indian Army because, in one way, it will be a very good thing.

RW: You will be able to capture lots of guns from them...

Prachanda: Yes, they will give us lots of guns. And lots of people will fight them. This will be a national war. And it will be a very big thing. They will have many difficulties intervening. It will not be so easy for them. But if they stupidly dare—and they will dare, they will be compelled, they will do that then...we have to prepare for that and for that reason we are saying we will also need a particular international situation. For us this has to do mainly with India, with Indian expansionism. When there is an unstable situation in India and a strong mass base there in support of the People's War in Nepal and there are contradictions within the Indian ruling class—at that point we can seize, we can establish and finally declare that we have base areas, that we have a government.

When we declare we have established a base area then we will formally announce the creation of a central government. We are thinking that when Rolpa, Rukum, Jarjarkot and Salyan become a liberated zone, then we will declare the People's Republic of Nepal—the government of the People's Republic of Nepal. That government will be in the centre, and there will also be base areas, guerrilla zones, some prospective base area zones—different kinds of zones. But when a base area is declared, then the People's Republic of Nepal will also be declared.

Therefore, just now, we are not saying we have established base areas. But in the practical sense you understand, when you were there in Rolpa and Rukum, you saw that there is a kind of base area where we are exercising power. We are collecting taxes, we are holding people's court, we are controlling the forests, all these things. There, we have the squad, platoon, and the Special Task Force and the police do not dare come into these areas. This is a kind of preliminary base area. This is the *process* of forming base areas.

RW: Let me just clarify. You said that once a base area is formed, the People's Republic of Nepal would be declared. You're saying this would be declared before the seizure of power nationwide?

Prachanda: We have not exactly drawn up a detailed plan. But, in general, our thinking is that when we are in the position of first declaring a base area in one region of the country, the other regions should be near to being base areas. Like in the Eastern and Middle Regions, a form of power will have to be openly exercised. Until that time, we cannot make a liberated zone in the West. But with that situation we can organise a big mass movement in Kathmandu and other cities also. We are thinking like this. It is not final and it has not been already decided. But we generally think that in Nepal we can do it like this, because we already have a central united front. And we have a plan to make this united front a tool for revolutionary struggle at the central level, and a tool for people's power at the local level. This is our definition of the united front. At the local level it should be an instrument of exercising power; at the central level it should be an instrument of propaganda and revolutionary mass struggle. When that kind of situation develops, then we can make this central united front a form of a people's republic, a form of people's republic for propaganda value, political value and to crush the enemy and arouse the masses. At the central level, we will have to make a form of government. But before this we are not saying we have a form of government—it is a united front.

RW: Declaring a new government would also have international implications because you would demand to be recognised internationally.

Prachanda: Yes, international recognition. In our Fourth Plenum these questions came up. Should we now say we have a formal government? No, it would be premature. We must say that now it is premature, it is not time to say this. But when we look at the whole process of development, we see that, ultimately, at one point we will have to declare a new government and the president and the republic, the ministry and all these things. And we will appeal to the world's masses to recognise that this is the people's government.

We are also saying that we will not liberate only two, three or four districts and not care about other regions or the capital city. In Nepal, when we liberate an area and declare our government—and our base area in the Western Region—then we will need a clear and well-defined plan for the whole country and masses. There should be a big mass upsurge in other parts of the country. Without such mass upsurge and mass struggle in all other prospective base areas and guerrilla zones at the time, then militarily we would not be able to sustain our base area. Because at this time India will come at us, and the Nepali security forces will be centralised to crush us. Then thousands of ordinary people will be slaughtered.

RW: So a base area can only be established if the People's War is strong throughout the whole country.

Prachanda: Yes, that is our perspective.

RW: Maybe you could speak briefly on the question of building a new culture among the people. In particular, there were two things that struck me in my travels. One was the particular culture of sacrifice and devotion to the party and what role that plays in developing the People's War and the revolutionary consciousness of the people. The second thing is more general, the question of developing a culture of rebelling against feudal traditions and revolutionising social relations among people.

Prachanda: On this question I want to say that training the masses in the spirit of sacrifice is very important because in the era of imperialism and proletarian revolution, in today's whole situation, without sacrifice, without bloodshed, we cannot seize power, and we cannot transform the whole society on a new basis. Therefore, there is the question of sacrifice, of shedding blood, just as you saw with the martyrs in the West. People want to be martyrs. The people feel that to be a martyr is to be respected. This is a great feeling, which will enable us to change the whole feudal, individualistic and anarchist outlook prevailing in this society. When you live among those comrades, those families of martyrs—martyrs' brothers, mothers, sons—you see that a kind of cultural transformation is going on inside them and in their feelings.

When one of our comrades is martyred we vigorously make it a question of pride and historical importance. The mother and father, the parents of that martyr, will then feel that, 'Now my son has died, but there are thousands and thousands of others who are now my sons'. This is the great feeling. This is the great change that has happened. Those parents see that 'everybody is my son—hundreds of young people are now my sons'. The whole feudal and individualistic sectarian culture that has prevailed is turned upside down. We encourage, for our cultural revolution, this kind of sacrifice, and we glorify this kind of sacrifice. Because we know, in this era, in today's world situation, thousands and thousands of people will have to be prepared to be sacrificed.

Mao said, if there is a third world war, everybody cannot be killed. Maybe half the population will be gone and half the population will remain and a new world will emerge. It's not that Mao was irresponsible to say this. The spirit of what he said is not that millions of people should die. It was the spirit of making a new world. It was the spirit of transforming the world.

In a more general sense, you asked about overall how to change feudalism. There are two issues here, I think. One is that the party should make a complete plan, and there should be a complete effort to do this; there should be a developed ideological and political line and training to change the feudal relations. The other is that we have to make a concrete plan for every region. Because, just as I said, although Nepal is small, then again, it is big. There are many kinds of culture here. Some are tribal cultures, some more primitive cultures, some upper caste cultures—there are all different types of cultures. And we cannot make one plan for all of these.

For the whole Himalayan region, we should make a complete plan, in accordance with the cultural problems, traditional constraints, the different kinds of specific problems that there are. In the mountainous region, in the Western Region, as you saw, there are not so many temples, but when you go to Kathmandu there are so many temples—it is a capital of temples. Therefore, we have to make a conscious effort for every region, for every nationality. What are their traditional constraints, what forms of feudal exploitation and feudal oppression are prevailing in that group—we have to make efforts to consciously crush these things.

The last point is that the main question is struggle. In the process of struggle, the masses transform themselves. Struggle is the main vehicle of transformation. Other things are secondary.

RW: To follow up this question, there is the particular role of women in the People's War and the question of breaking down the feudal oppression of women. One thing that we learned from the class struggle and revolutionary process in China is that there is a dialectical relationship between the ideological and political struggle—transforming the thinking of people—and transforming the actual social, economic and family relations that hold women back, that prevent women from playing an equal role in society.

As long as women still have the main responsibility of taking care of children and the housework, these kinds of things, they will be prevented from playing a full role in society and in the revolution. So, new forms have to be found in society to solve this contradiction. This is a process of class struggle among the people—to transform the thinking of the people in order to change the institutions and to develop new revolutionary institutions that change the relations between people and further transform their thinking. Maybe you could speak of this in terms of what has been achieved in the People's War in Nepal—and also what more needs to be done, including bringing women into higher levels of leadership and responsibility.

Prachanda: Before the launch of the People's War, 'the woman question' was not so seriously debated in our party. That was our weakness. In our society, male domination, feudal relations have prevailed for a long time. In general terms we agreed, 'Yeah, the woman question is important. As communists we know these things'. But in a concrete sense, in a serious sense, I must say that before the launch (of the War) we were not so serious on 'the woman question'; and because we were not serious, our women comrades were not at the forefront of the movement. There were some women sympathisers and some organisers, but there was not much effort to develop the women comrades.

Then right after the launch (of the War) the question came up—urgently it came up. I was especially thrilled when, during the first year, I saw the sacrifice women were making in the main region, in the struggling zones—their militancy, their heroism, and their devotion. When I saw the women masses come into the field, then we started to debate seriously the woman question. Now the situation in the party has changed, more or less, to seeing the woman question from a proletarian viewpoint. From different angles, we try to understand the woman question—what is the meaning of the woman question, what is the political and theoretical importance and what are the practical implications in the class struggle and in the broader historical perspective?

And from a practical point of view, I want to say that among the oppressed nationalities, there is not so much male domination. There is a kind of equality there. Among some nationalities, women are seen as more important—the wives are even seen as more important than the men.

RW: What nationalities are you referring to here?

Prachanda: Mainly the Mongoloid nationalities, mainly the Magars, and mainly in Rolpa and Rukum. Here there is not as much male domination. Women can easily obtain a divorce, and if a woman remarries the community does not regard her as a bad woman. The traditions are very different. More and more militant and revolutionary women cadres are coming from those nationalities. And we are trying our best to develop the leadership of those comrades.

Before the launch (of the War), there were not any women comrades in the district committees. Now there are. In Rolpa, there are three or four women comrades in the district committee, and in the secretariat also there are women comrades. There are women comrades who direct whole area party committees, who direct whole squads. All these things they are doing. Also there are some district committee secretaries, new women comrades who have been developed and they have done a good job: you saw in one district in the East, that the DCS is a woman comrade, and in another district, near the Indian border, there is also a DCS woman comrade. In district committees, there are now more than 40–50 women. This shows the big change in our national structure and how we are developing the leadership qualities of women. We are also trying to bring women into regional level leadership, and we are trying to develop them on the level of central committee leadership. Among the oppressed nationalities, there is a lot of potential for developing proletarian leadership from among the women masses. And we are focusing, centralising, our effort here to develop the leadership of women. There is also a lot of potential to develop the leadership of women from among labourers.

RW: What about the practical obstacles that women face in the home, in terms of playing a larger role? For example, when I was traveling around, I saw many women with small children, and this is a problem. Some women are able to have relatives take care of their children, but this is not always possible. Is there a vision of socialising more of the housework and childcare?

Prachanda: At this point, the practical problems women comrades are facing—we can say the whole party is facing—are mainly associated with taking care of small children. With squad members who get pregnant and have babies, there is a question of who will look after the child. Some women comrades have a strong will to continue working, but the practical problems of caring for a baby become a big obstacle. In the main region, what the party is trying to do, for the time being, is ensure that when a woman has a baby, she will be placed in a secure area among the masses for about 6 months. She will not go back to her own home, and she will be among the masses, still doing whatever work she can do in the local area. Then after 6 months, when she can travel with her child and other comrades can also carry the child, she can then go and speak and organize. This is the kind of thing hundreds of women are doing. When the child is 1-year old, then they can be cared for by the masses or mass organisations and the woman comrades can leave. Now locally, the party is discussing the question of how to organise collective childcare. This question is presenting itself practically at this time. In some places, there are plans to set up a childcare house where comrades who have good experience and spirit will go and work. This plan is not finalised but is being discussed.

Also, the party is not directly pressing, but strongly encouraging men and women comrades, couples, not to have children for the time being, to not have a baby for 5–7, or even 10 years, because it will be a big practical problem. We explain that on this question, it is also a kind of sacrifice. We should have to sacrifice—do not have a baby. There are so many cases of couples who are not having babies right now; but trying to not have children presents another problem, because Nepal is very backward and there are insufficient health centres, and insufficient doctors.

RW: You mean lack of birth control?

Prachanda: When a woman gets pregnant then the question arises of abortion—they want to have an abortion. And after several abortions the physical condition of the woman will be harmed.

RW: So actually birth control is a pressing question.

Prachanda: Yes, a pressing question. We tell comrades it will help if they do not have babies for the time being. But if they do have a child then we will organise the masses to solve the problem of childcare. There are many cases where a woman has a baby, and, when some kind of childcare is established outside the party's organisational setup, then the police will capture her. There are many woman comrades who are in jail in the Western Region because of this.

RW: Because they had to leave the safe areas?

Prachanda: If they leave safe areas outside the control of our organisation then they will be captured by the enemy. That kind of problem also exists. In terms of women, I want to say that another very big problem is developing leadership...

RW: And illiteracy is a big obstacle for women, right? Because the low theoretical level, educational level, presents an obstacle to women coming into higher levels of leadership.

Prachanda: Yes, that is also a question. Now on the local level we are trying to develop a local education system to teach women comrades to read and write in night school. Such things are in the process of being done. But this will be a long process, a protracted process. Five, ten, even 20 years are needed to make everyone literate. We should teach the women comrades how to read and write. There are many women comrades now who are already literate, and we are trying our best to develop them in leadership. But illiteracy is a big problem, and we are trying to raise the level of literacy among the general masses.

RW: Before we end, could you briefly tell us about your personal background, so that people know something about you. What is your political history? What shaped your revolutionary thinking and activities? How did the class struggle, in Nepal and internationally, affect you?

Prachanda: I am from a poor peasant family from the Middle region, from Pokhara. But because of the poor conditions there, my family, my parents, moved from Pokhara, from the mountain area, to the *terai* region—to Chitwan district. My whole youth, and high school, was spent in Chitwan district. And I started being influenced by communist ideology 28 years ago, when I was about 17 years old. At that time there were big mass movements in the area. There were student movements; there were anti-Indian expansionism mass movements. All these things impressed me. This is an area with a big Indian comprador bourgeois presence and a lot of exploitation. All these things made an impression on me. And even more, what impressed me, convinced me, was the Great Proletarian Cultural Revolution in China. Mao, the Cultural Revolution, all the anti-revisionist movements: all these things impressed me.

Twenty-eight years ago I became a communist; I became a party member. And after some time, there was a big two-line struggle, and I was in touch with the revolutionary comrades in the Fourth Party Congress. In the process of that two-line struggle, I came into contact with revolutionary comrades more senior than me, and we had close contact, discussion and debate.

And in the class struggle there was a big mass movement going on. Twenty years ago there was a big mass movement, and in my district, a big women's movement and peasants' movement. This also provided the environment within which to develop my revolutionary thinking. At the same time, there was a big two-line struggle inside the party, and I continuously went with the revolutionary line. And when there was a split with Dumdum (M.B. Singh), then collectively we comrades, the main team in the central committee, tried to study the whole international process, the international communist movement, the Nepali communist movement. And in that process my thinking developed.

RW: The struggle against revisionism has been very important...

Prachanda: My main thrust is that I hate revisionism. I seriously hate revisionism, and I never compromise with revisionism. I fought and fought again with revisionism, and the party's correct line is based on the process of fighting revisionism. I hate revisionism, I seriously hate revisionism.

RW: I'd like to explore some more your comments about the international situation and, specifically, the significance of the People's War in Nepal, as part of the world revolution. What is your thinking on that, from two sides—how the People's War in Nepal can give strength to the international movement and how the international communist movement can give strength to the People's War in Nepal, that dialectical relationship?

Prachanda: Objectively there is a dialectical relationship between the People's War in Nepal and the whole international situation and movement. And what we think, and I think, is that a new wave of revolution, world revolution is beginning, because imperialism is facing a great crisis. Some people are saying that economically and culturally imperialism is in deeper crisis than before World War Two. There are so many symptoms of radical change that the people's movements are seeing around the world. Economically, culturally and politically, we see that a new wave of world revolution is beginning. This is fact. We have to grasp this fact, because just like Mao said, there will be fifty to a hundred years of great turmoil and great transformation.

From a practical point of view, the People's War in Nepal is contributing to making and accelerating this new wave of revolution, and it is contributing to the organisation of the international communist movement on a Maoist basis. Maoism should be in command of this new wave of world revolution. The People's War in Peru has done a good job of establishing Maoism. We also think that the RCP/USA has done a good job, ideologically and politically, to fight against revisionism and establish Maoism. Our party and the People's War in Nepal is also accelerating this process.

Right now, subjectively, the proletarian forces are weak—after Mao's death and the counter-revolution in China. Nepal is a small country, we are a small party—but we have a big perspective. Our People's War may be a spark, a spark for a prairie fire. We have already seen that during these 3 years of People's War, that the Indian communists and Indian masses have been somewhat impressed. There have been thousands and thousands of masses gathering in New Delhi, shouting, 'Long live the People's War in Nepal. We will support the People's War in Nepal'. In every corner now in India the People's War in Nepal is the subject of debate.

We are carrying out the People's War under the banner of Marxism–Leninism–Maoism. We think this has played a very significant and important role among the Indian revolutionary masses and in the ideological debate in the Indian communist movement. It has also helped the RIM very much in exposing international revisionism, modern revisionism, revisionism in China and Russian revisionism. In Nepal there is a very big revisionist party and much revisionist influence; the People's War has played a very big role in exposing all this.

This war has changed the name of the country itself—the identity of the country. It was a very backward, poor and beggar country. But now it is a country of heroes, of proletarian heroes. Now on the world's highest peak, Sagarmatha (Mount Everest), the red flag is flying. This will be seen from all over the world. People will say, 'What country is Nepal? It is the country with the world's highest peak, Mount Everest. What is there? Heroic proletarian revolution, People's War is there'.

Therefore, we think we have a very big responsibility, we face a big challenge in this present international situation. We will do our best; we should do our best, to the end, to fulfill our duty and responsibility. When you are in a pond or in the middle of a lake you do not know the importance of water. But when you are in the desert, then you see that just one glass of water is very important. Today there are not many genuine People's Wars in the world. So in this desert of revolutionary war, the People's War in Nepal is one glass of water for all revolutionary people. And we will fulfill our duty to give water to the revolutionary people.

We also see that without the experiences of the whole

international communist movement—and without the help of the RIM and without the help of all the communist leaders and dedicated comrades who are keenly and seriously helping the People's War in Nepal—we will not be able to sustain and maintain the People's War in Nepal. Finally, I want to say that, although we are in weaker position subjectively, objectively a wave of revolution is beginning and we communists should dare to fight. We will win.

Chapter 4

The Political Economy of the People's War*

Babu Ram Bhattarai
Chairman,
United People's Front-Nepal

At a certain stage of their development, the material productive forces of society come in conflict with the existing relations of production, or—what is but a legal expression for the same thing—with the property relations within which they have been at work hitherto. From forms of development of the productive forces these relations turn into their fetters. Then begins an epoch of social revolution.

—Karl Marx

Context and Theoretical Premises

An armed People's War was initiated in Nepal from 13 February 1996, under the leadership of the Communist Party of Nepal (Maoist), with the proclaimed aim of establishing a new democratic socio-economic system and state by overthrowing the present socio-economic structure and state.

This move should be understood in the context of Nepal's gradual decline to the status of the second poorest country in the world in terms of various criteria of development. Seventy-one per cent of its population falls below the absolute poverty level; nearly half of the national income is in the hands of

---

* The statistics used in this article are mostly from government sources like Central Bureau of Statistics, Nepal Rastra Bank etc. and from reports of United Nations agencies, and some are from studies conducted by non-government organisations.

the richest 10 per cent of the people. More than 60 per cent of the total population is illiterate, more than 90 per cent of the population lives in rural areas and 81 per cent of the labour force is engaged in backward agricultural occupations. Ten per cent are unemployed and 60 per cent are under-employed or in disguised employment. Food grain production, the most important indicator of national production, has shown a decline over the last 30 years. The foreign debt is the equivalent of over 60 per cent of GDP and is increasing as years pass.

It is therefore only natural for everybody to be eager to know how the People's War and the New Democratic Revolution is going to change these statistics and solve the formidable problems that give rise to them. It is no secret that the present reactionary state has for the last 50 years been peddling various attractive slogans along with eight Five Year Plans, but after each plan or campaign the problems have been further aggravated and the socio-economic situation of the country has further deteriorated in comparison with other countries. In this context it is necessary to identify the root cause or causes of this condition and to provide a scientific solution, instead of merely looking at the visible symptoms of problem and trying to solve it in a partial or disjointed manner. For this, it is necessary to analyse the problem with a historical materialist methodology, using the concepts of Marxist–Leninist–Maoist political economy. Today, in Nepal, the Maoist People's War is trying to do just that.

In the process of producing goods required for satisfying their physical and cultural wants, people use certain objects and technology (i.e. productive forces), and in that process a distinct relation (i.e. productive relation) is established among them. It is through the interactive combination of productive forces and production relations that a particular social system (i.e. mode of production) takes birth. Similarly, the contradiction between the ever-changing productive forces and production relations provides the motor for social and economic development. In general, since the development of the productive forces is faster and the development of the relations of production takes place at a much slower pace, at some stage of development of society the production relations block the development of the productive forces and this leads to constraints and distortions in society. It then becomes necessary to smash the old production relations and to develop new production relations in their place. Only in this way is it possible to remove the prevailing distortions and obstacles and to develop new productive forces and give impetus to the forward march of society. This is the process and point of time of social revolution.

Against this dynamic, the reactionary ruling classes of society and their allies attempt to develop the productive forces without smashing the old production relations, which have become obstacles to the process of development. The first path to development is known as the 'revolutionary' path and the second as the 'reformist' path. However, the 'reformist' path will only remain viable as long as there is possibility of developing productive forces within the old production relations; when that possibility is exhausted, the 'revolutionary' path becomes necessary. It is important to understand here that, in Nepal, the attempt to create a New Democratic system by smashing the old system through a protracted People's War under the leadership of CPN (Maoist) has been made when all attempts to carry out reforms within the old semi-feudal and semi-colonial system of relations of production, long ridden with crisis, have failed.

It is important to note right at the start that the decisive factor in the development of society is the motion generated by its own inner contradictions (i.e. between productive force and production relations). However, under specific conditions the intervention of external forces affects the internal development process in significant ways. After the rise of capitalism to its highest stage, imperialism—because of the process of centralisation and concentration inherent in the capitalist process of development—no social system in the world is able to remain outside the influence of imperialist intervention. The more these social systems are primitive and backward, the more damaging is the influence of imperialist intervention on their internal development process. Particularly in the case of societies that are on the verge of transition from feudalism to capitalism, the effects of imperialism distort the internal production relations, promoting the growth of comprador and bureaucratic capitalism (i.e. a capitalism that functions as an agent of foreign monopoly capitalism, engages in financial and commercial activities instead of productive activities and assumes a monopolistic character from the outset by relying on the state) instead of indigenous forms of industrial capitalism. That is why it is necessary to smash the relationship with imperialism while bringing about a progressive transformation in 'internal' production relations through revolutionary means.

It is also important to understand the dialectical relationship between the development process of society and the spatial structure. This is because, along with the social processes, changes take place in physical/spatial structures too, although the nature and quality of the change may be different from, or less than that in the social structure. As far as the relationship between the two processes is concerned, it would be more appropriate to view the physical/spatial structure as a 'reflection' of the social structure than as the 'causative factor'. It is necessary to understand the transformation processes of the social and spatial structures in their inter-relatedness, as the distortion and malady of the social process is reflected in regional structures through uneven regional development. The importance of the Maoist protracted People's War, based upon the strategy of encircling the city from the countryside, can also be understood in this way.

Based upon the above short account of the conceptual premises, it is possible to analyse the external and internal class relations of Nepalese society and the resultant socio-economic and spatial problems, and to evaluate the capacity of the People's War to solve these problems.

Imperialism and Expansionism

Imperialist Oppression

The present era is one of imperialism or monopoly capitalism. Because of the nature of unequal and uneven development inherent in capitalism, most of the world's capital and wealth has become concentrated in the hands of the few imperialist countries of the West and the North, whereas most of the countries of the East and the South (i.e. Asia, Africa and Latin-America) are suffering from underdevelopment and poverty. That the gap between the rich and the poor has never been so wide in the history of mankind and that this gap is growing ever wider, has been documented by the statistics of the imperialist organisations as well as others. For example, the annual sales of the 200 largest multi-national companies of the imperialist countries exceed the gross domestic production of all countries in the world, except the richest economies (USA, Japan, Germany, France, Britain, Russia, Italy, Canada and Australia) and they own one-third of the world's wealth. The income differential between the world's richest and poorest countries in the 1960s was 30 times, whereas it is more than 60 times today (in the 1990s).

The siphoning of wealth from the poor oppressed countries to the rich imperialist countries takes place on a world scale, through the profits of capital investment in industries, interest on loans, commercial profit from trade in goods and services and so on. Whatever capital investment the imperialists make in the poor oppressed countries—whether through multilateral agencies like the World Bank, the International Monetary Fund etc. or through unilateral mechanisms like the transnational corporations rooted in their own country and supported by their own state, they remove 10 times more capital to the imperialist centres from the oppressed countries than is transferred the other way. Besides this, through their monopoly over science and technology, communications and capital, the imperialist countries have ensured that the overall development process of the poor oppressed countries has been distorted and dependent.

According to the imperialist logic of 'bigger fish eats smaller fish', there will always be fierce competition among monopoly capitalist groups to expand and consolidate their hegemony and there will be war in order to maintain areas of influence (or territories), or to re-divide the old economic territories. This is demonstrated by the fact that after the advent of imperialism in the 20th century, two world wars and more than 160 other wars have occurred, and six times more people have lost their lives in wars in this century as compared with that in wars in the 19th century. The very fact that imperialists spend 1000 billion US dollars a year in armaments (almost half of which is spent by the United States alone) proves the nexus between imperialism and war. That is why imperialism is also called 'the era of war capitalism'. Thus, on the one hand, the contradictions between imperialism and the oppressed nations are sharpening intensely while, on the other, inter-imperialist rivalries are pushing the whole world to the brink of war. Under such circumstances, it becomes not only natural but also inevitable for oppressed nations to fight wars of liberation, relying not on capital, armament or technology (the resources of imperialism) but on the oppressed masses (the resources of the oppressed nations).

Among the oppressed nations of the world, Nepal stands amongst the most oppressed. The very fact that it has declined from 13th poorest in the 1970s to the 2nd poorest in the world today indicates the degree of stagnation of the country. The poor and underdeveloped state of the country is not, however, because of lack of natural resources or due to the laziness of the ordinary people but due to internal and external exploitation and oppression. This can be proved by comparing Nepal's position before and after the semi-colonial Sugauli Treaty of 1816 with that of other contemporary countries of the world. Nepal, in the lap of the Himalayas, sandwiched between the giant states of China and India and surrounded on the southern, western and eastern sides by India, was historically first oppressed and exploited by British colonialism, and then, after the 1950s, by various imperialist powers and principally by Indian expansionism. After the Sugauli Treaty and indeed up until now, the internal development process of Nepal has remained stunted and distorted by the destructive effect of external imperialist and/or expansionist forces.

All the economic and non-economic indicators of social development reveal this. Particularly since the decade of 1950s, when it first experienced imperialism through ties of trade, finance etc., the process of underdevelopment, distortion and dependency has become all the more intense. The fact that today the foreign debt has mounted to more than Rs. 150 billion, the annual trade deficit has reached nearly Rs. 50 billion (equivalent to the annual budget) and dependency in every area of the economy has been aggravated, provides enough indication of the oppressive effects of imperialism. According to the stipulations of the International Monetary Fund, any country whose foreign debt is more than 200–250 per cent of total exports and whose debt-servicing ratio is more than 20 per cent of exports is said to be in a 'critical' state. In Nepal, these parameters jumped in 1994–95 to more than 600 and 35 per cent respectively. There is no doubt that the condition of Nepal has become critical—and tragic—because of its entanglement in the imperialist net.

It has become necessary to wage a People's War in Nepal in order to gain liberation from the oppression of imperialism and to march forward along the path of self-reliant development. From this point of view, the People's War in Nepal is part of the world anti-imperialist national liberation movement.

Expansionist Oppression

The biggest direct manifestation of world imperialist oppression and exploitation in Nepal is Indian expansionist exploitation and oppression. 'Expansionism' is the process of exploitation and oppression of a smaller and weaker economy by a stronger economy that has not itself developed to the level of imperialism but derives its strength from the backing of external imperialist forces and its own state. Similarly because its hegemony cannot be maintained on the basis of purely capitalist competition, the expansionist power uses extra-economic coercion (military, political and cultural) to maintain its economic areas of influence or markets. That is why Indian expansionism, which is itself a jail-house of various oppressed nations, has been exploiting and oppressing various neighbouring countries of South Asia (and other Asian, African and Latin-American countries) with the backing of imperialist forces (such as USA, UK, Japan, France, Italy, Germany, Russia etc.) or of multinational companies, together with that of its own central state, headquartered in Delhi.

Indian expansionism has kept Nepal as its captive market through a series of unequal treaties, forced upon the weaker country at various times, taking advantage of the fact that Nepal is 'India-locked' from three sides and that it is largely through India that transportation, communication and trade connection with the rest of the world must take place. In 1816, British India forced the Sugauli Treaty upon Nepal, reducing it to a semi-colony. From that time onwards, Nepal's path of independent and self-reliant development was blocked and a process of socio-economic retardation and underdevelopment (i.e. distorted and dependent development) was initiated. If one is to compare Nepal's socio-economic development indices immediately before and after the Sugauli Treaty, this is very clear. Prior to the treaty, Nepal was self-sufficient in basic industrial production—cotton fabrics, copper and brass utensils, domestic instruments, military armaments (including modern rifles), sugar etc.—and in food grains. But after this treaty, with the penetration of factory-made goods from India and concomitant decline of Nepalese industries, Nepal was reduced to total dependency. This process did not take place all of a sudden, but it started with the Sugauli Treaty, was intensified particularly after the Nepal–India trade agreement of 1923 (which created a 'common market' of India and Nepal) and reached a pinnacle in the decades after the semi-colonial Treaty of 1950 with so-called free India.

At present it is mainly through the 1950 treaty and successive versions of that treaty 'agreed' every 10 years, that Indian expansionism maintains its semi-colonial commercial, industrial, financial and fiscal monopoly over Nepal. Expansionist oppression and exploitation in different areas have been safeguarded by the periodic trade and transit treaties, and by other treaties and agreements based on the unequal relations enshrined in the 1950 Treaty. Semi-colonial relations have multiple dimensions—economic, political, military and cultural—and in regard to Nepal, Indian expansionist exploitation and oppression has a multifarious character. However, all of these different forms ultimately support economic exploitation and oppression. In Nepal itself, the economy reveals the most striking characteristics of Indian expansionist oppression and exploitation.

Historically, Indian expansionism has used Nepal as a captive market for its industrial goods. That is why, up until the decade of 1950s, about 95 per cent of Nepal's foreign trade used to take place with India. In subsequent decades, with the increasing direct penetration of other imperialist forces into Nepal, India's trade share has been reduced to about 30 per cent, but the overall structure of trade is grossly un-favourable to Nepal (see Table 4.1). In addition, it is important to note that because of the open border between Nepal and India, almost one third of total trade takes place informally or illegally. This means that the real volume of trade with India is always larger than that indicated by the official statistics.

If one is to judge by the structure of the trade, Nepal's export/import ratio with India before the Sugauli Treaty was five times more favourable to Nepal and it remained twice as favourable (or more) during the period after the 1923 trade treaty.

TABLE 4.1
Import–Export Trade of Nepal, Classified by,
Countries and Commodities (1994–95)

Commodities	India			Other Countries			Total Trade		
	Imports	Exports	%	Imports	Exports	%	Imports	Exports	I/E %
Value[a]	5,242.1	2,161	41.22	19,861	276.4	14	16,427	2,437	14.84
% Primary goods	25.21	64.14	—	44.4	1.90	—	25.07	13.62	—
% by country	31.91	88.61	—	68.09	11.34	—	100	100	—
Value[b]	15,546.90	1,208.10	7.77	24,862	14,253	57.33	49,084	15,461	31.5
% Secondary goods by commodity	74.77	35.86	—	55.58	98.10*	—	74.91	86.38	—
% Products by country	31.67	7.81	—	68.33	92.19	—	100	100	—
Value[a]	3.2	0.0	—	11.7	0.10	8.50	14.9	0.1	0.67
% Not classified by commodity	0.02	0.0	—	0.02	0.00	—	0.02	0.0	—
% by Country	21.48	0.0	—	78.52	100	—	100	100	—
Value	20,791.20	3,369.10	16.20	44,735.50	14,529.7	32.48	65,526.70	17,898.8	27.32
Total % by commodity	100	100	—	100	100	—	100	100	—
% by country	31.73	18.82	—	68.27	81.18	—	100	100	—

Source: Nepal Rastra Bank, Foreign Trade Division, 1995.
a. Value in Rs. million.
b. Of the 'secondary products' exported to 'other countries', woolen carpets & garments together constitute 92 per cent.

After the 1950 treaty, however, the balance shifted against Nepal to twice as unfavourable, while by the 1990s it had become almost seven times more unfavourable to Nepal. It is clear that with an ever-increasing trade deficit, Nepal's economy is becoming irretrievably caught in the Indian expansionist trap. Secondly, if one analyses the commodity structure of imports and exports, then Nepal is seen to be exporting a smaller volume of value-added goods—mainly (64 per cent) unprocessed or semi—processed agricultural products—whereas it imports more (about 75 per cent) higher value-added industrial products from India. This adverse ratio is deteriorating every year, against Nepal. Thus the general process of imperialist oppression and exploitation through 'unequal exchange' is seen to be operating in the case of Nepal.

Thirdly, as the semi-colonial Treaty of 1950 provides for 'national treatment' with respect to the Indian monopoly capitalists, allowing them to reside in Nepal and to engage in economic activities on an equal footing with Nepali citizens, they are able to monopolise the economy of Nepal completely. At present about one dozen India-based billionaire capitalists (mainly Marwaris) exert strong control over Nepal's industry and commerce. According to the estimation of one Indian researcher some time back, about 80 per cent of Nepal's industry and commerce was in the hands of Indian capitalists or capitalists of Indian origin. The Indian expansionist state has tended to place restrictions on the international transit facilities that a land-locked country like Nepal is actually entitled to enjoy unhindered. In this way, it has facilitated its hegemony over the Nepali economy, by forcing upon Nepal adverse and unequal export–import trade and transit conditions. This is reflected in the conflict that arises every decade when the trade and transit treaty is renewed, when the Nepali people register protest against it.

Another important aspect of the way in which Nepal is maintained as a captive market of Indian expansionism is that multinational companies of various imperialist countries like USA, UK, Japan, Germany, etc. sell goods produced in their India-based branches to Nepal, or they open subbranches of their Indian branches in Nepal. For example, products of multi-national companies based in India—like Bata (shoes), Hoecht (medicine), Proctor and Gamble (soap, chocolate etc.), Hindustan Lever (soap)

Nestle (coffee, milk products etc.), Brook Bond (tea) etc., and products of Indian joint-ventures with multinational companies such as Maruti–Suzuki (automobiles), Hero–Honda (motorcycle) etc.—are freely sold in Nepal. In this way, world imperialism enters Nepal, riding an Indian expansionist horse.

This combined intrusion of imperialism and expansionism has not only stunted the development of new industries in Nepal but has also created a situation where previously self-reliant domestic industries, such as soap, tea, shoes, biscuit, paper, etc. are now beginning to collapse, one after the other. Even those industries—like woolen carpets and garments—that have emerged since the 1980s and are now the principal exporters to third countries (more than 92 per cent of total exports), tend to be overtly or covertly controlled by Indian expansionists through their hegemonic control over raw materials, labour, capital and trade. Similarly, the tourism sector—one of the major sources of foreign currency—is also largely under the control of Indian capitalists. This is demonstrated by the fact that out of four five-star hotels, at first all four and now three 'enjoy' collaborations with Indian capitalists (and one is fully owned by Indians), while the forward and backward linkages of the tourism industry are intimately connected with the Indian economy.

Besides ensuring that Nepal constitutes a captive market for its industrial goods, the other feature of Indian expansionist exploitation and oppression is its control over Nepal's natural resources, mainly the latter's rich water resources. Most of the rivers that irrigate the heavily-populated northern Gangetic plains flow through Nepal and the cheapest and the easiest sources of the energy required by India for future industrialisation, agricultural development and general consumption are the huge water resources of Nepal (which has the second largest water resource potential in the world— out of an estimated potential of 83,000 Megawatts of hydro-power only 0.5 per cent has been tapped so far). That is why Indian expansionism usurped Nepal's water resources (mainly for irrigation purposes) through the Sharada Darn Agreement in 1920, the Kosi Agreement in 1954 and the Gandaki Agreement in 1959. However, in 1996, through the 'Integrated Mahakali Development Project Agreement' they have taken full control of whole of the Mahakali river for irrigation and power purposes. The earlier Kosi and Gandaki Agreements were nakedly semi-colonial treaties as they deprived the *terai*—the grain basket of Nepal—of irrigation, by diverting the water to India through dams constructed, ironically, on the Nepal side of the border, allowing only a negligible amount of water to Nepal and prohibiting the building of other dams upstream for a considerable distance. The Mahakali Treaty, however, has adopted a more devastating form of neocolonial exploitation and oppression by talking equality in theory but in practice ensuring monopoly in the use of water and electricity to the Indian expansionists and imposing trillions of rupees of foreign debt upon Nepal. Potentially even more far-reaching than all of these specific 'agreements', the 'Joint Communique' of June 10, 1990, has opened the door for the exercise of an Indian monopoly over Nepal's most important water resources in future by declaring all the rivers of Nepal to be 'common resources' for Nepal and India as well.

Another form of exploitation and oppression by Indian expansionism is the recruitment of innocent, diligent and militant young men of the hills of Nepal into the Indian army and police, and into the private sector as cheap labour, thus perpetuating a long 'tradition' of British colonialism and imperialism, and ensuring the continuing reproduction of Nepal's semi-feudal agricultural economy. This 'foreign' exploitation of cheap Nepali labour through temporary and 'relay' (i.e. the son following in the father's footsteps) migration, which started immediately after the Sugauli Treaty, has had a disastrous effect on the historical development of the industrial proletariat and of indigenous capitalism in Nepal. Finally, the common market and open border maintained by the trade treaty of 1923 and the 'peace and friendship treaty' of 1950 has made Nepal's financial and monetary system totally dependent on the Indian financial and monetary system, and this has had a very adverse effect on the development of national capital and industrialisation in Nepal.

Given all this, it is clear that 180 years of uninterrupted semi-colonial relations with Indian expansionism has had a very negative and destructive effect on the development of class relations and socio-economic structures and, in essence, on the development of national capitalism in Nepal. That is why one of the most important objectives of Maoist People's War is to break the chains of semi-colonialism and to usher in a new type of national capitalism (and a New Democracy) by mobilising people of all ranks and classes suffering under all forms of semi-colonial exploitation and oppression.

Internal Social and Spatial (Regional) Relations

While there can be no doubt that the evolution of Nepal's economy and society has been affected by the various interventions of imperialism and expansionism, the main cause and basis of its historical development must be sought in the structure and dynamic of its internal class relations or production relations. It is necessary to seek the root cause of Nepal's underdevelopment, socio-economic and regional inequality, poverty and cultural degradation in the internal social and spatial relations and thereby attempt to chart the path of its progressive transformation. In general, Nepal is in the process of a transition from feudalism to capitalism, but it has been stunted and degraded to a semi-feudal and semi-colonial state as a result of the combination of external imperialist/expansionist intervention and internal reactionary class relations. Nepal has its own geographical and historical specificities. For example, 79 per cent of the total land area comprises hills and mountains, and only 21 per cent plains *(terai)*. There is immense geographical and ethnic diversity. It has had no direct colonial experience. For the last two and a quarter centuries it has been characterised by the uninterrupted rule of broadly the same reactionary classes within a formally independent state. Given these specificities, it is necessary to analyse in some detail the present socio-economic of Nepal and the major issues of development.

Semi-Feudal Relations and Underdevelopment in Agriculture

The basic economic foundation of the contemporary Nepali society is agriculture. This is because more than 81 per cent of the labour force is engaged in agriculture and nearly half of the gross domestic product comes from the agricultural sector. This is why the level of development of productive forces and productivity in agriculture has a decisive effect on the development of economy as a whole and why the existing production relations in agriculture play a decisive role in determining the nature of the overall social structure.

The productive forces in Nepalese agriculture are extremely backward and are almost primitive in nature. First of all, the nature of the means of production reflects the level of development of the productive forces. The lower and more backward the level of development of agriculture, the more it has to rely on the traditional means of production such as land, human and animal labour, and primitive equipment. In general, even today nearly 99 per cent of the total investment in Nepalese agriculture is made in land, human and animal labour, and primitive equipment and only about 1 per cent is invested in 'modern' means of production (e.g. machine, fertiliser, pesticide, high yielding seeds etc.). Furthermore, over 81 per cent of the total labour force engaged in backward forms of agriculture indicates a very primitive stage of the economy. Labour is underutilised (through disguised employment or underemployment) and this ultimately has an adverse effect on overall national production. (The more developed an economy, the smaller the proportion of the labour force engaged in agriculture and the more the 'surplus' labour is engaged in more productive sectors, like industry or services. For example, in the United States, less than 7 per cent of the total labour force is engaged in agriculture.) In Nepal, on average, three persons are engaged per hectare of land and in the hills it may rise to six persons per hectare. Another important index of the development of the productive forces in agriculture is the availability of irrigation facilities. In Nepal, up to 1991–92 only 13 per cent of total cultivated land (some 26 million hectares)—18 per cent in the *terai* but just 8 per cent in the hills—had permanent irrigation. This is not due to any natural lack of water or the mountainous topography, but to purely social factors. According to a report produced by the Asian Development Bank, 60 per cent of the total cultivated land in Nepal (80 per cent in the *terai* and 25 per cent in the hills) could be irrigated. Mainly because of the lack of irrigation, the cropping intensity in Nepal is estimated to be just 90 per cent (less than one crop a year), which indicates a very low level of development of productive forces in agriculture.

A primitive structure of agricultural production and declining rates of production generally also indicate a low level of productive forces in agriculture. The more backward or 'lower' is the society, the greater is the ratio of production of use values. From this point of view, in Nepal, 80 per cent of total agricultural production is in food grains and the production of cash crops is negligible (and highly concentrated in the eastern *terai*). The most depressing feature is the declining rate of agricultural production. According to the official statistics for the decade 1984–85–1994–95, the annual rate of growth for agricultural production as a whole was negative (–0.7 per cent) whereas for food grains it was even worse (–7 per cent), particularly for the principal crop, paddy rice (–16 per cent). Thus Nepal, which was once a food grain exporting country, has now become a food importing country. The net import of food grains (worth Rs. 3.5 billion in 1994–95) from India and other countries indicates this. The conversion of most of hill districts, which were traditionally self-sufficient in food grains, into food-deficit districts provides an indication of the declining and alarming state of agriculture in the hill regions.

The most important index of the development of the productive forces in agriculture is the productivity of land and labour, and their rate of growth. It is not difficult to appreciate the abysmally low level of productivity of both land and labour in Nepal where the population/land ratio is very high and the use of irrigation and modern inputs in production is very low. According to one estimation, made some years back, the average output per hectare of 10 crops was Rs. 2,700 at current prices whereas the productivity of labour (annual) was only Rs. 1,461. This very low level of productivity is actually decreasing every year and, except for few districts in the eastern *terai*, the state of agriculture is very delicate and alarming throughout the country, particularly in the hills.

What is the explanation for the extremely low level of productive forces and mounting crisis in agriculture, the backbone of the country's economy and society? To answer this, it is necessary to analyse the relations of production in the agricultural sector. The most important means of production in agriculture is the land and the condition of ownership of cultivable land determines the mode of organisation, extraction and utilisation of surplus product (i.e. production relations). In the absence of reliable data on land distribution in Nepal, it becomes very difficult to make an objective analysis of land ownership. However, some generalisations can be made on the basis of the data collected from existing sources. The first impression one gets about current land relations in Nepal in general is that the distribution of land is very unequal and that the large majority of the population is of landless, semi-landless and poor peasant status.

Given the current availability of cultivable land and its productivity, one could define those who own less than 1 hectare of land as 'poor peasants', those owning from 1 to 4 hectares as 'middle peasants' and those owning above 4 hectares as 'rich peasants' or (if more) 'feudals'. On this basis, the statistics suggest that about 70 per cent of poor peasants own about 25 per cent of the land, 25 per cent of middle peasants own around 45 per cent of the land and about 5 per cent of rich peasants and semi-feudals own 30 per cent of the land (see Table 4.2). According to one early report, by a

TABLE 4.2
Distribution of Household (HH) &
Area Owned by Size of Landholding

Size of holding (hectare)	1961		1971		1981		1991	
	HH	Area	HH	Area	HH	Area	HH	Area
Landless	1.43	0.0	0.80	0.0	0.37	0.0	1.17	0.0
<1	73.89	24.03	76.77	27.20	66.32	17.33	68.63	30.5
1–4	19.56	35.68	18.39	39.29	28.05	46.13	27.68	50.8
>4	5.13	41.42	4.03	33.74	5.35	36.54	2.51	18.7
Total	100.00	100.00	100.00	100.00	100.00	100.00	100.00	100.00

Source: Central Bureau of Statistics, *Agricultural Census of Nepal* (1961, 1971, 1981 and 1991), Kathmandu.

Values are given in percentages.

specialist from the FAO, who came to Nepal to evaluate the effects of the so-called land reform of 1964, the structure of land ownership is even more unequal. According to this report, 8 per cent of the Nepali population was totally landless and of those who had some land, 65 per cent of poor peasants owned only 10 per cent of the land, 25 per cent of middle peasants owned 25 per cent of the land and 10 per cent of rich peasants and semi-feudals owned 65 per cent of the land. In the *terai*, those big landlords with more than 10 hectares each owned more than 50 per cent of the total land, whereas in the hills, poor peasants constituted more than 80 per cent of the population (see Table 4.3). From this, it is

TABLE 4.3
Territorial Distribution of Households (HH) and Area Owned After 'Land Reform' by Size of Holding

Region size of holding (hectare)	Ktm.Valley HH	Ktm.Valley Area	Eastern Terai HH	Eastern Terai Area	Western Terai HH	Western Terai Area	Eastern Hills HH	Eastern Hills Area	Western Hills HH	Western Hills Area	Nepal HH	Nepal Area
<1	80.28	39.90	43.27	5.63	14.61	1.14	91.33	44.51	46.17	25.71	65.13	9.67
1–5	19.72	60.10	41.28	29.20	36.52	12.41	6.98	25.81	22.65	57.45	24.57	25.79
5–10	—	—	7.50	15.77	29.21	32.14	1.34	14.64	0.50	4.12	5.84	21.63
>10	—	—	7.95	49.40	19.66	54.31	—	—	0.64	12.63	4.46	42.91
Total	100.00	100.00	100.00	100.00	100.00	100.00	100.00	100.00	100.00	100.00	100.00	100.00

Source: Zaman, M.A. (1973). *Evaluation of Land Reform in Nepal*, Ministry of Land Reform, His Majesty's Government of Nepal, Kathmandu, pp. 93–94.

easy to argue that the principal reason for the low development of productive forces in Nepalese agriculture is the lack of cultivable land in the possession of the majority of labouring peasants, and the overwhelming proportion of land concentrated in the hands of the better-off and often non-labouring minority.

Apart from the ownership of means of production, how the labour is organised and how the produce is distributed and how it is consumed will determine the social class relationships and finally the social relations of production. In Nepali agriculture there is a dearth of reliable statistics. However, the broad pattern of class relations can be discerned by generalising on the basis of the available data. There is no doubt that there is a majority of 'owner-cultivators' who own small pieces of land and who work on their own land. However, even those landlords who own more than 10 hectares and have never stepped onto their farmland to work are also enumerated as owner-cultivators in the official agricultural census. The number of owner-cultivators increased from 60 per cent in 1961 to 80 per cent in 1971 (see Table 4.4). That is, however, misleading. In order to circumvent the tenancy law, most of the landlords made false declarations that they had been cultivating their own land; hence the number of owner-cultivators was grossly inflated. Also, not only big landlords but also rich and even middle peasants, may—for various reasons, for example, because of physical disability due to illness or old age and engagement of other members of the family in other occupations etc.—rent out land to tenants for cultivation instead of cultivating themselves, but they are still registered as owner-cultivators rather than the tenants. Consequently, the figures provided in the FAO report, according to which the number of owner-cultivators is 65 per cent of the total and the land cultivated by them about 49 per cent, may be nearer to the truth (see Table 4.5).

Except for those who cultivate their own land with family labour, the remainder either rent it out to tenants or have it cultivated by different forms of paid labour—from bonded to 'free' wage labour. Because up until now, the rights of tenants have not been secure and the number of unregistered tenants far exceeds the number of registered tenants, it is impossible to make a reliable estimate of the number of tenants and the amount of land tilled by them. According to the official agricultural census conducted

TABLE 4.4
Landholdings by Types of Tenure and Territorial Zones (1961 & 1971)

Type of tenure	Owner-cultivator		tenant		Owner-tenant			Total	
	HH	Area	HH	Area	HH	Area Own	Others	HH	Area
High Mountains									
1961	—	—	—	—	—	—	—	—	—
1971	82.00	76.50	2.30	1.56	15.62	13.91	8.02	100.00	100.00
Hills									
1961	65.62	56.56	2.95	2.19	31.43	27.56	13.68	100.00	100.00
1971	89.32	84.26	1.03	0.67	9.63	9.74	5.68	100.00	100.00
Kathmandu Valley									
1961	38.13	35.00	12.19	7.51	49.61	27.64	29.85	100.00	100.00
1971	54.27	58.19	19.96	12.89	25.77	15.84	13.09	100.00	100.00
Inner Terai									
1961	71.34	59.56	10.52	14.43	18.14	16.12	9.89	100.00	100.00
1971	88.88	81.22	5.35	8.66	5.95	5.27	4.96	100.00	100.00
Terai									
1961	47.40	49.58	15.00	12.25	37.60	21.42	16.75	100.00	100.00
1971	68.59	69.96	8.46	7.99	22.95	11.18	10.87	100.00	100.00
Nepal									
1961	59.64	51.84	7.17	9.79	33.19	22.64	15.72	100.00	100.00
1971	80.99	73.65	4.38	6.48	14.61	10.62	9.32	100.00	100.00

Note: 'Mountains' are included with 'Hills' in the figures for 1961. HH Represents Households.
Source: Central Bureau of Statistics, *Agricultural Census of Nepal* (1961 & 1971), Kathmandu.

TABLE 4.5
Land Tenure Distribution After 'Land Reform'

Land tenure	% of households		% of cultivated area	Average size of holding (hectare)
	Total HH	HH with landholding		
I With Land	92.2	100.00	100.00	—
1. Landlords	1.8	3.31	26.91	18.33
2. Owner-cultivator	62.0	65.22	49.11	1.67
3. Owner-tenant	19.1	20.70	15.36	1.64
4. Tenant- cultivtor	2.3	10.77	8.62	1.74
II Landless	7.8	—	—	—
Total	100.00	100.00	100.00	—

Source : Zaman, M.A. (1973). op. cit.

every decade from 1961 to 1991, the number of tenants as a percentage of total cultivating households varies from a maximum of 40 to a minimum of 10, while the land tilled by them as a percentage of the total cultivable land varies from a maximum of 2 to a minimum of 6, which as mentioned above is clearly on the low side. The report of the FAO consultant gives the number of tenant households as 30 per cent and the land cultivated by them as 24 per cent, whereas according to other studies conducted, by non-government organisations, the number of tenants may be 40 per cent and the land tilled by them 30 per cent. From our own practical experience, we feel the latter estimations are more nearer to the truth.

The ratio of owner-cultivators is higher in the hill regions and that of 'tenants' is higher in the *terai* and inner *terai*, which is to be expected considering the availability of cultivable land and the pressure of population. Nearly two-third of all tenants till the land on a share-cropping basis and the rest pay a fixed rent, either in cash or kind, or have other tenurial conditions. In share-cropping, tenants in Nepal generally surrender half of their produce to the landowners, whereas in other parts of the world they usually 'share' only one-third to one-sixth of the produce. Although the tenancy system exists under the capitalist mode of production as well as under feudalism, in Nepal, especially in the share-cropping system, tenants are forced to till the landlord's land under arrangements that provide for bare subsistence needs rather than securing capitalistic profit. The rights of tenants are not secure, the rate of rent is high and the tenants are often 'bonded' to the landlord through high interest rates charged on loans and other labour-service conditions, apart from the rent of the land. From this it is clear that the principal mode of surplus extraction in Nepali agriculture (and which extends to other sectors of the economy) is 'semi-feudal'; this plays a major role in the underdevelopment and backwardness of Nepali agriculture (and by implication of the whole economy).

Apart from the owner-cultivators and the tenants, the remaining (nearly 5 per cent) landowners regularly make use of bonded labour and wage labour to cultivate 20 per cent of the land. A bonded labour system, variously known as *Haruwa, Kamaiya* etc., exists in the central and western *terai* region while farming by seasonal wage labour exists widely in the the eastern *terai* and in areas around urban centres. The system of bonded labour, in which the labourers are kept under control, like serfs, and forced to work on the land, is a continuation of a mediaeval feudal form, and constitutes the most primitive, oppressive and retrograde labour relationship existing in Nepali agriculture. Although the wage labour system is basically of a capitalistic nature, in the case of Nepal, not only is it relatively limited (in quantitative terms) but, if analysed in detail, can hardly be seen as indicative of progressive capitalist relations of production. This is because a majority of those who employ wage labour do so, not with the purpose of expanded reproduction of capital in the agricultural sector, but either for their own subsistence or with a view to investment in trade or finance in the urban areas. As a result, the employment of wage labour plays a limited role in the development of the productive forces in agriculture.

On the whole, although different relations of production exist in Nepali agriculture, there is no doubt that the semi-feudal relation remains the principal and determining relation, both qualitatively and quantitatively. Here it is necessary to be clear that although numerically the small owner-cultivators are in a majority, since they are tied with various economic and non-economic exploitative chains to local landlords, usurers and feudal landowners, they are not 'free'. They do not in fact have the 'independent' standing they outwardly appear to have, and they too are subordinate to the laws of the prevailing dominant semi-feudal relations of production.

Besides the ownership of land and relations of production, the characteristic reactionary role of moneylending (usury capital) has also contributed to the reproduction of semi-feudalism and has retarded the process of development. Peasants are usually in need of loan for both production and consumption purposes; taking undue advantage of this situation, the feudal usurers provide credit to the peasants at high interest rates and under oppressive conditions, and by entrapping them in a vicious cycle of indebtedness they enforce and reinforce semi-feudal exploitation through the payment of interest and through labour-service payments. This practice has been going on for a long time in the rural areas. In recent times, the centre of gravity of this form of 'exploitation' has been shifting gradually from 'feudal usurers' towards 'merchant usurers', without lessening the peasant's oppression in any way, either in quantity or quality. Finally, in addition to these historic forms of usury, imperialist financial capital has entered into the agricultural sector over the last few decades in the form of bureaucratic capital with state backing. The main vehicle for this bureaucratic capital is the Agriculture Development Bank, which injects imperialist financial capital into the backward Nepali agriculture sector at high interest rates (i.e. 19 per cent) and actually represents some 85 per cent of so-called institutional credit.

However, according to a recent rural credit survey, conducted by the Nepal Rastra Bank, even now, 80 per cent of all rural credit is under the control of 'traditional' usurers, while institutional bureaucratic capital is able to capture only 20 per cent. According to the same survey, more than two-thirds of peasants are caught in a debt trap, owing money to either traditional or 'institutional' usurers (or both). Poor peasants tend to be more highly dependant on traditional usurers, who charge interest rates at least double (and often three or four times more than) the institutional ones. But, if one analyses the purpose for which credit is advanced by the Agriculture Development Bank, we find that instead of investing on such sectors like irrigation, which would enhance the development of the productive forces, more is invested in such sectors as 'agricultural marketing', which under present conditions ensures that Nepali agriculture remains a mere appendage of world imperialism. New bureaucratic capitalist relations may have been superimposed on the old semi-feudal relations, but instead of developing the productive forces in agriculture in Nepal, this has only contributed to its dependent development.

Because of backward semi-feudal relations in the Nepalese agriculture sector, on the one hand, there is rampant disguised unemployment and underemployment as a result of the entanglement of surplus labour in the net of oppressive social obligations, and on the other, there is large-scale seasonal and temporary emigration of labour from the rural areas to the urban areas and to India to supplement inadequate farm incomes with non-farm earnings, thereby perpetuating the reproduction of backward semi-feudal relations in Nepali agriculture. According to a study of the National Planning Commission undertaken some time back, rural labour was unemployed or underemployed for 63 per cent of total labour days. As a result, nearly one-third of the labour force heads away from home as seasonal or temporary labour in order to supplement the farm earnings. The existence of this rampant disguised unemployment and underemployment is thus both the cause and the consequence of backward agriculture. Without a large-scale transfer of this massive labour surplus to the non-agricultural sector within Nepal it is impossible to develop either the agricultural sector or the overall economy.

Since the 1950s, many attempts have been made to introduce reforms in Nepali agriculture without destroying the basic class relations—specifically to develop the productive forces while preserving the existing production relations. After the Second World War and especially after the end of the Rana rule, attempts were made to implement limited 'land reforms' with a view to bringing about agrarian change without destroying the old feudal structure and to facilitate the penetration of imperialist financial capital. Attempts were made first in the 1960s to implement various growth-oriented 'development' plans based on the model of 'the Green Revolution'. After the failure of that model, and recognising the increasing danger of agrarian unrest, programmes such as the 'Small Farmers Development Programme' were introduced in the 1970s. During the 1980s, as part of 'structural adjustment' and in the 1990s as part of 'globalisation' and 'liberalisation' once again the emphasis was on making agriculture 'export-oriented' and 'enterprise-oriented'. All of these contradictory and largely ineffective programmes were supported by a range of agencies, including the World Bank, representing the interests of imperialism, and implemented by the state apparatus of Nepal directed by feudal and bureaucratic capitalist interests.

But just as with the demon acting as exorcist, it proved impossible for programmes designed and directed by imperialists and implemented by feudals and bureaucratic capitalists to transform a rural economy dominated by feudalism and imperialism without a radical transformation. As a result, Nepal continues to have an agricultural economy marked by rampant poverty, disguised unemployment and underemployment, very low productivity, declining rate of growth and general backwardness. The ruling classes and their planners have been trying to cover up the pathetic state of the agricultural economy by referring to the mountainous terrain, unfavourable environment etc. But the truth lies elsewhere, as the land, water, climate and labour needed for agricultural development are often nowhere near as favourable elsewhere as they are in Nepal. Thus, the principal objective and rationale of the People's War in Nepal is to develop the productive forces in agriculture and to lay the foundation for the overall development of the economy by establishing new and progressive relations of production after smashing the prevailing reactionary production relations backed by the reactionary state.

Decline of Industry and Expansion of Comprador/Bureaucratic Capital

The most important criterion for judging the economic and overall development of society is the quantity and quality of industrialisation. Because, unlike agriculture, which is more dependant on the natural means of production, industry depend more on the man-made means of production, in that the production process can be organised on a large scale and in a more flexible manner and hence the overall development of society can be faster due to the potential for rapid growth in social productivity. The higher the level of development of a society, the larger is the proportion of the total labour force in industry and greater the share of the social product contributed by industry.

Although the emergence and continuing existence of cottage industry as an adjunct and part of agriculture is seen from the most primitive society onwards, it is the case that the rise and development of modern large-scale factory industry has taken place together with the rise and development of capitalist society.

Historically, the birth of industrial capitalism was accompanied by several concomitant processes—the primitive accumulation of capital that resulted from the concentration of the surplus product from the old feudal agriculture sector as capital in the hands of a few merchant capitalists; the separation of the petty producers of old feudal society from their means of production and their transformation into 'free' workers selling their labour power; and the production of both the means of subsistence and the means of production as commodities to be exchanged in the 'free' market. It was necessary for industrial capitalism to have both a 'capitalist class', investing capital in the process of production and constantly seeking greater profits, a 'free' working class, able to sell their labour power without any hindrance and a 'free' market where subsistence goods and the means of production could be sold and the raw materials needed for industrial production could be purchased (unlike the restricted market of small ruling class consuming only luxury goods). If, for whatever reasons, one, two or all three of these are deficient or lacking, then the development of industrial capitalism is not possible.

The birth and development of merchant capital can be traced back to the beginning of human society, for trade in goods is necessitated by inequalities and diversity in production and consumption in different communities. Similarly, inequality between producers and consumers within the same community led to the birth of usury capital (or, interest bearing capital, which may be called financial capital after the birth of modern banks). These two forms of capital do not directly contribute to the process of production. But merchant capital helps in realising the value of capital invested in production by ensuring that the products (commodities) reach the consumers, and for this it usurps part of the profit of production capital, while usury or finance capital usurps part of the profit of production capital in the form of interest in return for promoting and assisting capital investment. That is why, when they operate within the capitalist mode of production and under the hegemony of industrial capital, merchant capital and financial capital do not have such independent strength and play a generally progressive role in society.

In pre-capitalist feudal or semi-feudal society, however, they constitute independent players and, just as parasites in a tree or on an animal, the bigger their size the more destructive and negative the influence they exert on the development of the society. After the rise of world imperialism, the merchant capital and usury or financial capital of the third world's feudal and semi-feudal societies have turned themselves into comprador and bureaucratic capital as agents of imperialist capital. Their expansion serves a doubly negative role in the dependant and oppressed nations of the world, through, on the one hand, blocking the development of free industrial capitalism and, on the other hand, by transferring 'third world' capital to world imperialist centres as super profits from trade and as interest. In this context, it would be useful to analyse the decline of the traditional industries, the stunted growth of national industrial capital and the expansion of comprador and bureaucratic capital in Nepal.

Until the beginning of the 20th century the state of traditional industry was quite encouraging in Nepal, but when factory-made goods began to be imported without restrictions from British India then the local industries were gradually undermined. During the global imperialist economic crisis of the 1930s and with the demand created by the Second World War, the Biratnagar Jute Mills was established in 1936 and the era of modern factory industries began in Nepal. However, if one considers the state of industrial development in Nepal 60 years later, one finds a situation of backwardness; today, the role of industry in the country's economy is insignificant. This is demonstrated by the fact that both the proportion of the total labour force engaged in industry and the share of industry in the gross national product are very low and that instead of increasing, are stagnant or even decreasing. For example, of the total labour force, the percentage of those engaged in industry was 2.2 in 1952–54, 1.32 in 1971–72 and a mere 1.25 in 1991–92. Similarly, the percentage share of the industrial sector in GDP was 16 in 1964–65, 10 in 1974–75, 6 in 1984–85, and 10 in 1994–95 (whereas in developed economies, both tend to be above 40 per cent).

The industrial structure-type and quantity of goods produced—also indicates the very backward and distorted state of industry in Nepal. Production of basic goods (e.g. cement, electricity etc.), capital goods (e.g. agricultural equipments, machines etc.) and intermediate goods (e.g. construction material, thread, paper etc.)—all essential for the overall development of the economy—is very low. The production of consumer goods, and particularly of consumer non-durables (e.g. foodstuffs, liquor, cigarettes etc.), is high— more than 80 per cent of total capital investment and more than 60 per cent of the total number of industries and of workers. Even this subsector is distorted, with the production of luxury goods (e.g. beer, wine, cigarettes, soft drinks etc.) consumed by a very restricted upper class high and growing fast, and the production of subsistence goods used by the majority of middle and lower classes low and declining. For example, in 1994–95, the production of beer and soft drinks (e.g. Coca-Cola, Pepsi Cola) was such that they could be distributed at the rate of 1 L each for the whole population of Nepal, whereas production of cotton fabric was such that only 1 m was available for every three persons and only one pair of shoes for every 30 persons. During the last 10 years, the production of beer has increased five times, whereas the production of cotton fabrics and shoes fell to one-third. Industries that lend themselves to a quick profit and that have no guarantee of stability (e.g. stainless steel in the 1960s, carpet and garment industries in the 1980s) have mushroomed and then vanished in no time, by comparison with industries based on indigenous raw materials, labour and markets, or which have greater value-added within the country.

Those basic industries that were established within the country at state level with external help at the time of international conflict and the Cold War, in the 1960s, are now either in a disastrous condition due to negligence or corruption, or are being sold at a throwaway price to the comprador bourgeoisie. Many industries are closing down, either due to lack of raw materials or because they are not able to compete with foreign goods, and nearly 50 per cent are operating at less than 55 per cent of their total capacity. Even after the decade of 1980s, when the much propagated 'liberalisation' campaign was launched as directed by world imperialism, the multinational companies have not been investing as much as expected by the ruling classes and where they have invested it is mainly in the sectors that benefit them most in terms of quick and large profit returns, such as in beer, liquor, soft drinks (Pepsi-Cola, Coca-Cola), hotels etc. 'Fake' industries, which assemble only imported parts (e.g. T.V., radio etc.) or just paste on local labels, are increasing. In a word, the development of national industrial capital has been stunted and only a distorted and dependent kind of fake and rootless industry is developing to any extent. It is not difficult to understand the reasons behind the backwardness and decline of industries in Nepal: the principal factors are, on the one hand, the dominance of semi-feudal relations and prevalence of backward agriculture and, on the other, the lack of development of the capital, labour and markets needed for developing industrial capitalism, due to the hegemony of imperialism and expansionism.

Historically, in Nepal, as the primitive accumulation of capital from agriculture and trade sector has been centralised in the hands of the big feudals of the ruling classes and an India-based comprador bourgeoisie and because up until now they have maintained their hegemony over the economy, the development of a national industrial capitalist class has been inhibited. For example, the first modern factory, the Biratnagar Jute Mills, was started as a joint venture between an Indian Marwari (Radha Kishen Chamaria) and the then Prime Minister (Juddha Shamsher Rana), and even today the collaboration of the Rana–Shah ruling families and the Marwaris continues to dominate the big industrial and commercial houses. The comprador class, working in collaboration with Indian expansionism, finds it more profitable to be involved in foreign trade or to work as the agents of foreign capital than to invest in developing national industrial capitalism. As this very class has been exclusively enjoying the patronage of the state so far, the emergence of any independent national capitalist class has been impossible.

The development of a 'free' working class has not taken place in Nepal to any degree as semi-proletarian labourers remain tied to a backward, semi-feudal system of agriculture, the surplus labour from the rural areas migrates to the cities (in Nepal or

India) as temporary or seasonal workers, and labourers from India are engaged in industries in Nepal, particularly in the *terai*. Finally, because of the backward nature of agriculture and widespread rural poverty, and the limited development of the urban areas, an adequate internal market for industrially produced goods and industrial raw materials has failed to develop; whatever internal market existed has been captured by imperialism and expansionism. Because of extreme economic inequality in the country, the majority of the people do not have significant aggregate purchasing power and thus whatever limited industrial development has taken place produces only luxury goods for the consumption of the minority of the rich, and since they too have limitations, these industries cannot flourish. As for foreign markets, Nepali industry cannot compete effectively because of backwardness and low productivity, and in any case, access to the Indian market—and to third country markets beyond—is constrained by any number of hurdles of trade and transit. For all of these reasons, the development of national industrial capitalism in Nepal and the industrialisation of the country is impossible in the context of the existing internal and external class relations and structures.

In striking contrast with the stagnation and decline in industrial capital invested in production within Nepal, the volume and value of merchant and usurer or financial capital engaged in distribution and in facilitating the flight of national capital abroad in the form of commercial profit or interest has been expanding rapidly over the last decades. Although the absolute scale of merchant and financial capital in a relatively small society dominated by backward semi-feudal agriculture and a subsistence economy is not substantial as yet, the rate of their expansion has accelerated in recent years. For example, of the total labour force, the proportion of those engaged in the commercial and 'services' sectors has increased from 4.5 per cent in 1952–54, to around five per cent in 1970–71 and to over 8 per cent in 1990–91. Similarly, the share of the trade and service sectors in GDP was 13 per cent in the year 1964–65, 14 per cent in 1974–75, 27 per cent in 1984–85 and 31 per cent in 1994–95. The faster growth rate after the decade of 1980s can be attributed to the so-called liberalisation policy and it is not difficult to appreciate the basically foreign-inspired and reactionary nature of this growth.

If one considers the state of merchant capital in Nepal, although its history is very old, its size and influence has never been so big in the overall economy. But the main characteristic of merchant capital in Nepal is that right from the beginning its role has been associated more with external trade than with internal trade. Hence, its links with production within the country were limited and it was easily transformed into comprador capital instead of into national industrial capital. Nepal's geographical location, on the main north–south trade route between Tibet and northern India, explains why entrepot trade dominated commercial activity from the outset. Particularly after the opening of the route via Sikkim to Tibet at the beginning of 20th century and the inundation of Nepali markets by Indian factory-made goods during the first half of the century, merchant capital in Nepal became closely associated with trade with India.

Even today, the scale of internal trade within Nepal is limited, because only about 30 per cent of agricultural produce goes to the market and (according to one survey) internal trade is worth only Rs. 15 per person per month. But against this, the volume and value of foreign trade and particularly of the import trade has increased exponentially. In 1964–65, the share of foreign trade in GNP was 17 per cent (of which 11 per cent was trade in imports); by 1994–95 its share had increased by more than two and a half times to reach 40 per cent (of which import trade accounted for over 30 per cent). About one third of the state's annual budget revenue comes from foreign trade and that, too, mainly from tariffs on the import trade; and when sales tax is included, about 60 per cent of the state budget revenue depends upon the trade sector. From this it is clear that the state is highly dependant on merchant capital; it is also the case that the funding of state expenditure in this way contributes to expanding bureaucratic capital. Although tourism—regarded as one of the main sources of foreign exchange—is called a 'service industry', most of the materials used in it are imported from foreign countries and 50 per cent of the total earnings goes back to the foreign countries, so that tourism under the present circumstances is deeply integrated in the international trade sector and is largely funded by comprador capital.

In totality, if one is to analyse the structure of Nepalese merchant capital there is no doubt that its nature is 'comprador' as it mainly helps in realising the value of foreign capital by selling the industrial goods of the imperialists and the expansionists. Similarly since it remains largely 'independent' of the production process within the country and helps in the flight of domestic capital towards foreign countries in the form of commercial profit, it is clear that its expansion has a negative and destructive effect on the development of national economy. Historically, Indian traders and the landed feudals of Nepal have had a monopoly over merchant capital operating in Nepal—75 per cent of the wholesale trade of Kathmandu and the *terai* is in their hands, and all major tourist hotels have joint investment from Rana–Shah families and Indians. Merchant capital, instead of being integrated with the internal production process, is concentrated in the foreign trade sector, and the foreign trade sector has been devoted largely to the fulfilment of the demands of the wealthy minority for consumer goods. Nepali merchant capital has in this way transformed itself into comprador capital instead of developing into national industrial capital. Unless this process is corrected, by destroying comprador capital and by nurturing national capital, it is not possible to develop the country's economy.

As far as financial capital is concerned, the usurer's capital levying high interests and other service charges has existed for a long time in Nepal, and even today has a wide network in the rural areas. The birth of modern organised financial capital in Nepal took place only after the establishment of the Nepal Bank Limited in 1937. Until the 1960s, foreign currency was under the control of Reserve Bank of India, whereas internal individual usurer's capital was the main source of credit. After the establishment of various financial institutions under the aegis of the state (e.g. Nepal Industrial Development Corporation, Agriculture Development Bank etc.) and the development of the private commercial banks, at the end of the 1950s and throughout the 1960s, the expansion of bureaucratic capital in the form of financial capital took place at a faster pace. In the 1960s the gross assets of all financial companies constituted probably around 15 per cent of GNP, but by the 1990s these had increased to about 50 per cent. Foreign banks started entering into the country after the 1980s, and in the last 2 years eight foreign banks have been established. The gross assets of the commercial banks have increased by nearly 10 times from Rs. 7.7 billion to Rs. 75.99 billion.

If one examines the structure of this fast growing sector, however, it is easy to discern its reactionary nature. First of all, the landed feudals and merchant comprador capitalists, instead of investing in production-oriented industrial ventures, invest their surplus from agriculture and profits from trade in this new form of usury where higher interests and quick returns can be achieved. This retards the development of agriculture and industry. Secondly, since most of the investments made by these financial institutions (approximately 50 per cent) are in trade and in consumption credits and less in productive sectors of agriculture and industry, this will have a negative impact on the long-term development of the economy. Thirdly, as these financial institutions are basically appendages of imperialist finance capital, they will assist the process of capital flight and thus thwart the development of industrial capitalism in the country. The very fact that the present fast rate of expansion of financial capital has no positive correlation with the development of agriculture and industry in the country, conclusively proves the reactionary nature of this financial capital.

Another example of the penetration of imperialist financial capital and its destructive activities in the form of bureaucratic capital is so-called foreign aid. After the decade of the 1950s, when the entry of imperialist and expansionist financial capital in the form of foreign 'aid' was initiated, its quantity has been constantly increasing and along with it the total foreign loan dependency of the country has also increased. Nepal has now become caught in the vicious circle of the debt trap, requiring further foreign loans to pay back the foreign debt. In 1970–71, the foreign loan per capita was Rs. 15, but after 25 years of 'development' (i.e. in 1994–95), the figure had increased 400 times, to more than Rs. 6,000, and one quarter of the annual budget revenue had to be spent on servicing the foreign debt. Another indicator of the country's external dependence is the fact that while in 1975–76, 41 per cent of the total 'development budget' was dependent upon foreign loans and aid, in 1994–95 that dependency had increased to 62 per cent. The principal objective of foreign loans, apart from earning interest, has been to expand imperialist and expansionist markets. This is shown by the fact that for the last 40 years more than 60 per cent of foreign 'aid' has been used in the area of transportation and communication. Also, in keeping with the imperialist plan of checking the mounting crisis in oppressed nations after the decade of the 1970s from breaking out in revolutionary upheavals, billions of rupees have been pumped into the rural areas of Nepal, through INGOs and NGOs.

Thus, to develop national industrial capitalism by destroying the comprador and bureaucratic capital and to pave the way to self-reliant development by breaking away from dependency, a revolutionary transformation of society and the process of the People's War have become inevitable.

Regional Inequality and the National Question

Social processes take place in geographical space; the social division of labour is manifested in a geographical division of labour. Along with the historical development process goes the process of the organisation or reorganisation of geographical space. In other words, according to the system of production, distribution and consumption of goods in society, the structure of human settlements, systems of transportation and communication and the overall regional structure is established. In pre-capitalist societies, particularly in feudal mode of production, which is primarily based on agriculture (in which land, the principal means of production, cannot be transported from one place to another) and in which market exchange has a negligible role, there is a very low level of regional differentiation. There exist only a few towns, as military forts or political–administrative centres and as centers for the consumption of the miniscule parasitic classes of society, and rest of the productive classes of people live in small rural settlements or widely scattered hamlets. As a result, a regional structure marked by a big capital city at the centre and more or less homogenous small rural settlements all around is characteristic of feudal society. It is only after the advent of the capitalist mode of production that big modern cities develop as centres of production, distribution and consumption, and unprecedented changes in the regional structure take place. Significant regional disparities and spatially uneven development are a geographical manifestation of growing social inequality resulting from the process of concentration and centralisation inherent in the dynamics of capitalism.

The regional structure of a feudal or semi-feudal society locked in a colonial or semi-colonial relationship with international monopoly capitalism (i.e. imperialism) is like a hybrid of feudal and capitalist structures. In other words, on the one hand, the overwhelming majority of the agricultural hinterland is characteristically backward while, on the other hand, there exist limited urban centres and islands of extraverted 'development' that accumulate the surplus product from backward regions and transfer it abroad, and which import foreign products to distribute throughout the country. This phenomenon of 'unequal development' generates, particularly in the exploited and backward regions, the consciousness of a regional identity and sense of autonomy or independence, which often takes a 'nationalistic' form. Because those inhabiting the backward and oppressed regions are often indigenous peoples, where there is a confluence of common territory, language, economy and culture, such regional oppression manifests itself as national oppression and in this way regional issues and question of nationality become intertwined with each other. Regional unequal development is the main reason why the question of nationality often becomes more intense after the advent of capitalism or imperialism. It is in this way that we should understand regional issues and the question of 'nationality' in Nepal, which is in a stage of transition from feudalism to capitalism.

In the period immediately following the unification of Nepal, the only settlements that could be called urban centres were Kathmandu, Lalitpur and Bhaktapur—the urban population of Nepal was concentrated in the Kathmandu Valley. This urban–rural structure conformed precisely to the mono-centred structure of the feudal society. This was prior to the establishment of a number of trading centers in the *terai*, following the extension of the Indian railways up to the border with Nepal at the end of 19th century. In 1953–54, the urban population of Nepal was still only 3 per cent of the total population, and of the 10 urban centres having more than 5,000 people, five were in the Kathmandu Valley and five in the *terai* (with the Kathmandu Valley having 83 per cent of the urban population and the *terai* 17 per cent). Even today, after 40 years, 90 per cent of the total population lives in the rural areas and only 10 per cent lives in the towns. This is the manifestation of a limited geographical division of labour, corresponding to the low social division of labour of a semi-feudal agriculture-based society (whereas in developed societies, 80–90 per cent of the population lives in towns and cities and only about 10–20 per cent live in villages in the countryside).

The process of urbanisation and the development of transportation and communications in the last 40 years, however, indicate some important changes in Nepal. Today, out of the 33 settlements officially designated as 'urban centres' in 1991, 3 were in the Kathmandu Valley, 8 elsewhere in the hills, and 22 in the *terai*. The distribution of urban population in these is 35 per cent, 12 per cent and 53 per cent respectively. It is evident that as the economy of Nepal was increasingly entangled with imperialism and expansionism, urban centres mushroomed along the Indian borders, and the overall regional structure of Nepal started to become outward-oriented. The earlier primacy of the Kathmandu Valley as the capital region was retained, but it also increasingly became a hub of links with the 'outside world'. Within Nepal itself, the flow of road and air traffic and of the communication systems generally is mainly oriented towards Kathmandu and then towards cities in the *terai*, with 40 per cent of total vehicular traffic going to and from the Kathmandu Valley. Such a monocentred and extraverted regional structure reflects the semi-feudal and semi-colonial social structure and the process of unequal and distorted development in the country.

If one considers the condition and pace of development of the main geographical regions of the country, then one sees a very alarming picture of overall backwardness combined with increasingly unequal and distorted development. Physically, Nepal can be divided north to south into the Himalayan mountains, the hills and the *terai* plains (including the inner *terai*) and into Kosi, Gandaki and Karnali watersheds from the east to the west, with the Kathmandu Valley situated within the hills, but distinctive because of the specificities of Nepal's historical development. Leaving aside the prehistoric period, the east–west spine of the central hill regions has been the main habitation zone for some 3,000 years, with the Kathmandu Valley as the most developed area. It is only after the end of the 19th century, when there was massive deforestation of the *terai* (as the economic importance of timber was transformed by the extension of Indian railways up to the border) and even more dramatically after the 1950s with the eradication of malaria, that human settlement in the *terai* started to increase significantly. In the hill regions, prior to the establishment of the unified state of Nepal, the level of development was almost identical everywhere. Afterwards, however, the Gandaki region in the west central hills became more developed, as did parts of the eastern hills (albeit for different reasons, to do with climate and agricultural potential, links with India and political–administrative factors) and the Kathmandu Valley. The regions further west (today the mid-west and far-west) remained particularly backwards and were increasingly marginalised, as indeed were parts of the central and eastern hills.

The fact that before the 1950s, 60 per cent of the total population of the country lived in the hills and mountains, five per cent in the Kathmandu Valley and 35 per cent in the *terai*, clearly indicates that the hill region was at that time, and before, the main settlement zone. However, by the 1990s the spatial distribution of the population had undergone a change; now 42 per cent live in the hills, 11 per cent in the Kathmandu Valley and 47 per cent in the *terai*. Given the continued dominance of agriculture in the economy and limited development of industry, this population change is less an indication of an economic sectorwise vertical transfer (i.e., from agriculture to industry, which is historically progressive) than a geographical regionwise horizontal transfer (i.e., from agriculture to agriculture). But migration from agriculture in the hills to agriculture in the *terai* will not solve the problem in the long term; it merely shifts the problem from one place to another and postpones the crisis for a while. Arguably, it in fact further retards the development of the hill region, which constitutes 80 per cent of the total area of Nepal.

As regards the increasing trend of migration towards the capital region of Kathmandu Valley, it is to a certain extent due to the availability of non-agricultural employment opportunities and to the distress flight of semi-proletarian peasants as 'informal refugees'. Also, because of the physical concentration of the major economic and social services, including the central administration and other facilities, the rural feudals and the *nouveaux riches* from all over the country flock to Kathmandu to invest their agricultural surpluses in financial and commercial activities, or in real estate. Some indication of the extent to which capital from all over the country pours into Kathmandu so that Kathmandu itself consumes most of the share of 'development' is provided by these figures: 60 per cent of the deposits and 50 per cent of the credits of commercial banks are centred in Kathmandu; one third of the internal trade of the country takes place in Kathmandu; 69 per cent of investment in tourist hotels is in Kathmandu; 60 per cent of motor vehicles in the country are registered in Kathmandu; 60 per cent of industries in the country are located in or around Kathmandu.

By contrast, most of the rural areas, especially in the hills, are without basic physical infrastructure (roads, water, electricity etc.) or social services (education, health etc.). When a districtwise composite development index (with indicators of agriculture, industry, finance, social service, physical infrastructure development etc.) is constructed, the districts of the Kathmandu Valley (Kathmandu, Lalitpur and Bhaktapur) rank first; the far eastern *terai* districts (Morang, Sunsari and Jhapa) come second; districts like Parsa, Kaski, Banke and Chitwan, with big urban centers (mainly in the *terai*), come third; and the rest of the *terai* comes fourth; the mountain and hill districts come last, and among these, the districts of the Karnali watershed are the least developed. Despite the general backwardness and underdevelopment of the entire country, regional inequality is increasing under the present semi-feudal and semi-colonial dispensation. Unless the process of mono-centred and extraverted development is rectified, it is certain that regional disparities will, in future, become even deeper.

The most disadvantaged regions within the country include those inhabited by indigenous people since time immemorial. These regions, which were independent tribal states prior to the formation of the unified state in the latter half of the 18th century, have been reduced to the most backward and oppressed condition due to internal feudal exploitation and external semi-colonial oppression. They have been left behind in the historical development process because of the blockade of their path to independent development and the imposition of socio-cultural oppression along with economic oppression, with the backing of the state, by forces that came from outside. Thus, it is quite natural that the question of the oppression of the eastern, central and western hills, where Mongoloid peoples are numerically predominant, or of the *terai* regions where Austro-Dravidian peoples still survive, appears as a form of national oppression. In these areas, the regional and the 'national' questions are intertwined. The problem of the Khas-dominated far western Karnali region by contrast may be dealt with as a regional question alone. There is a real and urgent need to solve the problem of the oppressed regions and nationalities by granting regional and national autonomy, depending on the specific concrete circumstances.

The Economic Policy, Programme and Process of the New Democratic Revolution

On the basis of the preceding analysis, it is clear that the main constraint on the development of the social productive forces in Nepal is the entire structure of internal and external relations, that is, the social relations of production under the prevailing semi-feudal and semi-colonial dispensation. It is not possible for Nepal to forge ahead through reforms or changes in the superstructure while retaining the base of the old society intact. It has become a historical necessity to establish a fundamentally new kind of socialist-oriented capitalist, or New Democratic, system of production by destroying the old semi-feudal mode of production chained to imperialism and expansionism.

To put it more clearly, history compels us to dispense with the feudal, comprador and bureaucratic capitalist classes hindering the development of Nepal and to hand over the responsibility of organising a new and higher form of social system (the New Democratic system) to the progressive classes (i.e. workers, peasants, petty bourgeoisie and national bourgeoisie). The People's War is the inevitable instrument of this historic New Democratic revolutionary transformation. The People's War, waged under the leadership of the Communist Party of Nepal (Maoist) and with the joint participation of all the progressive classes of society, is aimed at building a New Democratic base after destroying the base of the old semi-feudal and semi-colonial economy and society, and ultimately at creating a classless society without exploitation. The economic development policy, programme and process of the New Democratic revolution can be presented as below.

Economic Development Policy

The main economic development policies of the New Democratic revolution in Nepal will be as follows.

Revolutionary Change of Production Relations

The main economic policy of the New Democratic revolution in Nepal would be to change the old relations of production in order to develop the productive forces and to give a faster pace to the development of the economy and society in general. Although there exists an interactive relation between production relations and productive forces, and any change in one affects the other, at the present historical stage of development in Nepal, the retrograde semi-feudal and semi-colonial relations have become the main obstacle to the development of a new and higher form of capitalist production. In this situation, any attempt to develop only the productive forces (capital and technology, much of it foreign!) while keeping the old relations of production intact would not only be completely retrograde but has already, in practice, proved a failure.

The main policy of the revolution would be to confiscate the means of production that have been in the hands of the reactionary classes—mainly the land that has been in the hands of the feudals and the capital of the comprador and bureaucratic capitalist classes—and to hand these over to the progressive forces (the workers, peasants, petty bourgeoisie and national bourgeoisie) and to organise the mode of production in a new way. It is only by unleashing the revolutionary initiatives of the working and progressive masses that the revolutionary transformation of a backward economy like that of Nepal is possible. That is why it can be said that the slogan 'Grasp revolution, Promote production' advanced by the great Mao applies also to Nepal. However, because of the backward semi-feudal state and very low level of development of the productive forces in Nepal, the principal form of the new production relations would not be socialist at the outset but capitalistic, and only after going through a transitional stage would a socialist transformation be carried out. In the New Democratic stage, the key basic industries and financial companies would come under the social ownership of the state, some of the larger means of production would be jointly owned by the state and private enterprise and in agriculture, the largest sector of the economy, there would be widespread private ownership by the peasants while in small and medium industry and trade there would be ownership by private industrialists and traders.

Independent and Self-Reliant Development

The other principal development policy of the New Democratic economy would be to achieve independent and self-reliant development, free from the oppression and exploitation of imperialism and expansionism. The country's development is impossible without freedom from the trap of imperialism and expansionism. In the past, the process of underdevelopment in Nepal undoubtedly accelerated after it became entangled in an unequal and exploitative relation with world imperialism and particularly with Indian expansionism, and at present, it is caught in an irretrievable foreign debt trap, unbearable trade deficit, all round dependency and plundering by foreign capitalists and multinational companies. Hence, instead of the present extraverted and dependent development policy, an inward-looking and self-reliant development policy, relying upon its own natural resources, capital, labour, technology and markets, would be followed. This does not at all mean that there would be no economic ties with foreign countries or that there would be no use of modern science and technology, as falsely alleged by the imperialists and their agents. There would be a policy of maintaining trade and other relations with all, but on the basis of equality, mutual benefit and national needs, utilising modern technology to the extent possible. However, these relations in practice would depend upon the policy of the foreign forces towards the revolutionary state.

Planned Development

The other important policy would be to achieve the planned development of the economy through a scientific assessment of the available and potential resources and the physical and cultural needs of society. At present, there prevails a tendency to produce and distribute goods in an anarchic manner, with a view to making profits for the few monopoly capitalists through markets effectively under the control of imperialists and expansionists (despite the rhetoric of 'free markets') or for the conspicuous consumption of the minority of the upper classes. Because of this, there is massive wastage of the productive instruments and resources of society, on the one hand, while the majority of the people are deprived of even the minimum basic needs of life, on the other. Thus it is right, both in terms of economic logic and social utility, to organise the economy scientifically and in a planned manner according to the needs of the society, rather than in such an anarchic, wasteful and inhuman mode of production. However, when talking about planned development one should not envisage the negative experiences of the former Soviet Union (especially after 1956) and a command economy. Here, planned development means the creation of a genuine mass-oriented and efficient economy functioning under the guidance of a centralised leadership but with decentralized initiative and management, such as was, to a large extent, practiced in China during the time of Mao Tse Tung.

Balanced Development

The other important economic policy of the New Democratic revolution would be to bring about balanced development, both economically and geographically, by maintaining a correct balance and harmony between country and town, between hills and *terai*, between agriculture and industry, between small-scale cottage industry and big modern industry and so on. At present there is increasing inequality and an imbalance between different economic and geographical regions. Balanced development in the country will be achieved by ending the pre-capitalist and bureaucratic capitalist monopoly over the economy, by granting national and regional autonomy to the oppressed nationalities and geographical regions and by pursuing an overall planned development strategy. The main strategy of balanced development would be to treat industry as the leading sector and agriculture as the foundation in the development of the national economy, and, in the context of regional development, to pursue the policy of the 'urbanisation of the countryside' and not the 'ruralisation' of the cities.

Economic Development Programme

To remedy the grave economic distortions and problems prevalent in the country, the following economic programmes would be carried out, with full commitment and as a national campaign in keeping with the above basic policies, during the course of the New Democratic revolution and on its completion.

Revolutionary Land Reforms

In a semi-feudal agriculture-based economy like Nepal, the New Democratic revolution means basically an agrarian revolution. Revolutionary land reform is, therefore, the biggest and the most important economic programme of the New Democratic revolution. The principal objectives of land reform would be (1) to make maximum use of the productive capacity of majority of the peasants and to accelerate the development of social productive forces by making landless peasants the owners of the land and by making available adequate means of production (land, credit etc.) to the poor peasants; (2) to increase social production by bringing to maximum use the wasted or underutilised means of production (land, money capital etc.) belonging to the feudals; (3) to make available capital and raw materials for the country's industrialisation by increasing agricultural production and productivity and by diversifying agriculture and (4) to ensure an adequate internal market for the products of industry by raising the incomes of the peasants and workers who constitute a majority of the country's population.

The principal strategy of land reform would be to usher in capitalist relations of production by destroying completely the feudal, semi-feudal and bureaucratic capitalist relations prevalent in agriculture. It would be primarily based on the policy of 'land to the tiller'. In other words, the land of those feudals (and also *guthis*) who do not put their labour or capital to use on the land would be confiscated without compensation and distributed to the landless and poor peasants, and the tillers would be made owners of the land. However, the land belonging to the middle or rich peasants (who may have rented their land out to others for various reasons) will not be confiscated, although a ceiling to landownership, tenancy rights and the rate of rent would be fixed and implemented. All forms of debt incurred by landless and poor peasants would be completely nullified and all labour-service and other forms of payment forced upon them would be cancelled. In order to enhance production and productivity of agriculture and to protect the backward agricultural sector from the competition of the industrial, commercial or financial sectors, adequate institutional provision—of irrigation, modern inputs (e.g. fertilisers, seeds, pesticides, machines, implements etc.), credits and markets—would be made to the farmers, and in order to guarantee proper prices for agricultural produces, the appropriate monetary and price policy would be implemented at the state level.

The process of implementation of the land reforms would be most important. It would be scientific and revolutionary. It is not possible to implement a revolutionary land reform programme without making the peasants conscious and organised, as they have been subjected to oppression and exploitation from time immemorial and tend to be culturally and politically backward. For this reason, it would be necessary to build cooperation through local peasants associations and to mobilise the peasant masses to prepare the actual records of landownership, to determine the class status of rural households (i.e. landless, poor, middle and rich peasants and feudals) and their role in the village, to identify the actual tillers and to implement themselves the land reforms at the village level. The land reform programme would be implemented in stages (i.e. in terms of both social class and geographical regions!) and by taking local specificities fully into account. In that process, maximum caution would be exercised so as to avoid both 'leftist' and 'rightist' errors. Special attention would be paid, while implementing the land reform programme, to mobilising the 70 per cent of landless and poor peasants actively behind the revolutionary land reforms, to bring the 25 per cent of the middle and rich peasants to support them, or at least not oppose them, and to strictly enforce the programme that will dispossess the five per cent of feudals and bureaucratic capitalists. There are 2.6 million hectares of cultivable land currently available in the country. If only the 40 per cent of land belonging to the 5 per cent minority (the surplus land is about 1 million hectares) were to be distributed among the 70 per cent of landless and poor peasant families then it would amount to more than 0.5 hectare per family, and if it were to be distributed among the 44 per cent landless and semi-proletarians (i.e. those owning less than 0.5 hectare) each would receive nearly 1 hectare. At present only 0.25 million hectares of land has permanent irrigation, whereas it is estimated that 1.4 million hectares of land could be irrigated. If the huge labour surplus that is available could be mobilised to bring irrigation facilities to the additional 1.15 million hectares, then even with the present technology, agricultural production could be increased many times over. There is no doubt that dramatic transformation could take place in the agricultural sector and in the overall economy as a result of revolutionary land reforms.

National Industrialisation

The other important economic programme in the New Democratic revolution would be to bring about the industrialisation of the country at a rapid rate by making industry the leading sector. The principal objective of industrialisation would be (1) to increase general social production and productivity of labour (and that of the overall economy) by putting the surplus labour stuck in the backward semi-feudal agriculture sector into productive use; (2) to make way for the development of a superior mode of production (i.e. capitalist and socialist mode of production) in agriculture, and ultimately in the whole economy, by producing the necessary capital goods for the agricultural sector, by providing markets for agricultural products and by providing productive employment for the surplus labour in the agriculture sector; (3) to prevent the flight of capital away from the country and to end dependency by producing necessary capital goods, basic goods, intermediary goods and consumer goods, (4) to promote exports by producing goods with a comparative advantage in the international division of labour and (5) in general, to cater to the higher material and cultural needs of the society.

The coordination of capital, labour and markets essential for national industrialisation will be achieved primarily through the revolutionary transformation of the existing society. Capital originating from the agriculture sector and lying idle in the hands of feudals or being spent on conspicuous consumption or in circulation for usurious purposes, and the capital in the hands of big comprador and bureaucratic capitalists, would be confiscated and brought under state control. Besides this, protection and encouragement would be given to the many small and domestic industrialists, to the small and medium traders and to the national bourgeoisie. Capital accumulation from the agriculture sector and its investment in industry would be promoted, for ultimately it is the agriculture sector that would be the main source of capital for industrialisation. The major emphasis would be on labour-intensive industrialisation, since there would be dearth of capital and a surplus of labour within the country for a long time to come. Special attention would be given to the development and use of indigenous technology. There would be a stress on harnessing the immense hydropower potential of the country, through small hydroelectricity projects, for the supply of necessary industrial energy and to ensure self-reliant, pollution-free and sustainable development. From the beginning, attention would be paid to primary and medium level technical education for the production of skilled labour and technical manpower that would be increasingly needed as part of the process of industrialisation. As for the market for raw materials and finished products, a policy of relying primarily on the internal market would be pursued; at the one end, the supply of raw materials would be ensured by enhancing the production of medicinal herbs, animal husbandry, horticulture, cash crops, the processing of minerals etc., taking full advantage of the country's geographical diversity, while, at the other end, the necessary market would be created for the industrial products by eliminating existing socio-economic inequalities and increasing the purchasing power of the general masses. The creation of a large domestic market for the means of subsistence and means of production for the general masses instead of the current narrow market for the luxury goods meant for only the limited upper classes would accelerate the process of industrialisation. Similarly, special measures—the cancellation of unequal treaties, control of the open border, adoption of correct tariff–financial–monetary policies etc.—would be taken by the state to protect national industries from the interference and domination of world imperialism and particularly of Indian expansionism.

It is obvious that the state would have to play a special role in the industrialisation process of Nepal because of the country's semi-feudal and semi-colonial condition and due to the backward state of the productive forces. Nevertheless, industrialisation in the New Democratic stage would be of a capitalist nature rather than of a socialist nature. The state would provide leadership and guidance to the overall process of industrialisation by its ownership of basic industries and financial institutions, and through central planning and fiscal/monetary policies. On the other hand, private ownership and enterprise would be encouraged and promoted in modern industries, small and domestic industries, and small and medium trade. Only by becoming liberated from imperialist and expansionist oppression under the leadership and guidance of a progressive state would the development of industrial capitalism be possible in Nepal and the base be prepared for the construction of a higher level of society.

Regional Balance and Integrated Development

The other important development policy and programme of the New Democratic revolution would be to coordinate national economic development with regional development from the very beginning, and to ensure balanced and integrated development throughout the country. The principal strategy for this would be (1) to accelerate the pace of social development by making maximum use of the productive potentials of different geographical regions; (2) to make the economy self-reliant and to protect it from the danger of external interference and oppression through economic and geographical decentralisation; (3) to orient the society towards a more advanced and democratic stage by controlling social and geographical polarisation and (4) to ensure sustainable development through interdependence between different social sectors and geographical regions.

Programmes to promote regionally balanced and interdependent development would include controlling the polarisation between city and countryside; developing a settlement system based on the interdependence of big, medium and small towns and villages; developing interactive relations between hill and *terai* regions by ascertaining the division of labour between them; establishing production zones based upon integrated development of big and small industry and agriculture; enforcing national autonomy in oppressed nationality-dominated areas; implementing regional autonomy and local self-government in the oppressed and remote areas. Under present circumstances, particularly because of the centralisation of the basic economic, social and physical services and infrastructures in the few urban centres, an uncontrolled process of population concentration in the big cities takes places, leading to the ruralisation of the cities. By contrast, in the New Democratic system, economic, social and physical services and infrastructures (e.g. industries, banks, colleges, hospitals, electricity, motorable roads etc.) would be provided in the rural areas and a policy of urbanisation of the countryside would be followed. These policies and programmes would be carried out through integrated development planning and necessary economic and other policy measures.

The Process of Revolutionary Transformation

The transformation of one social system into another, or the destruction of the old by the new, always involves force and a revolutionary leap. The People's War is such a means of eliminating the old by a new force and of taking a leap towards a new and higher social system. There would be two important specificities of the process of New Democratic transformation through the protracted People's War in Nepal.

Dialectical Process of Destruction and Creation

Because Nepali society is currently in a semi-feudal, semi-colonial stage and is characterised by unequal development and a very low level of material and cultural development, it is necessary to destroy the old mode of production bit by bit, starting from its weakest spots, and to create a new mode of production systematically from the same place (i.e. a strategy of protracted People's War). To put it in concrete terms, as the contradictions are sharpest in the rural areas, the process of destroying the old structure and creating a new one should commence from there. Hence along with the development of the People's War in Nepal, the process of destruction of the old relations of production and the creation of the new relations should go on concurrently from below. The existing semi-feudal relations of the rural areas should be destroyed and in its place the policy of revolutionary agrarian reform, industrialisation and balanced development be implemented, on a New Democratic basis. However, it would not be possible to implement economic reconstruction without consolidating the new state power, and even if it were implemented, it would be impossible to preserve it. That is why the policy of organising the New Democratic system of production would start from below in line with the stage of development of the new state power, and only after capturing state power throughout the country would the New Democratic system be implemented fully.

Transitional Capitalism and Continuous Revolution

The New Democratic system is basically a capitalist system. However, in the present era of imperialism and in a situation where the productive forces are very backward, as in Nepal, it is impossible to develop the capitalist system in the traditional way and ensure its viability. It is not possible for the owners of small plots of land and small capital to increase productivity simply by labouring individually or to protect themselves from the monopolistic assaults of big capital. It is only through the gradual cooperativisation of agriculture and through state protection for industry, and by moving generally and systematically ahead along the path of socialisation, that the large number of small producers can preserve their existence and increase their productivity. In that sense, the New Democratic system is only a transitional capitalist system and its contradictions would have to be resolved through the higher form of a socialist system. Only through a process of continuous revolution would it be possible to solve the newly emerging problems and resolve the social contradictions at a higher plane.

The process of the People's War is a link in a chain of just such a continuous revolution in Nepal to solve its current economic and social problems. The principal objective and rationale of the People's War in Nepal is, thus, to develop the social productive forces and create a higher form of society through a continuous revolution of the base and the superstructure by putting 'politics in command'.

> *We must not go by the short-sightedness of the small producer. We should learn the wisdom of the Bolsheviks. The naked eye is not enough, we must have the aid of the telescope and microscope. The Marxist method is our telescope and microscope in political and military matters.*
>
> —*Mao Tse Tung (Problems of Strategy in China's Revolutionary War)*

> *Without planning, victories in guerrilla warfare are impossible. Any idea that guerrilla warfare can be conducted in haphazard fashion indicates either flippant attitude or ignorance of Guerrilla Warfare.*
>
> —*Mao Tse Tung (Problems of Strategy in Guerrilla War Against Japan)*

Chapter 5

Women's Participation in the People's War

Com. Parvati

Anybody who knows anything of history knows that great social changes are impossible without the feminine ferment.

—Marx

Introduction

Ever since an armed People's War was initiated in Nepal on February 13, 1996, under the leadership of the Communist Party of Nepal (Maoist), about 800 people have been martyred amongst whom nearly 100 are women *(figures prior to November 2001,* AK & DS). Along with hundreds of men, many women are being jailed and sentenced to long prison terms, many have gone missing and many have been raped and tortured. The spark of the fire that started from Rukum and Rolpa districts in Western Nepal has now spread to all parts of Nepal. Today even the government and foreign media are forced to acknowledge this.

What has baffled them is the degree of participation by women in the People's War in Nepal. This is particularly the case in the context of a country that, although semi-feudal and semi-colonial, is chacterised by a predominantly feudal economy—with 88 per cent of the total population living in the rural areas and 81 per cent of the population engaged in the agricultural sector, and with agriculture accounting for 42 per cent of total GNP. The feudal character of the land ownership structure can be judged by the fact that, broadly, 65 per cent of poor peasants own only 10 per cent of the land while 10 per cent of rich peasants and landlords own 65 per cent of the land. This class inequality is reinforced by gender inequality in production relations, as women are barred from inheriting their parental property.

Sources of Women'S Oppression

Women's Economic Oppression

Women's economic oppression is firmly rooted in the present feudal and semi-feudal mode of production, which is dominated by petty peasant production. Land being the chief means of production, women's economic oppression is firmly rooted in the present structure of land-ownership relations, which is patriarchal, patrilineal and patrifocal in nature. The chief source of gender contradictions, and hence of the alienation of women within the present production relations, lies in the fact that despite bearing a double workload at both household and farm level, a woman cannot legally own land and parental property on equal terms with her male counterpart. Women cannot inherit tenancy rights to land on a par with men. As a result they have limited access to credit and other similar facilities, thus further constraining their scope for economic upliftment. This puts them strategically at a disadvantageous position vis-á-vis men.

In addition to this, the remnants of medieval relations, such as serfdom in the *terai* and debt slavery in both the *terai* and hill regions, make women particularly vulnerable, as they have to often provide 'voluntary' sex and labour services to the landlord and his household, in addition to labouring on their own plots. Women's economic oppression is further reinforced by the low level of the productive forces in agriculture in Nepal, which are extremely backward with hardly any modern inputs. Labour in agriculture is predominantly human labour, supplemented by animal labour with the help of basic equipment like sickles, hoes, shovels etc. In addition, the absence of basic infrastructure at the level of the household—including lack of easy access to sources of fuel and water, and general dependence on manual processing of agricultural products—makes household work tiresome and time-consuming. It is a well-known fact that in unequal societies, the more labour-intensive the work, the more is the work burden that falls upon women.

On top of all this, due to the basic subsistence nature of agriculture and the obligatory semi-unemployed state of most household labourers during parts of the year (as a result of the predominance of rain-fed cultivation), there is mass migration of able-bodied male members of many households to the urban areas of Nepal, to India and elsewhere, leaving women and children behind to bear the burden of toil on the land and in the home. One can easily infer from this that women are the backbone of the subsistence rural agricultural economy. Because women are socially marginalised at the household level, however, their work is undervalued: they are paid less—sometimes as low as half the amount—than men, for the same job and same input of labour.

The position of women in the urban areas is little better. If women in the rural areas are suffering from backward 'medieval feudal' oppression then women in urban areas are suffering under 'modern imperialist' oppression. They too are undervalued and underpaid, and are often sexually as well as physically exploited in sweat shops run by bureaucratic capitalists backed by imperialist and expansionist forces, in such enterprises as garment and carpet factories.

Women's Social Oppression

The roots of women's oppression must not only be sought in the economic structure but also in social and cultural structures. Equally, the sources of women's exploitation must not only be sought in her productive life but also in her reproductive life. Women's social oppression is firmly rooted in the state-sponsored Hindu religion, which upholds feudal Brahminical rule based on the caste system, which disparages women in relation to men. In this tradition, women are looked upon as mere 'daughters' before they become 'wives' and until they die as 'mothers' of children (particularly sons). Because of the strength of patriarchy and of patrilineal inheritance law, Nepal has one of the highest indices of son preference in the world. Thus females (girls and women) face discrimination from the womb to the tomb. This can be seen manifested in their high mortality rate: they die younger than men (52 years for women and 55 years for men). Nepal has one of the highest maternal mortality rates in the world (875 per 100,000). It has also one of the highest child mortality rates: nearly 1 child in every 10 dies before reaching the age of 1. All this is accompanied by early marriage, early pregnancy and multiple pregnancies—making huge demands on the mental and physical health of women. Because women are seen as a means to beget son/sons to inherit private property, women are forced to any lengths to beget sons, even at the cost of their own health, in order to secure their marital status and to ensure their share of the land via their sons. Thus women without sons are mostly abandoned, or socially ostracised, or become co-wives.

The caste system makes women belonging to the scheduled (or 'untouchable') castes even more vulnerable economically, socially and sexually. In fact, the imposition of Hindu culture on Nepali society is so strong that it has even affected women who belong to less feudalistic non-Hindu groups.

Women's Political Oppression

Women's political oppression is rooted in the patriarchal economic and social structures and relations that are upheld by the present monarchical parliamentary system. The fact that the heir to the royal throne must be through the male line, together with the personification of the king as a living god, both symbolises and reinforces male dominance and ensures that men are more powerful than female members in society. Thus, men are the rulers and women the ruled, even within the household. The king thus represents a patriarch, in body and in spirit. Unlike in the bourgeois republican countries, where women have at least legal access to parental property, women in Nepal do not even have this legal provision, putting them strategically at a disadvantage in all respects, including entering into political life within the present political system. Thus, in parliamentary politics, women are ultimately used only as a ready-made source of votes—a sort of vote bank— through their male relations. The present parliamentary system, which makes it necessary to have money and capital to be able to stand, let alone win, in an election, is a big hindrance to women. The limited number of women who have managed to enter into politics tend to be widows, or the wives or daughters of already well-known male politicians.

Women and New Democratic Revolution

Without revolutionary ideology there cannot be revolutionary movement.

—Lenin

Women in Nepal have reasons to fight for the New Democratic revolution as it addresses their economic, social and political oppression in totality. As mentioned earlier, the source of women's economic oppression is primarily their lack of access to land-ownership on an equal par with men. This is directly addressed in the New Democratic revolution, where the central economic feature is the agrarian revolution. Under this system a revolutionary land reform is to be carried out under the slogan of 'land to the tiller'. Along with this, a revolutionary land relationship between men and women is to be developed under the slogan of 'women's equal right to property'. In the rural areas, women's access to landed property will make them an important and powerful core of the rural agriculture economy; in the urban areas, this 'right to property' will allow them to inherit urban land, and other means of production such as industry, business enterprises etc., thus making them part of the urban economic system. This prepares the first 'foundation' for woman's economic emancipation, which will have important bearing on developments in other socio-political arenas.

Since the New Democratic system is anti-feudal, it will at once remove any religious tint given to the state, making it a secular state. With the end of feudal Brahminical Hindu rule, women will become culturally independent from men. This will gradually remove the bias against daughters, making them as important as sons within the household. Under the New Democratic system, there is no question of accommodating the feudal monarchy, which is the symbol of patriarchal rule over women. So, politically, the New Democratic system prepares the ground for removing patriarchal rule and in its place women will emerge to constitute one of the most important groups, along with other oppressed groups, in the anti-feudal and anti-colonial united front government. For these reasons, women in Nepal have good reason to fight tooth and nail to establish the New Democratic system.

The anti-imperialist nature of the New Democratic revolution will abolish unequal relations with imperialist, expansionist countries, thus saving women from sweat shops where they are exploited sexually and economically. This also prepares the ground for removing prostitution, consumerisation and the commodification of women in Nepal.

Revolutionary Trends in Women's Mass Organisation

Having grasped the essence of the New Democratic Revolution and its relevance to women's emancipation, women's organizations—particularly the All Nepalese Women's Association (Revolutionary)—have initiated a revolutionary trend in the women's movement in Nepal. This should be understood in the context of the women's movement in Nepal, which can be broadly categorised into three distinct trends. The rightist and reactionary trend openly serves the interests of the feudalist and bureaucratic capitalist forces. These women talk of women's emancipation but support the system of the constitutional monarchy, uphold the state-sponsored Hindu religion and are openly engaged in imperialist-sponsored NGO/INGO activities. They grumble about the commodification of women, but dare not protest against beauty pageants etc. They condemn revolutionary violence but condone state violence. They are closer to the ruling parties such as the Nepali Congress Party, the United Marxist–Leninist Party (UML) and other official 'Marxist–Leninist' Parties. The second is the revisionist trend. These sound revolutionary in word, but in deed they practice reformism. They say they are republican, but they are involved in the monarchical parliamentary system. They condemn the activities of NGOs and INGOs in theory, but in practice many of them are engaged in such activities. They are close to groups like 'Masal', the 'Unity Centre' etc.

The third category belongs to the revolutionary trend. This is represented by the All Nerpalese Women's Association (Revolutionary) or ANWA(R), which is close to the CPN (Maoist). This group of women has taken a clear stand regarding male supremacy and private property. It is very clear about the class nature of the present state, which is maintaining class oppression and gender oppression. Similarly it has taken a clear stand against NGO/INGO activities in both words and in deeds, as they consider these organisations to be extensions of imperialist and expansionist forces whose ultimate aim is to prepare the ground for expanding their own interventions, while at the same time checking the growth of genuine revolutionary movement of the people.

Pursuing the policy of unity and struggle ANWA(R) has been forging broad alliances with other forces, particularly with anti-feudal and anti-colonial forces, to protest against beauty contests, pornographic literature, the sale of liquor etc. It has formed a broad alliance to protest against the state repression of women, particularly the rape and torture perpetrated on sympathisers of the People's War. While other organisations condemn revolutionary violence, this organisation considers it as a legitimate defensive measure of the masses against the present armed state repression.

Women's Participation in People's War in Nepal

Women hold half the sky

—Mao Tse Tung

In Nepal, women's active participation in war can be traced back to the days of the centralised feudal state expansion campaign in the late 18th and early 19th century, particularly back to 1815 in the battle of Nalapani in Dehradun (at present in Northern India) where Nepali women and children, together with their menfolk, offered heroic resistance against the British army, who not only outnumbered them but also had better equipment. Despite their advantages, they (the British) were able to seize Kalanga fort only on their third attempt after incurring heavy losses.

Similarly, women were mobilised during the anti-Rana movement by various anti-Rana political parties during 1947–50, culminating in the overthrow of the Rana regime in the year 1950. Women demonstrated their active participation in the democracy movement of 1990, which ended 30 years of the autocratic monarchy's non-party 'Panchayat' regime, replacing it with a monarchical parliamentary system. However, in all such movements, most of the women involved were drawn from known political family backgrounds or from among the urban educated women, and were mainly based in urban areas.

It was only after the CPN (Maoist) started the People's War that women from grassroots, mainly rural women, began to be mobilised. Today, they are professional fighters in the guerrilla war. The traditional weapons, such as stones, sickles and sticks, with which women threatened their enemies in earlier movements, have now been upgraded to rifles, automatic weapons and explosives. Initially, they were looked upon as mere helpers or as a reserve force for political movements, but today they are also leaders, and commanders of guerrilla squads constituting of men and women. The significance of this development can be understood when it is realised that Section 10 of the government's Army Act 1960 bans the recruitment of women into the Royal Nepal Army. Recognising the double exploitation of women, the CPN (Maoist) has rightly targeted them, to unleash their doubly repressed energy to attack the system that has been responsible for their present sorry state. In each guerrilla squad it has made it policy to recruit at least two women guerrillas (in each squad there are 9–11 members). Women guerrillas fight as combatants at night and do propaganda and production work during the day time. Where circumstances demand, exclusively women's guerrilla squads have been constituted, but this is more of an exception than the rule. One incident in Rolpa is worth mentioning. where an all-women's guerrilla squad was responsible for eliminating a feudal tyrant who was also known to exploit women sexually.

At village, area and district levels, women have been mobilised under women's mass organisations. In revolutionary stronghold areas, people's courts have been established, in which, along with other cases, cases against women's exploitation have been brought to trial by the combined efforts of the Village Defence Committees, women's mass organisations and the people as a whole. Many cases of land usurpation of widows or of single women have been brought and their land restored to them through such courts. Many defaulting husbands who have taken to drinking and beating of their wives or practicing polygamy, and sexually exploiting women, have been disciplined through such courts. One interesting case in Parbat district is worth mentioning. A school teacher was known to exploit women sexually while promising to help them find matches for their marriages. He was brought before the people's court and was made to stand up and sit down, holding his ears, for several minutes, and was made to apologise for his crime; eventually he was let off, after a warning of more serious consequences, should he continue with his criminal behaviour.

Where women are not directly involved in guerrilla warfare, they are working as a support force for the People's War. They function as organisers, as propagandists, as cultural activists, as logistics suppliers, as nurses for wounded fighters and cadres, as espionage workers, as cover for the party cadres or combatants, as visitors and as a source of inspiration in jails and in martyr's family households. They are also trained to prepare locally made explosives.

Because, culturally, women have been associated with household work, women activists have been most effective in mobilising the masses in new areas, where they are easily accepted at household level. This has helped male cadres to gain access subsequently to households in new areas. It has been generally observed in places where local women were mobilised, that such places eventually became stable bases for sustaining the movement. Also because of women's multiple role inside and outside the house, they provide good cover for many logistic and espionage activities by party cadres and guerrillas.

In regards to women's commitment to the People's War, it has been generally found that they often take time to decide to join the movement, but once they are committed they stick to it more consistently and more firmly than do the male cadres. There have been fewer cases of surrender or running away from the battlefield by women. They are also less liable to disclose party-related secrets. They are thus found to have greater perseverance and patience than men, although they may lag behind men in their theoretical knowledge. This may be because women have more to gain from the movement than do men; that is, for them it is not only a question of escaping from class oppression but also from gender oppression. After all, breaking off double chains requires greater strength and greater will power!

The following heroic examples exemplify the different roles women have been playing in People's War in Nepal:

Dilmaya Yonjan: The first woman combatant, who heroically gave her life in the successful Bethan armed raid. She was killed while she was igniting a bomb. What makes her martyrdom even more meaningful is that she belongs to the oppressed nationality of the Tamangs.

Lali Rokka: A social activist and health assistant in remote Rolpa district. She was picked up by the police from her health post and shot dead. Her 'fault' was that she actively exposed the reactionary role of a local NGO in her area.

Bindia Chaulagai: A young woman in an advanced stage of pregnancy who was tortured in police custody for providing food for guerrillas in the jungles. The torture resulted in the premature delivery of the baby, which ultimately led to its death, and was followed by her own death few days later.

Sunsara Budha: The wife of a Party activist, who was tortured in front of her 2-years-old child when she did not reveal the whereabouts of her husband; her child was also tortured but she still did not buckle. The police then brutally killed her, leaving behind the injured child.

Kamala Bhatta: A teacher and President of ANWA(R) in Gorkha district who was raped and killed by a special commando force of the armed police while she was returning from mass work amongst women in the villages.

Devi Khadka: A living symbol of barbaric state repression, who was repeatedly raped in police custody, leading to laceration of her womb. She was raped because she did not yield to police pressure and sign the death certificate of her brother who was languishing in jail. Today she is alive and actively engaged in the People's War.

Savitri Chaulagai   *Jaya Dahal*   *Nirmala Devkota*
Subhadra Sapkota   *Juna Choudhary*   *Dila Thapa*
Some names of the Women Martyrs

Chiniya Lama, Nirmala Deykota, Manju Kuwar and Suvadra Sapkota: These three women, along with three male cultural activists, were killed by police at the direct instigation of reactionary revisionist UML local leaders. Their 'fault' was that they had been mobilising and organising villagers with progressive culture shows.

There are many other individual examples that could be cited. But, in addition to the widspread brutal treatment of individuals, the mass rape of women and incidents of airlifting women in helicopters to be raped elsewhere and then killed have all been reported in the revolutionary stronghold areas. In the initial stages of the war, women were just (sic) tortured and raped, but the recent trend is to kill them as well. This shows that even the reactionary armed forces have now acknowledged women as an invincible fighting force. The mass scale of state repression of women also demonstrates the unwilling acknowledgement by the state of women's participation in various capacities in the People's War.

The Role of the People's War in Women's Transformation

People's War is a total war.

—*Mao Tse Tung*

The People's War has affected women in different ways. First of all, it has brought fundamental changes in the party activist's family life. Earlier, before the party launched the People's War, there were many contradictions in theory and practice relating to gender issues within the household and in the wider social arena. For example, the strong preference for sons, early arranged marriages for daughters, the practice of polygamy by men combined with an insistence on strict monogamy for women, feudal cultural customs such as fasting on auspicious dates, the practice of 'untouchability' with respect to menstruating women and lower caste people, a strong attachment to private property, the relegation of women to household activities while men engaged in active politics and so on were all pervasive. But today, with the launching of the People's War, many wives have left home with their husbands to join the movement, leaving children to alternative support systems. Those wives who have decided to stay at home have become more economically independent and are more highly politicalised because of the necessity of circumstance, the subjective efforts of the Party to politicise them and the overall political atmosphere created by the People's War. Repeated search operations, warrants, threats and torture, sometimes even rape, have made them even more defiant and aggressive with regard to the state machinery. Even children have not been spared from such attacks, thus politicising them at an earlier age. They are found actively assisting village defence committees, taking part in cultural activities, helping in propaganda and espionage etc.

Since most of the able-bodied males who support the movement are forced to go underground in the revolutionary stronghold areas, women and children are left to look after their property and to face the police. The absence of men from the household has reversed earlier gender roles. For example, today women are found ploughing the fields, although this is officially not permitted by Hindu religion. They are found roofing their houses, something that is not normally culturally accepted. Today, women in revolutionary areas are refusing the widowhood ceremony when their husbands are killed by the security forces. At the same time, the Party is consciously trying to transform their bereavement into a source of strength, so as to avenge their menfolk. These days, newspapers carry such resolutions from these women. Take the case of Sangeeta Budha, a resident of Rolpa. Her husband was killed by the police in 1997. According to her, it was she who worked in her father's house when her father was arrested. Today after the killing of her husband she has taken to the jungle to join the guerrilla war to avenge her husband's death. The people's War has effectively transformed the normally reactionary Hindu festival of "Teej"* into a revolutionary platform for propaganda in support of the People's War and to expose state repression in Nepal.

The absence of men, together with the police atrocities, has made women more cooperative amongst each other. On top of

---

* *"Teej" is a day long fast imposed on women in order to pray for longevity of their husbands or for those unmarried they keep fast to pray for eligible husbands. Women in their bridal dresses and make-up sing on this day in public areas.*

this, the Party has launched campaigns for community-based system of exchange, with cooperative labour such as the *parma* system (a traditional form of labour-exchange practiced between several farm households) on a larger scale, building new and maintaining old roads, installing community water sources, organising community-based fodder and fuel collection, installing new *chautara* (public rest places) etc. Take the instance of one such *chautara* constructed at the border of Rolpa and Salyan districts, which was built by local villagers in remembrance of local women martyrs, Kumari Budha, Sunsara Budha and Lali Rokka.

Collective farming has particularly helped those de-facto single-parent households where husbands are either away to serve the People's War or have gone away to work in remote urban centres or abroad. In some places it has even managed to win the heart of families whose male members are serving the reactionary military and police forces. With the establishment of people's courts and trials women now feel more secure in their own homes and outside, as defaulting husbands and roving men are duly punished. Also, women have become more aware of their legal rights and their oppressed state. Furthermore, repeated rape and molestation by the police force and the protection given by the state to goons and rapists, have exposed the class character and gender bias of the state. This also has enhanced the political consciousness of the masses.

Earlier rape victims were stigmatised, but today with the institutionalisation of rape and murder by the state, the earlier sense of shame has given way to a sense of class hatred, and revolt against the state apparatus. On the one hand, indiscriminate sexual harassment by the police has alienated even women of the ruling classes from the existing state, on the other, it has strengthened cooperation among the oppressed masses against the state.

The People's War has given an alternative revolutionary life to aspiring young men and women. Women's lives, particularly in rural areas, are so tedious and monotonous, set in a repeated pattern of reproductive activities; marriage being arranged at a relatively young age, they have no way of escaping from this beaten track of a life cycle. For aspiring women to venture out of village means almost always getting trapped into prostitution or being trafficked to India (it is estimated that about 150,000 women from Nepal are trafficked to the urban centres of India!) or trapped in low paid sweat shops where sexual harassment is rampant. Thus, for such aspiring women, the People's War offers a challenging opportunity to work side by side with men on equal terms and to prove their worth mentally and physically. The People's War has also given a dignified alternative life to many socially abandoned women—women abandoned by their husbands, women who have been left in the lurch after losing their virginity to cheats and women who could not afford to get married, are all found helping the People's War in various capacities. For them, a heroic death in the course of the People's War is more attractive than the everyday 'death' imposed on them by conventional society.

The People's War has helped instill progressive norms in people's lives. Today the new generation of women activists are defying the traditional arranged marriage system and opting more and more for love marriages on ideological grounds. They no longer fall head over heel for the idea of begetting sons; in fact they are limiting the number of children to a bare minimum, so as to continue their revolutionary activities. Men are found to be more sympathetic and cooperative in running family life. Today, strict monogamy has been enforced on men by the Party. Married men found indulging in illicit relationships are severely punished; similarly married women found indulging in illicit relationship are also not spared. Those who have reasons to divorce, however, are encouraged to divorce and remarry. There have been cases of remarriages: women and men who have lost their spouses in war have remarried. Such cases, although limited, are being encouraged by the Party.

The People's War has also ushered in a creative environment for literacy for women. As a result, many new women are coming forward to share their experiences of the People's War, police atrocities etc. by writing their memoirs, poems, feature articles and theoretical articles in newspapers and journals. The People's War has also thoroughly exposed the sham activities of NGOs/INGOs like Ama-Milan-Kendra (Mothers' Get-Together Centres) that construct temples and spread religion in the name of organising women. They have been exposed and discredited.

Nepal being a country of diversities, the People's War has affected women of different nationalities—Indo-Aryan, Tibeto-Burman and others—in different ways. The People's War has helped Indo-Aryan women to break the feudal patriarchal restrictive life imposed by the puritanical Hindu religion, by unleashing their repressed energy; it has given meaningful lives to Tibeto-Burman and other women who are already relatively free and have greater decision-making rights, by giving them challenging work to do. The People's War has not only released them from their class and gender oppression but also from their ethnic or nationality oppression. The People's War has particularly affected women of so-called lower castes, who are economically, socially, politically and sexually exploited, by unleashing their hatred against the state.

The Peoples' War has qualitatively and quantitatively changed the women's movement in Nepal. While it has shifted the geographical 'centre' of the women's movement from the urban centres to the rural areas, within the urban areas it has qualitatively changed the women's movement from a middle-class feminist movement to a broad-based women's movement with a class perspective as the key unifying feature. Today, wider issues, such as state repression of women, the rights of women, state repression of the masses etc., are being considered along with other feminist issues. The rampant mass rape of rural women perpetrated by the state is seen to affect urban feminist activists as well. They are now increasingly becoming involved in human rights organisations, to show their concern for the human rights abuse of women and children. Atrocities perpetuated by the state in revolutionary stronghold areas resulted in the sending of a team of six women journalists to investigate women's condition in Rolpa, Rukum and other districts. They exposed the atrocities perpetrated by the government in both the national and international media.

The People's War has also forced different women's organisations to come together on the same platform to organise protest rallies or joint press conferences against state repression, to rally against beauty contests and so on—which was rarely possible before the People's War started. The coming together of seven women's organisations, owing allegiance to different political parties, to organise a protest rally against the brutal rape and torture of Devi Khadka in police custody, is one such example.

The Role of the Revolutionary Party in Mobilising Women

In the overall context of Nepal, feudalism is the principal contradiction that women have to face. As a result, remnants of feudal values tend to seep into even Party organisational structure. This affects women in particular, as they have to fight on two fronts, from a class perspective and a gender perspective. This becomes particularly challenging for women and the party organisation when women in leadership in various committees and guerrilla units are not easily accepted because of feudal prejudices. This is where the policy of the CPN (Maoist) of encouraging women's participation in the People's War at every level becomes important. Similarly, with the increasing influence of imperialism in urban areas, there is a danger that women will be swayed towards a sectarian feminist influence. This is especially true for well-to-do educated women, who have joined the movement, revolting against feudal and patriarchal domination at home. Because of their class background they may be more sensitive to gender issues than to class issues; this, if not checked, may lead to reformism or right deviation within the Party. Hence, the Party should counter this danger by bringing class elements into the picture when debating the leading role in the women's movement. This can be achieved only if the Party genuinely follows the 'mass line', as advocated by Chairman Mao, whereby the Party is deeply rooted within the downtrodden masses while at the same time not antagonising other anti-feudal and anti-imperialist forces. On the other hand, however, one must also be careful that gender issues do not simply get postponed due to overzealousness in applying class consciousness. This may lead to adventurism and 'left' sectarianism in the Party.

Both these extreme tendencies (rightist and leftist) must be checked by making well-to-do educated women more class conscious and poor women and men (in particular) more gender sensitive. Also one must be theoretically clear that the aim of an exclusive women's organisation in a Marxist–Leninist–Maoist organisation is to prepare women activists who are already class conscious and are also gender sensitive so that they can effectively represent themselves in other mass organisations and local united fronts. Objectively, there are many grounds for women's participation in the People's War. However, subjectively they still lag behind men because of their long history of subjugation, their poor literacy level, their lesser exposure to the outside world etc. Hence, the subjective input by the CPN (Maoist) regarding its women's members is very crucial.

Today the People's War faces a new situation, where young men and women are fighting together on the war front, and in underground organisational work. In such a situation, the question of sexual morality must be faced in such a way that the movement does not fall into anarchism, in the name of sexual freedom. On the other hand, because the culture is predominantly feudal, one must be aware that conservatism may often prevail, in the name of restraining sexual freedom. The Party has issued certain rules and regulations to handle such situations. In fact new cultural values and norms are being promoted to break away from decadent feudal culture.

Today the People's War has reached the stage of preparing base areas. Today the challenge lies in mobilising women's power not only to destroy the old society but also to construct a new progressive society. This can be done by enabling women to participate in productive activities and in the decision-making bodies of the embryonic local anti-feudal, anti-imperialist New Democratic state in the prospective base areas. One should bear in mind that not solving or postponing women's issues at the Party level will hamper the proletarian cause in a long run, as women are the most oppressed force among the oppressed classes and groups. Such shortcomings will ultimately affect the Party's political line and drive it towards either rightism or ultra-leftism. This is where the spirit of Great Proletarian Cultural Revolution must be inculcated into Party life, right from the beginning. The slogan 'it is right to rebel' is an apt action-oriented slogan that arms women to rebel against feudalism and to fight against right and left tendencies in the Party.

Conclusion

War, particularly class war, is by itself a great educator for the masses, in the sense that it exposes the class character of the state. Particularly for women, it also exposes the patriarchal nature of the feudal-bourgeois state. This is particularly the case in Nepal, where women are being triply punished for challenging the existing class structure and the patriarchal structure of the existing state by being tortured, raped and killed.

Since women suffer most as a result of feudal economic relations, backward and oppressive feudal culture (and perverted imperialist culture in urban areas) and patriarchal state apparatus, they can be a reliable force in the anti-feudal and anti-imperialist New Democratic Revolution. Women are also the most reliable force to push the New Democratic Revolution forward to Communism, as their total emancipation can be realised only after abolishing private property, which is possible only under Communism. The women's question has become an important question for all classes. In today's class war, the imperialists are trying to use women as peacemakers to maintain the status-quo while the Marxist–Leninist–Maoist forces are steeling women to strike violently against the system that has been responsible for their double exploitation.

Let us therefore hail, 'Working Women of the World, Unite. You have Nothing to Lose but Your Double Chains!!'

Chapter 6

Maoist Statements and Documents

THE MAOISTS' 40-POINT DEMANDS*

These demands were submitted by the political front of CPN (Maoist) United People's Front to the coalition government headed by Nepali Congress party.

These are the same demands that were raised during the 1990s People Movement, including the demand to end the banning of political parties. The UPFN continued to make these demands for 5 years after the so-called democratic negotiation with the monarchy. But successive governments (notably the Nepali Congress governments) acted directly against the spirit of the demands.

Thousands of supporters and workers of the Communist Party and UPFN were imprisoned or ensnared in false charges, and more than 100 sons and daughters of Nepal were killed when they mader these demands peacefully.

Now the government is asking 'what were these demands'? It means they threw away the demands in the dustbin. Here the demands are reproduced once more (INSOF-JP).

Demands Related to Nationalism:
1. Regarding the 1950 Treaty between India and Nepal, all unequal stipulations and agreements should be removed.

---

* The above demands were put forward by the Samukta Jana Morcha, led by Dr. Bhattarai, and handed over to the Prime Minister, Sher Bahadur Deuba. (Original translation by Barbara Adams, published in *People's Review*; revised by David Seddon for this collection).

2. HMGN should admit that the anti-nationalist Tanakpur agreement was wrong, and that it, together with the Mahakali Treaty, which incorporates the former, should be nullified.
3. The entire Nepal–Indian border should be systematically controlled. Vehicles with Indian number plates, which are today freely plying the roads of Nepal, should not be allowed free entry.
4. Gorkha recruiting centers should be closed and decent jobs should be arranged for the would-be recruits.
5. In several areas of Nepal, where foreign technicians are given precedence over Nepali technicians for certain local jobs, a system of work permits should be instituted for foreigners.
6. The monopoly of foreign capital over Nepal's industry, trade and economic sector should be stopped.
7. Sufficient income should be generated from customs duties for the country's economic development.
8. The cultural pollution of imperialists and expansionists should be stopped. Hindi video, cinema and all kinds of such news papers and magazines should be completely stopped. Inside Nepal, the importation and distribution of vulgar Hindi films, video cassettes and magazines should be stopped.
9. Regarding NGOs and INGOs: Bribing by imperialists and expansionists in the name of NGOs and INGOs should be stopped.

Demands Related to the Public and Its Well-being

10. A new constitution must be drafted by the people's elected representatives.
11. All the special rights and privileges of the King and his family should be ended.
12. The army, police and administration should be under the people's control.
13. The Security Act and all other repressive acts should be abolished.
14. All the false charges against the people of Rukum, Rolpa, Jajarkot, Gorkha, Kavre, Sindhuphalchowk, Sindhuli, Dhanusha and Ramechap should be withdrawn and all

those people falsely charged should be released.
15. Armed police operations in the different districts should immediately be stopped.
16. Regarding Dilip Chaudhary, Bhuvan Thapa Magar, Prabhakar Subedi and other people who disappeared from police custody at different times, the government should constitute a special investigating committee to look into these crimes; the culprits should be punished and appropriate compensation given to their families.
17. People who died during the time of the Movement, should be declared martyrs and their families, and those who have been wounded and disabled as a result, should be given proper compensation. Strong action should be taken against their killers.
18. Nepal should be declared a secular state.
19. Girls should be given equal property rights to those of their brothers.
20. All kinds of exploitation and prejudice based on caste should be ended. In areas having a majority of one ethnic group, that group should have autonomy over that area.
21. The status of dalits as 'untouchables' should be ended and the system of untouchability ended once and for all.
22. All languages should be given equal status. Up to middle-high school level (*uccha-madyamic*), arrangements should be made for education to be given in the children's mother tongue.
23. There should be a guarantee of free speech and a free press. The communications media should be completely autonomous.
24. Intellectuals, historians, artists and academicians engaged in other cultural activities should be guaranteed intellectual freedom.
25. In both the *terai* and hilly regions there is prejudice and misunderstanding in backward areas. This should be ended and the backward areas should be assisted. Good relations should be established between the villages and the city.
26. Decentralisation in real terms should be applied to local

areas, which should have local rights, autonomy and control over their own resources.

Demands Related to People's Livelihoods

27. Those who cultivate the land should own it—the tiller should have the right to the soil he/she tills. The land of rich landlords should be confiscated and distributed to the homeless and others who have no land.
28. Brokers and commission agents should have their property confiscated and that money should be invested in industry.
29. All should be guaranteed work and should be given a stipend until jobs are found for them.
30. HMGN should pass strong laws ensuring that people involved in industry and agriculture should receive minimum wages.
31. The homeless should be given suitable accommodation. Until HMGN can provide such accommodation they should not be removed from where they are squatting.
32. Poor farmers should be completely freed from debt. Loans from the Agricultural Development Bank incurred by poor farmers should be completely written off. Small industries should be given loans.
33. Fertiliser and seeds should be easily and cheaply available, and farmers should be given a proper market price for their production.
34. Flood and draught victims should be given all necessary help
35. All should be given free and scientific medical service and education; education for profit should be completely stopped.
36. Inflation should be controlled and labourers' wages and salaries raised in direct ratio to the rise in prices. Daily essential goods should be made cheap and easily available.
37. Arrangements should be made for the provision of drinking water, good roads and electricity in the villages.
38. Cottage and other small industries should be granted special facilities and protection.

39. Corruption, black marketing, smuggling, bribing, the taking of commissions etc. should all be stopped.
40. Orphans, disabled people, older people and children should be given special help and protection.

We offer a heartfelt request to the present coalition government that they should fulfill the above demands, which are essential for Nepal's existence and for the people's daily lives, as soon as possible. If the government does not respond by Falgun 5, 2052 (February 17, 1996), we will be compelled to launch a movement against the government.

MARCH ALONG THE PATH OF PEOPLE'S WAR TO SMASH THE REACTIONARY STATE AND ESTABLISH A NEW DEMOCRATIC STATE!*

APPEAL OF THE CPN (MAOIST) TO THE PEOPLE

Dear masses of the people,

Today Nepalese society is in a state of grave crisis, economically, politically and culturally. Where has the present regime, which has been harping on about development and construction for the last 50 years, landed Nepal economically? It has landed Nepal in the position of second poorest country in the world after Ethiopia. This regime, which does not manufacture even a needle in the name of self-reliant and national economy, has handed over the whole national economy to a dozen families of foreign compradors and bureaucratic capitalists. This handful of plunderers have become billionaires, whereas the real owners of this country and the national property—the toiling masses of Nepal—are forced to eke out a meagre existence of deprivation and poverty. The sons and daughters of Nepalese peasants and workers, reeling under the burden of unemployment and poverty, are compelled to lead a miserable life of dishonour and neglect, in India and other parts of the world, to earn their daily bread.

---

* This leaflet was distributed in hundreds of thousands all over the country along with the initiation of the People's War on February 13, 1996.

After piling a massive foreign debt burden on even the future generations, the feudal and comprador and bureaucratic capitalist rulers are making merry with it. In the name of privatisation and liberalisation—under the guidance and for the benefit of foreign capitalists—the process of mortgaging the whole country to the comprador and bureaucratic capitalists is now in full swing.

The burden of this economic degradation has been borne largely by the peasantry, which constitutes 90% of the population. That every new government formed under this state structure pushes and will push the country economically into further bankruptcy has been demonstrated historically.

To maintain the hegemony of one religion (i.e. Hinduism), language (i.e. Nepali) and nationality (i.e. Khas), this state has for centuries exercised discrimination, exploitation and oppression against other religions, languages and nationalities and has conspired to fragment the forces of national unity that is vital for the proper development and security of the country. On the contrary, it has prostrated itself before the foreign imperialists and expansionists, repeatedly mortgaging Nepal's national honour and sovereignty to them. The present state has shamelessly permitted the foreign plunderers to grab the natural water resources of Nepal and to trample upon our motherland. If this process is allowed to continue, there is no doubt in the minds of the patriotic, conscious and self-esteemed Nepalese people that the very existence of Nepal will be in jeopardy.

The present state has declared war against the development of the national culture of the Nepalese people by flooding (the country) with the corrupt, licentious and distorted imperialist culture. The feudal and imperialist forces are doing their utmost to replace democratic cultural values and ideals with Freudian, nihilist and anarchic values. This is a sequel to the conspiracy of the reactionary classes within Nepal to corrupt the people culturally and preserve their own heaven of plunder. These corrupt cultural values are no less responsible for the burgeoning of drug-trafficking, smuggling, thievery, black marketeering, looting, murder and rape in society today.

Within this moribund state structure, a coalition government of Panchas (i.e. royalists) and Nepali Congress Party hacks, defamed in Nepalese history for their anti-national and genocidal deeds, has recently been in power. This (government) has forced not only the peasants and workers of Nepal but also other people of different categories and professions to live in a state of scarcity, injustice and terror. The state has treated women as second class citizens for long, but now it has intensified rape, trafficking and the process of commoditisation through advertisements against them. The whole educational system is tuned to produce slaves for this state and there is rampant anarchy in it. Thus, whether it is workers, peasants, women, teachers, students, small traders, lower ranking civil servants, doctors, professors or members of other classes, including the national bourgeoisie, all are victims of this state of feudals and of comprador and bureaucratic capitalists. Without radical change in all spheres, any possibility of reform has now become a mere chimera (illusion).

The reactionary ruling classes, though ever swearing by democracy, have repeatedly used their guns against those political activists or ordinary members of the population who hold political beliefs counter to the interests of the rulers. This state, which regards itself as the custodian of 'democracy', has survived on the blood of innumerable sons and daughters of mother Nepal (ranging from the infant to the aged), while the people have professed and spoken out in favour of nationalism, democracy and livelihoods. Hundreds of thousands of Nepalese people fighting for justice have been subjected to inhuman physical torture, confinement in jails and mental torture. Not only during the partyless Panchayat (i.e. absolute monarchy) period but even during the present monarchical–parliamentary period, fascist genocidal and repressive acts have been on the increase rather than on the decrease. This is a bitter truth experienced by the Nepalese people in their everyday life. This process has now developed into a campaign of armed repression against innocent people favouring truth and justice. The recent armed operation of state terror (Operation Romeo, AJ & DS) let loose in Western Nepal and in different parts of the country has testified beyond doubt that the ruling classes have openly embarked upon an unjust war against the people. The heinous game of the reactionary state, of enrolling the sons and daughters of the poor peasants and workers in the police and the army as mercenaries and forcing them to use arms against their own wretched parents, brothers and sisters, is now crystal clear. With the passage of time those in the police and the army will also come to know the realities. There is no alternative for the people other than to raise the banner of a just war against this unjust war.

How did we reach this crisis of nationalism, democracy and livelihood and situation of open warfare of the state against the people? What is clear on the basis of historical and scientific materialism is that the seeds of this state of affairs were sown a long time back in the history of Nepal. With the advent of the era of imperialism and proletarian revolution, as in almost all the oppressed nations, in Nepal also a semi-feudal and semi-colonial socioeconomic structure based on the alliance of feudalism and imperialism was established. The process of feudalism prostrating itself before imperialism and of imperialism plundering the masses while protecting feudalism, was initiated. In Nepal, this process was initiated in a concrete form after the conclusion of the Sugauli Treaty of 1815–16 with British India. The inevitable consequence of this process was that it obstructed the development of national capitalism and instead opened the path of development of bureaucratic capital in the interest of both landlords and imperialism. This long historical period has been in fact the period of the process of birth, rise and demise of the same bureaucratic capital.

In Nepal, the 104 years of Rana autocracy (i.e. from 1846 to 1950), the later partyless Panchayat autocracy (i.e. from 1960 to 1990) and the current so-called monarchical multiparty system (i.e. from 1990 onwards) have all reproduced broadly the same structures, under broadly the same dispensation. Principally as a result of the struggle of the Nepalese people against these (socioeconomic) structures, and secondarily due to the complex evolution of the international political economy, the names of the system and the government have changed (sometimes liberal and at other times conservative), to effect the redistribution of the spoils of power. But the basic structure of the political economy and of the state has remained unchanged. The political developments of 1951, 1960, 1979 and 1990 can only be understood in this way. If we view the history of Nepal from 1951 onwards alone, what is amply evident is that within the womb of petty reforms carried out within the reactionary state there has been developing an ever-greater crisis for the country and the people.

The Nepalese people have constantly struggled against this state of affairs. In the process of such struggles, they have been the victims not only of the repeated repression and intrigues of the reactionaries but also of the betrayal and treachery of the reformists. Today the biggest traitors of the people have been those so-called communists (the revisionists), who have sought the crumbs of reactionary state power by licking the boots of feudalism and imperialism. The Nepalese people and Nepalese history will never forgive those traitors who have sat on the chairs of the reactionaries by betraying the people's faith in radical change and the Communist Party, and by stepping in the blood of thousands of martyrs. If somebody talks of limiting the struggle to the reformist struggle within the reactionary state, that will be merely another aspect of this treachery. This has now become a historically verified truth.

The other thing that should not be forgotten at this point, however, is that the negative recurrence of reactionary repression and intrigue, and of reformist betrayal and treachery has given rise to the positive enhancing of the political consciousness of the general masses of the people and the growing recognition by the people of the potential for their liberation through the people's class struggle and a long and intense ideological struggle of the unique revolutionary ideology of Marxism–Leninism–Maoism against such reformism. Today, the Marxist–Leninist–Maoist Party guided by this almighty revolutionary ideology has developed like a beautiful and blossoming flower, through the long struggle of the labouring masses of Nepal, irrigated by the blood of thousands of martyrs. While all kinds of reactionaries and revisionists are madly after it to nip it in the bud, the revolutionary masses are taking care of its preservation and development.

Dear Masses of the People,

What is clear from the above is that the present crisis is the result of the development of contradictions between the exploitation and oppression of the people by the state power of the feudal, comprador and bureaucratic capitalist classes, on the one hand, and the relentless struggle carried out by the people against it, on the other. To defend their moribund and crisis-ridden reactionary state, feudalism and imperialism have openly imposed on the Nepalese people an unjust war. If the Nepalese people cannot raise the banner of a just people's war against this unjust war and become victorious in it, the Nepalese people and the Nepalese nation will be doomed to a prolonged darkness.

Conscious of its duty towards this historical necessity, the Communist Party of Nepal (Maoist)—the proletarian party of the sons and daughters of the masses of the people—has resolved to initiate the process of forcibly smashing this reactionary state and establishing a New Democratic state. This resolve is based on the feeling of service and devotion towards the people, on the commitment to the almighty ideology of Marxism–Leninism–Maoism to free humanity forever from the yoke of class exploitation, and on the study of history of the Nepalese society in that light. We are fully conscious that this war to break the shackles of slavery of thousands of years and to establish a New Democratic state will be uphill, full of twists and turns and of a protracted nature. But this and this alone is the path of people's liberation and a great and bright future. This path will unfold by making uses of all forms of struggle in keeping with the historical stage of development of Nepal and principally, as we have said all along, according to the strategy of encircling the city from the countryside, with agrarian revolution as the axis and from the midst of and in conjunction with the rural class struggle. The process of the People's War in the context of the present balance of forces will move forward through the process of a people's guerilla war within the stage of strategic defence. What we are confident about is that the masses of the people of all classes and categories will extend active support and help to this revolutionary process and it will be vigorous. Besides this, we are also conscious and confident that this struggle will gain support and help from communist revolutionaries and struggling masses the world over and this will in turn assist all those revolutionaries. because this struggle of ours will be a part and parcel of the world proletarian revolution, undertaken with a view to end exploitation and the oppression of man by man, and to end for ever war itself. In this context, we would like to make a special mention of the on-going people's revolution in Peru based on Marxism–Leninism–Maoism, and the Revolutionary Internationalist Movement (RIM) and revolutionary movements the world over based on the same convictions.

Finally, we appeal to workers, peasants, women, students, teachers, intellectuals and the masses of the people of all categories and trades to march along the path of the People's War to establish a people's New Democratic state and to extend to it all forms of support and help.

It is right to rebel!
Long live the people's war!
Down with the reactionary state!
Long live the new democratic revolution!
Glory to Marxism–Leninism–Maoism!
With revolutionary greetings,
Central Committee, Communist Party of Nepal (Maoist)

REVIEW OF THE HISTORIC INITIATION OF THE PEOPLE'S WAR AND FUTURE STRATEGY OF THE PARTY*

From the particular characteristics of war there arise a particular set of organizations, a particular series of methods and a particular kind of process.... Hence war experience is a particular kind of experience. And who takes part in war must rid themselves of their customary ways and accustom themselves to war before they can win victory.

—Mao Tse Tung, "On Protracted War"

Review

The plan of the Party to initiate the people's war has been implemented. A great process, representing a qualitative leap in the development of class struggle in Nepalese society and in the life of the Party has been initiated. While affecting all classes, strata and categories of society in an electric motion, the People's War in Nepal has shaken the 'heaven' of the reactionary state as well as its foundations and generated new questions and enthusiasm among the masses. The high morale, extraordinary

---

* Excerpts from a document adopted by the meeting of the Political Bureau of the Central Committee of the Party held in third week of March 1996.

bravery and self-sacrifice demonstrated by the Party, front workers and supporters in the first phase of the initiation of the People's War has exposed the cruel, fascist and cowardly character of the reactionary classes and added a new dimension to the glorious tradition of struggle of the Nepalese people. All these have been indelibly engraved in golden letters of the history of revolution in the specificities of the initiation of the People's War in Nepal.

This great beginning, and its impact and success, is an indicator of victory and glory of the almighty ideology of Marxism–Leninism–Maoism of the world proletariat in general, and of the Nepalese proletariat and oppressed masses in particular. In this context, the Party takes pride in all the immortal martyrs who have sacrificed their lives to make the plan of historical initiation of the People's War a success, pays revolutionary homage to them and resolves to fight till the end to make their dreams come true.

In this great process of the initiation of the People's War, the revolutionary thoughts, policies and plans of the Party were translated into practice as a physical force, and on the basis of this live practical experience, the door is opened for further development and refinement of those thoughts, policies and plans. In the history of the Nepalese communist movement, beset with metaphysics and idealism, this process has represented the correct implementation of the dialectical materialist theory of knowledge. This has been a scientific and powerful blow to the revisionist proposition of from 'thought to thought' and from 'reform to reform'. Apart from this, not only the positive aspects but the limitations and weaknesses in the organisational struggle and technical spheres of the Party have naturally come to the surface while making the qualitative leap from the process of peaceful and legal struggle to the armed struggle. This great process has opened a treasure house of knowledge for further information. The process of learning war through war has started in practice. Because of its long ideological, political and organizational preparation, the Party has been able to face, as a matter of course, the killing of 17 persons (till March 20, 1996) by the enemy, the condition of having to go underground of more than 1,000 leaders and cadres of the Party at a time and the arrest and inhuman torture of hundreds of Party members,

members of different front organisations and supporters among the mass of the people by the enemy. This is a question of considerable pride for the Party.

The historic launching of the People's War has given practical expression to the theory of the army as the principal form of organisation and of war as the principal form of struggle through different forms of armed squads and guerilla actions. Actions during the initiation and the continuation periods were able to put the Maoist People's War at the centre of national politics of the country. The level, nature and number of armed actions and the level of propaganda and publicity achieved within a short span of 1 month is itself a unique experience for a Maoist Party in any country in the present day world. In this process, the specificities of the Nepalese revolution, the crisis of the reactionary state and the level of development of the class struggle and the Party have all been manifested simultaneously.

One of the main goals specified by the Party in the plan for the historic initiation of the People's War was to put the politics of armed struggle at the forefront of political debate in the country. This goal has been achieved more than ordinarily expected. The politics of armed struggle in Nepal has now been established firmly, not only among the general masses of the Nepalese people but to a certain extent at the international level as well. Similarly, the goals of preparing the ground for developing certain strategic areas into guerilla zones and of transforming the forms of organisation and struggle have also been satisfactorily achieved.

The historical initiation of the people's war has created new problems, contradictions and crises for all the political groups and subgroups inside or outside the reactionary government in the country. This has intensified the crisis brewing within the entire reactionary state. Even the arch reactionary elements could not deny that it is a political issue for fear of being exposed before the masses, because of the appeal made by the Party to the wide masses of the people along with its analysis of the grave situation of the country at present, and because of the level, quality and range of armed actions and propaganda. This process has intensified the contradictions among different reactionary factions within the government and within those factions themselves.

On the basis of their reactions towards the People's War, it is clearly seen that there are three main political trends: reactionary, centrist and revolutionary. Despite differences of opinion within each group over whether to view it as a political or a purely terrorist activity, all in the reactionary camp are unanimous in regarding the People's War as 'anticonstitutional' and 'anti-democracy'; the Nepali Congress (NC), the Rastriya Prajatantra Party (RPP) and the Communist Party of Nepal (Unified Marxist–Leninist) (UML) are the main ones in this category. In this context, the UML clique was actually the most upset by the process of the People's War. The 'Bahudaliya Janabadi' (or multiparty democracy) faction of this clique has been particularly aggressive, calling on the government to instigate immediate repression and conspiring to form its own government to undertake repression.

In the centrist camp are mainly those small petty bourgeois reformist groups that talk of Mao thought and new democratic revolution. These groups are trying to save their existence by hoodwinking the ordinary masses and their cadres with a low theoretical level through their pretension of opposing both the People's War and the government repression. Despite a quantitative difference, as the basic character of these groups is reformist and parliamentary cretinist, they are hurling the identical accusation of 'ultra-leftism' at the People's War. This accusation of theirs has become in practice merely an additional voice to the cacophony of the reactionary UML clique. To get carried away by the reactionary propaganda, to have faith in the bourgeois elements and to distrust the proletariat, are their characteristic qualities, which have now been exposed. To attempt to tread a middle path in the struggle between revolution and counter-revolution is to serve counter-revolution. This truth is now being confirmed by these cliques. A new opportunity is now at hand to expose thoroughly such opportunist characteristics and to clear away any illusions amongst the genuine revolutionaries in their ranks. What has been seen in reality is that the honest and revolutionary cadres of these groups (particularly of the liquidationist 'Unity Centre' and the neo-revisionist 'Mashal') have been helping the People's War somehow or the other. Apart from this, wherever and to whatever extent these groups do take a stand against the reactionaries, there and to that extent, we must pay attention to forge some relationship with them.

Political parties, organisations, independent intellectuals and general masses of the people that have helped and supported in various ways the process of the People's War led by the Party, constitute the revolutionary camp.

In essence, the great process of the initiation of the people's war has made a direct and massive impact in the politics of the country and has enhanced the possibilities of utilising from new heights the contradictions developing in new forms. The Party should be alert in practicing Marxism–Leninism–Maoism in this regard.

Future Strategy

The initiation of the People's War was historic, but now the grave question of whether we are able or not to continue, to defend and develop it, is looming large before the Party. At the moment, the attention of the politically conscious masses, intellectual community and all others is centred on what will be the next plan of the Party and whether or not we will be able to preserve and develop what has been newly born. Only through a serious coordination of the sovereign principle of Marxism–Leninism–Maoism and the experiences of the historic initiation of the people's war can we formulate the future plan of the Party correctly. In this context, we should first of all pay serious attention to the following points:

1. We should constantly keep in mind that despite all the specificities, the character of the People's War in Nepal is protracted. In the present condition of the balance of forces, the enemy wants to drag us into a decisive war, but we on our part, want to avoid it and prolong the war. The enemy uses the strategy of attack but we use the strategy of defence. The enemy wants to incite us and draw us into confrontation according to his own convenience, but we want to harass the enemy, tire him out and attack him at his weak points at the time and place of our convenience according to our own plan.
2. The enemy wants to keep us apart from the struggle for the people's immediate problems and wants to cut off our relations with the masses. We, however, do not want to be cut off from the live contact with the masses at any cost.

Our policies and programmes should guarantee our constant interactions with the masses because the Party has no separate interest other than the interests of the masses, and otherwise there would be no rationale for the existence of the Party.

3. We should have a clear understanding that the danger of making wrong policies and programmes in the Party is inherent in the vacillating character of the petty bourgeois class in Nepal. This class has the tendency to become overexcited and jump into adventurism after a minor victory, and the tendency to become disheartened and move towards capitulationism after a minor defeat. We must wage relentless ideological and political struggle against the tendency to drag the Party in the direction of either adventurism or capitulationism. In the present situation where the enemy is on the offensive, the capitulationist tendency is the more dangerous for the Party.

4. The historical initiation of the People's War is a rebellion of far-reaching consequences, against the existing state and exploitation and oppression of thousands of years. Put in the present stage of socioeconomic formation and development of class struggle in Nepal, this is not an armed insurrection to capture central state power immediately. The process of protracted People's War is the process of construction—of the revolutionary Party, the revolutionary struggle, revolutionary power and the revolutionary army—from the simple to the complex. At the beginning of such a new and qualitative process, through the historic initiation of the People's War by the Party and the widespread propagation of the politics of armed struggle, it is necessary now to concentrate on the development of guerilla war in a planned way, based on the principle of protracted people's war and on our own specificities.

Weapons are an important factor in war, but not the decisive factor: it is people, not things, that are decisive.

—Mao Tse Tung, "On Protracted War"

ONE YEAR OF THE PEOPLE'S WAR IN NEPAL

—General Secretary,
Central Committee Communist Party of Nepal (Maoist)

The historic initiation of People's War in Nepal on February 13, 1996, was an epoch-making event in the history of the country and was hailed as having significant implications internationally as well by the revolutionary forces the world over. On the occasion of the first anniversary of this historic event, it is appropriate to make a brief review of the whole process of class struggle in the country leading to this People's War, the specific experiences of year one of the war and its multifarious implications, lessons and future perspective.

The Background
The Objective Conditions

Nepal is a semi-feudal and semi-colonial country. Nearly 90 per cent of the population is engaged in backward agriculture (with only 10 per cent of urban population!) and the country is fettered by various semi-colonial unequal treaties with foreign powers (particularly India). The present centralised state was founded two and a quarter centuries ago under the leadership of a feudal chieftain of Indo-Aryan stock (Prithvi Narayan Shah, the forefather of the present king) by subjugating different tribal states mostly peopled by Tibeto-Burman (or Mongoloid) and Austro-Dravidian groups. After 1816, the country was absorbed into a semicolonial relationship with British India (though it was never colonised by any foreign power) and since 1950 has been locked in semi-colonial relations with 'free' India and neo-colonial relations with a number of other imperialist powers. As bureaucratic capitalism has grown steadily within the womb of feudalism over the years, the external form of the reactionary state has undergone several changes, culminating in the present constitutional monarchical multiparty parliamentary system (after 1990), while retaining the essential hegemony of the feudal and comprador and bureaucratic capitalist classes. Hence the society and state are constantly beset with a set of irreconcilable contradictions in class, national and regional terms that have given rise to a cycle of one crisis after the other.

Currently this crisis is manifest in different forms and is becoming more acute every passing day. The total stagnation of the economy and absolute low level of productive forces is reflected in a mere 180 U.S. dollar per capita of GDP (second lowest in the world!), a pathetic 1.25 per cent of labour force engaged in industry, 71 per cent of the population below the poverty line, a 60 per cent illiteracy rate and so on. Combined with this low level of economic development is an extremely high degree of class polarisation and inequality— 10 per cent of landlords and rich peasants own 65 per cent of cultivable land while 65 per cent of poor peasants own a mere 10 per cent of the land, the richest 10 per cent of the society gobble up 46.5 per cent of national income, and so on. Furthermore, while even according to IMF standards a country's position is regarded as 'critical' when its foreign debt is more than 200–250 per cent of its export trade or its debt servicing exceeds 20 per cent of its export trade, in the case of Nepal the respective figures had exceeded 600 per cent and 35 per cent respectively by 1994–95 and are rising further every passing year. This is an unmistakable sign of crisis engendered by imperialist/expansionist domination and attendant burgeoning bureaucratic capitalism. There is thus no doubt that the primary contradiction in the social dynamics of Nepal is that between the general masses of the people and the dominant classes of feudalism and bureaucratic capitalism.

Moreover, ever since the days of formation of the centralised state more than a dozen nationalities mostly of the Mongoloid and Austric peoples (e.g. Magar, Tamang, Tharu, Newar, Gurung, Rai, Limbu, Danuwar, Sherpa, Sunuwar, Rajbansi etc.), who together constitute that majority of the population, have been subjected to political, economic and cultural domination by the ruling Arya-Khas peoples. In recent years, the contradictions between the state and the oppressed nationalities has sharpened further. Together with this, as a result of the dynamics of polarised development inherent in bureaucratic capitalism, vast mountainous regions and remote areas (e.g. the Karnali region in Western Nepal) have been turned into 'internal colonies' of the centralised state. The process of regional uneven and unequal development is giving rise to sharp regional contradictions in the country.

The reactionary state has increasingly failed to manage these multifarious class, national and regional contradictions within the framework of its existing structures. Consequently, the state itself has been progressively sliding into deeper crisis. This is manifest in the 'hung' parliaments, frequent changes of government, pervasive environment of instability and increasing recourse to naked fascist measures against the people. This calls for and provides an apt objective basis for the New Democratic restructuration of the society and state through revolutionary means.

The Subjective Factor

These objective conditions for the revolutionary transformation of the society, political economy and state had been generally in existence for quite a long time. What was essentially lacking was the conscious subjective efforts of a vanguard Party of the proletariat. Although the peasant masses and isolated revolutionary individuals had at times in the past spontaneously revolted against the exploitation and oppression of their feudal rulers, it could not have led to any meaningful revolutionary change in the absence of the organised leadership of the most advanced class of the society. In particular there was strong anti-colonial and patriotic sentiment against the British amongst the people, as the brave 'Gurkha' fighters had never become reconciled to their defeat against the British and the ignominious semi-colonial treaty of 1816. But there was no effective leadership to channel that sentiment.

The founding of the Communist Party of Nepal (CPN) in 1949 paved the way for the emergence of such a leadership, for an anti-feudal and anti-imperialist New Democratic revolution in the country. But the Party leadership was stuck in the quagmire of one or the other form of reformism and miserably failed to chart the basic path of the revolution, not to speak of leading the masses in a People's War. Consequently the occasional spontaneous armed revolts of the masses or the actions of small breakaway factions could not be sustained for long, and the first four decades of the communist movement in the country were frittered away in mere squabbles over inconsequential issues.

The Unity Congress of the reconstituted CPN (Unity Centre)— which was later rechristened as the CPN (Maoist)—adopted for the first time in December 1991, a clear-cut political line of protracted People's War to carry out the New Democratic revolution in Nepal with a Marxist–Leninist–Maoist ideological perspective. However, when the question of implementation of the political line within the party came up, there ensued a vicious two line struggle against a right liquidationist clique, which was finally defeated and expelled from the Party in May 1994. After the consolidation of the Party along the revolutionary line, the Third Central Plenum of the Party (held in March 1995) chalked out a detailed politico-military policy and programme outlining the strategy and tactics of a People's War (see, "Strategy & Tactics of Armed Struggle in Nepal" in this volume), and made the final decision to launch the war. This was followed by 6 months of hectic preparations, primarily to remould the old organisational structure into a fighting machine. Then, a Central Committee meeting of the Party (held in September 1995) adopted the 'Plan for the Historical Initiation of the People's War', which defined the theoretical basis and goal of the war and formulated a detailed plan and programme for the final preparation and initiation of the war. As part of the final politico-ideological preparation (while organisational–technical preparations continued underground), a series of countrywide mass meetings under the banner of the popular united front organisation, United People's Front–Nepal (UPFN) were held, culminating in a massive public rally attended by more than 50,000 people in the heart of the capital city of Kathmandu (on December 7, 1995). Meanwhile a vicious armed police operation, code-named 'Romeo Operation', launched by the reactionary state against the rural class struggle going on for some time in Rolpa district in the Western Hills, and a countrywide public outcry against this state repression, provided a perfect setting to initiate the People's War. In the light of these developments, the Political Bureau of the Central Committee of the Party met briefly in January 1996 and made the final selection of the date of the historic Initiation or Launch of the People's War for February 13 (i.e. the first day of the month of Falgun according to the Vikrami calendar followed in Nepal).

Thus, the vanguard Party of the Nepalese proletariat, steeled by years of inner party struggle and class struggle, made the final big leap to create history by leading the Initiation/Launch of the armed People's War on the day of February 13, 1996.

The First Plan: Initiation and Continuation

As outlined in the Third Plenum document, 'Strategy & Tactics of Armed Struggle in Nepal', there would be three strategic stages of the protracted People's War, namely Strategic Defense, Strategic Stalemate and Strategic Offense. Within the stage of Strategic Defense, there would be several tactical phases, namely Final Preparation for Initiation, Development of Guerrilla Zones, Development of Base Areas etc. After the completion of the phase of Final Preparation for Initiation, a plan for the Initiation itself was worked out, which was again to be implemented and developed in subphases. The First Plan was envisaged to cover the actual Initiation (the first day) and the continuation for some time thereof, say about a month or so. The basic objectives of the First Plan, as outlined in the "Plan for the Historical Initiation of the People's War", were to make a practical leap into and establish amongst the masses of the people the politics of armed revolution for capturing political power and to initiate the process of making the people's army the principal form of organisation and armed activities the principal form of struggle. Hence—with a clarion call of 'It is right to rebel'— the emphasis was placed on arousing the masses to rebel against the oppressive system and the state, and the selection of targets and the forms of actions were designed to give correct political message and derive maximum political propaganda rather than to make any material gain in the very beginning.

As planned, on February 13, one police outpost each in Rolpa and Rukum in the Western Hills, an Agricultural Development Bank branch and a distillery factory in Gorkha in the Central Hills, a police outpost in Sindhuli, the house of a feudal-usurer in Kavre in the Eastern Hills and the factory of a multinational company (Pepsi Cola) in the Kathmandu Valley, were systematically attacked by armed squads (accompanied by the supporting masses at several places) with great precision to herald the historic initiation. These seven targets in different districts and regions were selected purposefully in keeping with the geophysical and sociopolitical specificities of Nepal and not to allow the enemy to concentrate its repressive armed forces on any particular area. On the same evening hundreds of thousands of revolutionary leaflets and posters issued by the Party were distributed all over the country to spread the political message of the people's war among the masses.

From the next day, also as planned, a wave of guerrilla actions, sabotage and propaganda actions took place all over the country in continuation of the initiation. Within 3 weeks about 5,000 actions, mostly of propaganda nature, had taken place far and wide across the country. The national media were agog with the 'ghost' of the People's War. All political forces and politically minded persons were forced to take a position vis-a-vis the new politics. The politics of revolutionary armed struggle was firmly established in the country within a very short span of time.

As the basic objectives of the First Plan were already fulfilled, the Party issued an inner circular to restrain further actions of offense but permit defensive actions. This step was deemed necessary and important as otherwise the initial 'rebellion' could be misunderstood as an 'insurrection'. The essential protracted nature of the People's War had to be emphasied and grasped firmly from the very beginning.

A severe tremor and shock wave had rocked the reactionary ruling classes and their state by then. After an initial vacillation, the reactionary state went into a mad frenzy and let loose its armed might upon the revolutionary forces and the masses. Scores of persons were shot dead in Gorkha, Rukum, Jajarkot and Rolpa; thousands were taken into custody and brutally tortured and the arson, looting and rape of the peasant masses knew no bounds.

At the end of March, the Polit Bureau of the Party met to take stock of the situation and chart the future course of action. It was resolved that the initiation was a tremendous success and that the emphasis now would be to mobilise the masses in favour of the People's War and continue the war in a planned manner. Accordingly, overt and covert programmes were launched throughout the country to mobilise the masses and to build public opinion against government repression and in favour of the People's War. As the reactionary state, predictably, obstructed the open mass activities of the various front organisations, new methods and forms of organisation were devised to carry out open activities. The open denunciation of state terrorism and widespread human rights violations by leading human rights organisations and prominent public figures contributed significantly to take the winds from the sails of the repressive state. Meanwhile, armed squads continued to carry out selected guerrilla actions and propaganda campaigns. Soon the reactionary state was caught up in such a pitiable situation that the Prime Minister himself went on record to call for a dialogue with the revolutionary forces, and the formation of a committee to pursue the dialogue was announced in the Parliament. The Party rightly saw through the conspiracy underlying the whole exercise and exposed it as such through various means.

At the end of the month of June the CC of the Party made a final summation of the successful conclusion of the First Plan and drew out the second Plan.

The Second Plan
Planned Development of Guerrilla Warfare

The basic objective of the Second Plan was to develop guerrilla warfare in a planned manner so as to prepare the ground for converting specific areas into Guerrilla Zones in the near future. To achieve this, the emphasis would be on creating radicalised (or militarised) mass bases in specific areas, and upgrading and expanding the fighting capability of the armed detachments. Accordingly, a broad categorisation to identifiy Principal Zones, Secondary Zones and Propaganda Zones was undertaken and the forces and activities were directed and concentrated in accordance with the envisaged roles of the different Zones. As earlier, a short period of preparation would precede the launching of the Second Plan, and by the very objective and nature of the Plan it would not commence on a fixed date but would follow an approximate time frame.

There was a slight setback in the beginning of the Plan, as the enemy managed to sniff it out, and the important element of 'surprise' had to be partially compromised. However, by October 1996 the execution of the Second Plan had started in earnest, and gradually it unfolded in such a manner and on such a scale that the reactionary camp was again caught by surprise. Military and non-military actions were judiciously blended from the beginning and this, plus the gradual phasing of the major actions over time and space, provided the key to the successful launching and progress of the Second Plan.

Of the major military actions so far, daring guerrilla actions to seize arms have been the most notable ones. Armed guerrilla squads raided police outposts at Lung in Pyuthan on December 14, at Triveni in Dolpa on December 15 (both in the Western Hills), on the state-owned Nepal Bank Ltd. at Duradanda in Lamjung (in the Central Hills) on November 14 and at Bethan in Ramechhap (in the Eastern Hills) on January 3, 1997. Of these, the Bethan raid was the most successful and was rightly hailed as the best example of daring military action and supreme sacrifice so far. Arms were also seized from local tyrants in different districts, like Sallyan, Dolakha etc. Also during this Plan period, the selective elimination of local tyrants, police informers and policemen was undertaken. The elimination of a police sub-inspector responsible for killing Com. Ram Brikshya Yadav in Dhanusa (Eastern Terai), of a village committee chairman responsible for the arrest of Com. Dev Gurung in Gorkha and of several police informers in Rolpa, Rukum and Sindhuli were highly appreciated by the masses and were of immense political significance. Similarly, a large number of sabotage actions, including those against Agricultural Development Bank branches in Kavre and Baglung, against INGOs in Baglung and Myagdi, of the premises of comprador capitalists in Kathmandu and Kapilvastu—and others—were carried out all over the country. The setting fire to the house of the Home Minister in Kathmandu on December 10 sent chills down the spines of the ruling classes and was a favourite topic of media coverage for several days. Armed propaganda actions in the form of marches, corner meetings etc. have been organised regularly all over the country.

Apart from these military and quasi-military forms of actions, other non-military (or political, economic, social and cultural) actions have also been organised in an overt or a covert manner in large numbers for mass mobilisation or propaganda purposes. In this regard, the highly successful Kathmandu Valley Bandh (or general strike) on August 21 and Nepal Bandh on December 12 under the banner of the National Mass Movement Coordination Committee (a specially created front organisation) helped to mobilise the masses in their hundreds of thousands in favour of revolutionary politics. Various village development programmes, people's cooperative schemes etc. have been launched at the local level under the aegis of the UPFN, with a view to preparing the ground for establishing local control in future. Different front organisations have been organising open and legal activities to mobilise different classes and the masses of the people. Particularly in the urban areas, new forms of organisation have sprung up to propagate revolutionary politics and expose the reactionary grouping.

During the Second Plan period, the reactionary grouping had let loose its armed might against the revolutionary forces with greater vengeance. Instances of shooting and outright massacre had multiplied; so too had the instances of police brutalities in the name of combing operations etc. Villages had been set on fire, properties looted, women raped! The Western and Eastern regions had been the worst affected. More than a dozen persons were shot by the police in one village alone (Mirul in Rolpa). Thousands of people, including Com. Dev Gurung and a number of important leaders of the front organisations, had been arrested and kept behind bars in inhuman conditions. Leading national and international human rights organisations had decried the gross violation of human rights by the state.

The Polit Bureau of the Party met in December and made a preliminary evaluation of the implementation of the Second Plan. Progress was found to be quite satisfactory, despite some limitations. The meeting formulated an additional programme to celebrate the first anniversary of the initiation in a grand and fitting manner. The Second Plan is still in the process of implementation.

The Implications, Lessons and Future Perspective

The Implications

The qualitative leap in the social development process of Nepal marked by the historic initiation and continuation of the People's War has had important political implications across the country. The past year of the People's War was accompanied by a faster degeneration of the old reactionary forces and the rising up of new revolutionary forces, thus hastening the process of sociopolitical polarisation.

During this period the crisis of the old state was further aggravated and the contradictions within it sharpened. As the problems of poverty, unemployment, price rise, corruption, foreign domination etc. grew more acute and the state, managed by a weak coalition of extreme rightist forces, increasingly failed even to offer a patchwork solution, a situation of all-round instability, anarchy and total breakdown was created. Particularly, there was a great patriotic surge among the masses against the abject surrender of the mainstream parliamentary parties, including the renegade UML clique, to Indian expansionism and the ratification of the Nepal–India 'Mahakali River Integrated Development Project Treaty' by the puppet parliament. Later on a farcical attempt to bring about a change through the realignment of the government coalition, and the naked horse-trading of the MPs, thoroughly exposed and discredited the parliamentary system as a whole. All this prompted even the BBC radio service to comment that 'the ultimate winners and gainers in the national politics were the Maoists and the People's War'.

The initiation of the People's War has hastened the process of polarisation in the Nepalese communist movement as well. The attitude towards People's War has served as a good acid test to differentiate revolutionaries from opportunists and revisionists. While the renegade UML clique has by and large further degenerated into reaction, and attempted to endear itself to both the king and the Indian expansionists to ride to power within the present dispensation to check the revolutionary process, a significant number of its leaders and cadres at different levels have crossed towards the revolutionary camp. Similarly two-line struggles have developed within the neo-revisionist Mashal and right liquidationist 'Unity Centre' over the question of support to the People's War. A large number of independent intellectuals and others have overtly or covertly extended their support to the People's War. Thus, politically if not organisationally, the CPN (Maoist) has emerged as the rallying centre for all genuine communist revolutionaries in the country.

One year of People's War has had a very positive impact in the development of the three instruments of revolution, i.e. the Party, the Army and the United Front. The Party, long used to legal forms of struggle and organisation, has made a marvellously quick and smooth transition into a fighting underground organisation to lead the armed People's War. Except for isolated instances of revolutionary impetuosity or capitulationist tendency, there have been virtually no differences or inner struggle within the Party with respect to the implementation of the revolutionary line. Rather the People's War has significantly improved the ideological–political level, brought about unprecedented monolithic unity and given birth to a reliable hierarchy of revolutionary leadership from top to the bottom. Similarly on the question of the formation of the Army, the past year has seen a meteoric rise, both quantitatively and qualitatively. Starting from the lowest and simplest formations, speedier upgradations to higher levels and qualities of armed guerrilla formations have been achieved. The emphasis placed on militarisation of the whole Party and development of symbiotic links with the masses in particular has had a very important bearing on the rapid and qualitative development of the armed formations. And lastly, on the question of the development of the revolutionary United Front, the initiation of the People's War has prepared the material ground for building such a Front under the leadership of the proletariat, and new initiatives have been taken in this regard during the past year. Taking into account the historical experiences and specificities of Nepal, the building of the United Front has been attempted simultaneously at two levels. At the local level, where class struggle has developed to a significant height, clandestine United Front committees under the leadership of the Party have been formed to exercise embryonic local political power and sustain the People's War. At the central level, the already existing and high-profile United People's Front, Nepal (established in 1991 as a loose front of different Left and democratic forces and subsequently operating as an open forum of the Party until the initiation of the war) has been reorganised as an embryonic revolutionary United Front by incorporating representatives from different progressive classes, oppressed nationalities and depressed regions, primarily to carry out propaganda and agitation in favour of the New Democratic revolution. Enthusiastic responses to the People's War from different Organisations for the Liberation of Nationalities and from prominent individuals has brightened the prospects of building such a Front.

Lessons and Future Perspectives

The experiences of the first year of the People's War have

provided significant lessons both positive and negative, but mostly positive, which should prove valuable for the development of the war to higher levels in the future.

The pace and nature of development of the People's War in different phases from the initiation as a general 'rebellion', through the continuation with a judicious blending of armed actions and mass mobilisations plus the open propaganda, to the Second Plan of 'Development of Guerrilla Warfare in a Planned Manner' has brought out some of the specificities of Nepal and has highlighted the need to be creative while applying the basic politico-military and organisational tenets of Marxism–Leninism–Maoism. While the basic nature of the war would be protracted and the strategy would be that of encircling the city from the countryside, it seems that in the specific historical and geopolitical case of Nepal the pace of development of the war could be faster and it would have to be waged, though in varying degrees, throughout the country or at least at several places at a time.

Valuable lessons have been learnt about the dialectical relationships between military and non-military forms of actions (though the former would be principal), between offensive and defensive actions, between centralisation and decentralisation of forces and activities, between open and clandestine activities, between People's War and mass movement and so on. The Maoist formulation of 'the decisiveness of people over weapons' in the war has been experienced in practice, and the process of development of the People's War from the simple to the complex and from the lower to the higher levels has been observed on a significant scale. Also, the strategic role and importance of guerrilla warfare in the overall military campaign has been well understood and a number of basic tactics of guerrilla form of warfare have been practiced quite successfully. Some experiences have been gained in discerning and utilising contradictions within the enemy camp.

The importance of constantly practicing the mass line and devising ever newer forms of organisation and struggle to mobilise the masses in favour of the armed struggle has been grasped from the beginning and effectively put into practice. Due attention has been paid to organise propaganda and publications, and to expand international relations in favour of the People's War, though further effort and proficiency in this domain is desirable.

The all important role of the Party in leading the People's War and the crucial significance of the preservation of the leadership, particularly in the initial phase of the war, has been correctly grasped and inculcated among the cadres and the masses.

Apart from these lessons, certain shortcomings and limitations have also been encountered, but quite naturally at that and not of any formidable nature or degree. The arrests of some responsible comrades and the deaths of some others have occurred due to certain avoidable lapses, mostly as a legacy from the legalist work styles of the past. Some erroneous thoughts about the relationship of the People's War to the mass movement, the distinction between a national war and a civil war, the role of weapons in war etc. have cropped up from time to time in some instances, but have been corrected subsequently.

In sum, the achievements of the past year have been significant and the shortcomings relatively negligible. Building upon the foundation of this initial success and firmly grasping the invincible weapon of Marxism–Leninism–Maoism, the People's War in Nepal should scale greater heights in future and move towards an inevitable victory.

TWO MOMENTOUS YEARS OF REVOLUTIONARY TRANSFORMATION

—Com. Prachanda, *General Secretary, CPN (Maoist)*

Introduction

The process of revolutionary transformation of the present semi-feudal and semi-colonial Nepalese society through the People's War has now completed 2 years. Within this period, the Party has successfully implemented two strategic plans of initiation and continuation of People's War and is at present carrying out the Third strategic plan. Today the People's War has established itself as the only revolutionary alternative in Nepal by breaking through innumerable cycles of repression by the reactionaries and opposition of the revisionists. In the process of destruction of the old state power and construction of a new one, the People's

War has today reached the stage of exercising local democratic state power. Creating a challenging influence and debate in every aspect of national life, from the military point of view the People's War has reached the stage of 'development of guerrilla zones'. By practically opening the doors of a new state structure in the form of a revolutionary United Front of masses of different classes, nationalities and regions oppressed for centuries, the People's War is showing in the course of its development the path of its own consolidation, development and victory. In place of the corrupt, immoral, fraudulent and individualistic anarchist culture of the old state, the People's War has developed a new collective and lofty culture based on sacrifice, ideological commitment and self-sacrifice. In totality, amidst the process of intense repression and resistance over the past 2 years the People's War has performed a memorable role in revolutionary transformation.

Until now, 90 of the best sons and daughters of the Nepalese people have sacrificed their lives for the achievement of this historic success. Thousands of revolutionary fighters are braving jail, persecution and horrendous torture perpetrated by the reactionary regime. Hundreds of thousands of people are nurturing this historic process through innumerable instances of sacrifice, devotion and self-sacrifice.

The path of development and victory of revolution has never been straight, easy and normal anywhere. The dialectical law of development is such that everywhere and always the revolution forges ahead by giving birth to intense opposition and counter-revolution and through ascent and descent, ups and downs and losses and gains. The experience of the last 2 years of the People's War in Nepal is also no exception to that rule. Today, on the occasion of the completion of two glorious years and of the start of the third challenging year of the People's War it would be relevant to briefly review past experiences.

Two Years of People's War and the Condition of the Reactionary State

In the initial phase of the historic People's War, the Nepalese reactionary ruling class, just as the reactionary classes of the world, tried to play down the great role of the people. Because of their own class outlook, the reactionaries everywhere and always tend to 'belittle' and 'bully' the forces of the people. On this basis, the Nepalese reactionary ruling classes 'declared' that they would wipe out the people's forces within 1½–2 months and resorted to state terrorism with mass arrest, torture, pillage and genocide. The masses, the Party and the revolutionary fighters continued to resist this by setting historic examples of devotion and sacrifice.

What was the result? The result was consistent with what happens in genuine revolutionary movements all over the world. The result was according to the prognosis of the invincible ideology of Marxism–Leninism–Maoism. The reactionary rulers had thought that they could easily extinguish the fire of People's War by resorting to genocide, repression and terror. But, as has been proved by the law of science and the experience of history, the killing of the masses did not extinguish the fire of revolution, but added fuel to the fire. The negative act of state terrorism was transformed into the positive result of development of the people's revolution. Instead, state terrorism tore off the mask of the so-called democracy, constitution and human rights donned by the reactionary state and helped the masses to recognise the fascist nature of the state. The fascist repressive drive of the whole year did not only reveal the crisis within the ruling state but deepened the crisis even further. After 1 year of repression they realised that there was even bigger wave of people's sympathy and cooperation for the People's War; that thousands are replacing the hundreds, and hundreds of thousands are replacing the thousands! They realised that People's War cannot be easily wished away, that it was fundamentally a new type of war.

Along with aggravating crisis within the rotten state of the reactionary class, this great process of the People's War intensified contradictions within its different political factions. Among the various parliamentary cliques that serve as stooges for different imperialist and expansionist plunderers, the process of manoeuvring for power was intensified. Under the threat of the above crisis, and immediately after the celebration of the first glorious anniversary and commencement of the second year of the People's War, a new coalition within the reactionary state was installed, revealing naked perversion, immorality, hypocrisy and flunkeyism. The new government, with the participation of the renegade UML clique, under the leadership of the Panchayati butchers, was a mockery of even the limited achievements of the

1990 historic People's Movement. It adopted a new strategy of repression combined with diplomatic intrigue against the People's War. Under this strategy in the beginning, it was pronounced that the People's War was a 'political problem' and that it could be solved through 'dialogue'. However, in practice preparations were made for even more intense suppression by constituting different commissions, parti-cularly an intelligence commission. The people grasped the overall conspiracy of the new government when it decided to introduce an anti-terrorist bill and to mobilise the military against the people, even when there was no change in the objective condition.

By reflecting upon the teachings of Marxism–Leninism–Maoism, the universal principle of development of revolutionary war and the specificities of development of People's War in Nepal, the Party had already visualised the possibility of the enemy mobilising its army against the People's War. To resist this, the Party had prepared its entire rank and file, the combatants and even the masses to a certain extent, with a series of political and military strategy and tactics. Postulating the mobilisation of army against the People's War as a sign of success from the military point of view, the Party had already prepared itself for the great prospects and grave challenges.

The great Nepalese masses launched a countrywide protest campaign against the reactionary government's decision to introduce the so-called anti-terrorist bill and to mobilise the army against the People's War, thus rendering it dormant for the time being. Within the short period of 1½ months, the fascist nature of the new government had been exposed. More importantly, for the first time, the broader masses of people had the opportunity to identify and understand the reactionary nature of the revisionist renegade UML clique. Against the wrath of the people, the government was forced to retreat. To a certain extent, the Nepalese people rightly experienced it as a form of victory for their initiative.

Alarmed by this kind of development, the feudalists and the imperialists started looking for another formula for maintaining their state. In this context the much hated process of buying and selling, confining and kidnapping of parliamentarians started, mainly through the intervention and in the interests of the Indian expansionists! The hypocracy of parliamentary democracy was even further exposed. It became once more clear to everyone that the parliament and the parliamentarians were nothing but the sheepfold and sheep respectively of imperialism and feudalism.

Ultimately a coalition government was formed, consisting of the past fascist Panchas and the Congress, infamous as traitors, mass murderers and stooges of Indian expansionism. This new government, most hated and shunned by the people, in its first public declaration made known its policy of containing the People's War. It declared that it would 'wipe-out' the People's War within 3 months. The new government is going ahead with the use of government sponsored goons under the name of People's Defense Committee, killing revolutionary cadres with surprise attacks, making false and vicious propaganda against the leadership of the People's War and mobilising huge commando police and military forces through unannounced, countrywide campaign of repression, arrest and torture, and making armed assaults on peaceful programmes of different mass organisations. In this way nine revolutionary combatants, including Com. Dhanraj Pun, Suk Bahadur Rokka, Prem Bahadur Rokka, and Bhim Prasad Gharti of Rolpa district, a woman Comrade, Kamala Bhatt, of Gorkha district, and Com. Padam Bahadur Rokaya of Jajarkot district have been murdered by this government of Indian stooges as of January 1998.

However, the more important aspect is the new and unprecedented wave of people's support in favour of the People's War that has been gathering momentum as these declarations and activities of the government have been understood. Peasants, women, students and intellectuals in their thousands are forging ahead at greater speed in the process of militant struggle. The military actions of the people's guerrillas have not only expanded widely but also attained newer heights. This has been confirmed by the recent success of higher forms of guerrilla actions accomplished in Rukum and Dhading, among other parts of the country.

Amidst this growth in people's hatred, wrath and resistance, another drama associated with the formation of a new reactionary coalition has begun. Taking the immediate form of a meaningless debate as to whether a mid-term election or a special session of parliament will materialise, a power struggle between the Royal Palace, and the governments of the United States and India is taking place. For their own exclusive purposes of domination and plunder, the Indian expansionists and the American imperialists are now openly penetrating into the reactionary groups including the Royal Palace, Nepali Congress, UML and RPP. It is now as clear as daylight that the various contradictions and conflicts within the different reactionary cliques of the country are in essence the reflection of a power struggle between different imperialist and expansionist camps.

On the basis of the above analysis of the People's War and the reactionary state it becomes clear that the reactionary state is sliding towards its doom and that the great process of the People's War is heading towards victory. The present reactionary state is the root cause of the decline of the country, and the masses and the People's War represent the safeguard and spearhead for the liberation of the country and its people.

Today, the feudalists, the expansionists and the imperialists are conspiring through their Nepalese stooges, the Nepali Congress, UML, the Royal Palace, RPP etc., to let loose more intense repression against the Nepalese people and the People's War. It is not possible to attain easy victory in People's War. For this, wider participation and more unified efforts of the masses is required. There are great possibilities and at the same time serious challenges, too, ahead of the People's War.

Until now, the reactionary class has been adopting a strategy of disinformation politically and of encirclement and suppression militarily against the People's War. To counter this, the People's War is adopting the strategy of 'demystifying rumour' politically and 'breaking encirclement and mounting resistance' militarily.

We should not equate the failure of different reactionary political groups with the failure of the reactionary state as a whole. If needs be, the reactionary state can do away with the present political groups in favour of exercising extreme despotism against the people. It is only by preparing themselves to face the worse to worst state that the revolutionaries can fulfill their historic role. The main point is to dare to win over the fear of death, through adherence to the revolutionary principles of Marxism–Leninism–Maoism and commitment for the sake of the people. However arduous the path may be, the destruction of the reactionary state and the victory of the people is sure.

The Role of the People's War in the Development of the Three Intruments of Revolution
The Party

Comrade Mao declared that the three 'magic instruments' of the New Democratic Revolution are the Party, the revolutionary United Front and the People's Army. Even though the theory may remain same, the specific development of these instruments depends upon the specificities of historical development of different countries. Here there is no question of accomodating mechanist thinking. It is well known that amongst the three 'instruments', the Party is the one that will provide leadership to the other two.

The People's War, which has been forging ahead over the past 2 years, has played a historic role in developing and transforming the Party itself. In a semi-feudal and semi-colonial country like ours and in the era of imperialism and proletarian revolution, the process of protracted nature of the People's War is also a process of revolutionary transformation of the Party. We are realising with our own experience that, in comparison with 10 years of idealist talking and sermonising, the 2 year's experience of the People's War has played an amazing role in the revolutionary transformation of the Party.

The People's War has in fact played several important roles in the transformation and development of the Party, including strengthening the ideological unity of the Party through emotional unity; raising the ideological, political awareness and level of the Party to a newer height through the unfolding of specific characterstics of the Nepalese revolution; leading the whole Party towards the development of a proletarian revolutionary culture of renouncement, devotion and sacrifice essential for giving leadership to the people's revolution; raising consciousness about dialectical relationships and the correct handling of class struggle and inner struggle; qualitatively consolidating and expanding the relationship between the mass, class, Party and the leaders and increasing the role, responsibility and recognition of the Party in the national and international arena.

It was the process of resisting the reactionary state's fascist repression and of facing the venomous attacks of the old and the new revisionists that sped-up the revolutionary transformation process of the Party. The thesis that the development of the Party as the revolutionary representative of the proletarian class takes place through intense process of class struggle and ideological struggle has been proved correct in Nepal.

Based on the synthesis of the experiences, achievements and limits of People's War, the Party today stresses making the lessons of the Great Proletarian Cultural Revolution (GPCR) as its point of departure, so as to prevent the Party from changing its colour and to ensure that it remains revolutionary and grows more mature in the face of repressive, conspiratorial and divisive activities of the reactionaries and the opportunists. For the continuous and positive transformation of the Party as the leader of the revolution, for defending it physically and ideologically and for expanding and strengthening its relationship with the masses, there is no better scientific method in the present-day world than the teachings of the GPCR. The Party is the unity of opposites; as long as the Party exists, the phenomena of unity and struggle between the opposites will also remain. The more developed and complex the class struggle becomes, the more the Party also necessarily becomes more developed and complex. A maximum and continuous practice of democracy both within and outside the Party is then necessary, so as to preserve the revolutionary quality of the Party and to defeat different manifestations of revisionism and opportunism. To ensure the maximum participation of the general cadres and the labouring masses in the internal affairs of the Party is the only guarantee against revisionism. The Party is now able to visualise clearly, on the basis of the experiences of the 2 years of the People's War, that unless one adopts a system of generating innumerable revolutionary successors from among the rank and file cadres and the masses, it will be impossible to defeat feudalism, imperialism and revisionism. The important achievement of today is the realisation of the necessity of developing consciousness and initiatives among the cadres and the masses to 'bombard the headquarter' of opportunism so as to fulfill the role of providing leadership to the great revolution of the people against the exploitation and oppression of feudalism and imperialism and the betrayal and treachery of revisionism.

The Revolutionary United Front

Theoretically it is obvious that the success of democratic revolution is impossible without a broad Revolutionary United Front bringing different anti-feudal and anti-imperialist classes, sections and levels of people together under the leadership of the proletariat. Similarly it is clear that the basis of such a united front will be, and should be, the unity between workers and peasants.

However, the process of initiation and development of the Revolutionary United Front will be different, depending upon the situation. In Nepal, the greatest manifestation of opportunism has been on the question of the United Front. Although our Party had been developing the revolutionary line in theory on this question for a long time, it had not been able to put it into practice, and indeed it proved impossible without initiating the People's War. Today, however, the experiences of the People's War have given us a clear picture of tactical and strategic aspects of the Revolutionary United Front. Looking at the historical specificities of Nepal and the experiences of the 2 years of the People's War, the broad united front of oppressed classes and masses, oppressed nationalities and the people of oppressed regions will be the concrete manifestation of our Revolutionary United Front. This conclusion has an immense historical importance.

This will smash the present 'unity' imposed by the Hindu feudal state power based on class, national and regional inequality and oppression, and open the door for building a new unity based on democratic values. Today the People's War has had maximum impact on the oppressed classes and masses of workers, peasants, women etc. on different oppressed nationalities and untouchable *dalit* castes and on the people of the oppressed regions of the far West and the Terai.

The Party regards it as a historical necessity in Nepal to give maximum importance to the question of struggle against national and regional oppression as an integral part of class struggle and democratic revolution. Until the political, economic, linguistic, religious and cultural rights of different nationalities, usurped in the course of formation of the centralised feudal state of Nepal, are reinstated democratically and they are guaranteed full participation in the new democratic state, and until a great force of national unity based on democracy is created, it will be impossible to smash feudalism and imperialism.

In order to achieve that great national unity there is no other proletarian outlook other than to recognise the right of self-determination, including the right to secede politically, to the oppressed nationalities. Hence our Party has firmly accepted the right of self-determination of different oppressed nationalities, in order to ensure their participation as a necessary part of the Revolutionary United Front. Accordingly the Party has been undertaking initiatives to put into practice national autonomy as the concrete programme for the present.

In the present stage of development of the People's War, wherever there is an exercise of local democracy the Party has been trying to apply practically the concept of United Front in it, while also, at the central level, to build the United Front as an instrument of struggle against class, national and regional oppression. In order to ensure the victory of the Nepalese revolution, the relevance of the Party's concept of United Front should be propagated amongst the workers, peasants, different nationalities, oppressed castes and the people of the oppressed regions and given an organisational form as fast as possible and in the best way possible.

At the ideological level, it is necessary to launch a more vigorous struggle against the rightist revisionists who hanker after opportunistic alliances in the name of United Front.

People's Army

The People's War, which is forging ahead with the Marxist–Leninist–Maoist slogans such as 'The people without army have nothing of their own', 'The main instrument of the state is the army', 'In New Democratic revolution the main form of organisation is the army and the main form of struggle is the war', etc., is playing an important role in the formation of the people's army. Today the unarmed masses are systematically transforming themselves into armed masses, relying on the revolutionary theory that war teaches war. Using the strategy and tactics of total war in the face of an extreme imbalance in the military forces of the enemy as against those of the people, the People's War has been moving forward the process of building the army, with some Nepalese specificities.

By unfolding many concrete laws of dialectical relations between open and secret work, rural and urban activities, legal and illegal struggle, political and military activities, mass actions and mass mobilisation, the People's War has been developing military consciousness and power of the people.

The Role of the People's War in the Development of Revolutionary Mass Organisation and Mass Movement

The historic initiation of the People's War and its successive development has opened a new door to the development of revolutionary mass organisation and revolutionary mass movement. First of all it has created new waves of revolutionary mass organisation and revolutionary mass movement by making a mockery of revisionist cowards who refuse to see the possibilities of developing mass movements and mass organisations beyond the limits of reformism and parliamentarism and who indulge in self-gratification with respect to their monopoly over that area after the initiation of the People's War.

Today, workers, peasants, women, students, teachers, intellectuals, *dalits*, oppressed nationalities and cultural activists are fueling the fire of organisation and struggle as allies of the People's War with new zest and zeal. Waves of revolutionary mass movements and revolutionary mass organisations have been created throughout the country, chiefly in the principal areas of struggle, by challenging both the severe state terrorism perpetrated by the reactionary state and the cowardly twaddle of the revisionist renegades.

Has modern history of Nepal ever seen such amazing initiative as the thousands of labouring women of rural areas of the country who have raised the flag of revolt, defying all kinds of difficulties? Can the revisionist cowards have ever imagined the great surge of women's participation in the form of guerrilla fighters and commanders, defying death consciously and willingly? Amidst the terror unleashed by government-sponsored goons, the police and the army, thousands of labouring women from each and every remote district are today participating in women's meetings and conferences, shaking heaven and earth and fighting for their due rights. These initiatives have proved the new relationship between the People's War and the mass movement. The fact that women are the most inspired group emerging in the last 2 years of People's War itself indicates a definite victory for the Nepalese revolution.

Today a new horizon of peasant's meetings, conferences and struggles has opened up throughout the country. The way poor peasants are taking great initiatives in capturing thousands of quintals of grains, crops and lands and in destroying the forged bond papers of different feudal landlords of the country, and in all these actions and initiatives the People's War has definitely played a great role. Hundreds of thousands of peasants from the main areas of struggle are attempting to exercise New Democratic power by systematically resisting the enemy's mass killing, looting and terrorising. Have such scenes ever before been observed by the Nepalese Communist movement? It is by taking the path of revolutionary land reforms, consciously and in a planned manner in different parts of the country, that the flames of revolutionary peasant struggle will in future reduce to ashes the whole feudal system and relations of production. Similarly, the revolutionary youth and students are marching forward, spreading their organisation and struggles throughout the country, defying killing, repression, arrest and torture by the enemy. The People's War has given new energy for sacrifice and initiative to the students by qualitatively developing among them a sense of responsibility towards their country and their people.

Along with the development of the People's War a new consciousness of the need to fight for their own rights and liberation is spreading amongst many oppressed nationalities of the country such as Magars, Gurungs, Tamangs, Newars, Tharus, Rais, Limbus and Madhises. The People's War has speeded up the process of formation of various national liberation fronts and expansion of nationality organisations. Similarly, today, along with the development of People's War, a wave of organisation and struggle has been created among *dalit* castes at a greater speed and a wider scale than ever before. The *dalits* are today rebelling against the inhuman tyranny perpetrated upon them by the feudal state of high caste Hindus.

The People's War has also made teachers, professors and intellectuals more conscious and active with regards to their responsibilities towards the country and the people. It is a significant change that thousands of intellectuals are coming forward to give moral support to the great historic process of

People's War and are organising against the social evils and degeneration and the tyranny of the reactionary state. Similarly today the People's War is playing an important role in attracting agricultural technicians, doctors, engineers, lawyers, human right activists etc. towards the New Democratic revolution. On the cultural front, too, the People's War is helping revolutionary cultural activists in their initiatives and in their alignment against the present capitalist, revisionist and neo-revisionist hypocrisy. In the fields of literature, art and culture, the People's War is directly helping in the formation of a countrywide new cultural army. The role played by the cultural front in bringing hundreds of thousands of people to participate in the People's War has been unprecedented.

It is not only within the country but also outside the country, particularly in India, that the People's War has created a new spirit and confidence among the expatriate Nepalese to get themselves organised and participate in the People's War in Nepal. The Party's influence and work among hundreds of thousands of expatriate Nepalese have both increased.

From all this, it becomes clear that the People's War does not weaken mass movement and mass organisation but instead strengthens them and opens the door for their qualitative expansion and development. From the experience of the past 2 years it has become clear that it is the revisionists who have been hampering the revolutionary development of mass organisation and mass movement by claiming to support mass movement but actually espousing reformism and parliamentarianism.

The Role of the People's War in Exposing the Revisionists

Nowhere in the world proletarian movement has the success of the revolution been achieved without waging intense ideological struggle against revisionism. One of the essential conditions for the development and victory of the Nepalese revolution is also to liberate the people of Nepal from the fatal poison of revisionism. Comrade Lenin said that it is foolish to try to fight against modern revisionism only with theoretical debate. It is mainly through the development of class struggle, combined with ideological debate, that revisionism can be defeated. It is not so simple and trivial to fight against Nepalese revisionism, which has penetrated deep within the Nepalese Communist movement over the past five decades and poisoned the minds of hundreds of genuine people. As Lenin said, it is mainly the development of class struggle in the form of People's War, along with the ideological debate, that has started burning up Nepalese revisionism (in Engel's words, a 'colossal heap of garbage').

The fact that today the new and the old revisionists have become more terrorised by the 'spectre' of the People's War than even the old reactionaries and are madly attacking it, proves that the revisionist heap of garbage is on fire. Immediately after the initiation of the People's War, the new and the old revisionist pundits abandoned the common morality of class solidarity and showed their true character by putting their faith in the feudalist and imperialist propaganda, doubting and dishonouring the great sacrifice and initiative of the masses. They exposed their true selves by lending their voice to the reactionary state and by trumpeting the charges of 'terrorism' and 'extremism' against the People's War. It is not only the leadership of the UML that has degenerated into reaction, but also the new revisionist ringleaders—who claim themselves to be upholders of 'New Democracy' and 'Mao Thought'—that have been serving the reactionary state against the People's War, thereby revealing their true character. In this context it is worth specifically referring to Mohan Bikram Singh, who is becoming degenerate and marginalised as a result of his own immoral, hypocritical and revisionist character, Singh who exceeded all of the others by announcing that the People's War would be wiped out within 10 months. However, when the old and new revisionists alike saw that the People's War was spreading more and more (against their wishes), they started parroting that there was 'a reactionary hand' promoting the People's War, just as the Nepali Congress Party and the Royal Palace have been accusing each other in the same way. They lamented the fact that the reactionaries have not been able to repress the People's War, which in fact has been effectively resisting the reactionary massacre and state terror.

When the People's War entered its second year, it was transformed into the life process of hundreds of thousands of people, it started challenging the ruling reactionary state all the more and it also encouraged genuine cadres from the revisionist camp to join and support the People's War, overtly or covertly. Seeing this, the old revisionists openly encouraged the reactionary state to suppress the People's War. The new revisionist ringleaders, in order to ensure their own political survival, played nakedly into the reactionaries' hands. They encouraged the reactionaries against the People's War by making mountains out of molehills from insignificant events at local level.

The People's War has now entered its third year, after completing 2 years. It has established itself as the only revolutionary alternative in the country. For the reactionary state today, the People's War has become the greatest obstacle. It sounds ironic that along with the imperialists, expansionists, Nepali Congress, Rastriya Prajatantra Party and United Marxist–Leninist group, even the leaders of Mashal and Unity Centre should be branding the People's War as 'terrorism'. But this is a fact. Nowhere and never have those self-declared 'revolutionary' elements, which have now entirely embraced reformism and parliamentarianism ideologically and politically, ever helped the revolutionary movement. Even after the success of people's revolution in the future, such kind of people will continue to oppose it. It is well known that the Bolsheviks in Russia and the Maoists in China were attacked, even after the revolution, by revisionists who still called themselves communists.

Today the People's War is scaling ever-greater heights while exposing all the rubbish of the new and the old revisionists. So long as the revolutionaries are guided by Marxism–Leninism–Maoism and so long as they remain loyal to the Nepalese people and march forward to liberate the country and the people, the venomous attacks of the revisionists will not be able to stop the development of the People's War. Rather, with the passage of time, the revisionists will get thoroughly exposed. The revolution will triumph. The last 2 years of the history of the People's War has sufficiently proved this.

The People's War and the Expansion and Consolidation of International Relations

Before the historic initiation of the People's War, the Party pledged that the 'Nepalese revolution is an integral part of world proletarian revolution and this will serve the world revolution'. Today, with 2 years of experience this pledge has been proved absolutely correct. It is already known to all that our Party is a participating member of RIM, an organisation striving to build a 'New International'. Within this period our relationship with the RIM Committee and all other participating fraternal parties of RIM has become qualitatively more vital and stronger. The initiation of the People's War and its successive development has, on the one hand, given new inspiration to the participating parties of the RIM, and on the other, the Nepalese People's War has received moral support from all these parties. In the course of our development, the international responsibility of our Party and the revolutionary Nepalese people have increased qualitatively.

Today our experience and influence is not only spreading among the participating members of the RIM but also among those revolutionary Marxist parties and organisations who are outside the RIM. Similarly relations with revolutionary organisations waging national liberation struggles against imperialism and expansionism are also expanding along with the development of the People's War in Nepal. The way the Nepalese People's War, which is of protracted nature, has expanded its international relations and its influence, has itself become a specific manifestation of the Nepalese revolution. It is a matter of pride that the Nepalese People's War is getting warm support, love and inspiration from millions of revolutionary masses all over the world within such a short period.

Just as the Nepalese People's War is developing its relations with international revolutionaries, so too at the same time the imperialists, expansionists and various reactionaries are hatching conspiracies and intrigues against it. In this regard, the comments of the ruling classes of India and the American imperialists, the world gendarmes, are particularly worth noting. Many conspiratorial and repressive moves by these powers against the Nepalese People's War and the Party leading it have recently come to the surface. These elements are mainly instigating their stooges, the ruling class and various reactionary groups of Nepal, to suppress the People's War. The Nepalese People's War has proved to be a slap in the face of the world imperialist system, which is currently undergoing new economic and political crises. It is now becoming clear that the Nepalese People's War will have a historic role in contributing to a new wave of world revolution in the near future.

The continuous development of the Nepalese People's War has also started to expose not only the weaknesses of Nepalese revisionism but also those of world revisionism. The People's War has proved a major blow to the old and the new revisionists who have been swimming in the dirty pools of reformism and parliamentarianism and have betrayed the people's revolutionary movement all over the world. In this regard, the attacks of the CPI-M, the CPI of India and other revisionist renegades on the Maoist People's War in Nepal are particularly noteworthy.

Today in many other countries of the world final preparations for launching a Maoist People's War are taking place. It is a matter of pleasure for all Nepalese revolutionaries to know that the experiences of the initiation and continuation of the People's War in Nepal are directly helping in these preparations. Today requests have been received from revolutionary workers of different parts of the world to allow them to come to the war front in Nepal and to participate in order both to safeguard and develop the Nepalese People's War and also to learn practical lessons from it. These are the highest manifestations of the international impact of the 2 years of development of the People's War.

In this way, on the one hand, the Nepalese People's War has become a new challenge to international imperialism and revisionism, and on the other, a new source of inspiration for communist revolutionaries and the mass of the people. This situation has definitely placed more international responsibility on the shoulders of the Nepal Communist Party (Maoist), the revolutionary fighters and the general masses of Nepal. The leading districts, the great martyrs and all the revolutionary fighters of the People's War in Nepal have now been transformed into common assets for communist revolutionaries all over the world. It is this sense of seriousness and responsibility that has inspired the Nepalese revolutionaries to develop the People's War to greater heights and to set new examples of devotion and sacrifice.

Conclusion

The great process of the People's War is marching forward, giving birth to powerful forces of revolutionary transformation in all areas of Nepalese society. Its enemies and opportunists within and outside the country are conniving with each other to repress and thwart this great process of revolutionary transformation. The revolutionary communists and the masses of the people within and outside the country are becoming increasingly organised on a large scale to safeguard and develop this great process. Thus, on the one hand, the 2 years of People's War have opened the doors of historic possibilities, while on the other, a situation of bigger challenges and threats from enemies and opportunists has also been created.

The revolution is not following the subjective wishes of anyone, but rather the dialectical path of its own development. The 2 years of the People's War have inspired the Party to fulfill its historic responsibility of liberating the people with greater firmness, devotion and responsibility, while remaining committed to the invincible principles of Marxism–Leninism–Maoism. Let us unite in the service of and for the liberation of the great Nepalese people! However difficult and challenging the path may be, the people's victory is certain!

EXPERIENCES OF THE PEOPLE'S WAR AND SOME IMPORTANT QUESTIONS*

Although the main ideological political and military line has been proved correct, the process of the People's War over the past 2½ years has given rise to several important new questions. It is necessary to answer them on the basis of the experiences of the People's War. In this regard, it is particularly important to pay serious attention and to be clear on the following points:

1. First of all, the development of the People's War requires even more theoretical clarity regarding guerrilla zone and base area. We should be clear that the concept of 'base area' is a strategic concept within the protracted People's War. The question of base areas is indissolubly linked with the protracted People's War. Hence this is a theoretical question. Without a base area, there cannot be any protracted People's War surrounding the city by the

---

* Document of the Fourth Expanded Meeting of the CPN (Maoist).

countryside. However 'guerrilla zone' is not related to any strategic or theoretical question of the protracted People's War. Actually the guerrilla zone is a tactical and transitional issue, that arises in the process of building a base area. If guerrilla zones are understood to be as strategically important as 'base area' then it can lead to a serious danger of reformism in the military field.

In the International Communist Movement there has been a wrong tendency to assume that 'guerrilla zone' is a strategic and theoretical concept, instead of recognising it as a tactical and transitional concept. This kind of tendency represents reformism in the military field. If guerrilla zone is given a protracted form in the name of tactics, then it will become a strategy. This kind of thinking weakens the role of conscious effort required in building base areas and ignores the necessity of developing guerrilla warfare into mobile and regular positional warfare. In fact such thinking regards guerrilla warfare as 'roving rebel guerrilla-ism' and denies the importance of a qualitative leap in the war. That is why this tendency is reformist thinking in the military field. We must concentrate our attention on preparing base areas while fighting against such a reformist tendency. It is clear that the process of developing guerrilla zones is essentially the process of building a base area. Even though theoretically it was clear, however, such expressions in the past plans as 'Preparation of base for guerrilla zone', 'Concentrating all efforts to develop guerrilla zone', 'Establishing guerrilla zone" have given the impression of understanding the question of guerrilla zone in a strategic sense. It is important to be clear that such expressions were made in the context of immediate tactics and practice. 'Base area' is the only principal strategic question in the protracted People's War.

It would also be a serious mistake to assume that base areas will be or should be stable and permanent at once. Comrade Mao explained the different stages of development of base areas in terms of temporary, stable and relatively stable base areas. It is not impossible for a base area, even once established, to revert to a guerrilla zone or even to enemy territory, due to intense suppression by the enemy. In China, many old base areas were lost, then recovered and new bases formed, and it was by going through this long process that the People's War was victorious.

Along with this, it should be made clear that the base area need not or even should not be built through only one technique, wherever in the world the People's War takes place. Even in China, there were different methods of establishing base areas—by capturing base areas at once by the regular Red Army, by the development of guerrilla squads among the masses and by inciting rebellion on the part of the enemy's army units. The question of the technique to be applied in a particular place to establish base areas will depend upon the situation. In general, Comrade Mao gave emphasis to having a strong mass base, a strong Party, appropriate terrain for military actions and a people's army for establishing base areas. Even if this is theoretically correct, however, it should not be copied mechanically. Actually, one of the key questions in differentiating the guerrilla zone and the base area is the question relating to the exercise of people's political power. In reality, people's political power cannot be maintained in a guerrilla zone. In such places there is a struggle for new political power by the guerrillas. By contrast, people's political power will be established in the base area and the enemy would require the deployment of a major force to capture it. From the above analysis one can draw the correct conclusions about guerrilla zones and base areas.

Now it is necessary to discuss whether or not we have arrived at an agenda regarding the question of building base areas, on the experience of 2½ years of the People's War in Nepal and what are the concrete conditions regarding the building of base areas in Nepal. It has already been made clear in the previous analysis of the People's War that different levels of development of embryonic people's power have been seen in areas under the three regional commands. Amongst them, there is the extensive exercise of democratic people's power now taking place in the main area of the Western region. Such a situation has developed because of the strong mass base, strong Party, favourable terrain, mass movement throughout the region and elimination of social class enemies by the guerrilla squads, combined with the containment and even to a certain extent the defeat of the local military strength of the reactionary state. In keeping with the realities of uneven development, significant areas of the Central and Eastern regions are also developing systematically in the same direction. It is clear, therefore, that the question of building base areas in Nepal has been brought onto the agenda after observing the practical situation created by the development of the People's War. However, it is not enough to think only this far.

Today, politically, the People's War has become established as a parallel force against the reactionary state; however, militarily it is very weak. The present People's War, which is forging ahead by giving birth to three types of areas, i.e., main, secondary and propaganda zones, has taken a countrywide form. Taking advantage of the deep instability gripping the present reactionary state, the main zone and the overall People's War have been able to gain substantial support from the different forms of mass movement and mass mobilisation. Today, the enemy is pursuing suppression campaigns throughout the country, while concentrating in the main zones to nip in the bud this newly formed political power. In future, if there is repression on a larger scale than at present, is there any possibility of building or maintaining base areas in Nepal or not? If there is, then under what conditions is this possible? We should be clear in this regard: not only in the general theoretical sense but also through the practical experience of the People's War it has been shown that it is possible to have base areas in different parts of the country. However, this is possible only after the following conditions in the context of Nepal have been fulfilled:

(a) The Party should continuously provide centralised leadership based on a correct policy in a bold manner.
(b) Guerrilla activities must be pursued uninterrupted throughout the country.

(c) Guerrilla zone must be developed around the main zone.
(d) The process of building a strong people's army must be intensified.
(e) Various forms of mass movement must be continuously developed at central and local level.
(f) Constant efforts must be made to orient public opinion in favour of the People's War, in India as well as around the world.

It is in the process of fulfilling the above principal conditions that base areas in Nepal can take birth, develop and be sustained. Henceforth, the Party must pay attention and concentrate its forces in this direction.

2. Based on above analysis related to base areas and guerrilla zones, it is necessary to redefine the substages of development of the People's War as undertaken by our Party's Third Extended Meeting. These four substages, including final preparation, initiation and continuation, guerrilla zone and base area, have already been discussed. From the point of view of theory and policy there is no mistake in the categorisation of these substages. However, there is scope for mistakenly concluding—in the light of development and experiences of the People's War—that the placing of guerrilla zone and base area in the same level of substages may mean that both zones have equal importance in terms of strategy and theory. This we have clarified above. The four substages mentioned then were developed with the aim of solving the practical problem of our development; hence it would be wrong to understand this mechanically. Today, the development of the People's War has demonstrated that it has reached the stage of building base areas. The ensuing plan will be mainly the plan of building base areas. From the point of view of strategic stages, this plan will also fall within the plan of strategic defence. We should be very clear about this.

This means we are entering the fourth substage of 'base area' and making a plan for it, after passing through 'initiation' and passing through the second and third substages, of 'continuation of initiation' and 'guerrilla zone" respectively. While the last Central Committee meeting had designated the Third Plan as 'the transitional Plan of entering into the third substage from the second substage', it was in fact the Plan of transition from the third to the fourth substage. The reason why we were not able to define it this way last time was because we lacked clarity in understanding 'guerrilla zone' and 'base area'.

This analysis will help in qualitatively developing the Party, the united front and the army, keeping in view the preparation of base areas. This does not mean that there is no need for guerrilla zones. The conversion of the main zone into a base area cannot take place without converting secondary zones into guerrilla zones and without developing guerrilla actions and the people's movement throughout the country in a planned way. The fact is that only by putting the preparation for building base areas to the front can we take the necessary initiatives to raise the People's War to a new height. It can then give new impetus to the process of revolutionary transformation in all spheres, encompassing ideology, organisation and struggle. This new process of building base areas is going to be a long process, involving many plans and campaigns.

3. It has become clear that our main problem today is the problem of development of people's military capability. The experience of the People's War and the current campaign of reactionary military operations has repeatedly shown that people without military power will retain nothing for themselves. Now, it has become all the more clear that it is only on the basis of military power that the initiative of the people can be increased in future. That is why it has become necessary for the Party to concentrate its principal attention on the question of building the army.

In this regard the Party should first of all pay attention to the structure of military organisation. In the past there have been attempts to build military organisation in the form of guerrilla squads, local defense squads and volunteer squads. Based on the new demands of development it has now become imperative to have qualitative improvement in this structure. For this it has become necessary to develop people's military power in the form of three categories: main force, secondary force and basic force. The main force will be built of regular guerrillas and that force will be directly under the Regional Bureau. For the time being this force should be maintained at the platoon level, while keeping the aim of raising it to company level under all the three regional commands. It should be mandatory to have a member of the Regional Bureau as commissar of these platoons. For now, depending upon the mass base, technical capability, geographic area and favourable condition, one more platoon can be made.

The secondary force should be understood as regular guerrilla squads, currently functioning under the District Party or to be developed accordingly. This kind of secondary force organisation will also gradually develop through platoon formation and beyond. Depending upon the level of development of the particular districts, platoon formation may take place in a flexible manner. Even then they will remain as a supporting force under the leadership of the District Party.

When we say basic force we mean a people's militia, organised so far in the form of local defense squads. From now on these squads shall be developed as a people's militia. The main force should be given priority in terms of weapons training and technology so as to make it sufficiently powerful. Every effort should be made so that the main force assists the secondary and basic forces. While, for the time being, preference will be given to guerrilla types of actions, the main force will also be practicing mobile warfare. The main zone would be the main area of action for the main force, as it is directly related to the requirements of building base areas. But, depending on the needs of the situation, this force could be used in any action in any part of the region. We should be clear that building up such a force will play a qualitative role in actions against the enemy, in ending localism and guerrillaism, and building the people's army. Hence all regions, districts and the overall Party should take a special initiative and help in developing this kind of main force.

Among the three forms of forces mentioned above, the main and secondary forces will constitute part of regular army, whereas the basic force will be a people's militia connected with daily production work. Depending upon the state of the war and its requirements, different type of coordination between all the three forces will be maintained. Such coordination will be developed appropriately for any work like propaganda, organisation, production, attack, defense and so on. Volunteer squads can be constituted for mass actions, according to requirements. However, they are not going to be any permanent type of military formation; hence it is not necessary to talk about them in terms of permanent formations.

In propaganda zones, particularly within the Kathmandu Valley Region, one or more guerrilla squads must be formed. Right now, there will not be any formation at the level of platoon. The existing squads active in those zones will constitute the main force there. Similarly the squads working under the leadership of the District Party would be the secondary force and the defence squads will be the basic force. Even among emigrants, military formations should be built, depending upon the specific situation, and a mechanism should be developed so that they can be sent for military actions inside the country.

The above conceptualisation, relating to main force, secondary force and basic force, represents an important leap in the development of the military strength. Only by successfully implementing it ideologically and strategically will we be able to guarantee the defense and development of the People's War.

4. It has been shown above that building and operationalising democratic people's power is another important question brought about by the experience of 2½ years of People's War. Right now, various embryonic forms of local people's power at various level of development are seen to be sprouting in different localities under all the three regional commands. The enemy is exercising extreme fascism to eliminate these embryos of the new state.

Looking at the overall situation, two important questions have been raised for the Party, regarding people's power and the revolutionary united front. The first question is related to the defence and consolidation of local people's power and the second question is how to express, in terms of political power and the united front, the forces of the People's War facing directly the central power of the enemy in the specific situation of Nepal. If seen in depth, it is clear that in Nepal these two questions are closely interrelated. If centrally one is not able to face the enemy's state by taking appropriate measures of propaganda, organisation and struggle in a relentless manner then it will be nearly impossible to maintain local people's power and similarly, without the foundation of local people's power the central initiative cannot take a revolutionary course. These things have been made clear by our recent experiences.

For defending and consolidating local people's power it is important to give serious considerations to the following points:

First Point: Without defeating enemy's military offensive through the development of appropriately powerful military force, neither local people's power can be protected nor can it be consolidated. Hence, the first condition for defending local people's power and its consolidation is the development of people's military power.

Second Point: It is important to make sure that different classes, nationalities and sections of people, which are antifeudal and anti-imperialist, should be encouraged to participate in the new state power through a democratic process. In this regard, everybody should not be coerced to be Maoists. Instead, a serious and responsible initiative should be undertaken to involve various political and social organisations, which are against feudal, bureaucratic and comprador bourgeoisie classes in the new state.

Third Point: The process of building a new state should be based on a fully democratic system and it should be made clear that, if needs be, the people should have right to call back their elected representatives. Here the main point to be noted is the importance of guaranteeing people's participation in the process of total control, decisionmaking and running of the new state.

Fourth Point: An attempt should be made to develop the structure of local people's power at the village, area and entire base area level, and while doing so, the principle of democratic centralism should be followed.

Fifth Point: In areas where people's power is being exercised or is going to be exercised, the entire masses must be organised in one form or another. It is important to take seriously the saying that the organised mass is the only 'iron fort'.

Sixth Point: New state power should make efforts to fulfill people's daily economic, social and cultural needs and to bring continuous improvement in them and so on.

Because of the economic, political and geographical specificity of Nepal it is not possible to retain such local people's power and base areas, to coordinate them, to resist against the enemy's central state and to mobilise the support of people all over the country, without a central level initiative. If centrally, one is unable to resist the reactionary state by developing people's broad revolutionary united front and if one does not play a direct role in coordinating and assisting the local people's power, then there is a clear danger of the local people's power being reduced into a weak and helpless sham.

Today the People's War is no longer a local issue. For both the people and the enemy the People's War has become a central subject. The enemy is making all efforts from the central level to eliminate the People's War. Not only this, the imperialists and expansionists are also openly coming forward to eliminate it, as Nepal's People's War plays not only a national but also an international role. Along with this, the revolutionary masses at international level are also coming forward to support the People's War. The enemy has put forward the slogan of the so-called national consensus in order to defend its reactionary state against the People's War. It has resorted to a strategy of eliminating the People's War through vicious suppression and to isolate it by declaring the People's War as the enemy of democratic elections and by making all the reactionary, reformist and opportunist political groups participate in the coming parliamentary election. Judging from all these conditions it becomes clear why the Party has to take concrete initiations centrally against the enemy's similar strategies.

From this point of view special efforts should be made to

organise the central revolutionary united front in the form of the Central Organising Committee of the People's Republic of Nepal and in the same capacity to organise and mobilise for agitation various left, progressive, patriotic and democratic forces of the country against the conspiracy of the reactionary state. Such a central formation will principally work as a means of struggle for the time being and will work secondarily as a means of power. It will primarily emphasise coordinating, refining, defending and developing local people's power. It will represent the unity of antifeudal and anti-imperialist masses of the people against the conspiracy of national consensus by the reactionary state. It will propagate the question of 'new state or old state?' in the form of a national debate and it will take the initiative constantly to bring forward the revolutionary mass movements as an integral part of the People's War. At the same time it will put forward the economic, political and cultural policies of the new state in concrete form while exposing the anti-national and anti-democratic character of the reactionary state.

5. With this clarity on the main questions mentioned above, a new chain of new improvements and actions in all aspects of organisation including the Party, the Front, the army, the mass front, the forum and departments will be developed. It will be discussed concretely in the future Plan.

(Extract from the resolution adopted at the Fourth Expanded Meeting of the Central Committee of the Party, in August 1998.)

The building up of an armed force is the key to establishing a base area: if there is no armed force or if the armed force is weak, nothing can be done. This constitutes the first condition. The second indispensable condition for establishing a base area is that the armed forces should be used in co-ordination with the people to defeat the enemy. The third indispensable condition for establishing a base is the use of all our strength, including our armed forces, to arouse the masses for struggle against Japan.

—Mao Tse Tung (*"Problems of Strategy in Guerrilla War against Japan"*)

Whether originating in the desire for an easy life or in overestimating of the enemy's strength, conservatism can only bring losses on the War of Resistance and is harmful to guerrilla warfare and to base areas themselves.

—*Mao Tse Tung ("Problems of Strategy in Guerrilla War against Japan")*

The longer the scale of the guerrilla fighting the more important the position of the base areas, and the greater the threat to the enemy's strategic centres and vital communication lines, the fiercer will be the enemy's attacks. Therefore, the fiercer the enemy's attacks on a guerrilla area, the greater the indication that the guerrilla warfare there is successful and is being effectively coordinated with the regular fighting.

—*Mao Tse Tung ("Problems of Strategy in Guerrilla War against Japan")*

History knows many peasant wars of the 'roving rebel' type, but none of them ever succeeded.

—*Mao Tse Tung ("Problems of Strategy in Guerrilla War against Japan")*

THE THIRD TURBULENT YEAR OF THE PEOPLE'S WAR

—*Com. Prachanda*

Background

With a new Plan for the new stage of 'Advancing in the Direction of Creating Base Areas', the historic process of the Nepalese People's War has entered into the challenging fourth year, after passing a turbulent third year. The third year of People's War has been qualitatively different in character from the previous 2 years, from the point of view of its intensity, vigorousness and profusion of experiences. The Nepalese People's War has completed 3 years 'begetting a fierce and forceful counterrevolution and immense opposition and providing strong resistance to it', in the process of 'maturing the rebellious party', as Karl Marx stated. This historic advancement of the People's War is line with what Lenin said: it is 'creating an abnormal and complex situation by itself in the process of its own development'. It is advancing incessantly, as Mao said, 'with its own dialectical rules of dynamism of the People's War and with ups and down, losses and achievements and ebbs and flows'.

Setting aside the repression and conspiracy of reactionaries and revisionists, respectively, the People's War in Nepal has entered into fourth year with great success, which is in essence a tribute to the 500 martyrs of the revolution, the entire people's militia and the general Nepalese masses, to the communist revolutionaries and working classes of the world including the RIM and above all to Marxism–Leninism–Maoism and the great Communist Party of Nepal (Maoist) guided by it. On this historic occasion, an attempt is made to present a general review based on the experiences of the third year.

Wave of People's Support and Emergence of Local People's Power

The People's War entered into a third year with the initiation of Third Plan's second campaign along with great success achieved in various activities, such as capturing thousands of quintals of grains from feudals and landlords to distribute among poor peasants, incidents of seizing land, mass mobilisation and events of organisational expansion. Millions of people observed the second anniversary of the People's War with great enthusiasm as a celebration of real people's democracy, with various military and non-military programmes, on the historic occasion of the People's War entering into the third year. Against this enthusiastic background, the second campaign of the Third Plan—which gave priority to military action—moved ahead. Actions on different scales advanced nationwide, particularly concentrating intensified attacks on the armed forces of the enemy by means of raids and ambushes in the principal areas of struggle.

Along with the success of military actions and mass mobilisation, preliminary features of new people's power appeared openly in the proposed guerrilla zones, especially in the hills of Western Nepal. Practice of people's power started openly after the overpowering of the enemy's local agents and police force by the people's guerrillas in the areas where a political vacuum was created because of mass boycotting of reactionary local elections. People's cooperatives, collective labour and farming, construction of rural tracks, bridges, memorials for martyrs, registration, purchase and sale of land, people's security, people's culture, people's court and running of schools on so on became preliminary daily exercises of new people's power. People in those areas felt themselves, for the first time, the masters of their own destiny. In the first 4 months of the third year, the main areas of Western Nepal became a de-facto liberated area. With some differences in degree, many areas in Eastern and Central hills also exercised preliminary people's power.

During this time an extraordinary wave of people's support and organisational expansion developed in favour of the People's War, from the capital city to all over the country. The reactionaries and revisionists who were claiming the People's War to be 'terrorism and devoid of people's support' were dumbfounded to see the open endorsement of the people of the call for a 'Nepal Bandh' made by the underground Front Committee for the first time. It was clear from the nationwide support of the people during the 'Nepal Bandh' that the People's War is indeed the only revolutionary alternative for Nepalese society and that it has the support of the masses.

The valour and skill in war shown by people's guerrillas in numerous actions during this period demonstrated clearly the development of the military strength of the people. From the events of secondary districts in Western Nepal, where the masses by themselves confronted the enemy police force, seizing arms, to the guerrilla activities of Tanahu Kalikatar that symbolised the pinnacle of Third Plan, have proved this fact.

Thus the first 4 months of the third year become memorable, revealing enormous mass support in favour of the People's War and marking the exercise of the new people's power in different parts of the country, especially in the hills of Western Nepal. No hypocritical propaganda by the enemies and opportunists can erase this historic achievement from the heart of the Nepalese people.

Barbaric Feature of Enemy's Strategy

It is a well-known truth that the anti-people and antinational rulers of the old regime have tried to 'nip' the People's War 'in the bud', by resorting to genocide and state terrorism from the day of the historic initiation or launch of the War. The revisionist cliques, who were engaged in a tug-of-war for power and were effectively for sale, completely submerging themselves in corruption, were also in competition in the conspiracy against the great People's War. After the experience of 1½ years they saw that People's War had flourished among the mass of the people and grew stronger day by day.

In this context, the imperialists and (mainly) the fanatical Hindu ruling clique of Indian expansionism increased pressure on their lackey Nepali parliamentarist clique to suppress the People's War by all means. It is worth noting the vicious and conspiratorial series of propaganda made against the People's War through public statements by the American Embassy in Kathmandu and the linking of the Nepalese People's War with Pakistan by the Indian media. The fact that the single flame of the Maoist People's War can terrify imperialists and expansionists proves how hollow, weak and corrupt is the world system they claim to be so monumental. It is in fact a consequence of the fact that the imperialist world system is characterised by political and cultural degeneration and ensnared in severe economic crisis. This further confirms the analysis of revolutionary communists that the world revolution is on the horizon.

It is also a well-known fact that, against this background, the Nepali ruling class hatched a conspiracy to mobilise the army and introduce a so-called anti-terrorist bill in parliament against the Nepali people and the People's War. But the Nepali people immediately branded the bill itself as terrorist and resorted to a nationwide struggle against it. In the capital itself, people's pressure mounted against the terrorist bill and the mobilisation of the army. The reactionary ruling class was forced to suspend the idea for the time being in the face of people's wrath. People took this episode as their victory and as defeat for the national traitors and the mass murderers. The wave of mass support for the People's War and the emergence of the embryo of new people's power that ensued has been described above.

Experience from class struggle and Marxism–Leninism–Maoism has taught us that when the reactionary ruling classes foresee imminent danger to their rule, they present themselves against the masses quite differently. This different method of reactionaries is nothing other than to scrap and throw into dustbin the constitution rules, laws, democracy, human rights and values and institutions previously trumpeted aloud by them, and to swim in the pool of blood of the people. Under the Third Plan, our great Party had already alerted the entire Party, the fighters and the people against this lunacy of the reactionary classes.

At last, everything that Marxism–Leninism–Maoism had taught us, and that the Party had warned of, came to pass. To trample the people and the People's War underfoot, Girija Prasad Koirala, of the fascist Nepali Congress Party discredited for mass murder and treason, was placed on the Prime Minister's chair under the direct instructions of the Indian expansionists. In the post of Inspector General of Police, Achyut Krishna Kharel, a criminal and notorious mass murderer of the people's popular movement of 1990, was appointed. A so-called special security committee representing the army, the police and the government was constituted in an underground conspiratorial way. For them neither a Bill nor any formal decision was required, and neither parliamentary values nor human rights were respected. This started the barbaric rule of the reactionary class, from the second week of the fourth month of the third year.

Under the so-called Kilo Sierra Two operation, a fascist campaign to massacre all, burn down everything and plunder everything was launched. A rampage of murderers, called 'commandos', equipped with most modern means of communications, arms and helicopters, was unleashed. Especially in the districts most influenced by the People's War, the bodies of the best sons and daughters of people 'disappeared' after mass murder. There was killing en masse—dozens in one place, indiscriminate shooting at unarmed teachers, students and guardians observing Guardian's Day, mass murder of groups taking part in marriage processions, slaughter of popular leaders of the people after their seizure from their homes and plunder of villages after their encirclement. Barbarous crimes of mass rape and murder took place, the peaceful and lawful activities of Maoist supporters, students, women workers, peasants and oppressed nationalities were nakedly attacked, nationwide as well as in the capital. Undeclared war was waged on class organisations and attacks were carried out on newspapers supporting the Maoists. People were killed in false 'encounters'—while sleeping at home, eating meals or simply walking along the street. Supporters of the People's War were compelled to sign papers for their own arrest and surrender forcibly at gunpoint, and the homes of peasants were burned. False propaganda and a blackout on the activities of People's War by the media. All of these became daily occurrences under the reactionary rule of the fascists, from the last week of May 1998 onwards.

Within last 8 months of the third year, the fascist Girija Koirala clique of reactionary regime murdered 500 party members, fighters and supporters; hundreds of women were victims of rape; thousands of poor peasants had their households plundered; and thousands had been jailed and subjected to inhuman torture. Along with this vicious repression, the reactionary ruling clique intensified such activities as hatching a conspiracy for internal sabotage and misleading people about the Party and the central leadership spearheading the People's War. For these immoral and heinous acts, the Nepali ruling clique received the specific support and services of the U.S. imperialists and Indian expansionists to train its murderer gangs and also the assistance of Fujimori, the murderer of the Peruvian people. Months-long training programmes have been conducted, on genocide, repression and conspiracy against the people and the People's War both in Lima in Peru and in Kathmandu in Nepal.

It is clear that the present parliamentary fascist cliques of Nepal, like reactionary ruling cliques all over the world, has adopted the strategy of sowing illusion and creating division, of encirclement and annihilation, under the common policy of 'burn everything and kill everyone'. Over the last 8 months they have been adopting the same strategy against the Nepali people. The rhetoric of 'democracy', 'parliamentary norms', and 'human rights' has been proved to be entirely a farce in the eyes of the people.

Revisionism: The other side of Reactionary Coin

Since the historic initiation of the People's War, the old revisionist UML clique has been directly helping the reactionary regime, while the new revisionists have been doing so indirectly. The strategy of the revisionists has been to encourage the traitorous and genocidal ruling clique to indulge in greater suppression and barbarity by referring to the great revolutionary initiative of the people as 'extremist' and 'terrorist', suggesting that it is a 'People's War without people', a 'romance of petty bourgeois' and that 'armed struggle was a mistake' etc. The scientific truth of the lessons of Marxism–Leninism–Maoism, that in the age of imperialism and proletarian revolution no revolutionary movement against reactionary forces can occur without also becoming involved in a struggle against revisionism, has been experienced at first hand by the Nepali people in the realities of the last 3 years.

In this respect, the UML clique pursuing the reactionary strategy of 'multiparty democracy' and flouting the lofty words of Marxism–Leninism openly as a trademark for parliamentary elections, has emerged as the most reactionary of revisionists. This is the same revisionist traitorous UML clique that betrayed the nation with the Mahakali Treaty, acting as a naked lackey of Indian expansionism for the crumbs of reactionary power; this is also the same clique that prepared the bill against so-called terrorism and extended its full support to the mobilisation of the army, in its capacity of junior partner of the government last year. Thanks to the great Nepali people, whose resistance not only sabotaged the conspiracy of the UML clique but also allowed millions of people the opportunity to understand forever its fascist character, the traitor UML clique eventually split into two, amidst the whirlpool of people's wrath. In essence, this was a victory of the Nepalese people against revisionism.

It was, however, the same traitor UML clique that, under the direct instruction of Indian expansionism, extended support to the parliamentary fascist Girija clique (which was in a minority in the parliament) enabling it to form a government and commit crimes against the people. The UML clique is the one that saved the tottering government of the fascist Girija clique and participated in the government to become directly involved in national betrayal and genocide. People are also witness to the fact that the revisionist ML clique, which split on the issue of UML's national betrayal by chanting nationalist slogans, is no different in essence, ideologically or practically. People do not expect those raising slogans against national betrayal and state terrorism to plunge into the dirty pool of parliamentarianism. But as the ML clique is committed to pursuing the same reactionary strategy of 'multiparty democracy' and chanting the dirty songs of parliamentarianism, its slogan of nationalism is revealed as a phony slogan.

Besides the above revisionists, who have degenerated into the ranks of reactionaries, the activities of those revisionists who claim themselves to be protagonist of 'Mao Thought' and of the 'New Democratic Revolution', but spit venom against People's War and revolve around parliamenta-rianism, have also ultimately rendered service to the genocidal ruling class. In this context, the most mysterious stooge of the reactionaries is Mohan Bikram Singh, of the leading clique of Mashal. His entire efforts seem to be concentrated on discrediting and abusing the People's War from the level of the reactionaries. The Mashal leading clique (which in itself is on the verge of extinction) has come so low that its cadres have been degraded to the level of agents of the reactionary police against the Maoist guerrillas. Many stupid activities against the people have been perpetrated by Mashal in hiding and they have gone to the extremity of immorality by implicating the Maoists. By entering into an electoral pact with renegade UML clique to share couple of seats, Mashal is effectively reduced to serving the reactionaries. Ultimately Mohan Bikram has turned himself into a pawn of the reactionaries by accepting a pittance from reactionary regime and by hurling his choicest invective against the People's War.

Thus, the new and old revisionists of Nepal, like revisionists the world over, have proved themselves as the other side of the reactionary coin by setting themselves against the people's great revolutionary initiative. Today the Nepali people have witnessed in their daily lives what was taught by Marxism–Leninism–Maoism–that revisionism is part of the reactionary school.

Despite all this, however, the Nepalese revolution is moving ahead and will continue to do so, treading on the heads of the revisionists, as taught by Marxism–Leninism–Maoism. The flame of the great People's War has started to burn the rubbish-heap of revisionism in Nepal, and will succeed in turning it into ashes.

Fourth Extended Meeting of the Party Amidt Represion and Resistance

Our Party had envisaged the fascist moves of the enemy and the betrayal of revisionist group, under the Third Plan in particular, but more generally from the beginning of the historic People's War. No nervousness or deviation emerged amongst the militants and the mass of people as a result of the fascist moves of the enemy and the revisionists, because the Party, the militants and to a certain extent the mass of the people were alerted to prepare for it. Such developments were to be expected in a class war.

As indicated by the Plan, the Party militants and the mass of people continued with the task of countering disinformation, breaking encirclement and mounting resistance. The Party maintained lively contact with the masses in face of severe difficulties. New landmarks of sacrifice, devotion, bravery and self-sacrifice were created by responsible Party members and important guerrilla fighters against reactionary brutality, while staying amidst the people. Party members and fighters successfully set hundreds of examples of historic ideal of self-sacrifice for the Party and for the revolution. In the main areas of struggle, when massacres of dozens were carried out in one village after another, the poor peasants inspired the Party continuously asserting 'let the Party continue People's War, for which they were ready to sacrifice everything'. Hundreds of women victims of barbaric rape by the reactionary forces joined the People's War with hatred and helped to raise the revolutionary initiative of hundreds of thousands of working women to new heights. The Party itself got the opportunity to understand more deeply the level of patience, sacrifice, devotion and bravery that the mass of people possess for creating their own history under the leadership of the Party. Relations between the people and the Party have been further strengthened.

Under the circumstances of repression and resistance, the Party convened the Fourth Extended Meeting of the Central Committee in the middle of the third year. Understanding fully the sentiments, seriousness and feeling of responsibility brought about by the class war, the meeting, after intense discussion, passed unanimously the resolution 'New Plan for New Stage' to encourage a leap in the direction of creating base areas. Many concrete and important decisions were made by the Extended Meeting involving the three instruments of the democratic revolution, i.e. the Party, the army and the united front, with the glorious aim of creating base areas.

On the basis of the synthesis of the teachings of Marxism-Leninism–Maoism, the historical specificity of Nepali society and the experiences of more than 2 years of the People's War, the Party identified the principal conditions for creating base areas in Nepal.

With extensive theoretical analysis of 'guerrilla zone' and 'base area', the Extended Meeting laid special emphasis on the dangers of guerrillaism and reformism in the military field. This analysis and resulting decision provides the revolutionary line for the Party for a long time to come.

The Extended Meeting took most seriously the question of the process of continually transforming the Party, the main one of the three weapons of revolution, along a proletarian line according to the need to safeguard against conspiracy and pollution by our enemies and by opportunism, at a time when 'right revisionism' poses the greatest danger. It was decided to reinforce further the unified leadership of the Party, emphasising the need to link the concept of 'two-line struggle' with the synthesis of the Great Proletarian Cultural Revolution of China and Comrade Mao.

In order to strengthen Party unity against the danger of bourgeois pluralism and to wage struggle in unity against enemies and revisionists at the present point of the war, a decision was made to centralise further different levels of leadership and to establish consciously among the masses the role of different tiers of leadership, in particular the role of the General Secretary at the centre. The decision to establish the Party leadership amongst the masses in a more unified and centralised way is a decision of far-reaching importance, indissolubly linked with the decision of moving ahead in the direction of creating base areas.

Grasping with greater firmness the proposition that 'a people with no army has nothing of its own', the Extended Meeting decided to develop local military organisation as the Secondary force, under the direct leadership of local Party, to create platoons with the aim of developing them into companies under the direct command of regional commanders as the main military force of the people, and to develop the people's militia under each area command as the base force. Besides this, important decisions were made regarding centralisation, decentralisation and deployment to develop the war skills of military formations.

The Extended Meeting laid stress on making the revolutionary United Front still broader and as practical as possible as a means for the development of new people's power at local level and for propaganda and revolutionary mass struggle at the central level. For that purpose, a concrete decision has been taken to make a start to develop local people's power in accordance with the principle of Three-in-One committees, while at the central level a united front consisting of different fronts, nationalities and the left, progressive, patriotic and democratic forces would be developed.

Besides the above major decisions, the Extended Meeting undertook an evaluation of contemporary political situation of the country, synthesised a number of questions related to the Party's own history, decided to rectify the Party, and prepared a detailed framework of the new Plan. The Extended Meeting further decided to implement the plan to move towards creating base areas, from a particular date, with a special bang. The successful completion of the Extended Meeting, convened under adverse conditions but attended by 100 per cent of expected representatives, was itself a telling blow against the reactionaries and a symbol of victory for the Party, the fighters and the masses of people.

Declaration of New Decisions and Reactions to them

The convening of the Extended Meeting and declaration of its decisions provided a telling blow to the reactionaries and revisionists, who had been supporting mass slaughter and state terrorism for 4 months. The reactionaries, who clamoured that Maoist movement was under control, and the revisionists who parroted the same were equally dumbfounded by this declaration. After some period of guarded silence the media of reactionaries and revisionists centred their attack on the decisions of the Extended Meeting, particularly the centralisation of the leadership and its establishment. New and old revisionists appeared very active in such attacks. For months they tried to spread false propaganda regarding the decision on the role and establishment of leadership, labeling it a 'personality cult', 'dictatorship', the 'evolution of kingship', 'creation of a god' etc., and tried to mislead the masses accordingly. They resorted to the notorious Goebbels style of propaganda, by labeling a particular leader 'good' and another 'bad', with the objective of creating division among the Party leadership and setting one against the other.

But why are the reactionaries and revisionists attacking on the issue of centralisation of leadership and establishment? Are they really serious about such things as 'personality cult', 'dictatorship' or 'kingship' within the revolutionary Party of the proletariat? That is surely not the case because they themselves have accepted personality cult, dictatorship and kingship. They should surely have been elated to see the same being repeated in the revolutionary party. Why are they creating a storm about the revolutionary party of the proletariat and its leadership? This is a crucial question for all revolutionaries and the mass of people. Many honest people are confused on this question. The simple fact is that reactionaries resort to mass killing and state terrorism because they cannot accept it when the proletariat and working masses try to create their own state machinery against the reactionary state machinery. Similarly, when the proletariat and working masses try to establish their own leadership against the leadership of the feudals and bourgeoisie, that becomes intolerable to them. So they attack with their full might to discredit and not let the proletarian leadership get established among the masses.

Even here, when the Party proposed the Plan for creating base areas as the new political power and tried to centralise their leadership, and establish it in the form of new leadership, it became a matter beyond toleration to the old regime, the old leadership and its revisionist lackeys. Leadership is the key, but the question is leadership of which class? The entire history of revolution and class struggle in fact is the history of struggle for leadership. Again, the important point is leadership of which class is struggling against whom? It is obvious that proletarian democracy is dictatorship as far as the reactionaries are concerned and likewise the so-called democracy of feudals and the bourgeoisie is dictatorship for the proletariat and the working masses.

Similarly, the earth-shaking two-line struggles that took place in the International Communist Movement are nothing but ultimately the history of the struggle for leadership. From the First International to the Great Proletarian Cultural Revolution, the struggles waged by Marxist–Leninist–Maoists against anarchism, sectarianism and right-wing revisionism are all for the leadership of the proletarian class. Bakunin dared to call the great Karl Marx a 'dictator', Kautsky labeled Comrade Lenin a 'conspirator and dictator' and the whole world knows what Trotsky and Khruschev said of Comrade Stalin. Have not the modern revisionists labeled Comrade Mao a 'worshiper of the personality cult', a 'dictator' and a 'war monger'? So, there is no reason to be confused by the propaganda of the revisionists. When a rightist capitulator running away from class struggle goes to the lap of the feudal monarchy just to save his skin, leaving the Party, revolution and the people, then he exposes his hypocritical culture by labeling the great Party leading the People's War a 'monarchy' from the lap of reactionaries and rightist revisionists. We have seen how a common fellow who surrenders is carried on their shoulders by the reactionaries and revisionists with a great fanfare, as soon as they find him. It should, therefore, be understood that when somebody has no faith in the revolution, the Party and the people, and the revolutionary principles of Marxism–Leninism–Maoism, he first attacks the Party leadership in order to conceal his rightist, surrendering character. Objectively, that forms the part of the strategy of the reactionary class.

Among the conspiracies designed by reactionaries and revisionists the world over against proletarian revolutionary parties, the prominent ones are to try to alienate the leadership from ideology, policy and programme, the cadres from the leadership and the mass of people from the Party. The attack on our Party and its leadership is the result of a reactionary conspiracy to break such indissoluble relations, which in fact cannot be objectively separated out. How should a communist revolutionary react to the attack by reactionaries and revisionists? He should understand it the way Mao has stated: 'It is good if we are attacked by the enemy, since it proves that we have drawn a clear line of demarcation between the enemy and ourselves. It is still better if the enemy attacks us wildly and paints us utterly black and without a single virtue; it demonstrates that we have not only drawn a clear line of demarcation between the enemy and ourselves but have already achieved a great deal in our work'.

Process of Qualitative Development in People's Military Capacity

The third year of the People's War was of a qualitatively different nature from the previous years, from the angle of enhancing people's military capacity. The success of a series of high level military actions by the people's guerrillas during the so-called

Operation Kilo-Sierra-two by the enemy, and specially after the Extended Meeting, prove this. In the process of learning war through war itself, our guerrilla fighters have been vastly enhancing their war skills, albeit confronting numerous difficulties; incurring huge losses, but overcoming the natural limitations and drawbacks of their apprenticeship and learning from every event. The bravery shown by the people's guerrillas, their courage and instances of self-sacrifice have been inscribed in history as glorious episodes of Nepalese revolution.

When the fascist Girija Prasad Koirala, seated on the Prime Minster's chair after sucking the blood of hundreds of revolutionary warriors and of the people, arrogantly announced the Maoist movement to be 'under control' at a press conference, the very next day, the reactionaries and revisionists were met with a deadly blow from hundreds of successful actions, in the form of ambushes, raids, sabotages and propaganda actions planned nationwide, as special bang. This successful blow responded to state terror with red terror, and played a far-reaching role in entering into the great plan of creating base areas. It clearly showed that the massacres by the reactionary regime could not extinguish the flame of revolution but only served to fan the flames further.

In fact, the people's guerrillas successfully raided the Laliya police post in Dhanusha and captured rifles and ammunition kept there. In the process of the great 'bang', as part of high level and successful military actions, the guerrillas also raided Phalate police post, seizing all arms and ammunitions therein. The same day, guerrillas raided the police post at Nirmal Basti in Parsa, seizing all arms and ammunitions. Immediately after that the guerrilla platoon in Rolpa fought bravely with hundreds of enemy armed police force and succeeded in eliminating some, driving away others and later on breaking out of the encirclement of further hundreds of police force supported by helicopters to safety.

Presenting a model of intelligence and of the art of armed guerrilla warfare, the guerrillas attacked dozens of police force stationed at the Jhimpe tower at Saunepani in Salyan district and seized large number of rifles, bullets and other items. Here, the guerrillas granted an amnesty to 10 police personnel who surrendered and were given re-education. This incident once again clearly shows that the guerrillas of the People's War are not butchers, like the reactionary gangsters, but great revolutionaries who treat their prisoners of war well and grant an honorable amnesty to those surrendering before them. Immediately after this, guerrillas raided the police post at Bhattedanda in Lalitpur, as part of continuation of their valour in the historic Bethan action, and seized all rifles and ammunitions available there. After a few days, demonstrating another model of skilled guerrilla warfare, guerrillas ambushed a contingent of the police force, which was out to terrorise the people at Jhelneta in Dang, forced them to surrender and seized all the rifles and ammunition, but granted amnesty to the policemen themselves after 'educating' them. In Dolpa in the Karnali zone also, guerrillas successfully attacked a contingent of police by ambushing them and captured their arms and ammunition.

These are just examples of the many guerrilla actions that took place during the later months of the third year. In between, hundreds of actions—including the seizing of banks and arms in the banks, the capture of arms from feudals and the elimination of informers and criminals involved in genocide, the sabotage of the Minister's house in the capital, of police posts in many different parts of the country and of the factories of bureaucratic capitalists and the seizing of grain from landlords and its distribution among poor peasants—were successfully accomplished. Apart from these, if propaganda actions of different kinds are to be included, the number of actions would be in the thousands. The actions undertaken after the Extended Meeting or those undertaken specially after the historic 'bang' of October 17th, 1998, prove the failure of the enemy's so-called Kilo-Sierra-two operation, on the one hand, and the qualitative improvement in the military capability of the People's War, on the other.

Parliamentary Elections: Another Ploy of the Reactionary Conspiracy

The coalition government of the Nepali Congress and the United–Marxist–Leninist (UML) parties, notorious for national corruption and mass murder, has put forward the so-called general election as a 'magic wand' to solve problems of the country and its people. They are clamouring day and night that from the 'election', when either of the two parties gains a majority (not that they do get a majority but they announce it), political stability, law and order, development works and everything would miraculously prevail in the country. These rascals are taking people for a ride by shamelessly uttering all this nonsense.

In the last 8 years of parliament, 4 years were under the 'majority' government of this very same Girija Parsad Koirala. And what did the 'majority' government actually do? Kneeling down before the Indian expansionists it concluded the traitorous Tanakpur treaty, openly cheating the whole Nepali people. The lives of the people were ruined by the same majority government, which let prices rise and corruption go unbridled. Dozens were massacred in the heart of the capital in indiscriminate shooting by the government when people were making peaceful demonstrations. And was it not the same so-called majority government of Girija, which planted false cases, resorted to indiscriminate arrests and adminis-tered inhuman torture against political workers and ordinary citizens who differed from them ideologically? And was it not the same majority government, which under the banner of privatisation handed over whatever industries there were in the country to the Indian bureaucratic capitalists and impoverished the country?

Even in the last 4 years, the Nepalese government has been in fact under the Nepali Congress and the UML clique. Who prevented them from delivering other things for the people and the country besides the looting, corruption, national betrayal, genocide, extreme degeneration and distortion? Who forced them to quarrel for power like dogs fighting for a piece of bone or to reduce themselves to commodities for sale? Today the same traitors and mass murderers are presenting parliamentary elections as a panacea for all ills. This is yet further evidence of how the reactionaries despise the people's political awareness and historical memory.

What is the reality? The reality is that the great historic process of the People's War has aggravated the crisis of the reactionary state. The reality is that the drama of the election is being staged ahead of its due time under the guidance of the imperialists and the expansionists as a conspiracy against the People's War, when it flourished further despite genocide, plunder and state terrorism. It is quite clear that it is only as a conspiracy against the People's War that a coalition government of the two is formed, in defiance of the general parliamentary norm of government and opposition. In fact, however, both are declared lackeys of Indian expansionism; the UML clique has surrendered not only before Indian expansionism but also before the Girija clique of the Nepali Congress. Today, Girija, by declaring the election 'a war against the People's War', has verified this.

The reality is that the so-called parliamentary elections will offer the people and the country yet further betrayal and genocide, more inflation and corruption, more poverty and unemployment and more degeneration and distortion. What would be a bigger illusion than to expect any else from the same class, same system of thinking, same character, same clique and same persons? The reality is that because of the exercise of new people's power through the medium of the People's War, the feudal and imperialist forces are terrified and want to divert the attention of people elsewhere, so that they can isolate People's War and eliminate it; hence they have been following this strategy. When the old tricks of reactionaries are foiled, new moves like this are advanced. The way they are branding the parliamentary elections as a 'liberation war', a 'battle', a 'litmus test', a 'campaign against violence and terrorism', a 'new revolution' and so on makes it clear that the essence of the election is a conspiracy against the People's War.

But the People's War will not go in for confrontation just to suit them, in response to their provocation. The People's War will incessantly move ahead to fulfill its historic role according to its own plan, by exposing the reactionary parliamentary hypocrisy and by boycotting the mockery of elections. The People's War will continue to advance at its own speed before and after the elections, guided by the scientific principle of 'you fight your way and we fight our way', until the reactionary power is destroyed and people's power is established. The way the reactionary murderous cliques are presenting the so-called general election to parliament as 'the litmus test' against the People's War has exposed their terrified, defeated mentality and their impotency. Furthermore their lamentations demonstrate the qualitative level of success achieved by the great People's War in the last 3 years.

The old reactionary elements have openly and straightforwardly expressed the view that the People's War has become a serious threat to their entire system and hence the so-called general election is going to be held as a weapon against it. But the real threat is that of these revisionist traitors who try to hoodwink the masses in support of elections by putting forward a twisted argument to safeguard the moribund and barren parliamentary system as it exists and to serve the interests of proven national traitors and mass murderers. The People's War will continue to advance, however, as planned, exposing as it does the revisionists who are only betraying the people and the country by supporting a rotten system.

Conclusion

From the above analysis it is clear that the advancing historical stream of the People's War is further strengthened as it enters into its fourth year, after completing the third year. It has resisted successfully the conspiracy, suppression and terror of the enemy up until today. Today, the imperialist, expansionist, reactionary and revisionist elements, on the pretext of the so-called elections, are preparing for a more dangerous conspiracy and yet heavier repression against the historic tide of the People's War, advancing as an inseparable part of world proletarian revolution.

The great Party, the Communist Party of Nepal (Maoist), which has been leading the People's War based on the allpowerful principle of Marxism–Leninism–Maoism, has been attempting to forge broader and stronger unity with all left, progressive, patriotic and democratic forces inside Nepal and with communist revolutionaries and justice-loving people outside Nepal in order to resist the conspiracy of reactionary and revisionist forces. It is a matter of pleasure for the entire revolutionary Nepalese masses that the RIM Committee, which has been advancing steadfastly to establish a new International to advance the world revolution based on Marxism–Leninism–Maoism, and other parties and organisations under it have been extending strong support and sincere help to the People's War in Nepal in the true spirit of proletarian internationalism. Along with that assistance today, the international responsibility and solidarity of the Party and the people have been rising to new heights. Similarly, various initiatives have been undertaken in support of the Nepalese People's War by the revolutionary parties and masses of the people of India. The counter-revolutionary forces and the revolutionary forces are colliding at further, new heights. The path may be difficult, but the victory of the masses is inevitable. The Nepalese People's War will continue to advance, at the service of world revolution, whatever price it may have to pay. Ultimately the great ideal of communism, of a society free from all exploitation and atrocities committed on man by man, will be established on earth.

Long Live Marxism–Leninism–Maoism!
Long Live the Great People's War!
Glory to World Revolution!

February 1999

THE SECOND NATIONAL CONFERENCE*

The second conference took very important decisions regarding the Nepalese revolution with implications for the world proletarian revolution. The conference amended some of the articles of the Party constitution. The notified changes include the provision of a Chairman instead of a General Secretary. The role of Chairman is part of the development of the unified leadership of Party, Army and the United Front. The conference unanimously elected Comrade Prachanda to the position of Chairman of the Party. The conference also elected a new central committee. The first meeting of the central committee formed a politbureau and a standing committee.

The most precious step however was the synthesis of the ideology and the political line of the Party. The ideology of the party is summarised as Marxism–Leninism–Maoism and the political line as the Prachanda Path. The strategic plan of the people's war is agreed: strengthen and expand the base areas and local people's democratic power; move ahead towards the formation of central peoples government!

For the solution of the present crisis faced by the country an all party conference of the representatives of political forces of

---

* This document is based on a brief announcement by *A World to Win*. The second national conference of CPN (Maoist) took place in February 2001, on the fifth anniversary of the launching of the People's War in Nepal.

the coalition of present constitution, political parties, institutions and mass organisations is proposed. This would elect an interim government and this government would guarantee the formation of new people's constitution, as a tactical alternative.

The Conference passed a political document that explains the mass line in accordance with the experiences of the People's War. The document synthesises the joint adoption of the strategic lines of 'protracted people's war' and 'mass armed insurrection' following the analysis of changes after the 1980s in the world. It criticized the mechanical and dogmatic adoption of both the 'protracted people's war' and 'armed rebellion', which are different in form but same in quality.

The present world situation and recent Nepalese history are also analysed broadly in this document. It has proposals regarding the international relations and regarding the south Asian relations of the various revolutionary parties and the struggles for the success of revolution in this region, which would contribute the world proletarian revolution. The Conference formulated some new concepts regarding the world revolution as well as that of Nepal, while reviewing the whole international communist movement for the new 21st century.

The conference should be proud of the revolutionaries from Nepal and all over the world who contribute to providing the correct direction to the wave of proletarian world revolution.

A GREAT ACHIEVEMENT: PRACHANDA PATH*

As an inseparable organ of the international proletariat, the Party decided the line of the Nepalese revolution in the midst of class struggle and two-line struggle, based on the universal principles of Marxism–Leninism–Maoism. This was the first important achievement of the Nepalese revolution in the direction of the formation of ideas. A new historical epoch was initiated on 13 February 1996 with the historic initiation of the People's War, guided by this same line, with the great aim and determination of reaching communism through new democratic, socialist and

---

* This statement was excerpted from the Documents of the Second National Conference of the Communist Party of Nepal (Maoist) and is published in AWTW-2001/27.

cultural revolutions. Under the leadership of the Party, this historic attempt in itself was another great qualitative leap in the direction of defending and applying Marxism–Leninism–Maoism and revealing the specific laws of the Nepalese revolution. Today, the synthesis of the experience of 5 stormy years of People's War has developed into a set of ideas guiding the Nepalese Revolution, which is based on Marxism–Leninism–Maoism. This has been a great achievement of five years of the People's War.

This outstanding achievement stands on an immense foundation, the long history of untold grief, pain, bravery, courage, sacrifice and deep reflection by the millions of masses and revolutionary fighters. This achievement has been acquired at the cost of blood that has flowed into the soil, the blood of the thousands of the best sons and daughters of the Nepalese people. This great achievement has been attained through the consistent contribution of the whole Party and the leftist, progressive, patriotic and democratic forces, along with RIM and all the communist revolutionaries of the world. Throughout this process, the Party has resisted the reactionary regime's campaign of massacre, it has exposed revisionist treason and lies, as well as deviations inside the Party itself, and it has led all the struggles successfully, adhering to Marxism–Leninism–Maoism. Because of this successful leadership, today not only the Party's set of ideas but also a team of worthy leaders at the central level and a radiant section of thousands of cadre, our revolutionary heirs, have been developing steadily.

Because of the correct and consistent leadership of General Secretary Comrade Prachanda, a strong proletarian headquarters has been developed, as a centre of gravity of the Party, bringing Party unity up to the height of this ideological synthesis. So by 'Prachanda Path' the Party means the set of ideas that has developed as a form of centralised expression of the collective leadership. Developed in the context of prolonged discussion inside and outside the Party and the international communist movement, most importantly a high level of theoretical interaction with the RIM Committee, Prachanda Path, by enriching Marxism–Leninism–Maoism, expresses the set of ideas of the Nepalese people. This set of ideas emerging in the form of Prachanda Path will guide the basic line in the forward march of the Nepalese Revolution.

Marxism–Leninism–Maoism is the science of social revolution of the proletariat. As a science, it serves the development of the class struggle to change the world, and the synthesis of the experiences of the Party is Prachanda Path, the application of the universal principles of Marxism–Leninism–Maoism to the practice of the Nepalese revolution. This synthesis of Nepalese experience is based upon the indivisible dialectical relationship between international essence and national expression, universality and particularity, the whole and the part, the general and the particular, and it objectively serves the world proletarian revolution and proletarian internationalism.

This synthesis of experience has been acquired through the process of 'practice–knowledge–again practice–again knowledge', based on the dialectical materialist theory of knowledge. Marxism–Leninism–Maoism has taught us that this is a neverending cycle. Through the practice of class struggle and ideological struggle, the Party has developed the Party line as initial knowledge, applied that knowledge again to change the world, which has resulted in new knowledge in the form of the present synthesis. It is clear that this process is not going to end and be completed here; it is bound to continue all the way, through the process of 'again practice' and 'again knowledge'. To understand and guide the dialectical laws of the motion of progress in a correct way, communist revolutionaries should continuously try to be expert in applying the universal principles of Marxism–Leninism–Maoism.

HOWEVER TORTUOUS THE ROAD, THE VICTORY OF THE WORLD PROLETARIAN REVOLUTION IS CERTAIN*

—*Com Prachanda*

Chairman Prachanda, we would like to thank you for according an interview to our journal. Our readership has been following

---

* This interview with Chairman Prachanda, leader of the Communist Party of Nepal (Maoist) and the People's War in Nepal took place on 28 May 2001. It is taken from the RIM publication '*A World To Win*', No. 27, 2001.

the advances in the People's War since the beginning with the greatest interest and enthusiasm. How do you explain the spectacular success in advancing the People's War and arousing the masses, in only 5 years?

First of all, I feel honoured and express my heartfelt gratitude towards *A World to Win* (AWTW), which is well established as an important and leading ideological weapon of the international proletariat, for providing me with this opportunity for an interview. With deep appreciation of the genuinely internationalist support of AWTW, the Committee of RIM and the Revolutionary Internationalist Movement (of which our Party itself is a participant for the initiation, defence and development of the Nepalese People's War, a contingent of the international proletarian army) I wish you continuous progress in your endeavour.

There are definite subjective and objective factors behind the current success achieved by the Nepalese People's War during the short period of 5 years. Marxism–Leninism–Maoism and objective reality have taught us that in the present era of imperialism and proletarian revolution, there exists a universal objective basis, in general, for the initiation, defence and development of people's war in the oppressed and underdeveloped countries of the Third World. The main problem in implementing the strategy of protracted people's war in such countries is, in our opinion, the problem of subjective preparation. The principal aspect of subjective preparation is the question of the development of a militant communist party of a new type based on Marxism–Leninism–Maoism. The rapid development of people's war is inevitable today after this leadership problem is solved through intense struggle against alien tendencies in the proletarian movement, mainly right revisionism. For the masses there is no alternative to rebellion and revolution, given the objective background of exploitation, repression and poverty prevalent in the semifeudal and semi-colonial countries of the Third World.

In Nepal, our first effort was to correctly grasp the science of Marxism–Leninism–Maoism. To this end, we strove to link ourselves with the arduous and challenging ideological struggle waged by the genuine communist revolutionaries of the world against the Chinese counter-revolution after the death of Comrade Mao Tse Tung. Taking the synthesis of the Great Proletarian Cultural Revolution, the highest expression of conscious class struggle, as our starting point, we delved into serious study. We made a particularly fervent study of the ideological struggle that erupted in the process of the development of the Communist Party of Peru (PCP), the Revolutionary Communist Party (RCP) in the United States and in other countries. Through continuous ideological interaction with the Committee of the Revolutionary Internationalist Movement (RIM) we tried to acquaint ourselves with the principal tendencies in the world today and to attain the highest collective understanding of the international proletariat. Also, we made an attempt to draw lessons from the positive and negative aspects of the revolutionary and national movements of different countries including India, the Philippines, Turkey, Iran, Sri Lanka and others. In short, driven by a hunger for knowledge, we took pains to arm the Party ideologically, to whatever extent possible, with the advanced consciousness of the proletariat.

This search for ideological clarity was invariably linked with the class struggle of the Nepalese masses and the struggle against different types of right opportunism. From the starting point of the advanced consciousness of the international proletariat, we applied various forms of mass line to develop the understanding and desire of the Nepalese people for freedom. According to the principle of uniting with the masses under all circumstances, the Party applied different tactics, open and clandestine, legal and illegal, advancing and retreating etc. We summed up the experiences of splitting and uniting in the communist movement. To expand our ties to the masses, we laid emphasis on developing different mass organisations, forums and so forth. Throughout all this process, the Party has been following the policy of strategic firmness and tactical flexibility with particular seriousness.

In the end, after a serious investigation of the lessons of Marxism–Leninism–Maoism and the international and national particularities of the day, the Party concretised its theoretical commitment to the great march towards communism and proclaimed the People's War on 13 February 1996 through a countrywide shock of rebellion: The People's War has attained the current height after completing six strategic plans with such basic policies as decentralised actions within a centralised plan and command; balance between political and military offensives against the enemy; political justification of military action and military justification of political action; utilisation of the contradictions amongst the enemies to isolate the main enemy; organisation and mobilisation of the masses in the quickest and best possible way, as exhorted by Comrade Mao; and so on. In our opinion, the real key to the rapid development of the People's War is the fusion between the science of proletarian revolution, on the one hand, and the needs and the fighting spirit of the Nepalese people, on the other. In other words, the principal and decisive factor of this development is the correct ideological and political line of the Party.

In recent months we have read reports about military operations of the people's armed forces on a whole new scale. Where do things stand now in the process of building a people's army?

The Party has been striving to develop the people's army according to the universal principles of Marxism–Leninism–Maoism: 'without a People's Army, the people have nothing', 'political power grows out of the barrel of a gun', and the 'armed sea of masses', which are requirements for the revolution. The policy of the Party has been to develop base areas and guerrilla zones throughout the whole country and to build the total armed forces with a main force, secondary force and base (or local) force. In establishing our form of actions, the first, second, third and fourth priorities have been accorded to ambush and undermining, raid and commando attack, various types of sabotage and selective elimination, respectively.

To ensure direct participation of the masses in armed activities, the Party has been promoting armed mass actions and armed propaganda too, as part of its military campaign. Such campaigns have played an important role in ensuring the participation of the masses in the People's War. Following the principle of 'learning warfare through warfare', the people's army is now in a position to conduct successful actions at the level of the temporary battalion (several hundred soldiers) in terms of military formation; permanent and temporary companies have been built up under different regional commands in the country and dozens of regular platoons and hundreds of regular squads are in action. As base forces, the general masses have enrolled in the people's militias in their thousands. This process of enrolment in different military formations is advancing at quite a fast pace. The Party has recently resolved to organise this large structure of the people's armed forces—which has been successful in capturing enemy district headquarters and many other barracks of the commando forces—under a more unified and centralised command. Accordingly, it has been resolved, in principle, to establish a central general headquarters and general staff, to name the three armed forces collectively as the People's Liberation Army and to make a public pronouncement of this, to stress the development of mobile warfare, to centralise, decentralise and transfer according to needs etc., with the aim of converting every village into a trench against the enemy. Military activities have been shaking the country.

Where do things stand in relation to building up new people's power? What kinds of government exist in the base areas?

Beginning just 1 year after the initiation of the People's War, the question of the organisation of local people's power has always been on the Party's agenda. It is since then that the situation of a power vacuum has occurred in many rural areas of western Nepal. In such areas, embryos of new people's power have sprouted in the form of United People's Committees under the leadership of the Party. After the latest military victories of the people's army, the enemy has been confined to the district headquarters in the Western region, as well as other districts of the country. Thus, large rural sections of the country have become a form of liberated area. Of course, they are not fully liberated, as the enemy's last and main military force is yet to be defeated. Nevertheless, in the various districts in the main base area of Western Nepal, elections to the local and district level people's government have already been completed. Such local people's governments are in the form of a united democratic government of antifeudal and anti-imperialist patriotic, democratic and left forces. While the local government has been directly elected by the masses, the representatives of the local people's power have elected the district people's governments. These governments, known as Local United People's Committees exercise, in essence, both the functions of policy formulation and execution related to the legislative, executive and judicial organs.

To streamline the different functions under their jurisdiction, these people's governments, under the leadership of the Party, are composed of different departments, such as the Construction Department, Cooperative Department, Land Reform Department, Forest Conservation Department, Security Department, Education and Culture Department, Health Department etc. The system of recall of elected representatives of the masses, if the need arises, has been implemented from the beginning. At present, the Local United People's Committees have been growing not only in the main base area of western Nepal but also in the base areas under all the regional commands in the country.

As necessitated by new developments, the Party has now resolved to constitute a united front organism that will play the role of a newdemocratic government organising committee at the central level, for the defence, consolidation, expansion and coordination of the local people's government. The important point to be noted here is that the Party has been stressing for some time the development of a united front, such as the united front of the peoples of different classes, castes, nationalities and regions oppressed by feudalism and imperialism, according to the specific conditions of Nepalese society. While upholding the rights of the oppressed nationalities to self-determination, the Party has put forward the programme of autonomy for the peoples of various oppressed nationalities and regions. This policy and programme reflects a revolutionary policy of 'unite and struggle' on a democratic basis against the enemy's policy of 'divide and rule'. It is our Party's firm conviction that the central people's government organising committee will not only coordinate the local people's government but also play an important role in the preparation of the future insurrection.

At different times the Party has spoken of the possibility of negotiations with the old state authorities. Could you please explain your thinking on this?

I feel the question of negotiations with the old state power is a very sensitive question in the revolutionary movement. It is clear from the experience of revolution, from past history to the present day, that the reactionary ruling class has utilised the question of negotiations as a weapon to hoodwink the masses, to engineer a split in the revolutionary movement and to prepare the ground for large-scale massacre. Marxism–Leninism–Maoism has taught us that whether to negotiate or not to negotiate with the old state power depends on the concrete analysis of concrete conditions. The principal decisive factor in this is the defence of the basic interests of the people and the revolution. Our guiding principles on the question of negotiations are the experiences and summation of the BrestLitovsk Treaty under Lenin's leadership and the Chunking negotiations under Mao's leadership.

We consider the question of negotiation as a battlefront that has to be faced by the revolutionary movement under certain concrete conditions. We have launched a serious debate and study on the question of negotiations in the light of the negative experiences of the past and present, including that of Peru. On this question we have struggled, on the one side against narrow dogmatism, and on the other, and principally, against rightist capitulationism, and strived to develop a Marxist–Leninist–Maoist conception within the Party and among the general masses. The RIM Committee statement [see AWTW/21] and other material, such as Fighting the Right Opportunist Line in Peru, have acted as important motivating factors in this process. We are most serious about the whole Party and the masses not having any illusion about negotiations even if the main leadership of the Party were to fall into enemy hands.

We feel that this question should be understood correctly in the context of the particular conditions of the current international balance of power between revolution and counter-revolution and, principally, in the context of the concrete political situation in Nepal. It is self-evident that subjectively the power of revolution is weaker right now. To lead proletarian revolution to victory in a small and poor country like Nepal is definitely a challenging task. Making maximum use of the tactical flexibility of manoeuvring to the right and left, and advance and retreat, is the inevitable necessity of the circumstances. The Nepalese People's War has been advancing at a fast pace due to the proper balance between strategic firmness and tactical flexibility, and between political offensive and military offensive.

Today, the reactionary state in Nepal is reaching the extremity of its political crisis. The People's War is now at the centre stage of national politics. Every parliamentary clique is going through an extreme crisis of its internal contradictions, and the number one agenda for everyone is the People's War. Becaue of their own crisis, the ruling classes have, from the very beginning, clamoured about being in favour of negotiations and conspired to attract the urban middle strata to their side. In this situation, with a view to isolate the main enemy and to educate the middle strata, we made it clear that we were not against negotiation per se and were ready to fight at the negotiation table if definite conditions were fulfilled. This created another serious debate in national politics. Ultimately the conspiracy behind the negotiations hullabaloo was unmasked and a large section of the masses were won over to the side of the People's War. This we summed up as Mao's policy of 'fighting tit for tat'.

Now we are marching forward, focused on the main slogan of consolidating and expanding the base areas and marching ahead in the direction of establishing the central people's government. The latest towering military actions are the result of the same slogan and plan. Along with this, we have called for the dissolution of the parliamentary system and constitution, and for the convening of an all-section conference and the formation of an interim government, as immediate tactics. We have made it clear that if the old state is eager to negotiate on this political solution we are ready for it. In the present context of Nepalese politics, this slogan has played a significant role in isolating the hardline faction of the ruling classes, educating the masses further against parliamentary hypocrisy and raising the People's War to a new height of development. It is important to grasp that if the Party's policies and programme for negotiations were to be realised, if the situation so demands, it would draw the victory of the People's War in Nepal closer.

Lastly, we want to assert that there is no reason to be under any illusion or to be apprehensive about talk of negotiation aimed at advancing the People's War and revolution to victory. We are confident that we are making a creative application of Marxism–Leninism–Maoism against right capitulationism and sectarian dogmatism, with the aim of defeating the enemy on the negotiations front also, whilst assuming full initiative in our own hands in a situation of continuous victory of the People's War.

Some of our readers have asked what the difference is between your negotiation policy and that of the Right Opportunist Line in Peru.

There can be no comparison whatsoever between our aforementioned conception of negotiation and the Right Opportunist Line (ROL) in Peru. It has slightly surprised us that some of our friends abroad have such big illusions and gaps of understanding about the real situation in Nepal and the Party's policy. In this context, we regret not having been able to elucidate the concrete political situation and the essence of the Party's policies earlier. The ROL in Peru talked about negotiations with a view to liquidating the People's War, whereas we have talked about fight on the negotiations front as well, with the aim of advancing the People's War to the point of victory. The ROL in Peru has appeared in the form of capitulationism from inside prison, with an admixture of the enemy's conspiracy, at a time of serious setback faced by the People's War following the capture of the main leadership by the enemy, whereas we are talking about negotiations with full initiative in our own hands with the aim of destroying the enemy, when the People's War is advancing on a fast and victorious march. While the ROL in Peru has betrayed the revolutionary gains and revolutionary spirit of the masses, our talk of negotiation has been providing political training to the masses to participate more extensively in the revolution against the enemy. While the ROL in Peru is the product of a defeated mentality, our talk of negotiation is a revolutionary tactic advanced in a conscious and balanced manner after drawing lessons from the same negative experience in Peru. Hence, there is a difference of night and day between the two. I don't think I need to add anything more on this.

How do you see the relationship between the new democratic revolution in Nepal and the struggle going on in other countries?

The new democratic revolution in Nepal is an integral part of the world proletarian revolution. Hence it has a close and inseparable relation with national liberation, democratic and socialist movements in other countries. The basic characteristics of the era of imperialism and proletarian revolution, the murderous neo-colonial process of plundering the world through finance capital, under the pseudonym of globalisation and liberalization, by imperialism, and the massive impact of the qualitative change in information technology, especially electronic technology, define the specific relations among the revolutionary movements in different countries. This situation has further enhanced the practical importance of the great theory of proletarian internationalism. The present condition of instant worldwide impact of any positive or negative event in any corner of the earth has been preparing the material ground for world communism at an astonishingly fast pace. This situation has also qualitatively enhanced the capacity of the process of revolution in a particular country to exert influence on the revolutionary movements of other countries. Hence it is necessary to make new advances in the conscious efforts of the proletarian revolutionaries to further world revolution on the basis of proletarian internationalism.

We have made a deep appreciation in the context of the People's War in Nepal and concluded that its development cannot be effectively conceived if it is divorced from the experiences led by the PCP, RCP, USA, RIM and revolutionaries in India, Turkey, Iran, Philippines and other countries since the death of Comrade Mao. The present rapid pace of development would have been inconceivable without the support of communist revolutionaries and freedom-loving people of different countries, and particularly the Revolutionary Internationalist Movement, during the period of the historic initiation of the People's War. That is why we have conceived the new democratic revolution in Nepal as a base area of world revolution, internationalist in content and national in form. We have seriously sought to develop close solidarity with the struggles in other countries, whatever their level of development might be, to learn from their experiences and disseminate our experiences to them. The consciousness of this proletarian internationalist duty was responsible for highlighting with particular seriousness the Leninist conception of the fusion between the proletarian movement and the national liberation movement by the recent Second National Conference of our Party.

What is the goal of your struggle? How does it differ from the struggle that nationalist forces are waging in other parts of South Asia, for example?

It is open and clear that the ultimate aim of our movement is to contribute towards the attainment of glorious communism by ending all forms of exploitation of man by man from the face of the earth. Just prior to the historic initiation of the People's War we had clarified our theoretical commitment that this war would be advanced as an integral part of the proletarian world revolution and that weapons would not be discarded until the final construction of communism. Most importantly, it must be understood that only by marching forward under the guidance of Marxism–Leninism–Maoism, the invincible universal ideology of the proletariat, the last and the most revolutionary class in history, can this golden future of humankind be attained.

In South Asia various nationalist forces, which are a product of the state of social development, are valiantly fighting for the right of self-determination. Such nationalist struggles are not able to grasp the particularities of the era of imperialism and proletarian revolution. It is their limitation not to grasp that it is historically impossible for any national liberation movement to achieve success without being a part of the world proletarian movement under the leadership of the proletariat. On the other hand, the failure to provide correct leadership to the national liberation aspirations of the people has been a weakness of the political parties of the proletariat. The proletarian revolutionaries must do their utmost to overcome this weakness. The national movements on their own should not be seen as a drag on the proletarian movement, but as fraternal movements to be led on the basis of Marxism–Leninism–Maoism. It is also clear that unless they are led by the political parties of the proletariat such nationalist movements would ultimately be nothing but a tool of one or another of the imperialist cliques. If not a part of proletarian revolution, then surely a part of imperialism? Such is the historical destiny of national movements.

In Nepal, we have been stressing the question of national liberation ever since the time of the historic initiation of the People's War, according to the Leninist principle of the fusion of the national liberation movement with the proletarian movement.

The idea behind the concept of a 'new Soviet federation at the South Asian level', as advanced by our Party's second National Conference is the strategic objective of providing proletarian leadership to the national liberation aspirations of the peoples of this region. This is important to note.

Many observers have noted the massive participation of women in the revolutionary struggle in Nepal. What is the significance of this?

The important key to the intense development and the success of the People's War in Nepal is definitely the massive participation of women. The reactionaries and the revisionists are today 'astonished' by the massive participation of women and the records of sacrifice, devotion and dedication set by them in the People's War. As the first heroic event of its kind in Nepalese history, as a source of great inspiration for the women of the world, the women guerrillas have broken open the prison of the old state. In the vast rural areas, the working women have heroically faced untold savageries and atrocities of mass rape by the enemies. Even while their eyes were gouged and their bodies set ablaze by the enemy in the most brutal manner, the women have stood firm in their conviction for liberation. Objectively, the women have left the men behind from the point of view of sacrifice, devotion and dedication in the People's War. Today, thousands of women have come out of the confines of their kitchens to graduate into people's warriors. Thousands of women have borne untold misery to assist the People's War. The Party has now made organised efforts and plans to develop women communist leaders as a guarantee of the success of the revolution.

We feel that the motive factors behind such massive participation of women in the movement is the correct policy of the Party in providing an outlet vent for the spirit of rebellion created by the material conditions of Nepalese society. Because of its class character, the bourgeoisie never places confidence in the ability of women. On the contrary, because of its class character, the proletariat acknowledges the vast potential inherent in women. Hence, it is the proletariat alone that can genuinely lead the women to liberation. Our Party has, from the very beginning, upheld 'the woman question' as one of the decisive questions likely to decide the fate of the revolution. With the organisation of women alongside men in the guerrilla army, the women for the first time felt liberated from hundreds of years of feudal patriarchy and have taken their destiny into their own hands. Now the Party has formulated a special organisation and plans for the development of leadership quality in women in the light of its 5 years of experience. The Party is in the midst of a longterm plan to develop women leaders on par with men in the Party committees from the local to central level, in the different levels of people's power and in the people's army, from amongst the women subjected to double exploitation and oppression in both class and gender terms. It is our firm belief that the question of bringing forward communist successors from among the women in large numbers is important, not only for the success of the revolution but for preventing the future danger of counter-revolution.

Nepalese society is constituted as an admixture of Aryan and non-Aryan ethnic communities. From the point of view of intrafamily oppression, the women from Aryan communities are subjected to intense atrocities of Hindu feudal patriarchy, whereas women from oppressed Mongolian and other nationalities suffer relatively less from patriarchy. As our movement was more concentrated in the non-Aryan belt of western Nepal, it was culturally more conducive to the participation of women. In the Aryan community, as there was more exploitation and greater atrocities against women, the People's War provided a concrete method for women's liberation, and there has been increasing participation of women from this community as well. Thus, women's participation from the two different communities accelerated.

Recently your Party held its Second National Conference [see excerpts of Conference resolutions in this issue]. Could you highlight the main achievements of this Conference?

By breaking through the enemy's conspiracy and several suppression encirclements, we have been historically successful in concluding our Party's Second National Conference. The historic success of this conference has itself become a powerful blow against the enemy. The historic aspect of this conference is inherent in its far-reaching important resolutions, which the Party has summed up as epoch-making.

The main subject of the conference was the ideological synthesis based on the past 5 years' experiences of the People's War and chalking out the future direction of the People's War. The conference has been totally successful in fulfilling its aim, by unanimously adopting its ideological synthesis in the form of the 'Prachanda Path', through the document The Great Leap Forward: Inevitable Necessity of History. The document has presented the Party's set of ideas in the form of a summation of the international communist movement, an analysis of the specificity of the present international situation and the lessons to be learnt from it, a resolution on South Asia, a general summation of Nepalese history, a new review of the history of the Nepalese communist movement, a new evaluation of the Party's history, a summation of the three instruments of the revolution, a discussion of mass line, and a resolution on great achievement; and at the end an outline of a future plan was presented. The document, which was unanimously adopted through exercising a high-level proletarian democratic and lively debate, has unified the Party on a new basis. That is why the Party has summed up the Conference as the conference of Unity and Victory.

After the resolutions of the conference were made public, especially the resolution on 'Prachanda Path', they have created a big uproar within the reactionary and revisionist camp, while they have created a wave of excitement amongst the revolutionary masses. The military victories achieved in the following period and the successful mass meetings and demonstrations involving hundreds of thousands of people represent the transformation of the resolutions of the conference into a material force.

How has the Party itself changed since the People's War began?

As has been said by Comrade Mao, the People's War is not only an art of fighting against the enemy but it is also a means of cleansing oneself from within: we have made this clear right from the very beginning. Five years' experience has verified this in practice. First of all, the initiation of the People's War has produced a qualitative transformation in the Party's underground structure and its working style. Second, along with the development of the People's War, the Party has been able to concentrate on the class base, and there have been important changes in the class composition of the Party cadres. Third, the People's War has liberated innumerable Party cadres from the old reformist legacy, and this has given a new lease of life to the Party, and is continuing to do so. Fourth, the People's War has come out victorious against the Alok tendency*, including sectarian and anarchist deviations, and through this it has created an environment for new unity on a new basis. Fifth, the People's War has prepared the material basis for successfully implementing the Party's rectification campaign. Sixth, the People's War has established the Party as the sole revolutionary party among the masses in the whole country. Seventh, the People's War has raised the Party to the present height of ideological synthesis. In this way the People's War has contributed and is continuing to contribute in multifaceted ways in the process of ideological and material proletarianisation.

Your conference paid considerable attention to some questions of the history of the international communist movement. Why did you feel such a study to be necessary? What lesson does it hold for the future?

Yes! Our Party's Second National Conference has paid special attention to learning from the history of the international communist movement. Having reached the pinnacle of a historic victory in the fight for state power, why did our class have to face such a big setback in the world? This question by itself is a very important question. Certainly, it has often been said that it is the result of the laws of the ups and downs of class struggle, the treacherous betrayal of the revisionists and the conspiracy of the imperialists. However, this explanation is not enough to convey the total truth, and this will not be able to generate confidence among the masses for the revolution.

The principal factor in the development of any object or process will always be the internal. From this point of view the sensitive question is to find out where our class's revolutionary representatives in the past failed to pay attention or what their weaknesses were on the ideological questions. It is by using the

---

* Referring to the Party's struggle with a former leader, Alok, who degenerated.

telescope and microscope of Marxism–Leninism–Maoism that we can find this out. We have focused our attention on this subject, after 5 years of experience, for the success of the revolution, keeping in mind the necessity of shielding ourselves against the danger of future counterrevolution. In this process we have taken the experience of the Great Proletarian Cultural Revolution as the starting point of our study. This way, in the process of study and discussion our attention has been drawn towards the question of Comrade Mao's evaluation of the 30 per cent errors of Comrade Stalin.

We have tried to probe even more deeply Comrade Mao's evaluation that despite being a great and sincere Marxist–Leninist, Comrade Stalin had a fair share of metaphysics, subjectivism and dogmatism when it came to grasping dialectical materialist philosophy. By so doing, our Party has opened the door for studying such questions as to why Comrade Stalin's concept of party could not grasp the 'unity of opposites' and helped lead to the birth of Hoxha-ism; why he made several errors in grasping the nature and conduct of the class struggle under socialism; why he gave wrong directions/instructions on many occasions in regards to the relationship between Soviet socialism and world revolution; why he made the mistake of generalising the Soviet need to form a united front during the Second World War; why he laid one-sided emphasis on the growth of production and the development of the productive forces as a guarantee for the success of socialism; why he had some problems in grasping the Leninist concept of fusing oppressed countries' national liberation movements with the proletarian movement; why he was not able to grasp the importance of the contribution of the Chinese revolution and that of comrade Mao; and so on.

Throughout the experience of class struggle and ideological struggle we have come to see that many of the groups and old leaders of Nepal, who claim to be advocates of 'Mao Tse Tung Thought', have viewed Marxism from the Hoxha-ite dogmato-revisionist angle. They view and perceive Comrade Stalin not through Mao's eyes but through Enver Hoxha's eyes. This has created obstacles in the development of the Nepalese revolution for decades, and even now one has to struggle against that tendency. We feel that communist movements in almost all the countries of the world have been confronting this problem in small or big ways. In this situation, there should not be any hesitation on the part of the new generation of communist revolutionaries to learn from the errors of Comrade Stalin. This is because today the reactionary essences of Trotskyism, Khrushchevite revisionism, Euro-communism, 'Hoxha-ism', 'Ho Chi Minh's centrism', 'Juche' of North Korea and other wrong trends have been unmasked. For at least now there is no danger of such revisionists taking advantage of our sincere effort to learn lessons from history. On the contrary, this effort of ours to learn lessons from history will help substantially in grasping Marxism–Leninism–Maoism more firmly, in providing successful leadership to the revolution and in preventing the danger of counter-revolution in the future.

The Conference speaks of 'Prachanda Path'. Could you briefly explain this understanding?

Through the application of Marxism–Leninism–Maoism's universal truth to the Nepalese specificity, and mainly through the summation of the experience of five torrid years of the People's War, the Conference concluded that a definite set of ideas has been developed. That set of ideas has been named 'Prachanda Path'. The Party has put forward this nomenclature because it represents the centralised expression of the collective leadership and Comrade Prachanda's 'correct and continuing leadership'. The Party considers Prachanda Path as an enrichment of Marxism–Leninism–Maoism. Giving it concrete definition, the Conference has termed Prachanda Path as a set of ideas that is more than a general Party line but that has not yet developed to the level of 'Thought'. The Party has defined Prachanda Path in the Nepalese context as a new example of creative Marxism, opposed to both the right revisionists and sectarian dogmatists. The conference has correctly summed up the role of the immortal martyrs of the People's War, the general masses, the revolutionary fighters, the entire Party rank and file, the central team of leaders and RIM together with communist revolutionaries of the world, in developing Prachanda Path as a specific set of ideas. The Party is confident that the synthesis of Prachanda Path will serve the world revolution by giving direction to the forward march of the Nepalese revolution.

What has been the relationship between your party and the international communist movement?

The relationship between our party and the international communist movement has been particularly deep. The very fact that since 1984, the year of the formation of RIM, our party has been an active member, confirms this relationship. It was through RIM that we got great inspiration and help from the lofty experiences of the People's War in Peru. In its essence, the Nepalese People's War has been a joint effort of our party and the international communist movement because of the process of continuous debate and interaction throughout the whole process of preparation, initiation and development of the People's War. This reality reflects the specificity and grandeur of our relationship. Along with this we have been maintaining close relationships with revolutionary parties in India, who have extended great help in different ways to the development of the People's War in Nepal. Our entire party and the masses have given great importance to this relationship with the international communist movement. We have always said that if the People's War in Nepal faces a big setback then it will reflect not only the failure of our party but also that of the international communist movement to a significant extent. From this point of view, it is evident that our relationship with the international communist movement is somewhat different from such other relationships in the past. We are confident that, along with the development of the revolutionary movement under the guidance of the great ideology of Marxism–Leninism–Maoism and proletarian internationalism, this relationship will serve the world revolution even more profoundly.

How do you see the relationship between the revolution in Nepal and the rest of the South Asia region?

Because of South Asia's economic, political, cultural and geographical concrete conditions, we now feel it necessary to carry on the revolutionary processes of all the countries in this region in a coordinated manner. We have been stressing the importance of coordinating the revolutionary movements at the South Asian level in a context in which the region is growing into an important centre of world revolution, and in which the imperialists, especially the American imperialists, have been casting their evil eyes on this region, while the Indian expansionist ruling classes, who dream of being the big bully of the region, are kneeling before the American imperialists. It is by going through this process of joint efforts that we have pointed towards the possibility of developing a 'new Soviet Federation at the South Asian level' in the future. We have seriously considered the importance of advancing revolution in South Asia under a grand strategy. The Nepalese revolution and our party have for some time been maintaining a lively relationship with the revolutionary parties and movements in India, Bangladesh and Sri Lanka. In this respect we feel that the Indian revolutionary parties and the Indian revolution will have the most important role to play.

What suggestions would you offer to comrades in other countries who are striving to initiate or develop people's war?

To all those comrades who are endeavouring to develop various warfronts within a single campaign of world proletarian revolution, we, from the warfront in Nepal, would like to convey our well wishes that the comrades will be fully successful in applying the universal principles of Marxism–Leninism–Maoism to the specific conditions of their own respective countries. However tortuous the road may be, the victory of the world proletarian revolution is certain.

Thank you.

A REJOINDER ON SOME CURRENT ISSUES

—Baburam Bhattarai

The virtual civil war between the monarchist and democratic forces in Nepal has now been a matter of serious concern for all the enlightened citizens and political forces inside the country and the whole of the international community. The recent spate of 'joint statements' calling for a negotiated settlement by all and sundry in Kathmandu and new initiatives, both overt and covert, by the international forces, amply testify this. However, there is seen to be a discernible lack of clarity on some cardinal issues and outright misconception of many others. This is quite probable, given a long spell of emergency rule, with suspension of all civic and democratic rights including the right to information, and a sustained disinformation campaign by the royal armycontrolled media. It is, therefore, imperative that some of these misconceptions and lies be demystified and cleared and the real facts be put across, so that the path to a genuine political solution to the vexed problem may be paved.

The Reality of 'Civil War'

The first step towards the solution of the reigning problem is its correct identification or diagnosis. But the dilemma of our pacifists on the question has been no less hilarious than that of the proverbial blind men's speculation about the 'elephant'. Is it 'terrorism'? Or an 'insurgency'? Or a fullfledged 'civil war'? Without indulging in any semantic acrobatics, we can safely assert that what is going on is a fullfledged civil war. If you honestly and intelligently follow the definition and categorisation of 'war' in any international law book or articles of various Geneva Conventions and Protocols on war, you have no way but to acknowledge the ongoing fierce armed conflict between the Royal Nepal Army (RNA) and the People's Liberation Army (PLA) all over the country as a complete civil war.

It is no secret that the whole country is now divided between two armies, two states, two economies and two cultures. While the RNA is mostly confined to district headquarters, urban centres and roadside areas, the PLA controls the rest of the countryside, which constitutes more than two-thirds of the country. Regular armed clashes between the two rival armies are reported from 73 out of the 75 districts. Local people's power is being exercised by a network of revolutionary People's Committees, which is coordinated at the central level by United Revolutionary People's Council (URPC), an embryonic Central People's Government Organising Committee under the leadership of CPN (Maoist).

Is it just not ridiculous and an exercise in self-deception to brand or dismiss such a revolutionary political movement as mere 'terrorism'? Where on earth, or in history, have 'terrorists' enjoyed such widespread mass base? It is all the more intriguing that the Belgian government should fail to see through this objective reality and should agree recently to supply sophisticated weapons to the RNA in utter contravention of the 1998 Code of Conduct of the EU barring sale of weapons to parties engaged in 'internal conflict'. If it is not 'internal conflict', what is it, ladies and gentlemen?

The failure of the civilized world to recognise the ongoing armed conflict between two belligerent powers as 'civil war' or 'intra-state war', has prompted the RNA to indulge in widespread war crimes in the form of wanton execution of hundreds of prisoners of war, massacre of thousands of noncombatants in fake encounters and brutal torture, rape and arson against civilian population, and yet go scot free. A number of national and international human rights organisations have chronicled such war crimes, which have so far been conveniently suppressed under the emergency rule.

Hence the first and foremost task of any well-meaning pacifist eager to initiate a process of negotiated settlement should be to acknowledge the conflict as a 'civil war' or 'internal war' and to invoke the provisions of international law, conventions and protocols to check such war crimes.

The Core Issue: Monarchy vs. Democracy

Second, the core issue of the conflict, or the basic political agenda of the war, ought to be grasped correctly. For, as good old Carl von Clausewitz put it, 'war is the continuation of policy by other (i.e. violent) means'. However, there have been two diametrically opposite sets of misperceptions about the ultimate political goal, or the nature, of this war. While the one motivated (or ill-informed?) section prefers to believe the ultimate goal of this war to be nothing sort of a communistic republic, the other keeps on harping it to be mere pressure tactics to get a larger share of loaf within the present monarchical dispensation. Both the views are certainly not only wide off the mark of the objective reality, but also have effectively blocked any meaningful dialogue towards a satisfactory political solution to the problem so far.

Anybody who closely and correctly follows the official documents and public statements of the Party and the United Front, starting with the well known 40-point demands of the then United People's Front (the precursor of the current URPC) submitted in 1996 to the latest statement of Chairman Prachanda, should have no difficulty in comprehending that the bourgeois (capitalistic) democratic revolution is the immediate political agenda and abolition of monarchy is the core issue of the entire project. Of late, the immediate demands have been crystallised into an interim government, election to a constituent assembly and institutionalisation of the republic. The feudal autocratic monarchy has been principally targeted because it is the historical bulwark of all class, caste, gender, national, regional and religious oppression and main impediment to all round democratisation of the polity, economy, society and culture.

Of course, there is widespread illusion and misconception about the so-called constitutionality of the traditional monarchy after the restoration of the deformed and disabled parliamentary system in 1990. Subsequent events, particularly those after the infamous palace massacre of June 1, 2001, and more specifically the dramatic dissolution of parliament on May 22, 2002, should, however, dispel all such illusions and establish beyond doubt how the monarchy controls the real power of the state. We have always maintained that the faulty method of constitution-making by the nominated representatives of the King in 1990 and the continued allegiance of the RNA to the feudal palace have enabled the monarchy to retain absolute power and for ever dangle a Damocles' sword over the parliament. Recent course of events have fully corroborated this and some more are likely to follow in the near future. Hence it is our considered view that unless a new constitution is made by an elected constituent assembly and the country's armed forces are kept under the unqualified control of the people's representatives, no form of democracy can flourish and sustain in the country. This should clarify for once and for ever that the current fight in Nepal is historical fight between feudal monarchy and progressive bourgeois democracy as witnessed in 1648 Britain or 1789 France. Nothing more, nothing less!

And it is worthwhile clearing up a small but widespread misunderstanding about us at this juncture. It is often reported that we have since then dropped our cardinal demands of the republic and the constituent assembly, and are left with that of a mere interim government. Please note, ladies and gentlemen, this is not only utterly false but just ridiculous. How can we leave out such core issues, and that too after so much sacrifice? Then why should we wage the war at all? Yes, during the course of negotiations last year we agreed not to discuss the question of republic for the convenience of the other party, but had reserved our right to take the issue to the people during the elections to the constituent assembly. Our goal of a republic was retained, but only the means to achieve it was deferred to the constituent assembly in place of the negotiating table. It is as simple as that. As regards the constituent assembly, the issue was just raked up when it was not spotted in one of the public statements of our Party Chairman recently. Is it necessary and logical to chant all the demands publicly all the time? By no means. Therefore, let it be clear to all that the three demands are interrelated and constitute a single whole of the immediate political agenda of the democratic revolution, and remain valid to this day. If somebody wants to believe otherwise and live in a fool's paradise, it is his/her choice.

In the Vortex of International Conflict

Third, we would like to draw the attention of our pacifists towards the real source of danger of sucking the internal conflict of Nepal into the vortex of larger international conflict. Unless we correctly identify the role of international forces in the internal political dynamics of the country, it may not be possible for us to find genuine political solution to the problem. It is, however, quite disheartening that a large section of our intelligentsia (mostly Western-educated) and political parties fail to recognise the disastrous ramifications of the increasing hobnobbing of the ruling monarchist forces with the external powers and instead tend to cast unfounded aspersions against the revolutionary forces.

In this context it is first of all important to realise the obnoxious role of the international forces in carrying out the heinous palace coup d'etat of June 1, 2001. There is now increasing evidence of the involvement of the CIA in the coup. (see among others, Wagne Madsen, "Comparision Between Recent U.S.-Backed Coups", www.spiescafe.com). The recent patterns of judgment by the Supreme Court of Nepal in favor of Sher Bahadur Deuba and that of the Supreme Court of Venezuela in favour of the leaders of the failed military coup there (see *Frontline*, August 31–September 13, 2002) provide a strong resemblance of judicial manipulations by the CIA. Overtly active involvement of the U.S. government in shoring up the RNA and in prodding its allies (or satellites?) to do the same, is there for all to see. Hence such interventionist approach of the sole superpower of the world in a geostrategically sensitive zone sandwiched between two super states, India and China, naturally heralds the danger of the country getting sucked into the vortex of intermittent conflict.

The growing strategic stranglehold of U.S. imperialism in Nepal is basically designed to encircle China in the long term and to oversee India. This way both the giant neighbours are bound to get provoked and Nepal would be in an unenviable position of antagonizing everybody. Though in the shorter term the pro-U.S. monarchist forces may boast of support from all foreign powers, that is just transitory and soon the regime would be isolated from all. Even in India there is growing resentment against the pro-U.S. tilt of the Hindu fundamentalist BJP-led regime, and the recent support gained by the monarchist regime from the expansionist ruling classes of India may not last long.

It is in this context that the CPN (Maoist) and URPC have addressed to all foreign powers, particularly our two giant neighbours India and China, not to bolster the feudal autocratic regime and hinder the all round democratisation process in the country. The days of seeing the feudal monarchy as the factor of stability and peace are already over and now only a fully democratic and republican Nepal can guarantee sustainable peace and stability in the Himalayan region. Similarly, only by keeping the foreign powers out and letting the Nepalese people decide their own destiny themselves can the current conflict be resolved satisfactorily.

Let the gentlemen of the 'Foundation of Nepalese in America', among others, grasp this truth more firmly.

Emergency and Election are Antithetical

Fourth, there are some questions raised whether the emergency and elections can go together and whether there is any chance of our participating in the so-called midterm parliamentary elections in November. The plain answer to both is an emphatic 'no'.

It is a matter of common sense that an emergency rule, which suspends all civic and democratic rights of the people, is just antithetical to any form of election. Moreover, it is quite comical to note that the previous parliament was dissolved unceremoniously because it had refused to extend the emergency rule further, and the new parliament is to be elected under the emergency rule so that it can obediently endorse further emergency rule in future. So what is the use of any election or parliament if you are going to have indefinite emergency rule at the whims and fancy of the RNA? Just to hoodwink the gullible public, or the international community?

Now there should be no illusion to anybody that the limited democratic rights and parliamentary institutions gained after 1990 people's movement have been virtually usurped by the autocratic monarchy through its monopoly control over the RNA, and they can be regained and expanded not through any farcical elections under the aegis of the very same RNA but only through a new people's movement of greater heights and intensity.

As regards the question of participation on the farcical elections, if at all they are held even within the confines of RNA barracks, they would only help to legitimise the royal military dictatorship. While the mainstream Nepali Congress Party led by Girija Prasad Koirala has so far rightly seen through this royal conspiracy and reserved its final decision, it is quite intriguing and shameful that the opposition UML has hastily jumped into the election bandwagon. There are reasonable grounds to suspect that this most opportunist revisionist clique has been enticed by the royal palace and some foreign powers to provide a 'liberal face' to the royal autocracy and be pitted against the revolutionary forces in a 'diamond-cuts-diamond' manner. In that case it would only mean the degeneration of the UML clique into social fascism, whose tragic end only the future will reveal.

It is in this context that the CPN (Maoist) and URPC have recently proposed a broad political conference of all political parties, organisations and noted individuals opposed to the royal military dictatorship to find a political solution to the problem. We believe that time is now ripe for the democratic forces, both within and outside parliament, to take initiatives in their own hands and determine their destiny by themselves.

War and Negotiation Can Go Together

Fifth, there have been some queries and suggestions as to

whether we should not announce a unilateral ceasefire and call off the proposed 'Nepal bandh' (general strike) for September 16, given our repeated offer of negotiations for a political solution. Again we would say an emphatic 'no'. Because we believe war and negotiation can and should, if need be, go together.

As is well known, war and negotiation are just different means for a political end. And past history of all great revolutions testify that the two means are not contradictory but complementary. In our case, too, ever since the then government refused to negotiate over the 40-point charter of demands and the People's War (PW) was initiated in 1996, war and negotiation, in one form of the other, have been continuing and will continue till the aspired political end is met. We, therefore, appreciate the recent calls of the 10 parliamentarist parties, a dozen 'wise men' headed by Himalaya SJB Rana and others for a negotiated settlement of the problem, but fail to understand how we could clap with just one hand without the other side responding.

Also there have been repeated insinuations that since we had broken off the formal talks last time it is now our turn to make a new gesture for the resumption of the talks. We would again firmly reject such insinuations. What is basically missed, even by the enlightened political souls, while making such allegations is that talks are not held between two belligerent groups just for a tea party but for concrete political solutions to the shared problem. It should be known to everybody that the other party by not agreeing to our political proposals (the aforesaid 3-point demand, which was later slashed down to 2 point) and not advancing any alternative proposal of its own had in effect closed the door for any political solution and broken off the talks. We had formally pronounced this full 2 days in advance, before resuming the armed actions. So it is just ridiculous on the part of Deuba to make repeated outbursts against us on this question.

As regards the current countrywide mass actions and the proposed 'Nepal *bandh*' on September 16, these are the legitimate protest actions against the large-scale war crimes committed by the RNA. The 'Nepal *bandh*' is an indigenous form of mass political strike evolved over the years, which we feel is the most appropriate at the current juncture.

On the So-Called Military and Political Wing

And finally, there has been persistent disinformation campaign about the so-called contradiction between the military and the political wing of the Party. Again we would say this is totally baseless, preposterous and mischievous. Furthermore, we should proudly proclaim that in the contemporary revolutionary world our movement would perhaps be the most unified and centralised, where every military and non-military action takes place according to collective decision and plan.

Rather what our opponents fail to comprehend is that we have an integrated politico-military mechanism and no separate 'military' and 'political' wing as wildly speculated. While organisationally we are committed to ensure a concentric construction of the Party, the Army and the United Front under the supreme and unified leadership of the Party, the well-known dictum about the relation between the Party and the Army has been 'The Party commands the gun'. So there is no objective basis for any friction between the political and military fronts.

Another persistent rumor has been that Com. Badal is the 'military commander' and he is opposed to the Party leadership. It is quite interesting to note that now one Maj. Gen. Ashok Mehta (retd.) of the Indian army, who should enjoy access to RAW briefings, has also joined this rumour-mongering race. Gentlemen, we just pity your poor source of information! You are free to indulge in self-deception and live in a fool's paradise, but Com. Badal, a senior Party leader, is neither a 'military commander' nor is he ever opposed to the Party leadership. If you still want to grind the rumour mill, what can we do?

4 September 2002
[The author is Standing Committee Member of CPN (Maoist), and Convenor of United Revolutionary People's Council, Nepal]

THE FURIOUS ONE SPEAKS

In an interview with Bertil Lintner published in the Far Eastern Economic Review, 24 October 2002, Prachanda ('the furious one') gave a short reaction to the intervention by the king earlier in the month. We reproduce this interview here as the final 'statement' by the Maoist leadership in the collection.

BL: Are you willing to hold peace talks with the government?

Prachanda: I want to make it clear that right from the initiation of the People's War in Nepal, our Party has been upholding the strategy of political and military offensive against the old feudal state. To enter or not to enter into peace talks with the government is a part of our political strategy... It is not a question of willingness, rather than a form of struggle that we do not want to be disarmed.

BL: What would your demands be at such talks?

Prachanda: Our minimum demands are widely known: the formation of an interim government, election of a constituent assembly and organising the country as a democratic republic... It is quite clear that how far these demands will be fulfilled through peace talks will ultimately depend on the level of victory achieved in the actual battlefield.

BL: What is your final goal?

Prachanda: As a revolutionary communist party our final goal is socialism and communism. Right now our peoples are fighting against feudalism and imperialism. Therefore the immediate goal of our revolution is to fulfil the task of complete democratic revolution. We want to organise and develop the country with the full initiative of the masses through the abolition of the feudal and autocratic monarchy.

BL: How do you expect to achieve that goal?

Prachanda: No doubt we will achieve this goal through the politics of the People's War.

BL: What are your comments on the recent moves by the king?

Prachanda: The latest steps taken by this regicidal and fratricidal 'king' Gyanendra is nothing less than a feudal, autocratic, military coup. This desperate attempt of the feudal 'lord' will ultimately be smashed by our great people.

BL: Do you think it is possible to hold elections in the present situation?

Prachanda: Our Party has already decided that without any political resolution of the civil war, no election will be held.

Part Three
LEFT PERSPECTIVES

Chapter 7

The Maoist Movement in Nepal: A Class Perspective

Govinda Neupane

THE AGRARIAN POLITICAL ECONOMY OF NEPAL

According to the census of 1991, some 88 per cent of the population of Nepal lives in the rural areas (CBS, 1998, pp. 5, 11–13). The rural society is, for the most part, involved in agricultural production—81 per cent named agriculture as their main income source. Under these circumstances it is essential to understand the relations of production and structure of rural society. Nepalese Marxists have been using the term 'class' for 50 years with a specific meaning, but apart from reproducing the kind of 'class analysis' that Mao Tse Tung used in his analysis of classes and peasant movements in rural China, they have not attempted to study class structure of Nepal as it really is; thus, no serious attempt has been made to understand the class structure of contemporary Nepal.

According to Comrade Lenin, the great thinker of the world communist movement and leader of the Soviet Revolution, there are two paths in the capitalist development of agriculture. In the first path, a feudalistic landlord system gradually develops towards the controlled economic system of the Junkers. This retains the feudal subjugation and bondages of the farmers by providing a little capitalist form to them. In the second path, there is no capitalistic economic system or it is broken by the revolution. Instead, large tracts of land are seized from the feudal landowners and the land is redistributed. In this way, the peasants are converted into capitalistic peasants (Lenin, 1962, pp. 239–244). Be it is through the first or the second of Lenin's two paths, the rural economy and society of Nepal is currently in transition and is advancing through the process of the emergence of rural capitalists and proletarianisation of the rural poor. Seeing the process in a general way, it becomes clear that the landlord system, existing relations and the landlords themselves are disappearing from the rural areas. Since the process of proletarisation in contemporary Nepal is at a very early stage, the working class in the classic sense is not an influential class, and its numbers are also relatively small. Today, the biggest social class in terms of number and power is that of the workers in agriculture. These workers do not belong to the landless class in accordance with conventional definition. There is an urgent need for clarity with respect to these workers whose surplus value is being expropriated by the exploiters of other classes.

While looking at the different classes existing in the rural society of Nepal, we might bear in mind Lenin's two paths, but we also need to understand the specific history of the relations of production in Nepal. In the 1950s, the *Birta* Elimination Act was brought in; although it did not solve the problem of landownership, it had a major impact on the concept of landownership and the relations of production. The *Birta wallahs* now became like those tilling *Raikar* land. The Land Reform Act of 1964 imposed and fixed land ceilings, redistributed 'excessive' land above the ceiling, revised agricultural debts and introduced compulsory saving. This land reform was not definitive, but accelerated the process of change.

In eastern Nepal there came into existence many tea estates and fruit farms. Feudal landlords converted themselves into lords of tea estates and fruit farms, and agricultural tenants and landless labourers became estate workers. Many landlords kept 'excessive' land in a fictitious name and sold it off gradually. A few pieces of land were seized and distributed to middle class *khases** and to civil servants. This changed the pre-existing class structure and class relationship, and new transitional, class relations and classes came into existence. This was not any kind of 'revolution', because

---

* Group of the Nepalese people belonging to Indo-Aryan family.

it did not bring about a far-reaching qualitative change, but it did produce significant quantitative change. Although these changes were taking place, giving rise to new structures and relationships, there was little attempt to analyse the class relationships of Nepali rural economy and society, until very recently, when some have initiated a debate, with a view to clarifying some serious theoretical and practical questions (e.g. Bhattarai, 1989, pp. 98–104).

But field discussions held in some hill districts (Bhojpur and Salyan) and some *terai* districts (Morang and Banke) revealed that various indicators are used by the local peasantry themselves in developing a class analysis. These include the size, location and type of plot owned (or farmed), the wealth in livestock, the specialised skills available and the level and kind of income derived from non-farm economic activities (employment, business etc.). Even using these criteria, it is not easy to distinguish wealthy and poor people and the results of attempts to do so are not always correct. It is for this reason that locals also link assets and income to food security and labour input. In other words, they calculate the wealth and income represented by land, livestock, skills and non-farm income and add to this the months they can eat; this then reveals whether the household is obliged to work for others or is able to employ others. On the basis of these criteria, they divided the villagers into the rich, the medium and the poor. In current terminology, the rich meant the rich peasant class with minor exception, the medium level meant the middle peasants and the poor meant the poor peasants or workers. (Neupane, 1999).

Some landlords may live in the village who can be clearly identified as exploiting others, but their number in Nepal is relatively small. Today, almost all—rich farmers, poor farmers and agricultural labourers—are involved in the market and have come to depend on it. For agricultural inputs (chemical, fertiliser, insecticide, seeds etc.) agricultural producers depend on the market; their products (or some of them) are sold in the market. Many producers are involved in an undoubted process of differentiation of agriculture and are usually involved in the production of more than one agricultural crop or farm product (ghee, honey, vegetables, maize and 'cash' crops). It could be argued that, according to the traditional Marxist analysis, a 'rich farmer' who employs labour is an agricultural capitalist in this transitional situation, in so far as he appropriates surplus value through the imposition of a low rate of wages and long working days. Even middle and poor farmers who produce commodities for the market are producing surplus value.

There is a special group of peasants named 'squatters' *(sukumbasi)* comprising those people created by the Panchayat System, many elite people of the hill and some poor peasants also. Squatters do not constitute a class. They are only a group of the above-mentioned farmers. The generally talked about 'squatters' problem is in fact a process of diverting attention from the real problems of the peasants and to transfer the ownership of the public land to the relatives and cadres of the rulers.

In comparison to the villages, the urban areas are generally relatively rich. The urban poor remain in the shadows, obscured by the big buildings of the upper and upper–middle classes with their sophisticated life and showy lifestyle. The numbers of the urban poor, however, have been continually increasing. Thousands of child labourers also fall into this class of the working poor. They are in a very difficult situation as regards physical situation, livelihoods, social life and opportunities. These urban poor, who still often remain dependent on their own families and relatives in the rural areas, are an expanded form of the rural proletariat and although beginning to constitute elements of an urban working class are also often 'rural' (even 'feudal') in their outlook and work relations. They work, however, in a wide range of sectors, in industry, services and other areas. Their circumstances encourage a degree of fatalism, which provides the psychological basis for a certain passivity.

The establishment of industrial and financial institutions, such as jute mills, cotton mills and banks, from the mid-1930s onwards led to the beginnings of an industrial working class in Nepal. As the number of enterprises and institutions increased, so too did the number of workers. Apart from the industrial working class, wage workers are increasingly present in other sectors and occupations. Construction work, the transport sector, public sector employment and professional occupations are areas in which significant numbers of wage workers are to be found. The number of workers is increasing due to continuous expansion of service and occupations.

The growth of professional employment and the growth of 'the middle classes' (the 'new' petty bourgeoisie) has also been significant. The rapid expansion in south Asia generally (in Nepal also to a small extent) of computer and information technology as a sector of production and business, in particular, raises interesting and important questions about the relationship between manual workers and 'mental' workers, and the relationship between the workers and the 'petty bourgeoisie'. Therefore, now it is high time to think, consider and analyse the complexity and to find out the specialities in such new areas and fields. But, by and large, Nepali communists do not want to enter actively into this kind of debate and prefer to walk the less dangerous paths of unproductive traditional class analysis.

Among the upper classes of the Nepalese society there are some landlords, rich peasants, national capitalists and the comprador bureaucratic bourgeoisie or the capitalists having dual character. What new characteristic is notable here is that there is an intermingling of thinking, character or behaviour of the capitalists and the landlords among these people. This could be an important subject for a separate study.

TRANSITIONAL CHARACTER OF NEPALI SOCIETY

Today in Nepal, the society shows some characteristics of a capitalist society. Even in areas considered pre-feudal or feudal, there is the production and sale of commodities and the widespread sale of foreign goods imported from abroad. Such capitalistic relations can be seen in both the towns and villages. After the elimination of *Birta system* in 1959, the Land Reform of 1964, the eradication of the *Kipat system* and the need of land in the industrial sector, land has been redistributed to a large extent. But justice has still not been done in land redistribution because of the provision of high ceiling for home-stead, which is 28 Bigas in the *terai* and 100 Ropanis in the hill. In the *terai* there are many absentee landlords here and there. If the land registered in the name of relatives is also included, we can say that large tracts of land still remain. Thus, the slogan 'land to the tiller' has not been implemented. While analysing the hill agricultural society, however, it can be found that there were no big landlords even in the past. Deeper changes were introduced there as a result of psychological impact of the reform and the ownership over land is largely with those who till it.

Now also in some small areas, what might be termed 'prefeudal' production relations continue to exist. For example, the community-based economic system of the *Chepang* can be regarded as such. On the other hand, large areas of the countryside, particularly in the *terai*, continue to be characterised by 'feudal' production relations. But, if feudal relations remain characteristic in some areas of the *terai*, in others, particularly in the east, we can find farmers involved directly in agricultural production on their own land, paying wages to hired agricultural labourers, attempting to diversify their production, dependent on the market for farm inputs, and for the sale of agricultural commodities, and trying to use modern technology as the basis for capital accumulation. Under these conditions, such farmers may be regarded as agricultural capitalists in transition.

Distinct from this 'class', we find the largest category of rural producers, who produce for themselves for the most part, but who may employ others and also work for others, including neighbours. This kind of class is the biggest class of Nepali rural society. In so far as it includes those who are relatively self-sufficient and tend to employ others, we are dealing with rich or middle peasants. This could be seen as the 'petty bourgeois' class in terms of its outlook, practice and economic activities. The poorer rural producers, who are less self-sufficient and tend to work more for others, the marginal farmers and landless labourers—who are usually still referred to in Nepal as 'farmers'—are in effect the rural proletariat or agricultural workers. They tend not to see themselves as such and are not organised like workers, but this is because they lack class consciousness. If that were to change, they would recognise that their character is that of workers. If organised like an industrial unity, service academy, or in a fixed geographical unit (e.g. village), or had a fixed type of labour management (e.g. *Kamaiya*), or common profession or occupation (e.g. *Haliya*), they would certainly experience a greater degree of collective consciousness.

What needs to be understood is that although rural economy

and society in Nepal has not been unambiguously transformed into a capitalist economy and society, the expansion of capitalistic relations of production and exchange is taking place in exceptional forms. This is characteristic of a transitional condition. This must be seen in its totality and dynamism. Today, in Nepal, the number of agricultural labourers, share-croppers (tenants, including those working land in *Adhiya* and *Kut* relationships) and poor farmers is growing all the time. There are also increasing numbers of skilled workers both in agriculture and outside. The number of general or 'middle' peasants (what might be said to constitute a transitional rural petty bourgeois class) is in the numerical majority. The rich farmers or small capitalists are scattered here and there; their position is shaky.

Labour relations between these three classes can take several forms—mainly wages, but also through crop-sharing or labour-sharing arrangements. Low wages are common; producers of equivalent scale often exchange their labour. Under the crop-share arrangements, annual work brings an agreed quantity of material or cash payment. The shared labour relationship is found widely across the country, especially among so-called occupational castes (tailors, blacksmiths and cobblers/leatherworkers). Child labour is often provided for upper-class rural families, political leaders or wealthy businessmen's houses. Annually or bi-annually, parents receive a small payment for their children's labour. In addition there are the *beth-begari* and *Jhara* customary practices; the former is now transformed by being associated with political support and patronage, while people's participation is the form taken more and more by the latter, and constitutes a new feature.

All rural producers experience various forms of social discrimination and social injustice—on the basis of class, ethnicity and caste, and gender—which divide them and produce divisions of a socially complex kind. Female farmers suffer from patriarchal oppression and exploitation, and there is widespread gender discrimination throughout Nepal because of which women do not have equal opportunities in overall development of the country. There is also discrimination due to caste and ethnic affiliation. Regional lifestyles and traditions vary considerably and give rise to difficulties. Although the movements for reform in these areas have had some change in the life standard of the peasants, they have not yet achieved substantial changes in their political, social or cultural domains; but the movements continue to develop. The main issues of the rural society are 'the land to the tiller' and fixing of the minimum wages and the working hours. It is also necessary to redistribute the land and to prioritise it as an important work. Some discussion is required, however, of the subject of the Nepali working class. The first industrial action by workers in Nepal in the long history of the working class movement was a 20-days long action, starting on 4 March 1947, when the workers at the Biratnagar Jute Mill and the Morang Cotton Mill demanded the registration of their trade union and an increment in wages. The government suppressed the action by using the police force. The workers also participated in the movement against the Delhi Agreement (Samjauta) of 1951. Forty years later, in 1990, a coordinating committee in favour of the new democracy was established by the labour movement. In this way, the working class movement connected with the People's Movement (*Jana Andolan*).

It is possible to identify four major dimensions of the Nepali labour movement, which broadly characterise four phases in its development: 1. The establishment, expansion and consolidation of labour organisation, 2. Transformation of lifestyle and social security, 3. Defence and consolidation of Nepali patriotism and 4. Social and political change. As the priority was given to reducing immediate difficulties, the reformist influence remained strong within the labour movement, and the objective of the transformation of society was never really addressed. As a consequence, the twin tendencies of reformism and 'NGO-ism' have become strongly established among the working class in many different sectors and occupational groupings. They have tended to become a vote bank and to have turned their backs on the crucial issues of social justice and revolution. There has been a lack of political and critical class consciousness among the Nepali workers and the labour movement generally for a long time.

If on the one hand the Nepalese communists have been unsuccessful in providing effective guidance to the Nepalese workers' movement, the social democratic stream is engrossed in reducing the workers' movement to an NGO movement on the other. The CPN (UML) and other social democratic parties use it to purge themselves of the deviations. They also consider the workers' movement as a fertile land to reap benefit from. That is why they use their olfactory sense to pick up the beneficial issues, engage themselves in the NGO rituals and harbour the wish to limit the workers' movement within limited reform. The newly formed Nepal Teachers Association and many other professional or civil organisations have registered as part of the Nepal Trade Union Congress. This is a very old sickness to be found in the trade union movement of Nepal. In this way, the direct involvement of the associations of the petty bourgeois class has taken advantage of the size and scale of the Nepali Labour Movement, diverting and misguiding it, and using it for their own benefit and its own class welfare. The democratic socialists have systematically tried to weaken the revolutionary potential of the Labour Movement. One of the critical problems facing the Nepali Labour Movement today is how to free it from reformism, status-quo-ism and NGO-ism.

The other problem that has long existed in this movement is the lack of proper coordination of reform in lifestyle and social security, on the one hand, and the agenda of social transformation, on the other. Remaining aloof from the real and important issues of labourers' dignity, welfare and security and simply raising the empty slogan of 'the labour movement', rejecting their specific concerns with social security in order to speak of 'revolution', is unreasonable. As is excluding the basic work required for transformation from the agenda and peddling a dream of complete change in the labourers' lives; this is faulty theory and practice. These two things are now visible. A proper balance between the immediate and the long-term needs is required; so too is the rejection of the idea that one can be attained only if the other is abandoned. So, the present one-sided approach of 'either–or' must be opposed. What is needed is a unified approach to the problems facing the Nepali labour movement in which the forces of the revolutionary labour movement and the progressive social political transformational forces should work together, side by side, to solve these problems.

The other challenge for the labour movement remains the need to recognise the specific problems of specific sections of the working class (e.g. women, the unorganised sector etc.) and to see solutions in appropriately specific terms. This should be taken seriously and the nature of these specific issues and differences analysed. Otherwise, generalisation will predominate and the confrontation of reality be rendered impossible. By recognising the differences and inequalities existing as a result of their origin, working area and needs, a broader unity becomes possible within the labour movement. Labourers in Nepal today are different from European labourers today, or those of the 19th century. Their relationship with the villages remains intact, they still have some link in the villages, their families are still living in the villages and have a residence even if small. That is why, we should pay attention to their relationship with the rural soriety, the continuity of the fatalist thinking existing in that society and the complication of the values and norms of the feudal society. This means that even the Nepalese working class is in the process of transition from feudalism and its class behaviours are also affected by this transition.

CONTRADICTIONS OF TRANSITIONAL SOCIETY

Nepali society is, however, moving on from its specific transitional state. The old types of feudal relationship are breaking down. They are influenced by three significant factors. They are (1) a slow but undoubted process of capitalist development, starting in the mid-1930s, (2) the impact made by the 1964 land reform programme in land ownership and control and (3) the revolutionary change that has occurred in science and technology. Also, due to the diversity created by the massive expansion in trade and commerce, there has been a considerable increase in opportunities for the sale of labour power outside agriculture. Although there is a limited demand for labour in the industrial sectors in Nepal, the labour market and demand in service sector occupations has been expanding very fast.

In the agricultural sector also, the old feudal system is in decline and there are signs of a remarkable change. Five new characteristics have been seen in the present production system: (1) Except for a relatively small number of cases, the large landed feudal or semi-feudal estates are no longer in existence; (2) The initial stage of capitalisation of agriculture has started to emerge; (3) Agricultural capitalists have come into existence; (4) Diversification has started to emerge in the agricultural product for consumption and *(5)* Wages have become the main form of labour relation even in agriculture. In view of this it becomes clear that the agrarian revolution cannot be the main form of Nepalese democratic revolution. The rapidly developing 'capitalism' in Nepal is of a very strange type. To understand it and its significance, we need to pay attention to four things: *(i)* this is not the free developed capitalism as in Europe; *(ii)* this will not change the nature of the democratic revolution required for the transformation of Nepali society; *(iii)* it has increased the possibility of transition through the centralisation of armed power and a revolt and *(iv)* in spite of the long list of present day contradictions in Nepali society, the main contradiction is the contradiction between the reactionary class with the mixed charcter of the comprador and bureaucratic bourgeoisie on the one hand and the Nepalese working class on the other.

The relevance of the slogan 'land to the tiller', however, has not ended. It must have two elements: *(1)* Excess land, which cannot be ploughed by a single agricultural family, should not be allowed and *(2)* One farmer family should be allocated only as much land as it can till, on the basis of lawful distribution of land. But this alone cannot solve the problems of agriculture in Nepal. For this, capitalist development in agriculture is required, including diversification, industrialisation, mechanisation and cooperation. It will be necessary to fix minimum wages, recognise individual ownership of small plots, arrange access to the means of production and develop a cooperative framework for all aspects of the agrarian reform.

The most important issues are wealth, inequality and social justice. The key to dealing with all three at the same time is increasing the power of labour so as to increase its control over production, its skills and its productivity, thereby increasing and widening wealth creation rather than narrowing opportunities and presiding over the contraction and diminution of wealth. A new leadership, with effective plans and programmes, is demanded for such a programme of transformation, the construction of a detailed agenda and the capacity to implement it. A new state system capable of conceiving, planning and implementing radical change is required; a state that is practical and pragmatic, not abstract and ideological. Its structure and operations should be scientific in conception and execution, socially egalitarian and lawful, technically research-oriented, userfriendly, change-oriented and above all devoted and honourable in its service towards the people.

The other problem that must be dealt with is the current ideology of caste and ethnic difference. It has imposed a form of central ideology and control on all racial, ethnic and caste groups in Nepal, has restricted 'racial' freedoms and equality and discriminated against 'racial' minorities and 'lower castes'. The present superstructure has peddled an ideology of centralism. Whether in geographic or in caste and ethnic terms, there is an idea of the supremacy of the Hindu upper castes and classes; other castes and classes become 'marginal' and 'inferior'. Local structures are drained of power and forced to be dependent on the centre; in all aspects, whether the formulation of development policy or the management of resources, the administrative hierarchy is fixed. To change this, a programme of caste and ethnic 'freedom' or autonomy needs to be implemented on the basis of the distribution of castes and ethnic groups, languages, historical background and geographical potential. The right of self-governance should be given to the regional legislature, with regional governments having their own autonomy. This not only would fulfil the 'national' ambitions of different ethnic groups and peoples, but would also encourage administrative decentralisation and reduce the volume of work; it would increase the time and energy available within the administration to design, plan, implement, audit, modify and evaluate the main working agenda. Using the new technology and methods, the administration of the state in the 21st century can be conducted easily and without the old traditional red-tape. The key to change would be decentralisation. All of the ethnic groups and peoples of Nepal would have the opportunity of local decision-making. This system would offer social justice and carry it forward in a cooperative way and would make the present divisive and destructive theory and practice redundant.

Now our society is in the middle of different types of inequality. This has created various kinds of conflict. One kind is that between the minority of the educated and the majority of the uneducated—the mass of the Nepali people, in which the educated upper and middle classes of the urban areas are in conflict with the majority of the poor and disadvantaged classes of both urban and rural areas. Some intellectuals are creating the illusion that change today relies on intellectuals, and they explain their own role in the pages of the different newspapers and magazines. In short, the poor and socially excluded face trouble and pain on the one side, whereas many intellectuals waiting for the lottery of pomp and luxury are also there.

In our country, there is a need for technology, skills, excellent knowledge, service and also research centres. Both the rich and the poor comprise the country in their different ways; the task of keeping the balance between them is a tough one, but not impossible. The solution to this dilemma can be eliminated by giving first priority to the welfare of the labouring classes. By finding out and understanding previously unseen or ignored contradictions, the different needs can be identified in order of priority, and the proper solutions can be found by discovering correctly the situation of this transitional society.

Now another issue to consider is that of economic liberalisation, privatisation, structural adjustment and the problems raised by globalisation. There is now continual privatisation of state sector industries, of professional organisations and service-oriented organisations. The social contract accepted by the government in favour of the welfare of the working class is ever more strictly limited and, in the name of globalisation, the world is becoming an international market-place. These developments have created considerable damage. The employment of labour, development of vocational skills and individual and family psychology have all been adversely affected by these processes. In the context of Nepal, those who control the processes of liberalisation, privatisation and globalisation are those who direct the World Bank and the International Monetary Fund and the comprador capitalists (commission agents, local representatives, big import–export businessmen, smugglers), their political representatives (upper class political leaders, high positioned officials etc.) and most of the non-government organisations fed by the charity of the West and purporting to represent 'civil society'. The labour movement is made weaker by the direct or indirect involvement of these organisations. Now it has become necessary to fight against such distortions and disparities. Without eliminating the obstacles created by imperialism and its instruments, such as the IMF, the World Bank and other private and bilateral government banks and lending agencies, the process of new economic construction cannot be well balanced and managed.

In this current transitional social context, the movement in favour of classical and contemporary political freedoms has gained momentum and its central expression has been the Maoist People's War. The movement that gave rise to this War consciously paid attention to the contemporary social, economic and political contradictions of Nepal. Now, therefore, it becomes not only appropriate but essential to discuss the subject of the Maoist movement.

THE MAOIST MOVEMENT

Edward Muller argues that if there is significant inequality in the distribution of income in a country in which a democratic system exists, such inequality weakens the legitimacy of the government and democratic organisations may be replaced by more legitimacy of state and may be replaced by dictatorial organisations. The scope for the exercise of democracy can be reduced by substantial inequality. Therefore, to avoid such situation, democracy can be established and if necessary reestablished if inequality is to be maintained at or is reduced to a medium or lower level. Otherwise, a strong political party with a commitment to redistribution must maintain power for a relatively long period in order to be able to execute own policies and reduce the unequal distribution of income (Muller, 1988, p. 66). Although Muller was talking about the required environment for the establishment and maintenance of democracy with reference to Western states, the bitter truth for Nepal is that democracy cannot be maintained in any society with more than a certain level of inequality. Without the commitment of a strong political party in power, deepseated inequality existing in a society cannot be removed. The experience of Nepal tends to confirm this analysis and these conclusions. This is why the Maoist movement of Nepal has been emerging rapidly over the last decade as a way forward for the establishment of a new democratic state.

From the very beginning of the formation of the communist party in 1949, the revolutionary tendency was present, if in a relatively weak form. This tendency grew, however, over the next two decades and emerged visibly in the *Jhapa Bidroha* of 1971. This movement was the outcome of the positive influence of the Chinese Cultural Revolution and the Naxalbadi movement of India, and negative influence of the prevailing theory and practice of the ruling classes of Nepal and the political regime of the day. Imitating the strategy of killing class enemies, adopted by Charu Mujumdar and the Naxalites, an assault on the class enemy began in Nepal from Jyamirgadhi village in Jhapa District on 16th May 1971. As part of a conscious and planned movement, it chose the path of armed revolution and conducted the movement accordingly. Mistakes were made—notably the mechanical, blind imitation of the Naxalbadi movement, the neglect of the people's movement and lack of mass organisation, and the tendency towards petty bourgeois romanticism. This current was, consequently, unable to sustain itself successfully for very long. On the other hand, one faction of the Nepal Communist Party, which held a 4th national convention in 1974—and established itself as a new party, calling itself the Communist Party of Nepal (Fourth Convention)—determined to establish a democratic state on the basis of armed struggle. The plenum of this party, held at Ayodhya in 1981, concluded that the Chinese Communist Party was itself now 'anti-revolutionary'. This position was taken by several other parties across the world that had previously supported a broadly Maoist line. There followed a period of argument and debate about unity and division, and the party split on several occasions, as a result of disagreements relating to policy and leadership. Eventually, as a result of serious disagreement about the analysis of the immediate environment and the need to prepare for armed struggle, one faction separated from the others and the Communist Party of Nepal (Maoist) came into existence.

These major divisions at the beginning of the 1990s were between the parliamentary and non-parliamentary parties in Nepal, but through the first half of the decade, the divisions on the far left took place between groups that were, for the most part, committed to a non-parliamentary road. After the declaration of the People's War by the Communist Party of Nepal (Maoist) in 1996, the situation changed radically. This party now followed the strategy and military policy of the Chinese Revolution, including the progressive establishment of local rule, the development of base areas and the eventual establishment of a central government and a democratic republic, which is the long-term objective of the Peoples War. Now we shall turn briefly to a consideration of the People's War in Nepal.

THE PEOPLE'S WAR

The Communist Party of Nepal (Maoist) launched or initiated a People's War bearing in mind the historical context of the use of violence and the science of Marxist war. Those planning it started this long-term war consciously and in a highly organised way. The theory and practice of the Maosists reveal their commitment to a protracted People's War. This war is a complex phenomenon, carried out as a totality in which motivation, orientation, transformation and war work are carried on simultaneously. Therefore, a detailed explanation of the three major phases of a People's War is necessary. The War is firstly a guerrilla war, foundation of the base areas and a united front.

Guerrilla War

The Communist Party of Nepal (Maoist) is waging People's War Since 13 February 1996. Armed actions carried out in the beginning generated a qualitative difference in the devotion of the party towards the People's War, wide support from ordinary people and the level of preparation and organisation. After the attack of Dunai, Dolpa, it reached new heights. By capturing the district headquarters and holding it for several hours, the Maoist party confirmed its new and very specific identity. The successful military action helped the party win its psychological war with the police, it confirmed the party's success as a political as well as a military machine.

Three new features have been seen in the raids conducted by the Maoists. First, the military skills deployed against the enemy forces, the attitude of the insurgents and the coordination of people's participation. Large numbers of armed people were involved in actions directed against police posts and local collaborators, and substantial support was given to the guerrillas by the presence of large numbers of the masses. Second, this People's War is very strange, in the sense that it appears at one moment barely to exist, but at another bursts into action. After even substantial clashes at night, no guerrillas are to be found by searches carried out in the daytime. This is a peculiarity of the People's War. This brought disarray to the side of the enemy. Third, through talk and dialogue, it provided opportunities to those who were uncommitted and through action, it rendered passive those who were marginally opposed. It did what a skilfully waged war should do and bypassed the most active opponents from the political viewpoint and gained ground from the strategic point of view. The confusions, debates and delays that occurred with respect to the mobilisation of the army were the result of this skill in waging war. Until now, the Maoists have been successful in the conduct of raids. This success has shaken the heart of the enemy in the rural areas, the war with the police has been won psychologically and the military basis has been prepared for parallel rule.

Base Area

The Maoist People's War was the first war conducted in Nepal on the basis of a new theory and strategy aimed both at capturing local power and also at capturing central power. The objective of setting up base areas is new in Nepal, though it is not a new strategy for communists and Marxists. Even in the Jhapa uprising these elements existed but as they were arranged, subjective and uncertain in size and so did not seem the sun and moon of systematic planning and use. The concept of the base area is a concept in a new ideology, a new politics, a new culture, a new economic structure and management and totally a new set of norms, values, beliefs and attitudes. On the one hand, it gives the feeling of hope, faith and courage to the people and on the other hand, provides the experience of government in action, which instructs and trains the people's government. The achievement of a victorious sector, either permanent or temporary, not only becomes significant psychologically but also provides some thing concrete to the people, either of which is equally important.

Because of the development of the People's War and the people's participation in different districts of western Nepal such as Rolpa, Rukum, Jajarkot, Salyan, Kalikot, Dolpa and Pyuthan, the presence of the government is being reduced and possibility of establishing people's power is increasing. In these areas, there is primary exercise of labour power, new economic activities connected with new production relations and the construction of a new culture, and other areas are expecting the same sooner or later. Base areas can be established through the expansion of other areas as areas of guerrilla war, depending on the quickness of guerrilla warfare and the capacity of decentralisation of the opposition forces. In reality, the situation is developing rapidly in this regard. Now temporary base areas have been established countrywide and the central areas of influence have been expanded. As a consequence, the physical basis has been created for developing people's action. Temporarily, a political laboratory has been found and now provides the opportunity of executing specified policies in the areas under Maoist influence. By using this excellent opportunity, people-oriented activity in many areas—social, cultural and educational—is made possible. Movements against domestic violence, movement for gender equality, movement against gambling and other social evils such as alcoholism, movement for educational reform and action against the corrupt people all fall within these categories. These actions have had positive impacts upon the life of the common people. People are impatient to see such actions taking place even in areas including public health, agriculture, administration and justice. This shows that such administrative arrangement is possible not only in the base areas but also in other areas.

United Front

A united front is necessary for class unity and to establish cooperation for the revolution for which the party is responsible and which it is required to coordinate. In the social context of Nepal a special role is allocated to the so-called untouchable castes and minority ethnic groups. Because of the *Khas* hegemony, these marginalised groups are eager to take part in the revolution and they have a strong wish to contribute to the changes involved. In the class struggle, the coordination of caste and ethnic social contradictions, the issue of untouchability and other social issues should be managed together in the unified flow of the class freedom movement. This should unify the organisation of caste and ethnic groups and other marginal groups and special organisations. A broad united front in which all can be involved is an essential objective. In fact, however, the structure of the united front should not be uniform and centralised. Local fronts become active in specific local areas. Recognising the existence of specific circumstances and conditions, there should be many different 'fronts', based on different criteria (ethnic group, caste, geographical region etc.) and after a lapse of time, the fronts as a whole, or some of them, can be reorganised as a general federation or general united front. This kind of united front not only works well as regards people's mobilisation and the development of a united movement, it can also play a significant role in the development of a common regime for different ethnic groups. A united front established in the community can reflect in reality the potential of a selfgoverning system and provide the equivalent of a laboratory for this idea. A united front developed at the central level can provide an opportunity for effective intervention in the existing political power structure while at the same time it can provide a platform for the progressive forces to join their hands in the name of the people's welfare. The united front should be seen as a force for equality, justice and social transformation. In fact, in Nepal, the 'new democracy' means a system orchestrated by the united front, in which class, caste, and other progressive social forces work hand in hand. The party mainly pays attention to the class struggle in the village and remains the real force struggling against feudalism and imperialism and as the force behind the patriotic, democratic and leftist forces of the united front (Prachanda, 2000, pp. 8–9). Today, it is essential to study and analyse the role of the leadership of the communist party in the revolution, and the role of the people's united front in the new democracy. Given the experience of failure in attempts to develop different models of the new democracy elsewhere, the identification and pursuit of a non-traditional path has become a matter of urgency (Neupane, 2001).

SOME WEAKNESS OF THE MAOIST MOVEMENT IN A CLASS CONTEXT:

First of all, as a matter of Nepali history, the Peoples' War was launched as an exercise of armed class struggle. This created a new practice of concrete class struggle. The abstract slogan of class consciousness was left behind and consciousness was aroused in the context and during the process of concrete class struggle. The party that led this struggle is based on the labouring class, and most of the participants are also from the same class. In the rural areas under its control, economic and social reforms are undertaken in favour of members of the labouring classes. In the mobilisation of the People's War and in the establishment of base areas, a decisive role has been played by the organised armed forces of the labouring classes and the active participation of the ordinary rural people.

The weakness of this movement, however, needs to be addressed. From a class point of view, the movement suffers from three main weaknesses: *(a)* lack of clarity in the class structure of the Nepalese society and the core element of the revolution; *(b)* mechanical outlook in the handling of local class struggle and anti-*Munim** trend and *(c)* a lack of effective presence of the party among the working class.

(a) Lack of Clarity on the Class Structure of the Nepalese Society and the Core Element of the Revolution: Analysing the problem of land in Chinese society, Chairman Mao had reached the general conclusion that rural society was divided into three classes—the upper class of big and middle landlords, the middle class consisting of the remaining small landlords and rich farmers and the lower class comprising middle and poor farmers. In 1926, Mao decided that instead of three classes there were five classes of people living in China: the landlord and comprador class, the middle capitalist class, the petty bourgeois class, the semi-proletariat (including a large number of farmers who till their own land and others, such as poor farmers, small workers, business helpers, small farmers who plough and till the land of others on a mass scale and small traders) and the proletariat.

In present day Nepal, there are no big landlords as there were in China. In the past also there were no big estates as in China. In the land tenure system of 1950, Raikar land constituted 50 per cent, *Birta* 36 per cent, *Guthi* 2 per cent, *Kipat* 4 per cent and 8 per cent under state/*Jagir/Rakam* and other forms of tenures. Nearly two-thirds (60 per cent) of the total cultivated land was tilled

---

* *Munim* is a farm manager of a landlord and may be roughly represented by the word bailiff.

and ploughed by sharecroppers (Adhiya, *Thekka* or *Kut*). The proportion of farmers actually tilling their own land was 67 per cent. Some 30 per cent of the remaining land was under the fixed *Thekka* management and the remainder was under *Sewa-sharta*. This shows that in Nepal there was no real feudal landlord system. Imitation of the Chinese model in this regard is inappropriate. Only a small proportion of the land was farmed under a feudal system; in Nepal there were small landlords and rich farmers but no big landlords. The big estates were under the *Thekka, Adhiya* or *Sewa–sharta* systems. So while comparing our agrarian structure with that of other countries we have to recognise the distinctiveness of our own. The land reform of 1964 further divided the land and expanded land ownership. So the number of owner-producers increased significantly. Many big estates were divided and fragmented or transformed into commercial operation. The tea estates of eastern Nepal are examples of this. Farm labourers were converted into industrial workers or agricultural wage workers.

Nepali rural economy and society has been rapidly progressing towards capitalism by the same two paths that Lenin described in the Russian case. In Nepal, the semi-proletariat is numerous, as in the analysis of Chairman Mao. The village is linked to the market and thus influenced by the dynamics of the capitalist world economy. This suggests that a traditional rural revolution cannot be the central factor in the new democratic revolution. The Communist Party of Nepal (Maoist) has to pay attention, while analysing the class structure and dynamics of Nepali society, to the historical development process and the evolution of class contradictions. Instead of simply accepting the traditional model, an objective investigation and analysis should be undertaken. This kind of work has not been done well by the party.

(b) Mechanical Outlook in the Handling of Local Class Struggle and the Anti-Munims Trend: The Jhapa movement had a rather mechanical concept of the mobilisation of class struggle. While recognising some exceptional cases, the so-called class enemies killed in this uprising were not necessarily real class enemies and some of them belonged to friendly classes also. What actually happened is that in our country the landlords appear liberal and their *Munim*s (managers of the landlords) appear more flagrant.

The workers have direct relations with them and harbour more hatred towards them. A responsible political organisation should have understood this reality and instructed the people accordingly. In fact, the opposite was the case; the limitations of the local people's perspective affected the party, and as a result, unfortunate incidents also took place. One example can be cited to make the point clear. In a certain village, at a party meeting identifying 'class enemies', the local farmers identified a person who was a middle farmer and was ill-regarded because he was accused of stealing oxen and selling them in India. In fact, there the poor and landless farmers had no oxen and the accused was actually stealing from the rich or wealthy middle farmers. As it happens the local people made up a death squad and finished him off. This was the kind of action that the Jhapa movement undertook. In the beginning of the Maoist People's War many such incidents occurred. Now, they are fewer, but still take place. The Maoists should consider the criticism made above and leave this ill-considered kind of action. So, the decision must be taken to be truly revolutionary in class consciousness and actions must conform to this approach.

(c) Absence of Effective Presence Among the Working Class: The workers' movement is in its infancy stage in Nepal. There are five major causes for this. First, the number of workers is limited as a result of the slow and weak development of industrialisation and of industrial employment; second, workers do not clearly exist as such except in the industrial sector; third, the workers lack organisational strength in part as a result of differences between leftist and democratic socialist politics; fourth, there is a tendency to passivity among the working class and fifth, employers and the ruling class generally have been successful at organising repression. There is also a tendency for the workers to struggle for immediate objectives and to be satisfied with their limited achievements. This all has far-reaching implications for revolutionary struggle. The working class have learnt a lot from their wrongdoings and are becoming clearer about the concept of aiming for the ultimate freedom of their class, making their thinking more strategic and linked to long-term plans for revolution.

They are now more aware of the importance of participation in the movement and of the need to fulfil their historical responsibility. The Communist Party of Nepal (Maoist) has also fallen behind in regard to workers' awareness, unity and struggle. As a result, its presence in the urban areas remains stronger among the petty bourgeois class, with all its limitations, than among the working class.

CONCLUSION

In Nepal, the Communist Party of Nepal (Maoist) has been developing a total transformational agenda, as the new organisational backbone of the communist movement. It has not only conducted a People's War but has also raised questions relating to each and every sector of society, in every branch of ideology, worked on every aspect of understanding and tried to develop solutions to every one of the problems raised. The party is conscious of the dangers of left and right deviations plotted by anti-democratic individuals and forces, and foresees their likely effect in time to come. It also understands seriously what it means to claim to be the real revolutionary party for the complete transformation of Nepali society. Given the social and political infrastructure of Nepal, there are many possibilities for the rapid development of class struggle in both rural and urban areas; there is dynamism in the new emerging production relationships, giving rise to major changes in the balance and nature of class forces. In this context, priority should be given to land redistribution and the establishment of a fair wage system, capital investment and diversification in agriculture, realising the potential for class consciousness in works and organised force. Previously, there was no coordinated attempt at social transformation, but now the Communist Party (Maoist) has adopted the proper strategy to promote the speedy transition of Nepali society from feudalism towards capitalism and the previous void has been filled by the struggle with current realities. Apart from adjusting both strategy and policy, people-oriented welfare work is also being undertaken. Other new trends seen in the Maoist movement include the revision of the strategy that was previously adopted, and its re-naming as the Prachanda Path. This has given birth to many new possibilities.

In fact, this new movement has brought together various progressive tendencies and movements for the construction of a new range of thinking. This, consolidating the unity of the labouring classes, has provided a concrete base for the significant task of linking class struggle with the long-term objective of transformation. The Maoist movement, with the rapid transformation of present-day society, has taken a great leap forward from a historical point of view. The specific implications are that the campaign for social transformation has started concretely and it will continue. The process of transformation may accelerate or slow down, depending on the success or failure of the Maoist movement. But the people have been given new hope, and their enthusiasm and mental outlook has been positively affected by the reality of today's rapid process of change. As a consequence, there is an upheaval in Nepali society and this upheaval is changing political, economic and cultural practice, creating a new 'world record' as it moves forward.

Chapter 8

The Royal Palace Massacre and the Maoists' Pro-King Political Line

Mohan Bikram Singh

This draft of this chapter was almost complete when the massacre at Narayanhiti royal palace took place on 1st June 2001 in Kathmandu. The incident brought about major changes in the politics of the country and I was obliged to make significant changes, not so much regarding the subject matter as the format and presentation. The analysis focused on the Maoists and their political relationship with King Birendra. Clearly, the assassination of King Birendra and his family was certain to influence the political line of the Maoists. Without including their latest statements and actions, my chapter would have been out-dated. So, I revised the piece accordingly.

1

We have continuously criticised the 'pro-king' political line of Maoists over the years, and they have denied the charge. But, after the assassination of the royal family they themselves revealed their 'hidden alliance' with King Birendra. The chairman of the Maoists, Prachanda, expressed the view that it was the late King Birendra's 'patriotic stand' and 'political liberalism' that led the national and international reactionary forces to conspire in his assassination (Tarun Weekly, June 4, 2001). Indeed, the Maoists even went to the extent of praising all the kings of the Shaha dynasty over the last 200 years for their 'patriotism'. Dr. Baburam Bhattarai has stated that 'the main contribution of the kings of the Shah dynasty, from Prithivi Narayan to Birendra, has been to defend the integrity and independence of a Nepal struggling first against British colonialism and later against Indian expansionism'. He further asserted that "the Nepali people have an endless and high regard for them" (Kantipur, June 6, 2001). Modnath Prasrit, a leading intellectual of the CPN (UML) remarked that 'such blind support to the monarchy by republicans is unique in world politics. Dr Baburam Bhattarai surpassed even the loyalty shown to the monarchy by mediaeval courtiers. By showing such blind respect to the Shah Dynasty, Bhattarai has encouraged a slave mentality with respect to the kingship in Nepal, which is quite contrary to the tenets of historical materialism' (Kantipur, June).

The daily newspaper Kantipur asked a pertinent question: 'If the Maoists had such a perception of the monarchy, then why did not they declare it, when the king was alive?' (Kantipur Daily, Editorial, June 6, 2001) Shankar Pokhrel, a member of central committee of the UML, attempts to answer the question. According to him, there are two possible reasons for their open support for King Birendra at this point; 'Firstly, to gain maximum benefit from the people's popular reactions to the massacre, and secondly, their alliance with the Palace and other forces hostile to the parliamentary system and the constitution' (Budhabar Weekly, June 13, 2001). He further suggests that, if the first is correct, it indicates their 'extreme opportunism'; while if the second is correct, then it proves that 'our criticism against them' regarding their pro-king line is justifiable. It seems to me that the basic feature of their character is 'extreme opportunism'. Only such an opportunism would lead them to adopt both 'ultra leftist' politics and a pro-king political line. The very same fundamental character might at any time lead them into a rightist, or a pro-Congress, or indeed any other opportunist stance. It seems clear that their political line of action is not in fact decided on the basis of Marxist–Leninist principles or an analysis of the objective conditions, but by pure pragmatism. For them, the instantaneous benefits, personal interests or careerist ambitions are the main guiding principles.

Such a fundamentally non-revolutionary character leads them to adopt a policy of following each and every apparent opportunity—a policy of spontaneity and populism.

2

In the Political Resolution—'A Great leap Forward, an Inevitability of the History'—adopted at the 2nd national conference of the CPN (Maoist), it was stated that in spite of 'great sacrifice and heroism' shown by children, old, women and others, the royal palace signed 'a very humiliating and insulting treaty' (referring to the Sugauli treaty of 1816 A.D). Describing the role of the 'feudal ruling class', the resolution states: 'The insulting defeat of Nepal in the war against British India and the nature of the treaty demonstrates the tendencies both of struggle against imperialism and of collaboration with it. Although Nepal became a semi-colonial country after the treaty, it helps us, on the one hand, to understand the character of the feudal ruling class on the one hand, and the existence of a patriotic and national sentiment in modern sense on the part of the people. The 'Bhimsen tendency', which was strongly opposed to surrender to the British, contrasts with the tendency of Jung Bahadur to accept subordination to the British—a trait still found in present rulers'. Needless to say, the reference made to the feudal ruling class refers also to the kings of the Shah dynasty. According to the Maoists' resolution, firstly, there were those consistently opposed to the British (Bhimsen Thapa and others); secondly, there were those, notably the feudal ruling class (including the Shah kings), who represented 'collaboration' and 'national surrender'. According to the resolution, the Sugauli treaty itself is a manifestation of the anti-national character of the Shah Kings. Those historical 'facts', presented by the Maoists themselves, contradict the so-called patriotic struggle of the Shah kings, against British imperialism.*

---

* Prachanda, Mahan Agragami Chhalang, Itihasko Apariharya Abashyakta– 'Resolution' in short, p. 27.

The highly advanced 'capital, technology and superiority' of the British army also played an important role in defeating Nepal, but that was not the decisive cause. Because of the 'captious enjoyment and luxuries', 'unlimited series of conflicts within the ruling class' and 'curtailment of people's rights', Nepal was bound to lose the war (ibid, p. 27). The Maoists themselves suggest that, ultimately, the royal palace was responsible for the shameful defeat of the country. Both democracy and nationalism are closely linked; where rights of people are curtailed and totalitarian rule prevails, the basis of nationalism is weakened. The resolution states that 'feudal political power obstructed real national unity and development by imposing feudal and Brahman caste and social domination upon the linguistic, religious and cultural traditions of the people and by suppressing the people's democratic system and the rights of various nationalities, tribes and regions (ibid, p. 32). In such a situation, created by the kings of the Shah dynasty themselves, it was not possible for them to fight for the sovereignty and integrity of the country or to defend it effectively. Moreover, their 'awful attack' upon such a 'comparatively patriotic' feudal as Bhimsen Thapa, who adopted the attitude of 'non-compromising struggle against the British', also weakened the Nepali people's struggle against the British. The resolution also refers to 'the freakish nature of quarrels within the Palace and the attacks on Bhimsen and others who adopted a comparatively patriotic stand and supported a united front against the British at the Asian level' (ibid, p. 27).

After the Sugauli treaty, Nepal became a semi-colony. But the contradictions between those committed to uncompromising struggle against the British and those willing to accept servitude to them (the British) 'remained, with the ruling class of Nepal largely following the second tendency' (ibid, p. 33). The resolution has analysed the Shah dynasty over the last 200 years, and according to the Maoist analysis, the monarchy in Nepal has shown a compromising character first with British imperialism and later with Indian expansionism, sacrificing national interest for its own political survival. The analysis contained in the resolution clearly contradicts their more recent analysis, according to which all Shah kings, from Prithivi Narayan to Birendra without any exception, struggled against British imperialism and Indian expansionism to defend national sovereignty and integrity.

3

In 1950, the 104-year period of Rana rule came to an end and the Shah kings became free from the Ranas, who had kept them under their control for more than a century. The resolution refers back to the treaty concluded in 1950 between the Ranas and the Indian government and considers it an unequal treaty, working against integrity and sovereignty of Nepal, arguing that the Nepali people have been struggling against it for about last half a century. The 'resolution' compares the Indo–Nepal treaty of 1950 with the later Delhi treaty. The Delhi treaty involved the Nepali Congress, King Tribhuvan and the Ranas in New Delhi in 1951. Regarding this later treaty, the resolution states that 'the Delhi treaty was conducted between the King, the Ranas and the Congress to share power among feudal, bureaucratic and comprador bourgeois classes to safeguard the interests of Indian monopoly capital. It was signed under the direction of Indian expansionism and it was a betrayal of the nation (ibid, p. 29). The resolution concludes that "there is no basic difference between the nature of both those two treaties" (ibid, p. 29). This means that the Delhi treaty also was against the sovereignty and integrity of the country and constituted a betrayal of the nation. King Tribhuvan was directly involved in the anti-national Delhi treaty of 1950. From this it is not difficult to conclude that he, King Tribhuvan, had betrayed the nation instead of struggling against Indian expansionism. Such a conclusion, it is crystal clear, does not conform to the theory of 'the patriotic struggle of the Shah kings against British imperialism and Indian expansionism'. Not only that, but according to the Indian press, King Tribhuvan was actually willing to annexe Nepal to India.

The national conference of the Maoists reached the conclusion that "on the basis of the experiences of the present era of imperialism and proletariat revolution, it is obvious that feudalism and imperialism cannot go against each other" (ibid, p. 30). But after the royal palace massacre, which took place only 3 months after their conference, both Prachanda and Bhattarai have come forward with the idea of King Birendra being against both Indian expansionism and American imperialism. Dr Bhattarai speaks of the 'relatively patriotic outlook' and 'liberal political character' of King Birendra (Kantipur Daily, June 6, 2001). Such a view also does not agree with the analysis accepted at the Maoists' conference. Their resolution asserted that "a nasty and obnoxious disease of the communist movement—involving taking as comparatively progressive one or another enemy's point of view concerning nationality or democracy and defending it— has created a serious problem for the success of the revolution" (Mahan Chhalang, p. 30).

At that time they could not have even imagined that within a few months they would not only be a victim of the same 'obnoxious' disease, but would praise such a disease boldly and openly and would think themselves proud of it. Bhattarai has also emphasised the need for all 'honest and patriotic' Nepalis to recognise the king's 'relatively patriotic perspective and liberal political character' in spite of his 'feudal birth' (Kantipur Daily, 6 June 2001). Does such a conclusion conform with reality? Can the king's role during the Panchayat period be taken as an example of his 'liberal political character'? The Maoists themselves admit that 'in the past, attempts were made to defend the corruption and state terror of the dictatorial Panchayat System by invoking the danger of Indian expansionism (Mahan Chhalang, p. 31).' It is a well-known fact that King Birendra, after the death of his father Mahendra in 1970, ruled the country as a dictator and it was only after the great historical democratic movement of 1990 that people succeeded in abolishing the dictatorial Panchayat system headed by him. Describing any exercise to support the policy of supporting the corruption and state terror of dictatorial Panchayat system in the name of danger of Indian expansionism as 'revisionism' in their 2nd national conference, the Maoists emphasised the need 'for the whole Party to be alert' against such revisionism. But only 3 months later, they themselves were trying to conjure up pro-king and revisionist illusions in the country, by talking about 'the relatively patriotic outlook and liberal political character' of the king in the same breath as of the 'danger' of Indian expansionism. Their latest personification of King Birendra as a patriot and a liberal runs counter to the entire philosophy of Nepali communist movement (except that of Dr Rayamajhee, former general secretary of Nepal Communist Party and a renegade, who was nominated as chairman of the state council by the king) and contrary to the conclusions of the 2nd national conference of the CPN (Maoist).

The reinterpretation of King Birendra as a patriot does not conform to the theory of class analysis of Mao or of the Nepali Maoists themselves. The resolution clearly asserts that "the comprador bourgeoisie in particular protects the interests of imperialism" (ibid, p. 30). They agree with the view of the CPN (Mashal) that 'both the king and the Nepali Congress Party represent the feudal, bureaucratic and comprador bourgeoisie' (Kiran, Retrogressive Journey of Mashal Group, 200, p. 41). For two decades, Birendra was king of Nepal. To regard the king as a patriotic force and a bulwark in the struggle against imperialism and expansionism, is an indication of ideological bankruptcy and unbalanced thinking. In this context it is also worth mentioning that the Maoists said not even a single word about the 'patriotic' role of the king in their conference resolution. But after the royal palace massacre they suddenly confessed that they had 'hidden alliance' with the king. If indeed the Maoist leadership had such a positive view of his 'patriotic stand and liberal character' and had an alliance with him when he was alive, then they had managed to keep their views and their alliance with the king secret from their own national conference and party. If they indeed were so positive about the king, then they were not honest and open, even to their own party and comrades, let alone the people as a whole.

4

Explaining the 'political liberalism' of King Birendra, Prachanda has said in an interview: 'King Birendra's relative political liberalism is not hidden to anybody. Instead of killing thousands of people in the street (who were opposing the system), it was his speciality to try to find out a way out. Despite his class limitation his proclamation of the referendum in 1979, his acceptance of the multi-party system in 1990 and his 'soft' policy towards the Maoist People's War are some of the examples that demonstrate his political liberalism. On the other hand, this type of characteristic of his also made us think that with the development of the Peoples War, at some point, Birendra will probably play the role of a 'Sihanuk' (Nepal Samacharpatra, June 15, 2001). It seems that, for Prachanda, the proclamation of the referendum in 1979 and the advent of the multiparty system in 1990 are the result of King Birendra's 'political liberalism'. But the proclamation of the referendum in 1979 was not a progressive step; rather, it was a conspiracy to suppress the emerging people's movement in opposition to the Panchayat system. The CPN stressed at the time the importance of the popular movement against the Panchayat system. The movement lost its momentum when the bourgeoisie and the reformists accepted the referendum. The CPN (ML) decided to boycott the referendum, but our party decided to take part in it and cast votes in favour of a multiparty system. At that time, the Maoists of today were also members of our party. During the referendum, the Panchayati dictatorship, under the leadership of King Birendra, conspired to defeat those supporting a multiparty system to the extent that they used duplicate ballot boxes. After that, people were obliged to struggle illegally against the dictatorship of the monarchy for a whole decade. All the major political parties and groups of Nepal struggling for democracy clearly opposed the conspiracy of King Birendra in the referendum of 1979. However, Prachanda has presented this travesty—that of the referendum—as one of the examples of Birendra's 'political liberalism'.

For Prachanda, the restoration of multiparty system and the end of the Panchayati system in 1990 was also the result of King Birendra's 'political liberalism'. In this way, he undermines the three-decade long people's struggle, as well as the popular movement of 1990, against the dictatorial Panchayat system, giving priority instead to the king's 'political liberalism'. It is true that on occasion, the reactionary forces have to fulfill people's just democratic or progressive demands, being compelled by the strength of the people's movement or people's opinion. Labelling a reluctant recognition of defeat and the onward march of history, however, as 'political liberalism', would lead us to accept the abolition of the sati system by Jung Bahadur Rana, the abolition of slavery by Chandra Shamsher Rana, the abolition of residual kingship or touchability by King Mahendra, or the introduction of a parliamentary system by Mohan Shumser Rana (Prime Minister in 1950) as the results of the 'political liberalism' of the ruling class. It would also encourage us to see the worldwide independence of former colonies as the result of the 'political liberalism' of imperialism, rather than as a consequence of national liberation struggles. If we hold such a view of historical change, we will end up supporting all the reactionary forces in Nepal, and in the world as well.

In this context, we have to consider also Prachanda's statement that "instead of killing thousands of people in the street, it was King Birendra's speciality to try to find out a way out". Has he forgotten the fact that during the rule of King Birendra, many activists of the communist party and the Nepali Congress Party, struggling against the dictatorship of the king and his Panchayat system, were maligned, subject to false allegations and trumped up charges, imprisoned, tortured and killed? If we accept the king's acceptance of the eventual dissolution of the Panchayat system (which we believe he was compelled to do because of the force of people's movement) as the king's 'political liberalism', we will have to accept the Treaty of 1950 as the outcome of the 'political liberalism' of Mohan Shumsher. Such thinking would ultimately lead us to the conclusion that in the development of history it is not the progressive and revolutionary power of the people that plays the decisive role, but rather that it is the reactionary forces who have the most important role to play. Even a beginner in Marxism–Leninism would recognise that Marxism–Leninism has nothing to do with such thinking.

During the historical people's movement of 1990, it was after the agreement between the King and the other political forces that the Panchayat system came to an end and the multiparty system was restored. However, sovereignty was not, in the true sense of words, handed over to the people, and therefore the multiparty system remains limited. The constitution proclaimed by the King in 1992 declared that sovereignty belonged to the people. But what followed proved how empty was that claim. Today, it is quite clear to the people, for example, that the army is under the control, not of the government but of the king. King Birendra was also concerned to retain control of the army, in the face of the multiparty system, to reduce in effect the power of parliament and the elected government of the day. This shows, not his 'political liberalism', but rather his deep-rooted desire to retain real power. King Birendra's unwillingness to use army against the Maoists is taken by them as a shining example of his 'political liberalism'. The Koirala government wanted to deploy the army against the Maoists, but the king rejected the proposal. They say that this proves the army belongs to the King. But we suggest, rather, that the underlying motivation was his deep-rooted desire to disempower and eventually to remove the limited multiparty system and restore his dictatorship. The constitution of Nepal gave him the right to take state power into his own hands, in case of famine, economic crisis, civil war etc. The evolution of the Maoists' 'People's War' into a full-scale civil war or the total failure of government to control the situation would provide the constitutional opportunity for the implementation of the king's strategy. In this sense, we would accept—as the Maoists have themselves accepted—there was an 'undeclared unity in action between the King and the Maoists'. Modanath Prashrit has argued that, "on the one hand, 'the unholy anti-revolution alliance' aims at restoring the partyless or one party system, banning those parties supporting the multiparty system" (Kantipur Daily, June 11, 2001). The same logic was in operation when the king showed his unwillingness to deploy the army against the Maoists. It was a means of further undermining the power of the elected government to deal with the situation.

Now let us consider the Maoist's view of the possibility of King Birendra's playing a 'Sihanuk' at 'some point of people's revolution'. We would like to refer to our own pamphlet, in which we suggest that "in this respect they do not deploy a materialist analysis.. it is merely a sweet dream of the Maoists to think that at some point the king might play a Sihanuk".* To dream of the king being turned into a Sihanuk with the help of vague phrases such as 'at some point', 'probably' and 'might', is not something that can be encouraged by a Marxist–Leninist party, group or leadership.

---

* (Mohan Bikram Singh, 'Mashal ko Atitmukhi Yatra ya Maobadi Samuhako Darwarmukhi Shuvyatra,' Parishistha Ka).

5

Kantipur Daily noted that 'the Maoists started the people's revolution with the slogan of 'the People's Republic'. In this context, Punarjagaran Weekly wrote: 'They started the people's war by shooting at pictures of the king.' How then did their armed struggle manage to incorporate praise not only of King Birendra, but also of all the kings of the Shah dynasty? We have already touched on this point. During a revolutionary war, in different conditions, we have to take advantage of the contradictions of our enemies and we have to support comparatively positive policies, at least to some extent. But, the support by Maoists of a feudal king would raise eyebrows under any circumstances. As we have already mentioned, with their statements after the palace massacre, they have not only supported the positive policies of Birendra, rather they have upheld the idea of his 'patriotic stand' and 'political liberal character' in general. Secondly, they have declared that all the kings of Shah dynasty have played a patriotic role, first against British colonialism and later against Indian expansionism. Needless to say, such remarks in favour of the kings of the Shah dynasty cannot be taken as simply 'taking advantage of the contradictions among enemies' or as supporting only some of the positive policies or actions partially. Dr Babu Ram Bhattarai writes: "Despite his birth in feudal class, King Birendra did possess patriotism and political liberalism" (Kantipur, June 6, 2001). It also claimed that this is why they (the Maoists) had had a soft policy towards King Birendra and in turn the latter adopted a liberal policy towards them (Prachanda, Nepal Samacharpatra, June 16, 2001). But it goes further than this. If the Maoists enjoyed the support not only of King Birendra, but also of all the supporters of the monarchy in general, then the Maoists, dropping their policy of struggle not only against King Birendra but also against the supporters of monarchy, should adopt a policy of 'unity of action' with all of them. In fact, they have stopped criticising the monarch and the royalists as a whole in their articles, documents, interviews and newspapers. Besides, it should be noted that while in the course of their so-called People's War they have killed/beaten/ kidnapped activists of the Nepali Congress Party, the CPN-UML and the CPN (Mashal), they have done nothing to the royalists or the old panchas. Does this mean that they see the characteristics of 'patriotism' and 'political liberalism' not only in King Birendra, but also in all the royalists? If not, what is the purpose of abandoning the struggle against them and emphasising a policy of 'unity in action' with them?

Now, it seems, the Maoists have adopted a policy of 'undeclared unity in action' not just with King Birendra, but with all the royalists. Perhaps it is because of their inability to give a logical ground for such a policy or because of their guilty feeling that they had not been able to accept it openly. In one of his statements, Prachanda emphasised the policy of the 'unity of action' with all of the political forces except the Nepali Congress Party. Dropping their prior policy of the 'unity of action' only with patriotic, democratic and left forces they have now adopted a policy of 'unity of action' with the royalists. What was the secret behind their overemphasis on the policy of action unity with all the royalists? They say that they have adopted this policy to safeguard sovereignty and nationality. Dr Babu Ram Bhattarai has stressed the unity of the communists and monarch for the same purpose (Janadesh Weekly). In one of his articles, Dr Bhattarai asked the King and all royalists to unite with the communists to defend the nation. Now to prove the appropriateness for their undeclared 'unity in action' they have emphasised the hands of 'foreign' forces behind the palace massacre. In his statement, Prachanda says:, "it was because of King Birendra's patriotic stand and 'political liberalism' that the die-hard national and foreign reactionaries massacred King Birendra's family". It is still under investigation whether there was any 'hand of foreign forces.' There are sufficient examples to cite of American imperialism and Indian expansionism in Nepal and South East Asia for this to be credible. But at present we cannot conclude for certain that any foreign forces were behind the massacre. Even the Maoists have not provided any evidence in this respect, and have only pointed to some possibilities. A focus on these possibilities, however, serves the purpose of showing the appropriateness of their policy of 'unity in action' with the king. Even if it is proved that the foreign forces were involved in the royal palace massacre, that would not be enough to prove that the king had taken a patriotic stand against imperialism and expansionism and thus that their policy of unity in action with him was the correct one. We shall have to consider many other relevant factors before reaching such a conclusion.

Last year, in their booklet, the Maoists quoted the general line: 'A large mass of people in Asia, Africa and Latin America have rejected the slavery of imperialism. These...include some patriotic kings, residual kings and aristocrats.' They further wrote: "We challenge Mohan Bikram Singh to deny the alliance of Stalin and the Third International against British imperialism, the alliance of Mao with Chang Kai-Shek against Japanese imperialism and this kind of general line of the CPC" (Kiran, Mashal Samuhako Attimukhi Yatra, p. 36). This absurd 'challenge' merely aims at proving their futile notion of the policy of unity with the king. They emphasise that the principal contradiction in Nepal is not with imperialism, but with feudalism. But the king is the main leader of the feudalists. In such a situation, it is evident that they should have given main emphasis to the struggle against him, the king. But, because of their guilty feeling, they cite examples of the 'united front' in the period of struggle against imperialism or Fascism, or of policies associated with such an anti-imperialist united front. They are, however, only trying to camouflage and justify their policy of leaning towards the monarchy and the royalists.

6

The Maoists, in their resolution, denounced the existing parliamentary system as the 'torn loincloth of imperialism', having reached the conclusion that in the present era the bourgeoisie has a completely 'reactionary' character, losing whatever 'progressive role' it may once have had (Resolution 29). Thus, according to their analysis, both the parliamentary system and the bourgeoisie have become reactionary forces. It is true that in this age of imperialism and the Proletarian Revolution, the parliamentary system has generally taken on a reactionary character. But the same thing is not true in all historical circumstances and for all countries. Even the New People's Revolution is basically a capitalistic democratic revolution in those countries where feudal and semi-colonial conditions still prevail. In countries where the capitalistic democratic revolution has not yet been completed, the capitalistic democratic revolution plays a progressive role. In countries governed by an absolute monarchy or even a constitutional monarchy, the parlia-mentary system is regarded as generally progressive by Marxists–Leninists all over the world. Lenin made this point clear again and again. In semi-feudal and semi-colonial countries, compradors and bureaucrats are analysed as reactionary by Mao. But he too, describing the national bourgeoisie as progressive, has encouraged the strategy of making it a partner in a 'united front' during the period of the New Democratic Revolution. In the developed capitalist countries, by contrast, the parliamentary or multiparty system has become reactionary in the context of the socialist programme of the revolution. But it is an outright anarchic view to deny totally that the parliamentary system can play a progressive role in countries where absolute monarchy prevails or where there is a danger of its restoration, where fundamental rights are still to be gained, or where there is fascist system or dictatorial rule in one form or another. In such a situation, the analysis of the bourgeois parliamentary system as absolutely reactionary is not in harmony with the principles of Marxist–Leninism or with the thoughts of Mao, of whom they claim themselves to be true successors. It is not difficult to show that the source of such non-Marxist–Leninist views is definitely anarchism, Trotskyism and immature revolutionary thinking. It is this inherently non-Marxist view of the parliamentary system that has led them to accuse us of being a 'guardian' of both the parliamentary system and the Nepali Congress, the ruling party of the country' (Kiran, *Mashal Samuhako Atitmukhi Yatra*, p. 19).

The justification for putting forward a slogan of abolishing the existing parliamentary system while emphasising the New Democratic revolution is self-evident from a Marxist point of view. But when a reactionary danger threatens the very existence of the parliamentary system, the duty of a Marxist–Leninist party should not be to enter into an alliance with forces working for the restoration of direct or dictatorial rule by the king, but to raise their voice and struggle against the danger to the parliamentary system posed by this threat. We united even with the Nepali Congress Party to fight against the absolute monarchy or so-called Panchayat system in 1990. If the danger appears before us in one or another form, we should be prepared to unite with any other forces supporting the multiparty system—even the Nepali Congress. In countries ruled by absolute monarchy, any struggle for a parliamentary system also plays a progressive role. So, it is against the thinking of Mao himself to consider the parliamentary system as reactionary in all circumstances.

It is no secret that there was an organised attempt on behalf of the royalist groups to subvert the parliamentary system during King Birendra's reign. They resorted to a signature campaign and organised demonstrations to bring back the direct rule of the king, in the name of eradicating corruption and restoring peace and security in the country. Former pancha leaders, including former Prime Ministers Kritinidhi Bista and Marich Man Sing, and politician Rishikesh Shah etc. were active supporters of the direct rule of the King. All those newspapers close to the royal palace were full of interviews, statements, articles or editorials supporting this retrogressive political line. Under such circumstances, when there was such an attempt from the royalists, was it not the duty of a Marxist–Leninist party to raise its voice against such a danger? But the Maoists of Nepal have spent their energy, not in warning against any such eventuality, but in opposing every voice raised against the clear and present danger posed by the king and the reactionary forces. Dr Babu Ram Bhattarai has said in an interview, that 'Mohan Bikram Singh has raised the bogy of the king's threat to the multiparty system, when the king is in a weak position (Niskarsha Monthly, May/June, 2001). By doing so, they stood up as the guardians of the reactionary forces. It is not still decided who will win the political struggle in Nepal—the absolute monarchy or the democratic forces. The question is raised, not only with reference to this or that particular monarch, but with regard to all royalists and reactionary forces that have raised their heads to restore the monarchy.

The above analysis of their activities is proof that they are fully against the multiparty system, and any force, especially the CPN (Mashal), which thinks that the present system is relatively progressive is castigated by them as 'taking the side of fascism', meaning that of the Congress government. No less than a member of Maoist politburo, Kiran, writes "that leaders of Mashal help preserve fascism by raising the bogus threat of royalist forces raising their heads to strike back" (Kiran, Mashal Samuhako Atitmukhi Yatra, Kathmandu, 2000, p. 20). For them, raising the issue of reactionary forces is a 'Congress slogan', though that party (Congress) has never raised any such issue. For them, Mashal's activities are directed to the past: Kiran has suggested that "Mohan Bikram has become Nepal's Kautsky to prove that multiparty system is more progressive than the Panchayati system" (ibid, p. 18). It is indeed true that we regard the present system as more progressive than the Panchayati system. In the past they were of the view that the multiparty system and Panchayati system were equally progressive/reactionary. But now they have changed their stand. With their analysis of King Birendra as a liberal and patriotic person, and also with the revelation of their 'secret alliance' with the late King Birendra, it is crystal clear that for them the Panchayati system was more progressive than the multiparty system. It is for this reason that they have shown no hesitation in announcing their open love for the late King Birendra. It is their supposed revolutionary character that has brought them close to the monarchy.

7

There is a well-known comment of Mao about 'united front' theory, which says 'unity–struggle–unity with friends; struggle–unity–struggle with enemy'. According to this theory, if the Maoists had had a 'unity of action' with the king, they should have emphasised struggle along with unity. But we cannot find even a word against King Birendra in their documents, articles or statements. Thus, their policy of unity in action with the king is clearly against the Marxist–Leninist theory of the united front or that of Mao. Their so-called policy of unity in action with the king, in reality, is not the unity of action; rather it is an unprincipled or unholy policy of alliance with the king. Whatever the intention behind their 'unity in action' policy with the king, in practice, it helps strengthen the king's power or establish his direct rule. We have sufficient grounds to draw such a conclusion. About a year ago, Dr Babu Ram Bhattarai asked, 'Is it not a good thing to try to find out a better model of democracy not only for us Maoists, but also for the Congress, UML, the King and other forces?' (Kantipur, June 28, 2001). Here we have a Maoist group, which had launched an armed struggle with the slogan of bringing about a People's Republic, putting forward, 4 years later, their proposal to find a 'better model of democracy' in the company of reactionary forces like the King and Congress. Will this (better model of democracy) not be a great leap backwards? Is it perhaps that their 'unity in action' is a tactical policy only? It does not seem so, considering their declared views. Dr Bhattarai has said that 'the new model of democracy' would be established after the People's Revolution; it would be 'suitable for 21st century' and drawn up on the basis of the guidingline of the Party or on the basis of the 'synthesised' thought of Prachanda. On this evidence, it seems, the so-called new model of democracy has a strategic and long-term nature. The attributes like 'to be established after the Revolution' and 'suitable for the 21st century' naturally mean the same. During the period of the New Democratic Revolution, feudal and comprador bourgeois classes are not normally seen as friendly forces. Their attempt to seek a strategic and long-term alternative in collaboration with the reactionary classes clearly implies a real shift away from their much trumpeted Maoism.

CPN (Mashal), since the very beginning, has been calling for the election of a constitutional assembly to transfer sovereignty from the king to the people. The Maoist group had been denouncing this, terming it a rightist and reformist policy. But now the Maoist group has also proposed the election of a constitutional assembly. Why did they do this, all of a sudden? Commenting on this puzzle, the Political Report passed at the Eighth National Convention of the CPN (Mashal) held last year (2000 AD) says, 'The Maoists, directly or in a roundabout way, have made it public that, in their view, the election for a constitutional assembly should be conducted by the government, formed under the king. Directly and indirectly this means bringing the king formally into active politics and thereby strengthening his capacity for direct rule. Because of this coincidence of policy of the pro-royalists and the Maoists, the former have been supporting the Maoists and it is on this ground that there is both a hidden and an open (or disguised) "unity in action" between them (royalists and pro-monarchs) (Mohan Bikram Singh, Rajnitik Pratibedan, Mashal January/February, 2000, p. 7). The slogan for the constitutional assembly put forward by Mashal aimed at "transferring power to the people from the king" or "weakening the position of the king" (ibid, p. 7). The Maoists opposed it. Ironically, they have raised the same slogan, but to strengthen the position of the king and establish his claims to direct rule.

Criticizing Mashal's policy, the Maoists write, 'Mashal says (a) kingship should be ended and the sovereignty should be transferred to the people; (b) constitutional assembly should be elected. This is the immediate concrete program of Mashal. However, for Mashal, the end of parliament is not the immediate programme; despite saying that we should oppose the Fascist rule of the NC, it does not say anything about its elimination. What else is this, if it is not their blind devotion and worship for the chief ruling party and the parliamentary system? Here, the fundamental difference of the policy between Mashal and Maoists group is quite clear'. What is clear from the above is that their focus is on the elimination of parliament—and by parliament, they mean the parliamentary system. They say that 'the struggle against the parliamentary system is the reality of concrete life' (ibid, p. 41). It is also clear from their views that the struggle against the parliamentary system actually means their struggle to eliminate it. They also talk of the election of the constitutional assembly. But this assembly will be formed after the elimination of the system. This is clear from the statement by Dr Bhattarai, which refers to 'the replacement of this constitution and the system', 'to make every effort to look for better model of democracy'. However, while speaking of the election of the constitutional assembly, they remain silent about the interim government; undoubtedly, we can conclude that the election will be held under the active role of the monarch.

In a communiqué issued 3 months ago, after their second conference, the Maoists talk of a multilateral conference, the election of an interim government by the conference and the election of the constitutional assembly under the interim government. It is remarkable here that instead of talking of a multiparty conference they talk of a 'multilateral' conference. Their intention must be to include the king in the conference. Their policy is evidently to include the UML, Congress, the royalist political parties and other persons in the conference. After the elimination of the parliamentary system, the king will be the supreme power and therefore the multilateral conference, the formation of the interim government and the election of the constitutional assembly will be conducted under his auspices. For this, the first and foremost condition is the disposal of the constitution and the parliamentary system and the transfer of power from elected government to the king. What the king does after gaining power will be up to him. With this new power, among others, the king will have the ability even to override the election for the constitutional assembly, as King Tribhuvan did in 1960 AD. The Maoists cannot even begin to imagine what the king will do after obtaining power.

The elimination of parliament and the parliamentary system is not a headache for Mashal. Even Maoists admit that it is Mashal that is struggling to the best of its ability against the fascism of Congress. However, like all Marxist–Leninist parties all over the world, the CPN (Mashal) does oppose the replacement of the present parliamentary system with a more reactionary system of government.

8

The Maoists have written that 'Mashal is in confusion as to who the main enemy of revolution is and who should be the target at present'. For them, the ruling Nepali Congress is the main enemy and the target. They have consequently killed many activists of the Nepali Congress, though all of them were at relatively low levels in the party hierarchy and many of them belonged to the lower classes. Indeed, they have killed many ordinary teachers and students belonging to the lower classes, because they were supporters of the Nepali Congress. Next to Congress, they have killed many UML activists. They have also killed some activists of Mashal (e.g. Rudra Timilsina of Jhapa). It should also be mentioned here that except for some cases in the beginning, they have not attacked even a single person belonging to the royalists' organisations. It shows that they regard the royalists as friendly forces.

The CPN (Mashal) has been opposed to their terrorist policy based on assassination to the extent that we have opposed not only the assassination of what we would have thought were friendly forces but also the assassination of Nepali Congress activists. A resolution passed at the Eighth Convention of the CPN (Mashal) declared that 'our party has been against the assassination on account of political differences of the activists of even the Nepali Congress' (Mohan Bikram Singh, Rajnitik Pratibedan, Mashal, January/February, 2000, p. 8). But the more important question is this: What is and what should be the main target of the present movement? Both the king and the Congress are the inimical forces of revolution. Both of them are the representatives of feudal and comprador bourgeoisie and are the enemies of revolution. Although, keeping their class in view, they are both enemies, politically there are many differences between them. Therefore, analysing their roles we have to struggle against them because in different situations their roles may be quantitatively and qualitatively different. Taking into consideration various interrelated factors, the struggle against the king takes priority in comparison to the Congress. One thing should be clear here. Shedding light on the decision taken by the Central Committee of the CPN (Mashal) in Chaitra, 2057 BS (March–April 2000), General Secretary of the Party, Ram Sing Srish, stated that 'because of the aristocratic policies and activities of the present Girija government, the danger of fascist rule is increasing. Therefore, we have to emphasise the struggle against such a danger. But when comparing the danger of fascism with that of the royalists, at present the struggle against the latter is more important because it is creating a threat to the achievements of the historical movement of 1990. For this reason, the Central Committee concludes that the struggle against the royalists merits the primary consideration'.

Another factor determining how one might answer the question is that of power. Among the different reactionary forces, we have to pay more importance to the struggle against the forces which are in power and which exercise most power. For the Maoists, Congress is the main ruling power and they are focusing on it. They also write, "while the NC, as a ruling power, is oppressive in a fascist way, the king is a 'flea and a trapped tiger."

With this they have tried to justify their policy of struggle against the Congress but, ironically, their own views prove it incorrect. Prachanda himself (or the Maoists) accept that one who has the army under his control possesses the power in reality. Prachanda writes: 'Ultimately the army is the chief organ of state power' (Kiran, Mashal Samuhako Atitmukhi Yatra). In a newspaper close to the Maoists, Mao is quoted to the effect that 'according to Marxist–Leninist principles, the army is the chief constituent of state power' (Mahima Weekly, November 24, 2000). This means that the struggle should be aimed at the power that controls the army. Today, in Nepal, who controls the army? The Maoists themselves accept that when the Girija government was going to deploy the army against them, King Birendra was against it. A newspaper close to the Maoists wrote: 'in the present situation of Nepal, the army is under the control of the king, while the police are under the government' (Mahima Weekly, March 21, 2000). According to their own analysis, in 'the present situation' the army is undoubtedly under the king and so he is more powerful than the government. Therefore, the target of the struggle must be the king. However, for Maoists, despite the possession of the army, the king is 'the powerless government' and the Congress is 'the powerful one'. The weekly further writes: 'At present, relatively the fascist government of the Congress is the more powerful government' (ibid).

Another weekly close to the Maoists writes: 'Mohan Bikram, the old leader, pays much attention to the dramatic (false) danger of the king and the royalists' (Mahima Weekly, January 19, 2000). A book published by the publishing department of the Maoists reiterates that 'for Mohan Bikram, it is not the fascism of the Congress, rather it is the danger of the royalists that is of primary importance' (Kiran, Mashal Samuhako Atitmukhi Yatra, p. 33). Yes, that is our stand. Even according to their analysis, this is the truth. But because of their view leaning towards the monarch, they take the Congress not the king as their main enemy. Criticising the Maoist policy of leaning towards the King, Mashal writes: 'The CPN (Mashal) is criticising them (Maoists), saying that they have given up the struggle against the king by taking the struggle against fascism as the primary one..... They themselves agree that the king is not powerless or helpless as they recognize that the army is under the king. Therefore, it is clear that by mistaking the secondary enemy as the primary one, they have abandoned the struggle against the primary enemy (Mashal, January/February, Anka 57, p. 28). That is where the essence of their policy of leaning towards the king lies.

9

It is written in the preface of the political resolution of the Maoists—'Great Leap Forward, the Inevitable Need of History' (Mahan Agragami Chhalang, Itihasko Apariharya Aavasyakata), published by their central publishing depart-ment—that 'the Resolution was "presented by Prachanda" and was passed unanimously.' In the resolution (presented by Prachanda himself), all the achievements of the party have been attributed to him (Prachanda), and he has been highly admired and glorified. Some excerpts from the resolution will demonstrate this: 'Under the leadership of Comrade Prachanda, the party was successful in expelling the "reformist and liquidationist lobby" led by Nirmal Lama' (Mahan Chhalang, p. 46); 'the five years' experience of the People's War manifests the height of Marxist–Leninist–Maoist thought developed by the whole party and especially by Comrade Prachanda' (ibid, p. 47); 'in the internal struggle, ultimately the whole party was united under the leadership of the General Secretary, Comrade Prachanda' (ibid, p. 50).; 'the leadership of Comrade Prachanda signifies a great leap forward as well as the beginning of completely a new practice' (ibid, p. 57); 'the strong proletariat headquarters of Comrade Prachanda developed as the focal point of party unity' (ibid, p. 62).

No Marxist–Leninist principles underlie the party's eulogy of Prachanda and his self-admiration. It is rare to find a leader praising himself in a political resolution presented by himself, even in bourgeois parties. Even kings and emperors, who are routinely praised by others, less commonly praise themselves. When we study the propositions and publications of the Maoist group, we find Prachanda adopting a personality cult and trying to have this established in a planned and sponsored manner from the very beginning. As a result of such efforts, the Maoists' second national conference adopted the 'Prachanda path'. In a booklet published last year by the central publishing department of the Maoist group, they quoted me as saying that 'first of all the Maoists put forward the idea of the general secretary as the supreme leader of the Party and then, in the name of establishing Party leadership, launched a campaign worshipping Prachanda. Then they presented Prachanda as the ideologue of the Party. In this way they are trying, very systematically and diplomatically, to establish "Prachanda thought", which is evidently no more than anarchic individualism' (Kiran, Mashal Samuhako Atitmukhi Yatra, p. 48). It is true that we criticised them in that way and all our criticisms are based upon good evidence. In their organisational resolution they put forward the principle that 'the General Secretary is the supreme leadership' (Mahal, the Organ of the then unity centre, May/June 1985, p. 23). By getting such a notion passed, Prachanda tried, for the first time, to suggest that the General Secretary is superior to the Central Committee. Then he launched a campaign in order to establish the leadership. Even the political proposal mentions that a decision was made by the extended meeting in favour of the centralisation of the leadership and its establishment (Mahan Chhalang, p. 61).

The establishment of the leadership meant the establishment of the leadership of Prachanda. Later, through the means of his biography, photos, posters, and articles in his praise, his sayings quoted in the articles of central committee members or other party leaders and the like, a nationwide campaign launched the 'establishment' of Prachanda's leadership. Then, the notion of the 'directive thought of the party' was announced. Linking the 'directive thought of the party' with Prachanda, the Maoists suggested that he is individually 'the director of the party'. Badal, a central committee member writes: 'The great achievements of the party have also produced its main explorer, synthesizer, and director. He is Prachanda—the General Secretary. Then in the Party they made efforts to establish "Prachanda" thought. They did this at their second conference as well. The Nepal Samacharpatra (referring to an interview with a politburo member of the Maoist group) reported that 'a proposal for "Prachanda Thought" was also presented in the conference. When it failed, Prachanda himself proposed "Prachanda path", as a way forward, which was accepted "unanimously" '.

Explaining how the 'Prachanda path' was decided, the monthly magazine Class Struggle (Varga Sangharsha) wrote: '...a proposal demanding the adoption of the 'Prachanda Thought' (was) presented by the Prachanda Lobby during the Second Conference, but the Maoist leaders themselves made a compromise when Prachanda was obliged to retreat, due to the opposition and criticism by another faction of the leadership' (Vishnu Paudel, Barga Sangharsha, April–July 2001, p. 29). Today, all the central leaders of the Maoist group, activists or their proximal newspapers are indulgent and reverent with respect to Prachanda and the 'Prachanda path'. Shedding light on the 'Prachanda path', Prachanda himself writes: 'the party names the set of ideas developed in the form of centralized expression under collective leadership as the "Prachanda path". He further writes, "Prachanda path is the line leading to unity and victory" (The Kantipur, April 15, 2001). Even the Politburo member Kiran writes about it: 'Prachanda is the prime representative of the party's long held assignment analysis and the inventor of the new opinion' '. But what is 'the new opinion'? It is not mentioned anywhere. He further writes, 'Now Marxism–Leninism–Maoism and Prachanda path have together become the guiding principles of the party. It has an indivisible dialectical relation between international content and national form, universal and particular, whole and part of ideas; it serves the international proletariat besides guiding the Nepali revolution. The Prachanda path is based upon the unity of 3 organisational elements—philosophy, political economy and scientific socialism. The development process of Prachanda path will take place dialectically, continually taking new and supreme qualitative leaps forward (according to the dialectical materialist principle of development of knowledge.) This conference has cleared the way for the great possibility of the development of the Prachanda path—the fourth stage of Marxism–Leninism–Maoism. Let us unite in another great project of the Nepali and the world revolution with firm belief, confidence and resolution; the world revolution of the 21st century will establish the Prachanda path on another new and qualitative level' (The Janadesh Weekly, March 7, 2000).

In the development of the science of the proletarian revolution, RIM and Maoists rank Marxism–Leninism and

Maoism in the first, second and third phase respectively. Now the leadership of the Nepali Maoist group has begun to dream that the Prachanda path is the fourth phase of Marxism and that 'the world revolution will establish it as the new qualitative apex of the 21st century'. Earlier, one of their leaders had written, 'Certainly this (Prachanda path), on its own, is a great achievement of the Nepali revolution. Our nation should feel proud of it'. He takes Prachanda path as the third great achievement, with the establishment of the Party and 'the Jhapa Revolt' as the first and second ones respectively. He further writes, 'It is our primary historic responsibility to protect and promote the great achievement i.e. Prachanda path' (Dishabodh, June/July, 2000). In no way can the idea of considering the protection and promotion of Prachanda path as 'the primary historic responsibility', rather than that of the country, people, party or revolution, be taken as a genuine Marxist–Leninist approach. Explaining how exaggerated this notion is, the General Secretary of the CPN (Unity Centre) writes, 'The Maoist leaders have said that the "Prachanda path" ...constitutes "an epoch-making initiative, guiding the world revolution of the 21st century" and "the point of origin of the fourth phase of Marxism", succeeding "the third phase of Marxism" ' (Janaekata, March 13, 2000).

The 'Prachanda path' of the Maoists has been criticised by many political groups involved in the communist movement, and by many intellectuals. In an article published in Barga Sangharsha, Vishnu Paudel writes, 'None of the scientific philosophers like Marx, Engels, Lenin, etc. proposed naming their own contribution to revolutionary thought "an ism". But Prachanda himself propounds "the Prachanda Thought" and when that fails to be accepted, compromises with "the Prachanda path" '. Concluding that such a trend is 'the climax of bourgeois capitalist individualism' and an instance of naked self-admiration, he further writes that this is also the climax of an ambition to become the authority of the Nepali and the world revolution: 'The leadership of a communist party is not established by hero worshipping, but automatically in course of class struggle and ideological struggle'. The General Secretary of the CPN (UML), Madhav Kumar Nepal writes, 'Now, they hope, the perspective brought forward by their Second National

Conference will, to a great extent, guide the world communist revolution. ...They have put forward the "Prachanda path" as the fourth step after Marxism–Leninism and Maoism. This is an overestimation of their reach, ability and experience' (Mahadav Kumar Nepal, Dishabodh, April/May, 2001, p. 36).

Comrade Prachanda has stated that the CPN (Unity Centre) is their 'nearest friendly force' as a Marxist–Leninist–Maoist party. That is why we will quote, in detail, some of the criticisms of the 'Prachanda path' developed by Prakash, the General Secretary of the Unity Centre. In his article, Prakash writes, 'It seems that another extremist approach, interpreting the party authority as despotic, has been developing. This must have caused the decision regarding the "Prachanda path" '. He adds that 'The CPN (Maoist) might have taken the decision to adopt the "Prachanda path" in its haste to take on responsibility for the World Revolution and its even greater ambition to be the leader of the World Revolution'. He notes that 'there is a powerful tendency within the dominant feudal culture of Nepal which has encouraged ...hero worship. The CPN (Maoist) must have been attracted to the "Prachanda path" for this reason also'. Commenting that the decision was highly shaped by 'metaphysical mechanical thought and blind imitation', that it provides no new theoretical approach and that it represents the 'blind tailism' of an irrelevant interpretation of Marxism and is likely to endanger democratic centralism, he further writes, 'The trend of leadership worship prevalent today in the Maoist party is equally likely to produce Lin Piao and Khruschev from within itself. Though the immediate emergence of a Lin Piao is more likely, it is evident that Khruschev was also the product of this trend. This is not a new theoretical approach conceived by a developing Marxism, but the Lin Piaoist error. The CPN (Maoist) has made a Lin Piaoist error by making an imperfect decision like that of adopting the "Prachanda path" ' (Prakash, Janaekata Weekly, March 13, 2000).

There is no close relationship between Marxist–Leninist principles and such an individualistic approach. In fact, the approach resembles more the philosophy of Nietszche or the anarchic world approach. The foundation of the philosophy of anarchism is the individual. The philosophy of Nietzsche inspires the notion of super humans (instead of ordinary people), and encourages hero worship or a slave mentality. The philosophical basis of such notions is not a by-product of a Marxist–Leninist outlook. It considers the role of kings, military leaders and, especially, of genius personalities as the decisive elements in the making of history, but certainly not that of common people. But the overestimation of the individual is not compatible with the Marxist–Leninist world outlook, no matter how great or much of a genius that individual. But this tendency clearly exists among the Nepali Maoists.

Nietzsche's philosophy provided the theoretical foundation of Fascism. Philosophical notions of this sort have given the views and activities of the Maoists a fascist pattern. This approach of theirs is expressed not merely in their individualism and hero worship, but also in their organisational working system and in their treatment of the leftist and friendly forces and the ordinary people. They have not only suppressed those activists within their organisation who dissent, but have killed them. In this connection, it is worth mentioning the murder of Ramesh Dhungel. He was a member of the Maoists, but they eliminated him because of his differences with the leadership. They also murdered Rudra Timilsina, just because he disagreed with them and joined the CPN (Mashal). A woman—a resident of Madikhola, Pyuthan—ran away because she disagreed with the activities of the Party. Later, they took her back, whipping her publicly and very severely. Today, many of their activists, terrified, have escaped from the Party and are in hiding. The Maoists have not only murdered activists of the Nepali Congress and the CPN (UML), but have also assaulted, looted, entrapped and abducted several CPN (Mashal) activists, and have even assaulted several activists of the CPN (Unity Centre), which they have called their 'nearest friendly force' and a 'Marxist–Leninist party'. They have punished ordinary people, assaulting them and extorting money and meals from them, and raping women. In a village in Tulsipur, Dang District, they raped a 50-year old woman named Kojmaya Thapa belonging to an ethnic group (the Magars) on the night of 14th Push, 2057 BS (December 2000). In protest against this kind of treatment, a press conference was held in Kathmandu and several protest meetings were held in Tulsipur. On the other hand, they protect those feudals and traitors who provide them funds. This policy contradicts the Marxist notion of class struggle and Mao Tse

Tung's mass line. As the result of their anti-Marxist–Leninist perspective, they are following this unpopular and fascist tendency. Because of their pro-king political line on the one hand, and the growing fascist character on the other hand, their so-called People's War is possibly facilitating anti-revolution as much as revolution.*

Discussing such treatment towards the people, the renowned progressive intellectual, critic and novelist Khagendra Sangraula writes, 'The character and conduct shown by the Maoist fighters in the past is, in no case, fitting to the beautiful name of the "People's War". In the name of cultural revolution, murdering policemen after they surrender, ceding weapons, mutilating the ears of the people who dissent from them, breaking their limbs or taking their lives, visiting the huts of the common people and snatching their food, terrifying ordinary people by letting off bombs in densely populated areas, shaving young men and stripping them of their underclothes, imposing every possible evil verbal attribute to those who disagree with them—these are all very common activities of the Maoists. Are these activities and conduct of the Maoists qualitatively different from those of the policemen deployed in the name of "control" by an authoritarian regime? Following the activities of the police, what is the destination of the Peoples' War—a Popular Republic or the same autocracy?' (Khagendra Sangraula, the Kantipur Daily, July 16, 2001). The Maoists' position is the natural consequence of their non Marxist–Leninist view and the development of their character into Fascism. The political resolution passed in the 8th National Conference of the CPN (Mashal) suggests that 'from the conduct of the Maoists it is clear that their organization has been adopting the Fascist conduct getting deviated from Marxist–

---

* Such anti-people activities of Maoists has been a countrywide phenomena and people are highly dissatisfied with it. Now people have spontanously begun to raise against it. In this context the uprising of the people in Parsa is worth mention. On..................more than four thousands people attacked upon a village dominated by Maoists and burnt many houses belonged to them. Two person wer killed in the incident, one Maoist by the mass and another by police firing. The Home minister, Khum Bahadur Khadka has to deliver a report on the incident in the parliament. In Jhapa two Maoists were abducted by the people, who latter were rescued by the police.

Leninist principles or assumptions' (Mohan Bikram Singh, Rajnitik Prativedan, p. 8).

10

In an article published recently, one of the central committee leaders of the Maoists writes, 'It was not possible to take on the new discussion about Stalin and the Comintern, going forwards in the International Communist Movement to a qualitatively new level, without freeing ourselves from the legacy of the Mohan Bikram school. In this respect, the National Conference's (Second National Conference) Declaration of Liberation from the legacy of Mohan Bikram School, heightening the propositions established by Mao concerning the evaluation of Stalin and the Comintern, takes on an epoch-making importance' (Shital Kumar, Janadesh Weekly, June 19, 2001). The 'new discussion' of the international communist movement regarding Stalin and the Comintern is nothing new. It is in fact quite a stale one. CPN (Mashal) had rejected those stale logics about two decades ago. What they call 'the Mohan Bikram school or legacy' is nothing more than decisions accepted by the central committee two decades ago, when the Maoists also belonged to our party (and later those were also adopted by the Fifth Congress of the party). The then central committee had prepared 'a proposal on the international communist movement' (draft). It was presented at the founding conference of the RIM in 1984 by M.B. Singh. In this conference Mohan Bikram also tabled a Note of Dissent, which was later approved by the central committee. Thus, the approved views in the 'proposal on the international communist movement' were not the personal views of Mohan Bikram, but those of the whole of the party, before the split at the Party Congress. Therefore, their 'liberation' from the legacy of 'the Mohan Bikram School', is also the liberation from their own legacy too. They have called the document 'The Counter Revolution in China' the biggest ideological victory of the Fourth Congress against revisionism. The document was an 'ideological victory' over Chinese revisionism.

After a few months, a document on the international communist movement was also passed—in the same year in which there was an ideological victory over Trotskyism in the international communist movement as advocated by RCP-USA. Thus, the Maoists' freedom from 'the Mohan Bikram School' legacy was in essence their freedom from the legacy of Trotskyism too. In this context one more point also should be made clear. They had already at this time gone a long way from the views they held when they belonged to CPN (Mashal) and this had been following the Trotsky Line in practice. The decision of their 2nd conference relating to the Declaration of Liberation from the legacy of the Mohan Bikram School is in fact liberation from a former 'declaration' to go ahead in the path of Trotskyism. In their 'Declaration of Liberation' they have claimed to have strengthened the evaluation of Stalin and the Comintern. But, in the resolution approved by the Fifth Congress, many of Mao's views on Stalin have been criticised. At that time their (the Maoists') view on Stalin was clear. It is a known fact that using the healthy and friendly criticism by Mao, the RCP-USA campaigned in antagonistic way against Stalin's actions during the Second World War specifically and against the Comintern in general. Apart from adopting the views of Trotskyism, in order to strengthen their propositions, they have reversed their own views which they held before.

Regarding the criticism of Stalin, the resolution states: '...Our starting point should be the evaluation of comrade Stalin by Mao. Dividing Stalin's works and views into two parts Mao has declared 70% to be right and remaining 30% to be wrong' (Mahan Chhalang, p. 7). They further write, 'Mao's evaluation of Stalin is directed against those reformists who negate him totally and also against those narrow dogmatist revisionists who also justify his mistakes' (ibid, p. 9). One of their central members referred to the first as the 'reformism of Khrushchev and the latter as Hoxha-ism' (Shital Kumar, Janadesh, June 19, 2001). Here a question should be raised— are they prepared to evaluate Mao himself according to the formula of '70 and 30 percent' applied to Stalin? They do not dare to do so. For them to point out even .001 per cent of mistakes made by Mao is an anti-revolutionary act. This means that on the question of the evaluation of Mao they adopt a 'narrow dogmatism' (Hoxha-ism in another way) and justify even Mao's mistakes. So far as we are concerned, we maintain that some of Mao's criticisms of Stalin were wrong. But we also maintain that Stalin also made some mistakes. Likewise we accept that Mao was not totally correct. At the time when Maoists were with us (i.e. in the Fifth Congress), they also shared the same views as we do about Mao and Stalin. But now, declaring themselves free from 'M.B. school legacy', they have blindly followed the 'Trotskyites' legacy and have given up their own views.

To make the point clear, we would like to quote a passage from the 'Proposal on International Communist Movement' which was adopted by the Fifth Congress and which in 1990 was published under the title 'Revolutionary Perspectives of International Communist Movement of the Counter Revolution in China'. The Proposal of the ICM mentions 'new and disguised danger of Trotskyism'. That is directly related to the RCP-USA. In 1981, in Revolution, an organ of the central committee of the RCP/USA, Bob Avakian, Chairman of the RCP-USA, wrote many articles in which he criticised Stalin's views about the establishment of socialism and the second world war. In these articles he tried to prove that Stalin had fundamentally departed from Marxism–Leninism, that he was the enemy of the proletariat world revolution, that he lacked dialectic vision, and that he was a chauvinist, reformist and rightist (refer to Mashal's struggle against trotskyism within RIM, appendix D, CPN (Mashal) publication, 1996, pp. 29–32). In the above-mentioned documents, without mentioning the name of the RCP-USA, all the criticisms made against Stalin and the Comintern have been denied by our party. But in the paper presented by M. B. Singh at the founding conference of RIM in 1984, mentioning the name of the RCP-USA, all of its positions regarding Stalin and the Comintern were criticised in detail. The paper says, 'Their inability to take into consideration the historical experience of later periods and to consider some particular questions, separating them from the whole, has led the RCP to evaluate the history of the ICM during WW II in a wrong way. The RCP has concluded that 'the line of the Soviet Union and the Comintern in regard to WW II... was basically wrong' and a deviation in the line of the Communist International occurred.*

---

* Outline of views on the Historical Experience of the International Communist Movement and the Lessons for Today, by Bob Avakian, Revolution, June 1985 p. 4.

According to them, the principal aspect of WW II, even after the attack upon the USSR, was interimperialist and the united front against fascism was a 'departure in significant aspect from Leninism' (Conquer the World? The international proletariat must and will, revolution, special issue no. 50, p. 3). They (RCP) even went to such an extent as to see a kind of antagonistic contradiction between the defence of the USSR and the interests of the world proletarian revolution. Their attack on Stalin has taken such an antagonistic turn that they have no hesitation even to say 'Stalin did what he could so (and in some cases it was not insignificant) to kill the revolutionary struggle of the masses in order not to bring down the wrath of U.S. imperialism' (ibid, p. 28). In this context, the Proposal of CPN (Mashal) says, 'We are not against evaluating the history of the ICM during WW II and afterwards, and drawing lessons from that. We also hold the view that Stalin made many mistakes. Such mistakes were made both in the analysis of objective situation and in implementation of policies. But basically his approach was correct, was dialectical materialist and he was a great Marxist–Leninist and promoter of proletarian internationalism (ibid, appendix B, p. 17).

The paper says, 'as it is clear, CPN (Mashal) has serious difference with RCP-USA' (ibid, pp. 19–20). The period from 1984 to 1998 was one in which CPN (Mashal) was ousted formally from the RIM. It was a period in which the RCP-USA was trying to change RIM into a pro-Trotsky organisation, whereas the Marxist–Leninists tried to struggle against this pressure. During the conference of 1984, and after it, the communist parties of Sri Lanka, Turkey, Greece, India and Nepal struggled against this direction. But soon they resigned or left the RIM, due to their differences with the CORIM, or they were liquidated in their respective countries. Only the CPN (Mashal) continued single-handed the struggle within RIM against the attempt of RCP-USA to turn it into a Trotskyite organisation. After the RIM was formed, 'Gonzalo thought' was accepted by the Communist Party of Peru. Likewise, the RCP-USA accepted president Bob Avakian as the 'authority of the party'. CPN (Mashal) opposed both of those decisions saying that they were based upon 'personal cult'. The RCP had campaigned against Stalin. But in the founding International Conference of the RIM in 1984, because of the pressure of many other parties, they were not able to include the condemnation of Stalin in the manifesto of the RIM as they pleaded it should be in their party organs. Both Mao and Stalin, defining the present era of imperialism and proletarian revolution, have called it the 'Lenin Era', referring to Leninism as the Marxism of the present era. At the time of The Great Proletarian Cultural Revolution, Leninism was depicted as 'the guiding ideology' of our thinking and that motto was included in the manifesto adopted at the founding conference of RIM in 1984. But later, adopting 'Maoism' in place of 'Mao Thought', the analysis of Mao, Stalin and the Proletarian Revolution of China was revised. Behind such revisionism was clearly the intention of undermining Lenin and Leninism. Otherwise Trotskyism could not have been put forward. The attack, first against Stalin and then against Leninism as today's guiding ideology, was the result of that Trotskyite conspiracy. They proposed that the Lenin era has ended, that the third stage (that of Maoism) has begun and that Maoism is Marxism–Leninism at present. Thus 'it is clear by their behavior that behind the objective of removing Stalin from the scene was their intention to weaken Leninism and make it passive'.*

After the resignation of the communist parties of India and Turkey, RIM became a plaything in the hands of RCP-USA, which made concerted efforts to change it into a Trotskyite organisation. It was CPN (Mashal) that struggled continuously against this. As a result, the committee of RIM sent a letter to the central committee of CPN (Mashal) in August 1996, saying, 'The dispute between RIM and the CPN (Mashal) is by no means limited to a question of terminology. The debate has revealed that the dispute over Marxism–Leninism–Maoism concentrates on a whole series of political and ideological questions'. It further says, 'If your party continues to maintain its opposition to the ideological foundation of the Revolutionary Internationalist Movement the correct and principled response on your part would be your voluntary resignation from our movement. We hope that you will give urgent attention to this matter and respond within three months'. A meeting of the central committee of CPN (Mashal) was held and a 'Resolution on the Letter of RIM' was passed. Taking the decision

---

* Mohan Bikram Singh, on the difference of NCP (Mashal) with RIM, Mashal, 2053, No. 42, p. 8.

to continue the struggle, the 'Resolution' says, 'The CORIM has written to tell us that if our party continues to maintain its opposition to the ideological foundation of the RIM, "the correct and principled response" on our part would be "voluntary" resignation from the movement (RIM). But contrary to the suggestion made by the CORIM, the CC of our party has decided that the correct and principled response on our part would be not "voluntary resignation", but continual struggle against the non-Marxist–Leninist principles, policies and style of work of CORIM' (Mashal's Struggle against trotskyism within RIM, p. 12). In the first half of 1998, CORIM expelled CPN (Mashal) from the RIM. Soon after they published a long article in A World to Win titled 'On the Expulsion of CPN (Mashal) from RIM'. In this article they write, 'We call all the rank and file of CPN (Mashal) to separate themselves from Mohan Bikram, who is an anti-revolutionary' (A world to win, 1998, p. 24). The Maoists in Nepal insist on a 'new discussion' in the international communist movement 'freeing themselves from the legacy of Mohan Bikram school'. But their 'new discussion' and a 'qualitative level' of it is guided by the Trotskyite views of RCP/USA. They themselves confess that 'In this context the documents and articles of the chairman of RCP/USA, Bob Avakian, have played an effective role in giving new height to the discussion' (ibid, p. 41).

11

If we study the whole body of literature of the Maoists in Nepal, it is clear that the position of Mashal has been a central factor in the political line and movement of the Maoists. Clearly speaking, from the time of their birth, the complete eradication of Mashal has been one of their main political goals. In 1985 AD (2042 BS), the then Centrist Group (the former name of the present Maoist group) completed the plenum of its central committee. The plenum gave them formal recognition. The plenum also adopted a resolution entitled 'Anarchical Individualism: the Nepali Dimension of Rightist Opportunism'. In a booklet published by the central publication department of the Maoists group, it has been claimed that 'a detailed analysis, with an historical overview of the Mashal group and its leader Mohan Bikran Singh, has been undertaken. The analysis provides valuable theoretical and historical materials to reveal the Mohan Bikram position'. In fact, these 'materials' are nothing more than a series of personal allegations and character assassination. The 'valuable theoretical and historical materials' used against M.B. Singh include various types of epithets, such as 'cunning', 'talkative', 'a notorious example of rightist', 'hypocrite', 'low level dishonest', 'capitalist element', 'a successful representative of feudal class capitalism in the party', 'feudal left over', 'a son of big feudal lord', 'dogmatic', 'unrealistic', 'very cowardly', 'desolate', 'Freudian', 'disguised', 'feudal character', 'a successful man disguised under his Marxist philosophy', 'an expert on all sorts of tricks', 'an agent of the reactionary class', 'a friend of King Tribhuvan and his class', 'pro-king and pro-Congress', 'a mixed character of the rightist wing', 'an element of hatred', 'the rebirth of Martov of Russia in Nepal', 'a self-proclaimed great leader and so-called inspiration of the Nepali revolution' and so on. Because the Maoists make use of the politics of personal allegation and character assassination, this has become an inherent part of their present day political culture also. For the last one and half decades, personal allegations and character assassination have become the Maoists' major weapons against the CPN (Mashal) and M.B. Singh. Now, the 'Prachanda path' has provided new height and added new dimensions to this tendency. In their document, 'New Dimension', the Maoists have declared that 'M.B. is not only an individual, but also a trend..... Thus, history has put the responsibility for his complete eradication on our (Maoists) shoulders'.

Even before the birth of the Maoists as an independent and separate organisation or, as they themselves confess, even before their labour pains, they had been working hard against the 'M.B.Trend'. In this context, it will be relevant to discuss the views expressed by the Maoists from 1974 to 1983 AD (2031–2040 BS). The Maoists call this period, the period of the United Fourth Congress. With regard to this period, Kiran writes, 'Mohan Bikram and Nirmal Lama emerged from the Fourth Congress of 1974. They created a great confusion in the communist movement of Nepal'. Prachanda has described the period of the Fourth Congress as the 'critical period of the most difficult and complex ideological struggle against a new revisionism full of a revolutionary buzzwords and eclecticism'. In a political resolution adopted by the national conference of the Maoists' group, it was argued that 'there was not a favorable climate in which honest revolutionaries could fight boldly against M.B. Singh, the main hero of the working direction of the Fourth Congress'. In this context, Kiran writes, 'As much as we could, we launched an ideological struggle for about a decade after the United Fourth Congress. We could not understand, however, the eclectical new revisionism of M.B. Singh and defeat it. Though we defeated the M.B. attitude from organisational point of view in the Fifth Congress, we again remained unsuccessful in defeating him in the ideological, political and military lines of action, as well as in many other important issues. ......We had our own organisational identity, but we had great labour pains too, to give birth to a novel ideological and political approach'.

The Maoists have accepted many positive aspects of the Fourth Congress period. In this context, they write, 'The positive aspects of the Fourth Congress include the correct analysis of the class character of the Nepali Congress. Before, the party had analysed the Nepali Congress as the party of national capitalist class, and a democratic and friendly force. But the Fourth Congress analysed it as a political organisation of the comprador bourgeois and feudal classes and a class enemy. M.B. Singh had already put forward such an analysis in 1969 (2026 BS) when he was in Bhadragol jail in Kathmandu. Later the 'Central nucleus' and the Fourth Congress accepted his analysis. At present, with very few exceptions, this analysis has been accepted by all in the communist movement of Nepal. In his autobiography, Nirmal Lama is said to have stated, on his death-bed, 'I took the Nepali Congress to be a party of the national bourgeoisie and as democratic. But Comrade Mohan Bikram Singh regarded it as the party of the comprador bourgeoisie. After a prolonged discussion among us over many months, at the last I was convinced by his analysis' (Mulyankon Mashik, May/June 2001).

After the plenum of 1985 and its declaration of an eradication campaign 'against the M.B. trend', the Maoists have been continuously attacking Mashal—for the last one and half decades. I will not refer here to all of their attacks against Mashal and M.B. Instead, I will concentrate on the decisions made by the recently held Second National Conference of the Maoists in 2001. After that conference, Prachanda made a statement which announced that 'The Resolution passed in the conference has decided to expose the M.B. trend and to reject the line of action of the so-called Fourth and Fifth Congresses as a revisionist line of action, and to accept the line of action developed under the leadership of Prachanda and revised and established during the united congress as the correct line of action' (see Dishabodh in Nepali, 2000, p. 13). According to Naulo Bihani, a monthly magazine, near to the Maoists, the most important achievement of the national conference was 'the declaration of Prachanda path and the protest against the M.B. trend'. The remarkable thing is that the Maoists still feel it important to put an emphasis on 'an eradication campaign' against Mashal and M.B. even after 15 years of continuous attack. This indicates that the Maoists have not yet succeeded in their eradication campaign. Prachanda's statement also makes it clear that the campaign against Mashal occupies a great and important place in the whole history of the Maoists. In a monthly magazine Dishabod (2000, p. 11), Prachanda says, 'in fact, the ideological struggle against Mohan Bikram Singh's new revisionism has contributed a lot to the development of the Nepal Communist Party (Maoist)'.

As stated earlier, the Maoists have expressed the view that the correct class analysis of the Nepali Congress was 'only one' positive aspect of the Fourth Congress. After that, on the next page, they have stated that 'a month after Mao's death, the capitalist revisionists have usurped political power in China by conspiracy. Naturally, this has had a negative effect on the communist movement of the world in general and on the communist movement of Nepal in particular. The Naxalite movement of India suffered a serious setback, particularly after the death of Charu Mazumdar, and this led the then ML leadership (who had mechanical thinking) towards revisionism. The Fourth Congress, however, led the genuinely revolutionary people in the fight against revisionism by protesting against the counter-revolution of China' (Mahan Chhalang, p. 41). Prachanda further writes, 'The successful decision against the counter-revolution of China in 1981 (2038 BS) was the major ideological victory of the united Fourth Congress. The decision properly established the right to revolt against revisionism and then begun the process of revolt against the disguised opportunism of M.B. Singh. The opportunism of M.B. Singh was made naked. He was made a no-where man' (the foundations of Prachandapath, p. 5). The surprising thing is that the Maoists have been struggling continuously for two decades against the man who was made 'naked' and was 'nowhere' in 1981, a decade and half before. Whatever else, we wish in this chapter, to remind our Maoist friends of the facts of history. The plenum of our party, held in 1981, unanimously adopted a document titled 'Counter-Revolution in China'. The text had been written by M.B. Singh and was presented both in the Central Committee and Plenum. How can we accept the allegation of the Maoists that M.B. was a disguised revisionist and that the process of revolt against his disguised revisionism had started?

The Maoists have said that the Fourth Congress had two positive points, i.e., the correct class analysis of Nepali congress and the decision against the counter-revolution in China which they consider as the great ideological victory. But history shows that in both of those positive and correct decisions of the Fourth Congress, the man whom they call a 'disguised revisionist' had taken the initiative.

12

Even before the royal massacre much had been clear about the position of both the Maoists and the king—about their relationship. But since the massacre, little has been evident regarding the relationship between the Maoists and the new King Gyanendra, or about the positions and policies they would adopt in relation to each other. The facts disclosed so far are not enough for us to decide clearly about those things, and only general and unspecific comments can be made on their basis. However, there are sufficient materials available to indicate that basically they are following the same 'pro-king political line' as in the case of King Birendra.

Immediately after the Royal Palace massacre, the Maoists spoke out radically against the present King Gyanendra. They argued that the 'traditional monarchy' had come to an end in Nepal and that the 'consolidation of the republic' must be the immediate programme. Prachanda's press release about it says explicitly, 'the end of the traditional monarchy is clear.... The patriotic people of Nepal have given the verdict that Gyanendra, the villain responsible for the regicide, both on legal and moral grounds, cannot hold to the ambition of becoming the king of Nepal. In these circumstances, all patriotic, democratic, leftist political groups and powers have to take freely the initiative, without delay, to bring about the establishment of a coalition interim government. In the present situation, of the objective end of the monarchy, that interim government will play the historic role of institutionalizing the peoples republic' (Janaahwan weekly, June 15, 2001).

The above statement makes clear their initial radical opposition to Gyanendra and their commitment to a People's Republic. In opposition to the new king, they launched various activities, including meetings, processions and effigy-burning in different parts of the country. Their declaration of the 'end of traditional monarchy' or the emphasis given to the need for 'institutionalising people's republic' in Nepal do not, however, seem to conform to reality. Has the monarchy 'ended' in Nepal? Is Nepal about to become a people's republic? There is no objective basis for such views. Gyanendra has, in fact, become the king of Nepal. The army is subordinate to him as king. The government is responsible to him. The threat to the existing multiparty system remains, from the king. In such a situation, the movement against the monarchy has lost none of its significance, even today. So, the declaration of the 'end of the monarchy' either reveals the grave childishness, political immaturity or reverie of the Maoists, or hides some crooked or fraudulent trick working behind the declaration.

In any case, the statement shows that they have adopted the policy of opposing radically the present. But the question remains: Are they really against the monarchy or just the present monarch? It is not easy to reach a conclusion, for two reasons. Firstly, not all policies and actions of the Maoists are open and clear. By speaking for a republic and covertly (now overt) setting up a 'hidden' alliance with King Birendra, they have shown that they are not honest with their words and policies. Secondly, many newspapers have reported that the Maoists had also been in collaboration, earlier, with the present King Gyanendra. In such a situation, we cannot fully rule out the possibility of their having developed a covert relation with the present king, Gyanendra. The weekly Yugbani, 14 June, 2001 suggests that 'there is the hand of present king in the rise of the Maoists... some people had put this aside as rumour and hearsay, but some had referred to "the joint mission of Maharajgunj" (the residence of the present king) and spoken of "the Maoists in the jungle against democracy". There is something which matches up here, and there are certainly some who hold the view that there exists an unholy alliance between the Maoists and the present king. An extraordinary incident has brought Gyanendra to the throne. Under these conditions, the Maoists can see no point in staying in the jungle. That is why they have not hesitated to state that they felt restless to come into the open'.

According to Yugbani, then, there was the 'hand' of the present king in the 'uplifting' of the Maoists and both of them had launched a 'joint mission' to end the present parliamentary or multiparty parliamentary system. Ram Chandra Paudel, the then Deputy Prime Minister and Home Minister, wrote during his tenure, 'Nirmal Niwas (residence of the present king) was the "paradise" of Maoists until only yesterday' (Himalaya Times, 2001). This statement by Mr. Paudel also hints at a close relationship between the present king and the Maoists in the past. There exists no authoritative proof to allow us to come to a definite conclusion regarding the truth of the Yugbani claims or of those of Mr Paudel. However, the Maoists' 'restlessness to come out into the open', indicated by Yugbani and Mr Paudel, is worth considering. Soon after Gyanendra became king, Prachanda said, 'in this moment of crisis, we are restless to devote ourselves openly to the service of the country' (Kantipur Daily, June 10, 2001). The 'restlessness' for being 'open' means in effect abandoning their 'underground movement' and suggests being 'restless' to work constitutionally. They had never expressed such a concern to be 'open' and legal/constitutional before at any time during the over 5 years' period of their People's War.

Parchanda has also asserted that 'there is no reason for those honest patriots who saw national safety in the king and monarch yesterday to be afraid of the Maoist movement seen by King

Birendra with his liberal eyes' (ibid). What does this mean? Maoists raise the slogan of the People's Republic on the one hand and idicate that supporters of king and monarch have no reason to be afraid of their movement, on the other. That surely means that despite their plea for the end of the monarchy and for a people's republic, their intention is not to harm the king, or kingship. That is why the supporters of the king and kingship should not be afraid. That statement of Prachanda alone provides grounds for raising the question as to whether behind their radical opposition to King Gyanendra there is not some sort of disguised alliance with Gyanendra, as they say there was with Birendra earlier.

Himal monthly once wrote that 'the CPN (Maoist) has mentioned that it has replaced its old plan to throw out the monarchy in favour of a republic with one to convert the king into a Sihanuk (the Cambodian king)'. (Himal Monthly, March/April, 2001). Three months after the publication of that statement in Himal, Prachanda made the following statement: 'What we also think is that, with the development of people's revolution, at some point, King Birendra might play the role of Sihanuk' (Nepal Samacharpatra, June 15, 2001). What becomes clear from this is that, as indicated by Himal, the Maoists—who had previously proposed dethroning King Birendra to establish a republic—now talked of making him into a 'Sihanuk' and protecting him, and working in 'unity of action' with him. Such an obscure indication as this hardly conforms to Mao's famous advice: 'Be open, and clear, do not stick to intrigue and conspiracy' (which the Maoists have quoted in their own resolution). The question arises as to why did not they put forth their 'Sihanuk theory' openly if they had begun to think like that? Even in the documents adopted at the Second Conference they have not written even a single word to indicate that they are thinking in that way. Under such circumstances, we cannot rule out the possibility of some disguised or crooked objective lurking behind their apparent radical opposition to King Gyanendra.

It should be recognised that while the Maoists were secretly in alliance with the late king, they were also at the same time conducting a violent war against the government and the police. Considering their double role then, we cannot rule out the possibility of a disguised collaboration with the present king simply because they continue to wage an armed struggle against the government and the police. King Birendra is dead, but the death of the king does not automatically break their tie, once established, with the Royal Palace. The same kind of relationship will bring them sooner or later closer to the present king too. So, it will not be surprising if they were to give up their radical stand against the king in the near future.

There was direct or indirect support given by the king, the royalists and the military to the Maoists' armed struggle at the time of King Birendra. It has always been an open secret that their successful assault in Dolpa would have not been possible without the support, albeit indirect, of the military. As the army is fully under the control of the king in Nepal, the support of the military means the support of the king himself. Last year the Maoists attacked the headquarters of Dolpa, captured all of the government offices there during the night and abducted a good number of policemen, along with all their weapons. There was a military post near by and the prime minister himself had instructed the army to help the police defend the district government headquarters. But the military remained silent and inactive throughout the night. Even a layman can guess what that implies. It seems likely that the king and the military helped the Maoists not only in Dolpa but elsewhere, in different parts of the country. The Congress government frequently asked the king to deploy the military against the Maoists. But the king did not agree. Prachanda himself has admitted that the king had a liberal policy with respect to the Maoists People's War (Nepal Samacharpatra, June 8, 2001).

How did King Birendra actually help the Maoists? Bimarsha weekly writes, in this regard, that 'despite government pressure on the king and the military, there was effective resistance. Even the budget allocated for weapons for the police was diverted. Strong obstacles were put in the way of the government's establishing an Armed Police Force. The order for this was delayed (by the king) and after the establishment of the Armed Police Forces, the agreed plan for their training was not put into effect' (Bimarsh weekly, June 23, 2001). Many members of the government, even the then Home Minister, raised questions regarding the role of the military in Dolpa. Mentioning the views of the then Home Minister, Govinda Raj Joshi, for his criticism of the role of the military, Nepal Samacharpatra reported that 'Home Minister Govinda Raj Joshi has expressed the view that the Dolpa incident can be ascribed to the fact that the military had not given the weapons in time'. Mentioning that though they were ready it was difficult to deploy them because of the unavailability of necessary weapons, Minister Joshi added, 'out of the total budget of 35 crores allocated for the purchase of weapons the military has not distributed the weapons yet' (Nepal Samacharpatra, September 28, 2000). In Nepal only the military have the right to purchase weapons. The then Home Minister had effectively raised a question about the role of the king himself. That is why he was compelled to resign from his post. Yugvani wrote, 'There had been comprehensive consultations between the Prime Minister and the Chief of the Army on how the Maoists activities would be controlled in Dolpa. After that, it was agreed that the military would blockade all the roads into the area, while the police would take action (against the Maoists). But the military did not act accordingly' (Yugvani weekly September 28, 2000). Nepal Jagaran also wrote, 'It is said that the Prime Minister had instructed the military to co-operate fully with the police as soon as he learned that the Maoist terrorists were occupying Dolpa district. But there has emerged the puzzling fact that the military remained silent while dozens of police were abducted, crores of rupees taken from the bank and property from the government offices was being looted. What was the explanation for the passivity of the military? Whose orders had been responsible for such a role of the military? The weekly magazine further asked, 'Is it not possible that we can identify the hand of the anti-democratic camp behind the role of the military in Dunai (District headquarters of Dolpa) incident? This suspicion is real and widespread. The question to be asked is whether we see here the protection of the Maoists from one corner of the palace' (Nepal Jagaran, October 2, 2000). Suryodaya Weekly wrote, 'The present NC government has concluded that the role of the military was conducive to the Dolpa incident (Suryodaya, September 28, 2000). Nobody, however, directly referred to the king owing to the present constitution, which prohibits criticism of the king on pain of accusation of treason.

The previous king had apparently not only prohibited the use of military against the Maoists, but also obstructed the training of the armed police and their provision with modern weapons. Now it is becoming more and more evident that the present king also is following the policy of the late King Birendra. King Birendra planned to strengthen his position, to restore direct or despotic rule by ending the multiparty system. The same is true of the present king also. What is yet to be made clear is whether the present king is secretly working with the Maoists, as Birendra apparently did, or not. We feel that it will not take long to be clear whether the Maoists' attacks on the police are their independent activities or whether they result from the undeclared 'unity in action' with the king, as during the rule of the previous king. In the coming few months, it should become clear to what extent the Maoists' movement is based upon their own organisation and to what extent it is dependant upon their 'unity' with the king, the royalists and the military. To the government's proposal to deploy the military in the Maoist-affected areas, the military has responded by 'suggesting that the government declare a state of emergency in the mostly-affected Maoist areas and transfer resources and responsibility for this deployment' (Kantipur, July 7, 2001).

What will be the result of imposing emergency law or giving the responsibility of that place to the army? Discussing it, the weekly Bimarsha writes, 'In an area under emergency law, laws of general administration as well as the fundamental rights of the citizens will be ineffective (inert) and suspended. Not only people will be prevented from demonstrating, and organising processions and strikes but also the publication and selling and distribution of papers may be prohibited. In the name of having encouraged violence and terror, the army or the police may not allow one to read any papers in that area (Bimarsha weekly, July 13, 2001). In this way the army is bargaining with the government in order to enjoy privileges in the name of controlling the Maoists. In Nepal, the army is totally under the control of the king. Therefore it is evident that the king's strategy lies behind the role of the army. In this way, in the name of employing the army against the Maoists, he is able to use it as the means to acquire more and more power for himself.

Now it has become evident that their alliance with the king and the royalists played a vital role in their (the Maoists) activities in the part. The above synopsis removes all the suspicions/doubts about the vital role of involvement of the king, army and the royalists. Maoists had adopted two policies simultaneously—unity with the king and 'People's War' against the government—in the past. Taking into account that kind of their background we cannot ignore both possibilities even today; firstly, despite the war against the government present policy of disguised unity with the king and secondly, the possibility of their secret understanding with the king despite their radical opposition of King Gyanendra. The ex-deputy prime minister and minister writes throwing light on the 'hidden' unity of King Gyanendra with the Maoists: 'They (the Maoists) had unity in action with the palace against democracy' (Himalaya Times, May/June, 2001). The present king neither is nor can be isolated from the conspiracy that has been made by the monarch and royalists since 2046 BS (1989–1990 AD). The present king has long been referred to as a strong critic of the parliamentary system. In that context we have to wait for a little while more to be clear how his conspiracy against democracy goes forward and what kind of relationship he will develop with the Maoists to achieve his goal. Now we have to see whether the present king and the army under him will assist them in the same way as in the time of Birendra or not.

We believe that the new democratic movement is the most committed to the abolition of the semi-feudal and semi-colonial system and that this revolution can be accomplished only through the long-term armed struggle. Marxism–Leninism and Mao tse Tung thought emphasise the importance of a concrete analysis of the historical and objective conditions. When we analyse the situation of Nepal in this way, we reach the conclusion that the time to start the armed struggle has not yet come. We conclude that the people's mass struggle should be the primary aspect of the present movement, though we should also strive further for the preparation and strengthening the basis for such struggle. We, therefore, consider the Maoist's 'People's War' as an ultra-leftist deviation. Their ultra-leftist deviation has taken a pro-king turn and in this it serves the interests of the retrogressive forces more than those of the revolution. That is why they wish to abolish the parliamentary system. They have a policy of concentrating their attack upon the multiparty system while maintaining alliance with the king and the royalists.

Because of this kind of perversion in their thought, instead of building their alliance with the people, they have made an alliance with the king and the royalists, which Modanath Prashrit terms as an 'Unnatural anti-Revolutionary Alliance with the King'. Such a deviation is a result of the influence of Trotskyite political ideology, political immaturity and childishness combined with their petty bourgois character and motivating ambitions. Considering their Trotskyite character and pro-king political line, and following the great tradition of ideological struggle against all kinds of opportunists held by the Marxist–Leninists of the world, we have always conducted a firm, principled and uncompromising struggle against them.

Since this chapter was originally completed, many political changes have taken place in the country, notably the failure of the government's military deployment in Rolpa, the development of the 'core' areas or strongholds of the Maoists, the resignation of the prime minister Koirala and the start of peace talks between the Maoists and government. In July 2001, the government sent the army to Rolpa to surround the Maoists there. The Maoists had abducted a number of policemen in Rolpa and the army was deployed with a view to rescuing them. But the army refrained from taking any action against Maoists. The failure of the planned military action to take place led G.P. Koirala to resign from the Prime Minister's post. He was succeeded by Sher Bahadur Deuba, also of the Nepali Congress. Soon after Deuba was elected prime minister, both the Maoists and the government declared a ceasefire and embarked on the first of a series of talks.

Now, it has been an open secret that the military took no action in Rolpa because of instructions from King Gyanendra. Soon after the deployment of the army in Rolpa, 'a change in the Maoists' line of radical opposition to King Gyanendra took place. Kantipur daily, reporting 'symptoms of change in the Maoist attitude towards the King', noted that 'the underground CPN (Maoist), which after the Narayanhiti massacre had been demonstrating objection to and making propaganda against King Gyanendra Bir Bikram Shah, has shown signs of having changed its attitude toward the king'. Claiming that a Maoist representative held talks with someone close to the palace last week, the party source told Kantipur on Sunday, 'There has been a slight change in our attitude toward the king'. The source has mentioned that this was in keeping with the request of representatives close to the palace to the Maoists to become more positive towards the king.

A highly placed source close to the palace, supposed to have been a mediator between late King Birendra and the Maoists, told Kantipur, 'there is difference between the situation then and now'. Despite the new situation, there have been talks between the Maoists and the mediators of H.M. King Gyanendra. The Maoist chairman, Prachanda, has not, in his press releases and interviews, attacked the king as before. The Maoists have expressed their desire to be involved in any interim government, if formed, after the resignation of G.P. Koirala. 'If an interim government is formed, under those circumstances we would participate in a government on behalf of the Maoists', said the Maoists, according to reliable sources (Kantipur, June 16, 2001).

There are grounds for guessing that such a change in the attitude of the Maoists toward the king led him to instruct his army in Rolpa not to take action against the Maoists. What is the basis of such an understanding between the Maoists and the king? Needless to say, as in the time of the previous king, the similar agendas of the Maoists and the king have brought them closer to each another. Thus, in one way or another, 'a hidden alliance' has been established between them, as in the time of Birendra. Both the leader of the parliamentary opposition and general secretary of the CPN (UML) Madhav Kumar Nepal and the former Prime Minister and current President of the ruling Nepali Congress Party, Girija Prasad Koirala, have hinted that the Maoists have a secret collaboration with King Gyanendra. One weekly stated that on 6 September 2001, both Nepal and Koirala expressed the view that the 'People's War' was guided and protected by the king, and by India (Gatibidhi weekly, September 8, 2001). Two days later, Koirala amended his statement, making a little less clear; he now said that he was confused about the relationship of the Maoists and the king and requested clarification from the palace on the issue (Nepal Samacharpatra, September 9, 2001).

As far as the present Prime Minister is concerned, he is supposed to belong to the pro-King lobby within the Nepali Congress. It is because of this that soon after he became prime minister, the Maoists agreed to stop their armed struggle and to start discussions with the government. There are grounds to think that this could not have happened without an understanding between them and the king. In the last few days, the king has again and again expressed the view that he could not remain passive, looking silently on at the political situation of the country. This means that he is thinking of being active in the politics of the country. Such an active role on the part of the king would pose a serious threat to the present parliamentary system. The Maoists and the government are currently involved in talks. The first round of talks has already taken place and the second was to take place on 13 September 2001. It is difficult to forecast what will be the outcome of the talks. The prime emphasis of the Maoists in the talks is on the ending of the present constitution and its replacement by an interim government, thereby replacing the present parliamentary system. They also are demanding a republic. But many people near to the Maoists, such as Rishikesh Shah, a well-known royalist, have said that in the resort, they (the Maoists) will give up the slogan of a republic and will be prepared to accept any compromise formula under the monarchy.

We think that the forthcoming few months will be decisive for the Maoists, the existing parliamentary system and the monarchy too. The data are still insufficient to analyse the situation fully and reach a conclusion. But we can guess. The main contradiction within the country at present is between the king, on the one side, and the people and the democratic movement, on the other. So, the main problem that the people have to face at present is the danger of the king and royalist forces. The importance and seriousness of so-called People's War is precisely that it is helping the king to fulfill his grand design against the existing multiparty system and the achievements of the great historical movement of the Nepali people in 1990. The danger of the restoration of direct or dictatorial rule by the king is serious, and it is becoming more and more serious. We are convinced, however, that in the last resort, not the reactionary forces, but the people of Nepal will decide the future course of the historical development of the country and all the reactionary forces, including the king, will have to give way to that.

Finally, I would like to conclude the chapter by quoting the following passage from the resolution adopted by the Central

Committee of the Nepal Communist Party (Mashal) on June 9 and 10, 2001:

> The June 1st massacre has made it abundantly clear that the monarchy is no longer practical or relevant in Nepal. This is one of the positive consequences of the event. Now that there is widespread discontent amongst the people, we must pursue a policy of exposing the evils of monarchy, if possible jointly with other like-minded political parties and groups. But at the same time, we must be cautious of the danger that the reactionary forces take advantage of the moment to establish fascist rule in the country or to hijack Nepal into another Sikkim....
>
> Now they (the Maoists) have openly declared that they had an undeclared alliance with the king in regard to many national issues. What is the basis of such an alliance between them? The royal forces were bent on demolishing the present democratic system, and the Maoists were proving themselves the means for that, through their immature, anarchist and ultra-leftist policies. For this reason, there was undeclared alliance between the Maoists and the Royalists.
>
> They (the Maoists) maintain that the struggle against feudalism is the principal struggle in the present political context of Nepal. They also hold the view that the king represents the feudal and comprador classes of the country. Their analysis of the patriotic stance, not only of King Birendra but of whole of the Shah dynasty, however, is not only not in accordance with the political analysis of the communist movement of Nepal, but it is also against the political analysis of the Maoists themselves up till now.

Postscript

Many months have passed since I wrote the above. In the meantime, various important changes have taken place in the country's politics and the political line and role of the Maoists too. It is, therefore, necessary, to discuss these changes, to further clarify and update the issues involved. In the earlier part of this chapter I stressed that even if the Maoists have adopted a pro-royalist line this is not the principal characteristic of their approach. The main feature of their character is pragmatism or, more negatively, opportunism. For them no theory or policy is primary. The immediate political interest has been and remains the matter of primary importance to them. Accordingly, they pursued a pro-royalist political line in the past and by the same token, they may adopt a pro-Congress or pro-Indian line at any time.

In my article entitled 'Guiding Ideology of the Party or the Politics of King, Come and Save the Country?' (published in No. 60 of the 'Masal' in 2000), I wrote, 'We have frequently pointed out that the Maoists have adopted a pro-royalist political line. But it does not follow that their opportunist line ends there. Once a political party takes an opportunist line and fails to meet the standards of Marxist–Leninist theory and ideals, it is likely to manifest this again, in any form, any time. In fact, the Maoists have been pursuing a policy of utilitarianism more and more. Utilitarians formulate their policy and programmes not on the basis of theory but on the basis of calculation of how much or less benefit can be reaped by supporting or opposing a political force. At present, the Maoists have been pursuing an extreme type of opportunist utilitarian outlook. On this basis, they will not hesitate to pursue a pro-Congress policy if they feel that it is more beneficial for them to do so than pursuing the pro-royalist policy'.

In another article entitled 'Palace Massacre and the Maoist's Pro-royalist Political Line', I wrote, 'The primary aspect of their (Maoists') character is 'extreme opportunism'. This is why they were drawn closer to the king or pursued a pro-king political line. But that is not their principal feature. According to their opportunist line, they may at any time change or discard any particular policy of theirs. That opportunist character which inspired them to pursue an extreme "left" line may lead them take a "right" opportunist leap at any time'.

In the introduction to my recently published book 'RIM and the Maoists' So-called People's War', I wrote, 'Their primary character is their opportunism. It is because of this that the issue of theory or revolution is of secondary importance to them and they do not hesitate to discard any theory or to engage in an unprincipled bargaining for their immediate interest. Because of these characteristics of theirs, they may as easily become pro-congress and pro-Indian as extreme "leftists". This type of opportunist pragmatism is "dialectics" for them. Due to this tendency of theirs, there exists a possibility of any domestic and foreign powers to use them in favour of their interest'.

After the palace massacre, they first strongly opposed King

Gyanendra and emphasised their call for a republic. But by the time the above was completed, the signals of change in their opposition to King Gyanendra were already perceptible and a reference to this was made at the end of the article. Soon, this became more evident. A secret pact was made between the King and the Maoists, when the army was sent to Rolpa to launch operations against the latter. According to the pact, the Maoists discarded their policy of opposing King Gyanendra and the army returned without starting their operations. That action on the part of the army was against the instructions of the government (led at the time by Girija Prasad Koirala). The Prime Minister tendered his resignation because of the army's failure to obey his orders. He made this clear subsequently in his statements. This resignation on the part of the Prime Minister constituted a clear and open infestations of the contradiction existing for a long time between the Congress leadership and the Palace in general, and between the autocratic monarchy and multiparty system in particular.

Sher Bahadur Deuba became Prime Minister after the resignation of Girija Prasad Koirala. Deuba was clearly the king's man. I have made this clear in several of my writings previously. He represented the king within the Nepali Congress. When elections for the new leader began within the Nepali Congress, the Maoists favoured Deuba to win. Immediately after Deuba became Prime Minister, Prachanda and Deuba both issued statements, on the same day, announcing a ceasefire and the opening of negotiations. It is common knowledge that the announcement of the negotiations was not an off-the-cuff decision but was the result of the secret understanding being built between the Maoists and Deuba. As a result, the negotiations were announced from both sides as soon as Deuba became Prime Minister. Dialogue took place between the government and the Maoists. Though the dialogue was ostensibly between the government and the Maoists, it was in fact a dialogue between the King and the Nepali Congress in a disguised form. In other words, the objective of the dialogue was to strengthen the position of the king under the cover of the Maoists. Sher Bahadur Deuba had opened dialogue with the Maoists for the same purpose. The Maoists put forward their demands for the consolidation of the republic, a constituent assembly and an interim government. The demand for a republic clearly did not conform to the interests of the King. That is why they soon withdrew it and laid stress for the most part on the constituent assembly and the interim government. The slogan of 'the constituent assembly' looks revolutionary from outside but serves the interest of a retrogressive strategy in reality. Our party has also laid stress on the same slogan for a long time. Our objective in laying stress on the constituent assembly is to weaken the position of the King and to transfer sovereignty to the people. But the Maoists have put forward the slogan of constituent assembly as a weapon to do away with the multiparty system. They have put forward the dissolution of the parliamentary system or the parliamentary constitution as a prior condition for their participation in the election for a constituent assembly. This constitutes the point at which the proposal for a constituent assembly meets the retrogressive strategy of the royalists. Once the multiparty system is done away with in the name of constituent assembly, the king will come forward to occupy the centre stage, in the interim period. Once power is in his hands, it is then up to him to decide when, or whether or not, to convene a constituent assembly or other elections. This is what the royalists have been trying to do for a long time and the Maoists' slogan for constituent assembly fulfils this very retrogressive need of theirs. This is why the royalists have generally supported the slogans of the Maoists for constituent assembly.

The slogan for the constituent assembly carries a great meaning for the fulfilment of the interests of the royalists. However, the most important demand of the Maoists is that of the interim government and access to power through participation in that government. This is not any revolutionary government, please note, but an interim government to be formed under the King in alliance with all the reactionary forces. The main objective of concern to the Maoists is their participation in government, and their needs would be fulfilled if they could participate in any kind of government. The dialogue between the Maoists and the government took place with these interests of the Maoists, on one side, and those of the royalist, on the other. It goes without saying that the objective of such dialogue was the end of the multiparty system in the country. It was therefore natural that the contradiction escalated between the King, on the one hand, and the Nepali Congress as the leader of the multiparty system, on the other. The voice of opposition started to be raised, however, from the establishment side of the Nepali Congress against the government–Maoist dialogue and against the Maoist demands for a constituent assembly and interim government. The government–Maoist dialogue broke off at this stage and the latter attacked the army garrison at Dang-Ghorahi. It was the Maoists who took the initiative in withdrawing from the negotiations. What are the political reasons behind the Maoist withdrawal from dialogue and their attack on the military garrison of Dang? It is difficult to say anything in concrete and official terms, at least at present. We can only explore various possibilities. Firstly, contradictions had increased within the Maoist ranks during the dialogue between the government and the Maoists. Evidently, the motive of the leadership of Maoists behind the dialogue was opportunism. They had taken initiative of dialogue not because they wanted to achieve revolutionary objective but because they wanted to fulfil their opportunist and careerist ambitions. This had escalated the level of dissatisfaction and anger against their leadership and voices of opposition had started to be expressed publicly. One possibility is that the Maoists withdrew from the dialogue due to opposition and pressure from their own rank and file.

Alternatively, the conspiracy on the part of the Palace to achieve its retrogressive political objective by bringing the Maoists to the fore or through dialogue with them did not appear feasible due to the opposition of the establishment side of the Nepali Congress. After 11 September in the United States, it became difficult for the King to maintain his closeness with the Maoists, which could adversely affect his relationship with international reactionary forces and put his very existence in jeopardy. In such a situation, Sher Bahadur Deuba who was working in effect for the Palace, could not take the risk of including the Maoists in the government. That is why the Palace rejected even the request of the Maoists to maintain the status quo ante. In this case, the Maoists withdrew from the dialogue realising the futility of negotiation. A third possibility is that the utility of negotiation ended for the king when he did not see any possibility of furthering his strategy of destroying multiparty system through the medium of the Maoists and under the cover of the constituent assembly. The revivalists would be able to prepare the basis for the fulfilment of their retrogressive strategy only if the Maoists started the armed struggle again, creating the situation of civil war in the country. The possibility cannot be denied that the Maoists had withdrawn from the dialogue and started armed struggle again in accordance with the strategy of the Palace. Fourthly, the possibility of India's involvement can also not be ruled out in connection with the failure of the dialogue. Just like the royalist forces, Indian expansionism has also adopted the strategy of using the Maoists and their so-called People's War for the fulfilment of its own interests. India would be pleased if it becomes difficult for the government to suppress the Maoists and they are obliged to ask for help from India. It cannot be completely ruled out that such an Indian expansionist strategy is at work behind the withdrawal from the talks and resumption of armed struggle by the Maoist. Which of the above provide the main, or at least a partial, explanation for the failure of the Maoist–government dialogue, the resumption of the armed struggle by the Maoists and their attack on the military (and nothing else)? Or have all the above reasons played their part separately? It is difficult to say anything definite about it right now. Probably, in the future more light will be shed on these events and an explanation found for them.

But the fact is that today clashes have been taking place in different parts of the country between the government and the Maoists, and the Maoists have again been opposing King Gyanendra vehemently. The analysis of the nature of the contradiction between the Maoists on the one hand and the King and the army on the other carries specific meaning and significance in view of the previous pro-royalist line of the Maoists and specially in the background of the collusion between the Maoists and the Palace after the incident of Nuwagaun in Rolpa. For a long time, the Maoists had tried to further their so-called People's War by establishing relations with the royalists. Their relation with King Gyanendra was established in accordance with this line. But it broke off, as the King was not prepared to encourage such a type of relationship in the context of the international situation following September 11. It has been already said above that it is opportunism, not the pro-King line, that is the main characteristic of the Maoists. According to their nature, they can as easily adopt a pro-Congress or a pro-Indian policy as they have pursued a pro-royal policy. At the time of analysis we have not yet reached the conclusion that they have already adopted a pro-Indian political line. But there is evidence to support the idea that they have already taken some steps in that direction.

Some time ago, the army intercepted one of their documents, which 'disclosed' that they had renounced the policy of opposing Indian expansionists. At that time, there was no basis to regard the news to be true. But considering the new facts before us, the 'disclosure' made by the army can not be taken as entirely baseless. Some time ago, there was a considerable debate in the Nepali press about an interview given by Krishna Bahdur Mahara, a Maoist politburo member, which was published in an Indian newspaper. Mahara had led the Maoist team in the dialogue during 2001 between the government and the Maoists. That is why this statement carries a special significance. In the interview he supported the construction of Ram Mandir in Ayodhya. Only the Hindu fundamentalists have launched such a movement, whereas all the secular forces, including Indian Congress, CPI, CPM etc. have opposed such idea as being communalist. Even other political groups, such as the People's War Group, which maintains fraternal relation with the Maoists in Nepal, have not supported the construction of Ram Mandir. Given this, Mahara's views on the issue of Ram Mandir could only raise eyebrows. The comment by Mahara was nothing but an unprincipled and non-political flattery of Indian ruling party, the Bharatiya Janata Party. Political circles in Nepal did not give much importance to his comment because it was not an authoritative comment of the leadership of the Communist Party of Nepal (Maoist). The comment, therefore, was considered only an individual view and not an official position of the Maoists. Considering all the related facts, however, there is enough evidence to think that this was a part of a premeditated pro-Indian line which the Maoists have started to take.

If we study the materials published and propagated by the Maoist group for some time, it can be perceived that their anti-Indian stance is becoming less and less strong, to the point of virtual non-existence. The letter sent by Prachanda to the seven parties in the parliament can be taken as an example. There is not a single word about Maoist opposition to Indian expansionism. In view of their high anti-Indian rhetoric in the past, the letter cannot but provide a clear and concrete clue of their changing policy towards Indian expansionism. Viewing this letter in conjunction with Mahara's statement on Ram Mandir, their remains no doubt that this group is changing its policy towards Indian expansionism. Having adopted a pro-royalist line for a long time now, this group has now started to toe a pro-Indian political line. When the Palace refused to continue relation with the Maoists, they appear to have started to establish relation with the Indian expansionists. Mahara's statement was the first obvious step towards this.

The Maoists have launched their so-called People's War without assessing the concrete, objective and subjective condition of the country. Their armed struggle is not based on the support and participation of the people. This is why they have been caught in a situation in which they cannot carry on their so-called People's War or maintain their own existence without falling back on one or the other reactionary power. It is the result of this weakness of theirs that they are trying to preserve themselves with the support of the Indian expansionists after being deprived of the support and cooperation of the palace and the royalists. The struggle against Indian expansionism has had a great importance in the leftist and national movement of Nepal. In such a context, the renouncement of their anti-Indian expansionist policy only shows how low they can stoop for the fulfilment of their immediate interests. There is a long black history of the Nepali Congress' collusion with and flunkeyism towards Indian expansionism. There are examples of other political parties also colluding with the Indian expansionists for their immediate political interests. Is it that the Maoists are trying to capture a place for themselves on that black list? There is scope for raising such a question. It is perhaps because of the pro-Indian trends emerging and growing in the policies of the Maoists that they have stopped raising voices in national issues like Laxmanpur and other similar questions.

It is no secret that in the Nepali Congress, Sher Bahadur Deuba and Girija Prasad Koirala represent the royalist and the pro-Indian lobbies respectively. In the country the royalist or revivalist forces have been raising their voice in favour of direct rule by the king in opposition to the multiparty system. In this debate, Sher Bahadur Deuba has stood on the side of the King and Girija Prasad Koirala on the side of multiparty system. In the process of moving towards a pro-Indian orientation and away from their pro-royalist political line, signals have started to appear that the political relationship of the Maoists with, and their views on, different political parties have been changing accordingly. Earlier, their inclination was towards Deuba. Now they are closer to Koirala. Earlier, their emphasis was towards the end of multiparty system or the constitution. Now they have started to lay stress on the achievements of 1990. Earlier, they were laying emphasis on 'unity in action' with anti-Congress forces. Now they are laying stress on solidarity with the colleagues of the 1990 People's Movement (see Prachanda's recent letter to the political parties represented in the parliament). In this connection, there is also another remarkable aspect. Earlier, Deuba supported dialogue, whereas Koirala opposed it. With the beginning of the process of transition of the Maoists towards pro-Indian line, the attitude of both Deuba and Koirala towards the Maoists has changed. Now Deuba has become an opponent of dialogue, whereas Koirala is clearly for it.

The emphasis which the Maoists have been putting on the achievements of 1990, should be seen as positive. But this kind of thinking of theirs, as usual, is not the result of their correct analysis of country's political situation or policy but rather the result of their opportunist and pragmatist way of determining their policies on the basis of their immediate interest or benefits. Therefore, there is very little basis to believe that they will act honestly on or stand by the ideas they have expressed in favour of the achievement of the People's Movement of 1990. Secondly, while they have been shifting towards a pro-Indian political line and at the same time moving away from a pro-royalist line, it is difficult to take the change as a completely definitive move. Though the Maoists have been shifting away from their pro-King policy, it is difficult to maintain that they are completely free from this political line. They vehemently opposed King Gyanendra after the palace massacre. But soon they changed their stand and established relations with the king. Their pro-royalist line, the 'undeclared unity in action' with King Birendra and the relation with the royalists that enveloped during that collusion, all suggest that they were prepared to develop an alliance with King Gyanendra following the incident of Nuwagaon. By the same token, it is difficult to believe that the Maoist's relation with the royalists, once established, has been completely broken off, even though they are now locked in a fierce struggle with the king and the military. It cannot be completely denied that some aspects of their relationship with the king have been retained and it is always possible that the pro-royalist political line may be revived again.

In the same vein, it is difficult to believe that the pro-Indian political line has also appeared all of a sudden. In this situation there is room for a question: Was there any kind of contact, relation or basis in favour of pro-Indian trend, even while the Maoists were vehemently opposing the Indian expansionism? It would have been difficult for this trend to appear suddenly, in the absence of such prior contact, relation or basis. It is difficult to say anything right now in regard to the form or quantity of any such contacts, relations or bases. They will probably become clearer in the days to come. When considering the character of the Maoists—principled, opportunist or pragmatist—it cannot be denied that there was a veiled pro-royalist line at the same time as there was an acute struggle with the king and a veiled pro-Indian line as they were strongly opposing Indian expansionism.

Did the palace play a role in aborting the government–Maoist dialogue in line with the strategy of weakening the multiparty system, and were the Maoists influenced by that strategy? The behaviour which the Maoists showed after that was rather more inclined towards fulfilling the political objectives of domestic and foreign reactionary forces than to helping the country, people and the revolution. During this period they escalated their looting, beating, extortion, conscription etc. They also increased their destruction of development structures directly related to the life of the people. They have destroyed or set fire to water pipes, schools, university, health posts, vehicles of the Red Cross, public buses, electricity supplies and telephones. These tactics are not acceptable under the principles of a Marxist–Leninist party. But we also have to ask in all seriousness: 'Is this happening either because they themselves are operating under the retrogressive and expansionist strategy of domestic and foreign reactionaries or because there is an infiltration of such elements into their ranks, or simply because their organisation is degenerating into a group of vagabonds, ruffians, undesirable elements and criminals?' Prachanda himself has had issued a statement saying that such actions taken by their groups shall be investigated. It is difficult to know how much credence to give to his statement. Apart from this, it is surely the case that Prachanda issued this statement because the Maoists were being widely criticised in the country. Public opinion has turned against them and even the leftists opposed their actions without exception. The statement itself indicates the extent to which the movement they have launched in the name of the People's War has started to degenerate into such hooliganism, social crime and anti-people actions that it is not possible to cover them up.

The king has recently dissolved parliament at the recommendation of the Prime Minister. It is generally believed that the Deuba government is a puppet of the king and the army. The dissolution of the parliament has strengthened the position of the king and the reactionary policy of the royalists has become successful. In this context, there are two questions which have remained unanswered: 'How will the dissolution of the parliament influence the contradictions, competition and balance between the parliamentary system on the one hand and the strategy of the revivalists on the other?' and 'To what extent has the Maoist activity helped (directly or indirectly) the retrogressive strategy that has played a key role behind the dissolution of Parliament?' We shall have to wait for some more time to get the answer to these questions.

Through a reliable source, it has become known informally that the Indian Chief of Army Staff advised the government to enter into dialogue with the Maoists and sign an agreement with them. But this has not been confirmed publicly. There is some evidence, however, that India has a close relationship with the Maoists. We have already mentioned above that Prime Minister Duba has been strongly opposing the dialogue, whereas Girija Prasad Koirala has been for it. When returning back from China, Mr. Koirala went straight to India, changing his programme to come directly back to Nepal. The newspapers have maintained that the purpose of his visit to India was to hold negotiation with the Maoists. The media have also reported that such a meeting had in fact taken place under the auspices of Indian's Defence Minister Mr George Fernandese. This initiative, taken by the Indian government at an official level, clarifies many important political issues.

Firstly, it makes clear that the Maoists are trying to preserve their own existence with the support of India and that they are moving towards a pro-Indian policy. Secondly, the president of the Nepali Congress has adopted a more friendly position towards the Maoists because of the Maoists' changed policy towards Indian expansionism. Thirdly, a relation is being cultivated between the Maoists and the establishment side of the Nepali Congress.

It goes without saying that in such relationship, the primary and decisive role has been played by India and the interests of Indian expansionism have remained decisive. In view of the pro-Indian political character and history of the Nepali Congress, it does not surprise anyone to see it pursuing such an attitude towards India. But the way the Maoists are developing relations with Indian expansionism and the change in their policy towards it only signifies the degeneration in their declared theoretical and political line. It is not possible to predict what form the growing relationship between the Maoists and India will take in the future. There is no doubt that the objective of India in developing a relationship with the Maoists is to use them in furthering their expansionist policy in Nepal. The Maoists have made it clear several times that the objective of their "leftist" activities is to pressurise the government for dialogue.

It will not be surprising in this context, if there is a political bargain between the Maoists and the King, on the one hand, and the Nepali Congress and the government, on the other. It is difficult to predict what form the relationship between the Maoists, the Nepali Congress, the king and Indian expansionism will take in the future. One thing, however, is clear—even if the Maoists may reap some immediate political benefits from this new set of contradictions and alliances, this strategy will take them further down the road of degeneration.

13 June 2002
Kathmandu

Chapter 9

The Maoist Movement in Nepal: An Analysis from the Women's Perspective

Sujita Shakya

INTRODUCTION

The discrimination and exploitation of women increased with the emergence of class society. Women were entangled ever more deeply in the net of social exploitation and discrimination as society developed from the ancient to the feudal and then to the capitalist mode of production and society, although before this they survived honourably, respectably and capably. Today, they are considered to be delicate and frail. A long history of discrimination and indifference towards them has been justified by the 'fact' that biologically they are incapable and cannot compete with men. In our society, there is a dominant view that 'nature' has made women weak. Even progressives and Marxists express this view. But biological difference is not the same as social difference. Women cannot be made free only by providing legal and other rights, unless and until women are themselves actively involved in the destruction of the old structure of feudalistic and male-dominated societies. Therefore, women themselves have to think seriously and put forward an alternative but objective analysis of the historical development of society.

Women are 'made' backward by economic, political, social and cultural forces. Religious books and religious suppression also 'minimise' women. But women themselves advocate the bearing of children for the protection of 'tradition' and 'the nation'; mothers protect daughters from becoming involved in politics; women are the preservers of caste, untouchability and other conservative traditions. Women are also hesitant about accepting new norms and values. This, however, is due to the effects of male domination. Under such conditions, the provision of constitutional and legal rights by the government is not sufficient. Women have to identify for themselves the roots of discrimination, the solutions and the way forward. In fact, now Nepali women have an excellent opportunity for gaining their constitutional and legal rights; the irony is that the Nepali women's movement is incapable of advancing as effectively as it should.

The Nepali women's movement today is divided broadly into two factions: the conservative, reformist faction and the revolutionary, progressive faction. The first is concerned only with improvements in society whereas the second is revolutionary and dynamic. The first does not agree fully with the concept of giving equal rights to women, whereas the second one is committed to changing the social structure to develop gender relations. The first encourages women to solve their immediate 'hand-to-mouth' problems, whereas the second upholds the idea of abolishing gender inequality to ensure equal rights for women and men. The former approach is characteristic of the rightist parties, namely the Nepal Sadbhavana Party, the Rastriya Prajatantra Party and the Nepali Congress Party, whereas the latter is adopted by the others.

When the Maoist party started the people's War illegally, thinking that social inequality and discrimination can be removed in this way, this extreme vision dominated the leftist women's movement also; many women were under its influence. The main aim of this chapter, however, is to analyse the different stages of the women's movement in Nepal after its formation in 1951, to examine the concept of a women's movement in the present context, to consider what kind of programme is necessary and to explore the challenges now facing this movement. Finally, we shall try to consider the present and future impact of the movement and in particular the activities conducted by the Maoist All Nepal Women's Association (Revolutionary).

The Concept of Women's Emancipation

The women's movement is mainly a social freedom movement but is not a class freedom movement although there is a close relationship. Marxists gave a theoretical foundation to the women's movement; Engels in particular contributed with his *Family, Private Property and the Origin of the State*, arguing that the condition of women basically depends on the economic system and its dynamic. This was true in the past and is equally applicable in the present, and future. Not only 'leftist' women, but other women too, are fighting to establish equality, through political and legal reform. The women's movement is concerned with the struggle against the hegemony and special privileges of men. The women's movement as such does not want to attach its movement directly to any class or social freedom movement. In short, the women's movement has made its target the manifest consequences of the central problem.

Clara Zetkin's contribution is memorable because, in 1907, a women's International Conference was held under her leadership. The Second Convention agreed that 8 March would in future be celebrated as international women's day. This is still celebrated across the world every year. After the success of the October Revolution in 1917, the women's movement divided into two main streams—the democratic and the communist. The Marxist women's movement regarded private property as the main cause of sex and class slavery and argued for an end to private ownership of the means of production and foresaw the freedom of women with the transformation of social ownership.

Marx stated that slavery and the slavery system was born 'in the womb' of the family. Even today, family structure is an important source of ill-treatment and subordination of women. The present family is a single economic unit and that is its main aspect. The family structure rests on small domestic or household economics. It will be relevant to recall Lenin's comments in this regard:

> Women are in a situation of domestic slavery because the petty domestic chore suppresses, strangles, confines, degrades and limits them in kitchen and the upbringing of children and forces them to waste their labour in cruel, unproductive, tense, narrow and boring activities. The real emancipation and equality of women will come only when there starts a widespread struggle against small scale domestic economy, in order to change it into a large scale socialist economy.

This is applicable in the context of our country also. It is not possible to introduce basic or radical changes within this very structure. Therefore, we should keep on hitting at the existing unbalanced and unjust social–cultural structure in order to bring about a change in the status of women within the present feudal and semi-colonial setup and to achieve maximum benefits through an unremitting struggle. This is the basic difference between ANWA (Revolutionary) and the CPN (UML)'s sister organisation ANWA. The revolutionaries have been inspired by a wrong guiding principle that a leap can be made to accomplish revolution within this very structure, which is impossible.

THE HISTORY OF THE NEPALI WOMEN'S MOVEMENT

During the Rana Regime

Nepal is proud of never becoming a colony and the women's movement is also proud of its antecedents. The history of the women's movement in Nepal is closely linked to the patriotic nationalist movement in Nepal. At the battle of Nalapani, Nepali women fought bravely, carrying their children on their backs, against the British colonial army. In 1846 Jang Bahadur Rana initiated a black period of history by establishing a family regime, which was to last through the second half of the 19th century and first half of the 20th century. Later, in the early 20th century, different Rana rulers tried to introduce social welfare reforms by abolishing slavery, opening schools and colleges, but equal opportunities were not provided for women. Women started fighting against oppression from 1974 BS (1917 AD) under the leadership of Yoga Maya Neupane. Her organisation, named 'Nari

Samitee', was established in 1974 BS (1917 AD). This organisation spread the message of reform through Vajan and Kirtan (recitation of religious hymns) as there was no other way at the time to make the society conscious and aware. Her 24-point list of demands was presented to Prime Minister Chandra Shamsher Rana and afterwards to Juddha Shamsher Rana. They found it hard to disagree with the demands, but their agreement paid lip service only, and in practice, the voices of reform and freedom were suppressed. In 1997 BS (1940 AD), four of her followers were killed; this made her sad and she jumped to her death with 68 followers in the Arun river, saying that 'to die is better then to survive in this sinful country. This incident is the first major sacrifice of the women's movement. In 1974 BS (1917 AD), Krishna Prasad Koirala attempted to form a women's organisation, named 'Nari Jagriti' (Women's Awareness). This was not sustained although it originally aimed at opening different branches across the country. Chandra Kanta Mathema also led a movement for women' study and eventually a women's school was established in the year 1993 BS (1936 AD), at Makkhan in Kathmandu. Almost all of the women who were active against the Rana regime were products of these two schools.

Nepali women also played a vital role in the movement against the Rana regime. The political parties began to put women's rights on their agendas because many women also participated actively in politics. Kamakchya Devi Basnet and Rewanta Kumari Acharya actively participated in the establishment of the first political party, the Nepal Praja Parishad in 1993 BS (1936 AD). Nurses at Bir Hospital, Asta Kumari and Chanchala Manandhar distributed leaflets in different parts of Kathmandu city at night, hiding from the police, under the pretence of going to the maternity hospital. These activities were very bold and courageous and this work created a sensation among the Rana rulers. In 2000 BS (1943 AD), two secret organisations were founded, in one of which were Pushpa Lal, Prem Bahadur Kansakar and Kamakchya Devi Basnet, while in the other were Bhuwanlal Pradhan and Sahana Pradhan. In due course, the Adharsa Mahila Samaj (Ideal Women's Society) was established to uplift the level of women and also to make them more aware. In the same year, the workers movement was organised in

Biratnagar; here too, the participation of the women was remarkable. In 2004 BS (1947 AD), Sadhana Pradhan, Kanak Lata Bajracharya and Shnehalatta Shrestha were arrested while taking part in a 'Civil Rights Movement' procession.

Four years later, in 2004 BS (1947 AD) the Nepal Women's Association was formed, with Mangala Devi Singh as Chair, Kamakchya Devi as Vice President, Shnehaltta as General Secretary, Shreemaya Shrestha as Treasurer and Sita Devi Sharma, Rana Laxmi Manandhar, Champa Devi Bajracharya and Hiradevi Yami as ordinary members respectively. That year, the committee demanded female education, employment and the right to vote (adult franchise), and the Prime Minister fulfilled the demand for the adult franchise for women. This created confidence in the women's movement. In the year 2005 BS (1948 AD), six women were arrested. In the year 2006 BS (1948 AD), the Nepali Communist Party included one woman member, Moti Devi Shrestha (Durga Devi), as a founder member. On the first of Poush 2007 BS (1950 AD) an All Nepal Women's Association was formed in Raxaul (an Indian city on the border with Nepal), chaired by Tara Devi, and another was founded in Kathmandu, chaired by Punya Prabha Devi.

At this point, the demands of the women's movement included a rejection of a variety of practices around marriage, education and employment: widow marriage, child marriage, polygamy, exploitation in the name of religion and culture, lack of female education, employment opportunities and the adult franchise.

During the First Democratic Period

Until the time of the uprising against the Rana Regime, all women had a single general set of aims. But when the Nepali Communist Party proposed that the Delhi agreement was acceptable, different views emerged within the women's movement. Mangla Devi and her followers strongly stood in favour of the motion, whereas Kamakchya Devi and Shnehalatta were completely opposed to the motion. After this, the movement polarised between 'reformist' and 'revolutionary' factions. Mangla Devi led the reformist line whereas Kamakchya Devi led the revolutionary line. On 1 July 1951 AD, the All Nepal

Women's Association actively took part in a demonstration, showing a black flag to the Indian Prime minister; seven women were arrested. On 7 March 1952, a new, revolutionary women's organisation named All Nepal Women's Association was established by Kamakchya Devi. The aim was to revolutionise the women of Nepal. Apart from that general objective, the association also fought in practical ways against different kinds of exploitation and discrimination. Some of the demands written into the manifesto included the right to equal work, the right to equal pay, fundamental rights, special maternity facilities and free education for children. The manifesto also called back the Nepalese youth from recruitment to foreign armies and the establishment of democracy in Nepal. After the party was banned, the All Nepal Women's Association raised its voice against the ban.

In 1951, Nepalese women also participated in the movement launched against feudalism and defended the movement strongly. The All Nepal Women's Association also actively participated in the movement against imperialism, mainly against American and European imperialism, and Indian expansionism. It took part in the 3–day 'Satyagraha', staged in front of the royal palace as no right to candidacy was given to women in elections. As a result, Mangla Devi Singh, Punya Prabha Devi Dhungana, Prativa Jha, and Maya Devi Shaha were nominated to the Consultative Assembly. A big protest meeting was organised against one-sided nominations, at which eight women were arrested. As a result of this, Sadhana Pradhana became the first elected women member in the municipality. In the election of 2015 BS (1959 AD), only six women contested the elections, and only one of them—Dwarika Devi Thakurani—was successful. In 2017 BS (1960-1961 AD) a women's bill drafting committee was formed, which prioritised equal rights for women in paternal property. After 2017 BS (1960 AD), a chapter in the history of the women's movement was closed as a result of the actions of King Mahendra in banning political parties and political organisations and establishing the Panchayat System.

The Panchayat Period

For more then a decade, the women's movement was unable to move ahead actively because of the political ban. International split in the communist movement also influenced the Nepali communist movement. The divisions and factions that developed in the communist movement had a negative impact on the revolutionary women's movement. The political activities of the women's movement also became very limited.

With the reformation of the CPN (UML) in 1978, a revived Nepal Women's Association was formed under the leadership of Shanta Manawi; it was founded on 28 February 1981 of with the same objectives as when it was established earlier under Kamakchya Devi Basnet. The association became active both openly and underground. It raised its voice for an end to inequality and social discrimination and oppression. At this period, the activities of the Nepal Women's Associations (government sponsored women organisations) were largely at a personal level and it did not contribute generally to the development of women's condition. The All Nepal Women's Association (ANWA) on the other hand was by now spread all over Nepal. Within a decade more than 50 women workers had become full-time women activists. The ANWA provided a base for women all over the country. It also undertook the work of changing the outlook of women of different classes, professions, levels and groups. Taking advantage of celebrations like Teej, Tihar and International Women's and Labour Day, women were brought into the streets through cultural programs, mass meetings, slogans and demonstrations. The first conference was held underground in 2046 BS (1989 AD). Women played a decisive role in the 2046 BS (1989 AD) People's Movement. Sahana Pradhan became the chairperson of the United Left Forum that led the popular movement of 1990. In the movement, women were now organised in different independent organisations and professional organisations actively. Women also took part in the movement courageously, both in the capital and outside.

The Previous Decade

The eight-point program for the new constitution was developed in a collaboration between lawyers, political activists, women workers and intellectuals working with the constitution reformation suggestion commission. The following matters were included: equal rights as between sons and daughters in paternal property, guarantees for women's social security and protection, guarantees of citizenship in cases where a Nepali women is married to a foreigner, arrangements for women representatives in constitutional organs, special provision for economic independence, 50 per cent women representation in the upper house of the parliament, constitutional arrangements regarding the formation of women's tribunal to deal with violence against women, and special protection for women. The constitution of the kingdom of Nepal reflected the concept of women's fundamental rights and of equality between man and women. By keeping a provision for 5 per cent of women candidates contesting a national election, binding on all political parties, women's participation in politics was made compulsory. But no consolidated and concrete gains were made in the social security of women and others vulnerable groups.

ANWA also recognised, however, the need for concrete measures to ensure the safety of those women who were raped and tortured during the interim period (1990–91), including minors and disabled people. The Women's Security Pressure Group was formed under the leadership of Sahana Pradhana and more than 55 women's associations participated. It organised processions and mass meetings against rape and violence. It also gave out information leaflets and launched a signature campaign. In the beginning, the pressure group was very active, but later on it was unable to maintain the same dynamic. Some organisations used it in their own interests and it did not become as effective as it should have. Now also, it is necessary to make women's pressure groups active to face common problems. ANWA is in fact busy in with an internal restructuring of the organisation. At this time, the association has to make tremendous progress to bridge the gap of gender inequality. The provisions made regarding women's participation in local elections proved effective—significant numbers have participated at that level, but the women elected have not mobilised effectively. The constitutional rights afforded to women are not in fact brought into practice. The women's movement is not sufficiently 'result oriented'.

REVIEW OF THE WOMEN'S MOVEMENT AND WOMEN'S CONDITION IN NEPAL

If one considers the present status of women, it might seem that women have not played any role at all, but this is not true. Dozens of Nepali women have sacrificed their lives, from the period of the opposition to the Ranas to the present time. Hundreds of women have been imprisoned and many have suffered the loss of their near and dear ones. Many women lost their husbands and had to take on the burden of child care and upbringing by themselves. Some women are obliged to undergo disrespect and dishonour whereas many now prefer to choose the very tough underground life. Thus, both 'democratic' and 'leftist' women have made an important contribution to their society. They have remained in the front line and fought, and fought continually until the announcement of multiparty democracy. But women are still lagging behind in the exercise of the rights enshrined in the Constitution of Nepal 1990.

Some of the suggestions of the Women's Association are included in the constitution of the Kingdom of Nepal. The constitution has guaranteed basic human rights. There is an obligation to the effect that 5 per cent of candidates for election to the House of Representatives must be women. This is, however, only a partial achievement. The irony is that they are kept to the 5 per cent reservation. Article 11 of Part 3 of the Constitution has provided for equality as a right, and Article 11(I) refers to all people being equal before the law and states that nobody can be deprived of the protection of equal rights. Article 11(2) outlaws gender discrimination and Article 11(3) gives priority to the passing of specific laws for the advancement of women. Article (1) states the concept of the Constitution as the main law of the land, and extraordinary jurisdiction is given to the Supreme Court to make any contradictory law null and void. Freedom to earn income and to make use of property is covered by Article 17. Moreover, Article 131 clearly states that any contradictory laws shall become inactive a year after the establishment of the Constitution. In totality, the Constitution is progressive. Unfortunately, the present Nepali Congress government is not.

Many NGOs and social organisations have been established in the name of women's empowerment and the advancement of women's rights, taking advantage of the multiparty democracy and civil freedoms. Many women have gained new opportunities in this way. The positive aspect of this is that many women who were previously severely confined have benefited from a more open environment. This has helped quantitatively, but not qualitatively. Women's emancipation has been diverted, which is a dangerous matter. This has meant that women have become entangled in minor issues and have left more important matters aside. The treaties signed in the United Nations are a case in point. The government has emphasised its concerns, has recognised March 8 as international women's day and often puts forward the slogan of 'women and development' and even of 'gender equality'. Still, however, there is little difference as regards the real social condition of the women.

If we spare a moment to consider the social status of women, they are still worshipping the moon as god and believing the story of *Swasthani Bratakatha*, which is superstitious and illusory. Although there is so much progress in science and technology, Nepali women are still deprived of education and are forced to spend their lives in collecting fodder, firewood and in farming. There are still many areas where the whole day has to be devoted to bringing water and fodder and looking after the animals. For lack of health facilities, women are still subject to high levels of illness. This in itself raises big questions about women's emancipation. NGOs spend much of their income on salaries but the funds are collected in the name of the poor and helpless. The funds used in different causes remain largely ineffective. All such resources have been captured by women close to the palace—previously some were close to the Nepali women's organisations, but now it is Sujata Jost or Aarju Deuwa or others who belong to aristocratic families and dominate the scene. They take part of the funds that are meant for the poor and helpless for their political and personal benefits. Nepal is also a party to the 4th World Congress on Women held in Beijing and the Convention on the Elimination of All Forms of Discrimination Against Women, but they have not been implemented. The Women's

Minister has been unable to exercise power or influence and remained on the sidelines. The Women's Commission is in place now but has failed to come up with a concrete plan of action against various forms of discrimination against women.

The point of view of different tendencies regarding the development programmes of different NGOs also differs. The All Nepal Women's Association affiliated to CPN (UML) opposes and exposes the misuse of resources by some NGOs, accepting this reality. It has a positive attitude that emphasises support for good actions and criticism of bad ones, whereas the All Nepal Women's Association (Revolutionary) is almost entirely critical and considers NGOs the agents of imperialists. This approach is very different from those of other women's associations.

MAOIST DEVIATION AND THE NEPALI WOMEN'S MOVEMENT

In totality, the Nepal women's movement is divided into a democratic and a leftist section. From the very beginning of the Nepali women's movement, the former has supported reform, whereas the leftist faction has supported radical change. There are also different factions within these two major groups. At certain times, extreme positions have been adopted against male domination. This has been found especially among socalled educated and leftist women. Extreme thought—seen in the ideology of both the right and the left—inevitably develops into distortion and disparity, resulting eventually in dissolution. Now, at the present time, Maoist extremist thought constitutes a serious issue in Nepal. Consequently, the sister organisations of the women's movement have become entangled in it. The ANWA (Revolutionary) has divided the women's movement into three parts. Among them, the Nepal Women's Association, connected with Nepali Congress, and the All Nepal Women's Association, connected with CPN (UML), are considered reactionary organisations by the Maoist sister organisation, i.e. ANWA (Revolutionary)

This analysis is completely wrong. The experience of only 6 years is nothing. The reality is that the women's association close to the CPN (UML) has been developing as the mainstream of the Nepali communist movement in Nepal. This fact should not be minimised. The work of the revolutionary ANWA (R) cannot be compared to that of the other left women's associations. ANWA has been successful in raising the consciousness and organissation of women throughout the country. To consider such an association a 'reactionary organisation' may itself be the consequence of deviation. The analysis of the situation in this negative way also reveals a narrow sectarianism. The important objective is not to 'come into the spotlight' by violence but to continue a principled struggle for timely reform and correction, constantly and without hindrance. The present analysis of the ANWA (R) suggests a degree of immaturity and childishness regarding political analysis. The injustice, tyranny, exploitation and oppression faced by women cannot be overcome just by beating someone with 50–100 bamboo sticks and breaking pots of local wine. The other characteristic identifiable is their opportunism, whereby all other organisations are stigmatised as reactionary when the situation is easy, whereas when the situation becomes difficult they ask for help from other leftist women's associations.

Contrary to the opinion of the revolutionary ANWA(R), the ANWA CPN (UML) wants to organise all women, collaborate with NGOs and INGOs, to gain maximum rights for women's emancipation. The democratic women can also be used to gain equal opportunities in certain areas, which is not recognised by the ANWA (Revolutionary). For instance, paternal property and the rape and the trafficking of women are some of the issues of concern to all women. Because at the present time our country is semi-feudal and semi-colonial, this permeates the entire state system, economic mechanism and social structure. So the demand for People's Democracy and associated structures is no more than a wild goose chase now. Such a big ambition can turn into a dangerous weapon to be used against women. Many 'revolutionary' political movements (in India, Peru, Cambodia, Philippines and Sri Lanka) are actually examples of the failure of the women's movement, but the Maoist women never accept this truth.

The Maoists think that they are the only real communists and the rest of the left, in the entire world including Nepal, are all revisionists. The reality of their 'revolution' includes looting national property, slaughtering individuals, including the proletariat and ordinary low-level people in the name of not giving shelter and charity, raping the women working in own party and using women as weapons in the war. They present themselves as an invisible force having magical power and as the incarnation of the divine, like a hero of the cinema or worker of black magic. But the change of a society must be for the people and by the people, and other social agents are only facilitators. This has not been understood at all by the Maoists.

THE MAOIST MOVEMENT AND ITS IMPACT

The Maoist movement is a serious deviation within the Nepali Communist movement. From the very beginning of the Nepalese communist movement we have seen many such deviations, but this is the most serious of all. Individual murder and white tyranny have harmed the leftist and democratic movement. The Maoist movement has also influenced the Nepali leftist movement as a whole. After the launching of the People's War, all of national life has been very much influenced by it. However, it has played a positive role to some extent, in spite of its terrorist activities and commitment to insurgency. The positive and negative aspects of its impact are outlined briefly below.

Positive Impacts

The first positive influence of the Maoists after the launching of the People's War is the feeling of sacrifice: the people killed by it are, of course, not all positively influenced by it, but 70 per cent are involved due to their devotion and dedication towards the party. According to the records of the Maoist party, more than 100 women have sacrificed their lives and the number of women who have became prey to the police is countless. Most of those who have died as a result of government repression have been people from the lower orders of society, but their number is very high. Those who died, however, are considered to have sacrificed their lives for a cause.

The second impact is the diffusion of the movement to different indigenous peoples, ethnic groups and communities of women. The Maoists have carried their politics into different tribes, ethnic groups, *dalits* and women, and produced plenty of cadres from there. If these workers are transformed into Marxists and given a Marxist education, this is a positive development.

The third is the development of the armed forces. The effect of the armed struggle has been to put the police in disarray and to oblige their restructuring. It has also created a challenge for all traditional Nepali security organs, including the Royal Nepali Army.

The fourth is the people's action based on armed struggle and direct action against traditional practices and local reactionaries by ordinary rural people. But the irony is that the corrupt and reactionary people who give charity to the Maoists are protected by them openly.

The fifth is the publicity and propaganda given to the communist movement everywhere in the country, whether in the jungle, the streets or in the corridors of power. They are the centre of all political debate as a major force for change. In the short term, this may be positive, but in fact such a situation is not at all good. It has blocked the clarification of the different party lines.

The sixth is the raising of political consciousness in the remote rural areas in the name of the 'class struggle' and the People's War. Earlier, the movement was only known in specific areas, but now it is active even in remote rural areas and draws the attention toward those areas.

The seventh is that it constitutes a challenge to the constitutional court and judicial system. It has given a basis for criticism of the constitutional judicial system, which is said to be controlled by the corrupt and the 'Mafia'.

The eighth is that it has drawn the attention of all the political parties, including the ruling Nepali Congress. The Maoist movement has also added some energy to thinking about the transformation of political, social and economic structures. But the CPN (Maoist) does not pay much attention to making use of this positive aspect. The 'extreme left attitude' of the Maoists was exemplified when they left these concerns and attacked the Army. The Maoists must address the situation quickly and try to resolve it by dialogue. Otherwise, this movement will also turn into one of the terrorist movements of the contemporary world and fall into rightist opportunism soon.

Negative Impacts

The negative impacts are more in number than the positive ones, and are given below. Because of the war, foreign investment and the tourism industry are on the verge of collapse. In rural areas also it has had a direct impact as able-bodied men and women have gone into the jungle to be Maoists and the remainder have gone to the city in search of jobs, while yet others are displaced by their fear of police and army suppression.

Because of the Maoist terror and government repression, regular development and constructive works are constrained. NGOs active in the rural areas are leaving their working places for reasons of security and safety. Because of this, economic activities have been reduced. The rural banks are also closed because of safety problems and the traditional money lenders are also afraid of giving loans to the rural people due to the fear of Maoist attack and the rural areas are becoming a money free zone. The economic sector is deprived of investment, production, development and financial activities.

Other activities, except Maoist violence and government reaction, have been blocked. The Maoists are creating obstacles in areas where they have full domination and the political activities of other parties, Nepali Congress, CPN (UML), CPN (ML), Mashal and Unity Centre, are banned in these areas. The Maoists do not allow others to undertake political activities in their areas, thinking that its hegemony will be lost, and if any political party tries to be active locally, the government is hostile to it, pretending its collaboration with the Maoists. As a result, more than 70 CPN (UML) cadres have been killed so far due to the violence and police suppression. The cultural sector is also terrorised due to violent activities conducted by the Maoists. Now the Maoists are trying to win the collective consciousness of people by the bullet. They say that everything is 'the people's war' and it is our cultural celebration. The Maoists have forgotten the extremes of Mao's Cultural Revolution. They are dismantling the people's culture and encouraging petty bourgeois culture and feudal thought. Such an influence can be seen in their attitude towards different fairs and festivals and celebrations; their boycott of Dashain and Maghi are examples of this approach.

The Maoists are now damaging traditional social organisations in the remote areas that they control in terms of local government and in other ways. They also control the developmental aspects of local economy and society, such as community forest users' groups, mothers' groups and other economic groups. In all such activities, the Maoists' guns dominate. This kind of control of activity is a form of dictatorship. This does not do justice to the people. From the government's side also, the same thing is seen—while mobilising the army, the government also show the same dictatorship mentality. This has had the effect of moving the nation towards a dictatorship, sooner or later.

THE INFLUENCE ON THE WOMEN'S MOVEMENT

The women movement is not exempt from the influence of the extreme thought of the Maoist party. The attraction of legal and constitutional struggle is systematically reduced in favour of illegal means of getting quick justice, which has become very attractive to the rural women. But in the long run, women will not be able to defend themselves from the adverse effects. The Maoist party has recruited many women as cadres; they are attracted because the Maoists recruit them as guerrillas and militia, but in practice such women are often ill-treated and raped. Those women who have escaped have said that their reasons for escaping included unwanted sex and rape. The party has not paid especial attention to the control of sex and rape, at least as far as can be gathered from those who have escaped from the squads.

In the name of opposing polygamy, rape and illicit sexual relation the Maoists have been taking actions without paying attention on the psychological impact on the future life of the concerned women. In this context, the Maoists organise a mass meeting, encourage the victim to spell out charges and take action against the culprit. This has greatly discouraged the victimised women. After such action, the concerned women are found to have become lonely. The Maoists have not taken any concrete initiative to put an end to such situation.

Whoever opposes the Maoist movement is often subjected to

worse torture such as submerging in water at night and forcing them to sign a paper. In one such case in Rolpa one Chun Kumari KC was arrested, submerged in water, beaten and was compelled to sign a paper that she had had sexual relation with a gentleman of a village. They were then tied together and were taken round the village after blackening their faces with soot. They even banned that women from going to her husband's house. Having been displaced from the society, the woman is seeking justice. There are many such cases of vengeful actions that the Maoists have taken against those who differ with them but these incidents do not become public knowledge owing to insurgency.

The women in Maoist areas started an anti-alcohol movement, boycotting local drink; this movement has been very active in mobilising large numbers of people. It has been particularly effective in western Nepal. Many VDCs (Village Development Committees) and DDCs (District Development Committees) have formally declared liquor-free zones. This movement has brought women greater awareness and involvement in action. But in trying to control alcohol use, the Maoists have tried to enforce it by force. This has weakened the anti-alcohol movement and outside the Maoist l area, the use of alcohol has increased tremendously. The Maoist women's organisations cut the long hair of boys and rip open the pants and shirt being worn by girls to demonstrate their opposition to 'capitalist' culture. In places like Dharan, where young people put on fashionable clothes, this has created a backlash against communist ideology. But the women guerrillas in their areas of influence wear only half-pants themselves and move around from village to village, which implies a double standard. This makes it evident to us that they are themselves not clear with respect to their ideological positions and such forcible intervention distracts the attention of women from real left ideology.

The Maoists are also forcefully attacking religion, culture and tradition. Women are still superstitious, due to ignorance and backwardness. But the Maoists' extreme position has created a negative impact upon the ignorant rural women and also created a negative impact as far as the women's movement is concerned by suggesting that it is in favour of complete change. The Maoists do not bother to correct such mistakes. In the Maoist influenced areas, women are facing a twofold terror. On the one hand, they are influenced by the negative effects of the Maoist movement itself and on the other, they are the victims of the actions of the army and the police, which have been mobilised to control the Maoist movement. In the period of Operation Romeo and Kilo Sierra II, many women were victimised by rape, but the Maoists were not able to control such inhuman acts and brutal behaviour. Just the opposite; they too have applied the same methods in their actions against their opponents. There is an example, from Dang district. In Tulsipur Town Municipality, a married woman who was a supporter of Mashal was raped in course of taking action. This kind of mean, vengeful act mars their reputation. The revolutionary women's movement is seriously affected by its ignorance of social control and balanced principles. This has increased suspicion of their motives and actions, even among those inclined towards reform. Therefore, a serious responsibility lies on the shoulders of these revolutionary women.

Now, because of these left deviations, a serious programme is necessary to carry the progressive women's movement as a whole to its correct destination. By analysing the serious negative impact created by the present situation, women should be guided and led to proper path consciously and materially. Guidance is necessary to save the women's movement from the present crisis. ANWA has been conducting an ideological campaign against dogmatic and insurgent activities, and the association will be more active and make more progress in the forthcoming period.

IMPACT OF THE PEOPLE'S WAR ON WOMEN AND CHILDREN

It is a universal truth that in times of violence and terror, the main brunt will fall upon children and women. When a situation of conflict and tension develops, the number of incidents of human rights violation increases and the ultimate effect of it falls heavily on women and children. There have been continual incidents of violence and retaliation in the name of the Maoist movement since this violent and illegal movement started in Nepal. Women and children are the victims in most cases of both the Maoist insurgency and the government's retaliation. Such an effect after the commencement of the Maoist movement can be understood as follows.

Use of Women and Children in the War

Although there is no rule and law against using women and children in dangerous activities, the Maoists are using a large number of women and children in highly risky situations. They are using children below 14 years of age as guerrilla fighters and also for bringing and taking explosive materials. In Salyan district, a 13-year-old schoolboy died as a result of torture applied to him by Maoists while trying to recruit him into the People's militia. As a result, one 14-year-old school boy, who was used to set off explosive material at the district headquarters of Rolpa, died. Four female Maoist guerrillas were shot dead in an encounter with the police in military action in Lamjung. Large numbers of women are killed by the police during searches, as a result of the difficulty of running away. In the light of these examples, we can say that the Maoists are using unskilled women in the war by force. The ratio of killed women is high in comparison to women's participation. Although both men and women are required to participate in the war, the number of women killed reveals that the Maoists are not very serious about this deplorable situation.

Use of Women and Children as Human Shields

Local people who do not even know where they are being taken are often used by the Maoists when attacking police posts and large military garrisons. Large numbers of ordinary people are also used by the Maoists to sing songs and dance in the war zones. The Maoists have also used women to carry loads such as arms, foods and other war materials from one place to another in processions and even just to carry loads from one place to another. Similarly, the police also use local people on their patrols and force suspected Maoist supporters to sleep in the police station in the name of safety. Women and children in large numbers are used in such situations by both groups, competitively. According to the rule of human rights principles such as the Geneva Convention, people are not to be used as shields for purposes of war. Such an act is termed as a war crime. But in our country there is scarcely any such consciousness and such things are repeatedly done, by both sides. Now the government has mobilised the army, and it is likely that such activities may increase to an extent significantly greater than when the Maoists and the government were in dialogue. Both sides must be made aware that human beings should not be used as shields.

Victim of Explosive Materials

The Maoists are using women and children to carry and use explosive material and it is heard time and time again that many of them die due to lack of minimum knowledge of safe handling. Many children are disabled and many others have died because they considered it like playing with dolls. Such a situation is a very serious matter, all the more so because few people know exactly what an explosive material looks like and what it can do.

Misbehaviour and Sexual Exploitation of Women

There is strong evidence to suggest that women are illtreated to a considerable extent by the police. At the time of operations Romeo and Kilo Sierra II, it is publicly known that many women who were suspected of supporting the Maoists were ill-treated and raped by the police. Within the Maoist party also, cases of raping and sexual exploitation are apparently common, and incidents are heard of in which women were raped because they held a different opinion in the party. After the dialogue started, such incidents did not decline in the Maoist party. The Maoist party actually acknowledged one such incident in which a Deputy Chairman of the "people's government", one Kaile Giri, raped a child. Almost all the women guerrillas who have left the Maoist party have complained that they were forced to leave the party due to rape. Many such incidents have been kept secret but some of them have been made public. Rural women cannot go safely in the jungle to cut grass and to search for faggots on account of the risk presented by the Maoists and the police respectively.

Forced Shelter and Regular Lodging and Food Provision

The people in the Maoist-affected areas are routinely forced to provide food and shelter to the Maoists. They have to manage food and shelter for Maoists—and for the police too. For this, the economic status of the people concerned is not a matter of significance. The Maoists use people for food and shelter on a daily and regular basis. Women are mostly responsible for the burden of providing shelter and food. Those who demand these facilities, never think of the impact of such demands on women and children. If people refuse to provide shelter and food, in the name of people's action, the Maoists may beat, mutilate or even kill them—all of these have happened. For example, the Maoists killed a poor farmer, Nimalal Rokka, because he refused to provide food and shelter for them. Such inhuman conduct must be criticised and opposed by all sections of the society.

Effects on Women and Children of the Absence of the Male Members of the Family

After the death or disability of the head of a household, its effect is felt by the women and children. In this way, women are forced to survive as widows and in future the children are extremely affected. They may become 'revolutionaries' or they may become cowardly and timid. Therefore, the conflict needs to be resolved urgently considering these long-term effects on the future generation.

Because of terror and fear of the Maoists, after the commencement of the Maoist war, large numbers of youth are displaced or have escaped. The villages are turning into the dwelling places of the old, of women and children. Women have to manage everything, as men are underground. In this way, women of the Maoist-affected areas are under a double burden: that of terror and that of managing to survive.

Because of the departure of so many men from the villages, women have to do most of the farm work as well as the domestic work—even to the extent, in some cases, of ploughing. Children below normal working age are also required to become involved in productive activities. The Maoists add another big problem for women who are generally busy from morning to evening in domestic and household affairs. Women have to come forward to face the Maoist terror and the fear of the police by hook or by crook. In this way, we see that women are becoming active in two ways as stated above.

Children Deprived of the Opportunity to Study

Many teachers have been displaced in Maoist-affected areas. The Maoist People's War has created a serious problem for children's education: teachers' displacement, lack of government resources for the management of school and stoppage of additional fees, all add to the problem. Another difficulty is the excessive use of school children for Maoist activities and in a terrorised environment. Another factor for prompting people to run away or go underground is the killing of father or mother or their disappearance. These things have a serious affect on children's education. The child's mind is very soft and these things affect them later. But the Maoists are not thinking about this very seriously.

Additional Hazard for Maternity

There has been a serious effect on women's health, particularly as regards childbirth and post-natal care, due to violence and tension. The reality in this regard is that governmental services and facilities are being displaced and that the Maoists have not paid attention to alternatives; this has affected the lives and health status and security of women. Even for the underground cadres involved in the Maoist movement, their health and safety have become more problematic. These aspects of the conflict and its effects should be negotiated as a matter of urgency so that more human loss is not suffered. The Maoists should also think gravely about the protection of the rights of women and children. They are not so thoughtful as to reduce the level of conflict so as to make the present tense situation normal; they have simply characterised the situation as natural or normal. So voices should be raised from outside to control the war, insist on dialogue and arrange peace and security for the people. The All Nepal Women Association is determined to carry on its efforts to solve the War peacefully: one aspect of its mission is to seek the peaceful solution of violence.

THE PROGRAM OF WOMEN'S EMANCIPATION

In Nepal, the women's freedom movement attained political direction with the establishment of the Nepali Communist Party. But there is still a problem in regard to the progressive development of the women's movement in a consolidated way. Internally, attempts are being made to achieve international standards, following the lead of the United Nations, but in practice, this has not given any positive result. Although Nepal has signed all the relevant international treaties and proposals, at a national level these agreed resolutions are not actively put into practice.

Now the problem has been seen in the context of transforming initiatives for community welfare into class struggle. Some components of the women's movement, as distinct from the more political women's movements, do not try to carry the movement forward as a single and consolidated and total programme, but are trying to take it forward subjectively and in different ways. In such a situation of potential split, the women's movement should move forward by establishing itself as an ideological vanguard, making a genuine effort to rally all the women round it on the basis of a concrete programme of the movement.

Struggle Against Class Exploitation

Matriarchal society was dissolved with the beginnings of class society. The development of the patriarchal class led from the tribe to the single family household. The present form of family is linked to domestic finance. The present society, based on small private economics, will develop into a society based on big social economics. The form of the family will change and become more social and collective. Class struggle will be the main basis of women's freedom and the women's movement is aimed against class exploitation.

Women's Participation in Politics

Women after achieving economic freedom cannot play an equal role in all sectors of society. First of all, women should be made politically conscious and aware. From now on, women's participation should be emphasised in each and every sector of the political movement. The capacity of elected women must be augmented. One very important task of the women's movement is to encourage women, and to ensure that they participate in politics in a balanced way, both qualitatively and quantitatively.

Women's Empowerment and Rights

To reduce male domination, in all respects, after encouraging the participation of women in politics, a women's empowerment programme must be launched as a campaign. The concrete aspect of such a programme would be formulated by the Women's Commission and would ensure the active participation of women by reservation of quotas in all sorts of domains.

Equality of rights in paternal property, achievement of equal rights for women in regard to the acquisition of property, earnings—equal wages for equal work, selling and buying, equal access to all facilities, recognition of domestic work and general social acceptance of women are some examples of concrete elements of a programme for the women's movement.

End of Legal and Social Discrimination

Although there is a provision in the constitution against the inequality between men and women on the basis of gender, there is still no provision in the constitution to declare the first issue of His Majesty the King, whether son or daughter, the successor to the throne of Nepal Patriarchy, in other words, still predominates. Equal rights are not honoured with regard to the possession of property. The right of women's inheritance has still not been established. Legal struggles are necessary to eliminate such discrimination. This would help a lot in introducing reform in the social sector. The women's movement should, therefore, give priority to organise such a campaign to end legal discrimination.

There is still discrimination as between son and daughter from birth onwards. There is a deep impact resulting from the relationship between a father and mother and their son or daughter. This has created unwholesome divisions between male and female socially. For this, gender equality is required and a campaign against social discrimination should be conducted. The important role for the women's movement is to create pressure against social discrimination and build an awareness programme for the same.

Women's Awareness

For women's freedom, men and women must be equally responsible. Women cannot take advantage of their formal rights unless and until the ignorance, superstition and backwardness existing in the women's community is removed. A women's awareness programme is necessary to bring women forward within the women's movement and to enable them to make use of the achievements of the women's movement.

Unless and until women leave behind bad practices and bad culture in addition to traditional religious culture, they will not be able to gain their freedom. For the elimination of these constraints, legal, administrative and political initiatives are required and the old, traditional culture needs to be replaced by a new type of people's culture and its further development.

Education is an important mechanism for social awareness. The level of women's education is very low. Attention should urgently be paid to the matter of emphasising women's education and to encouraging and protecting the same. While preparing the curriculum, strict attention should be paid to removing gender discrimination. Skills training and vocational and employment-oriented technical education should be given particular emphasis. In short and as a whole, the level of education should be lifted to raise women's own standards.

Social Security

The improvement of social security will require the setting up of family tribunals, the elaboration of strict rules for the elimination of all types of violence and crime, the implementation of ILO standards for maternal health and safety, the establishment of social responsibility toward families and children and the creation of child care centres. The women's movement needs to take the initiative to struggle for the introduction of these measures and facilities.

Women's Employment

Even after entering the 21st century, the policy of equality between men and women is not yet implemented in practice. Perhaps the most challenging issue is the very limited access of women to employment opportunities and their resultant lack of participation in the labour force. Concrete policies regarding employment for women are urgently required to increase women's access to employment in all sectors and to increase the proportional participation of women.

Campaign Against Women Trafficking

The trafficking of women continues to be a social evil in our society even in the 21st century. For some this is is a matter of power and control, for others a means of making money. But serious action needs to be taken against those who are involved in kidnapping, trafficking, sexual exploitation, and rape, and also against those who lure or tempt women into situations where they are vulnerable to these forms of abuse. Action also needs to be taken for the rehabilitation and resocialisation of those who have suffered from these forms of abuse. Here too, the women's movement should take the initiative.

CONCLUSION

The Nepali women's movement grew through its direct contact and involvement with the leadership of the political parties from the very beginning. In the beginning, social reformation was the main agenda together with the development of an independent identity. But later on, it could not keep its effectiveness as before. Two kinds of movement developed— the politically organised and the less political movement concerned primarily with women's emancipation. As a result, the women's movement is not able to operate as a single coherent organised social force. The achievements of the women's movement are not fully utilised today—passivity and deviation have been unfortunate characteristics of the movement. Given this, the development of the women's movement—their empowerment and development as an organised force—is the vital issue now. Additional clarity is required as the Maoist women become increasingly influenced by extremist ideology. In conclusion, we argue that

1. The principal values should be made clear—that only with the end of the class society will all kinds of social discrimination be ended and that an active role is necessary to develop the women's movement in Nepal as an important force within the class movement as a whole. Theoretically, the Maoist movement is clear although in practice many lapses have taken place.
2. Realising the true causes of the backwardness of the women's community over a long period of time, and recognising the continuing reality of exploitation, oppression and discrimination, it should be made clear that the elimination of constitutional and legal discrimination alone will not bring full responsibility and

rights for women. Even in 'socialist' countries, political leadership is needed. Consequently, social transformation takes a long time. If this is forgotten, then hasty and ill-conceived actions will follow.

3. Although the women's movement in Nepal has attempted to break out of the limits of the existing political movement, this is not sufficient. Whatever has been attempted to create a rights-oriented movement, strong leadership is required. Without it, the women's movement will not be able to take the right direction, and there is a danger that the movement will go backwards. The leadership should empower the women's movement so as to be able to develop the women's community as a progressive social force. But in the Maoist movement, the free leadership of the women's community is blocked. It is evident that the gun is the main power behind such movements as the anti-alcohol campaign.

4. The Nepali women's movement has been able to secure several important rights from the perspective of the political movement, but women are not still able to understand it and the message has not reached the target. In such circumstances, capacity must be developed to recognise the gains to be found in women's rights and to create the appropriate leadership among women. All women organisations committed to question of women freedom should be carried forward unanimously. But problems have been raised due to the narrowmindedness of the Maoists.

5. The women's movement exists as organ of a broader political movement. Women's participation in politics is low and in such circumstances advancement only through the political movement is not sufficient. But in Nepal, the women's movement is being affected by this situation. In fact, the political movement is a guide to show the way to be followed. To walk along that path is the duty of women activists. From this perspective, the Maoist movement is totally deviant.

6. There is a lack of strategic and policy thinking as regards programme development. The distinction between which

demands are strategic and which relate to immediate policy is not clear, and as a result the onward march is at a slow pace. The women's movement cannot achieve all in a great leap forward. Therefore, first of all, the Nepali women's movement must specify clearly its aim and programme. Being focused on immediate fulfilling matters is one way of achieving the main objective—the journey of a thousand miles starts with one step. From this point of view, the Maoist movement is an obstacle to the development of the women's movement. It has tried to use the women's movement to serve its long-term objectives, while leaving aside the immediate and critically important objectives.

7. The women's movement should, of course, address questions related to strategic objectives as part of the wider political movement because the strategic questions for the women's movement undoubtedly relate to the questions of class and social freedom. But immediate tactical questions should be responded to and an attempt should be made to collaborate with other parties. In regard to the tactical questions facing the women's movement, the wider political movement cannot play the leading role. But Maoist movement has not paid much attention to this point.

8. The Nepali women's movement has, from the very beginning, been centred in the political movement. But now, in the name of separation it has been affected by outside influences. The women's movement may be weakened, if it is not careful by following this external experience in moving forwards. Therefore, special care and awareness are necessary while taking advantage of external experience. In fact, until now the Nepali women's movement has not been community based. The Nepali women's movement needs to study the social situation and base itself in the community and work with the community while moving ahead. The Maoist movement is very weak in this regard.

9. Now the Nepali women's movement is increasing its involvement with NGOs. Because of its own lack of resources and generally poor economic condition, Nepal should certainly seek assistance for social welfare

and the use of external support in social reform is not necessarily a bad thing. But to align the women's movement in one direction and to confine it to one particular kind of work is not good for the development of local leadership as an organised force and for the construction and development of the movement. To subordinate the Nepali women's movement to the wishes of the fund providers would not be proper under any circumstances. The women's movement should be especially alert in such matters. But maintaining alertness is not the same as maintaining a negative attitude or even opposition to such relationships; this is not the aim. The Maoist movement, however, has been expressing a negative attitude towards the above-mentioned institutions.

Viewed from this angle, we can see that the Maoist movement has, on the whole, introduced extremism in the women's movement of Nepal though it has been able to draw the attention of the Nepalese society to some issues of women and to instil a sense of sacrifice among a certain section of the Nepalese women. It has also created an aversion to the reality-based women's movement. In order to overcome this situation we should try to launch an intense ideological struggle. We should also endeavour to establish the change-oriented women's movement based on the realities of the Nepalese society. This is the challenge for and the responsibility of the Nepali women's movement today.

Chapter 10

The Maoist Movement and Its Impact in Nepal

Pradip Nepal

BACKGROUND TO THE INSURGENCY IN NEPAL

The political history of Nepal includes many violent episodes and incidents, and many armed movements. The national character of Nepal is thus not without violence. All political movements and parties have used various forms of violence to achieve their desired goals. When analysing the insurgency currently conducted by the Maoist Party in Nepal, this historical reality should not be ignored.

The revolt of Lakhan Thapa against the Rana regime is generally regarded as the first serious and important armed movement in Nepal. Later, the Prachanda Gorkha conducted a bombing campaign against the Ranas; this was effectively the basis of that movement. There was a conscious element of violence even in the first organised political movement in Nepal—the Praja Parishad. The struggle of 1950 was a liberation movement that espoused violence and the armed struggle. In 1961, 1971 and 1975 two of the major political parties of the country, namely, the Nepali Congress and the Communist Party of Nepal undertook, a long and sometimes violent struggle against Panchayat rule. In the more recent history of Nepal, violent revolts have taken place not only at the level of organised political parties and political movements, but at the level of popular uprisings and people's movements. The struggle of 1951 launched by K.I. Singh and Ram Prasad Rai, the armed peasants' movement led by Bhim Dutta Panta in 1951, the revolt in Rukum led by Kami Buda in 1952, the peasants' movements launched in the eastern *terai* in 1953, the peasants' movement of Dang district in 1958–59 and the bomb explosions (*bombkanda*) organised by Ram Raja Prasad Singh—all of these made violence the basis of their struggle.

The violent movement launched by the Maoists cannot be separated from its historical context and background. The present violent struggle has not come into existence only on the basis of the theoretical concepts of Maoism; its development is not due to the ideological consciousness of the people. No one can deny the Nepalese tendency to extend opposition to its highest level, that of violence; this too is responsible for the exacerbation of violence—war as an extension of politics by other means. That is why one cannot find a pure political conscience even in the struggle launched by the Maoist Party.

PREPARATION FOR AND GENESIS OF THE MAOIST ARMED STRUGGLE

In the Nepali communist movement, all previous divisions were unsuccessful in gaining much political ground. But the Fourth Convention faction did become successful in this regard. This group established itself from the divisions within the Party and expanded. It became a nationwide consolidated organisation. The leader and principal instructor of this group was Mohan Bikram Singh. This faction did the best of several similar factions in the 5 years of its existence. It continued in existence after 1980 with the motto that 'division can make the party strong'. This group also, however, split many times even over minor issues because of its faith in dogmas and the rigidity that prevented it from understanding creatively how the situation in the country was developing. The tendency is for all these subgroups to be very hostile towards dissenting viewpoints—aggressive and intolerant, yet doubtful and partial.

The Maoist Party is inevitably one of such subgroups; these same attitudes are to be found also in the Maoist Party. This is why there is intolerance, aggressiveness and one-sidedness in the thinking of the Maoist leadership. This is the explanation of the fact that when the nation was involved in the Jana Andolan—the movement for the attainment of multiparty parliamentary democracy—this Party tried to clearly distinguish itself from this movement by direct action, blackening the statue of the King and pelting the police on their beat with stones while other parties were trying to move ahead in the direction of a peaceful People's Movement. But these activities were later thought to be inadequate, and the campaign of assaults on the police became the embryo of a wider armed struggle. The Maoist Party moved to centres in the rural areas to launch a full armed struggle after the strategy of assaulting the police had proved unsuccessful.

The 1990 (2046 BS) People's Movement and its success were not looked for by the Maoist party. The Maoists were neither ready for the Movement nor believed in its success. Its success threw into disarray the Maoists' plan for violent struggle. The Maoist Party therefore changed its working policy and decided to use one faction to exercise its parliamentary rights openly. In the parliamentary elections of 1991 (2048 BS), the Maoist Party was elected in a number of seats, with the help of CPN (UML) and demonstrated its significance. In the local elections held in 1992 (2049 BS), it was successful in many local constituencies, again with the assistance of CPN UML. In this way, within 5 years, the Party had become a party of parliamentary politics.

The situation did not remain like this. In 1994 (2052 BS), the Party entirely abandoned any parliamentary involvement and made the Peoples' War the only form of political struggle. The deeper causes of this will be discussed later; here, a short description and explanation of the start of the violent struggle and analysis of the causes of the primary phase will be provided.

Before starting its People's War, the Communist Party (Maoist) presented a 40-point list of demands to the then Prime Minister, Sher Bahadur Deuba in Mangshir 2052 (November/December 1995 AD), giving the final date for their fulfilment as 13 February 1996. The demands were broadly similar to the demands made by all of the opposition political parties involved in parliamentary politics and could have been fulfilled by the general decision of the cabinet. Even pure rightist parties like the Nepal Sadvawana Party and the Rastrya Prajatantra Party are raising similar demands today. In reality, it would have been a way to prevent the start of the Peoples' War. The move towards a People's War was not justified then; it is not justified now.

In fact, it was only a pretext for launching a violent struggle. The Maoists might have intended to start their struggle on February 15 (Democracy Day), 2 days after the end of the period indicated in the ultimatum, because of the deep symbolism of that date in the minds of the Nepalese people. But they evidently could not exercise patience. Fearing that they would lose the pretext for their launching armed struggle if the government did fulfil their demands, they initiated the People's War before the date of the ultimatum arrived, attacking two police stations and slashing posters of King Birendra. It is easy for anyone to conclude that their movement did not, from the outset, bear the character of a considered protracted struggle.

The important point here is that the Maoist party opposed the People's Movement of 1990, at the beginning, during and for a long time afterwards. It adopted an ambivalent position towards the new multiparty political system and the Constitution of 1991 (2047 BS) established by the people's representatives—first supporting, then opposing, first participating, then boycotting. The party initially participated in the parliamentary and local elections. But after its involvement in the Peoples' War, it was, for a while, opposed totally to the Peoples' Movement of 1990 (2046 BS) to parliament and to the parliamentary system, to multipartyism and to the Constitution of 1991 (2047 BS). It saw nothing positive or progressive in any of these.

After 6 years of the Peoples War, however, the Party has now adopted the policy of opposing the constitution while supporting multipartyism, the parliamentary system and the People's Movement of 1990 (2046BS). The Maoist Party has not been able to explain the contradictions it has demonstrated over the last 10 years, from the 1991 elections to the present time. In view of its inconsistent outlook towards multiparty system, the People's Movement of 1990 and the Constitution of 1991, one is compelled to say that this party is an opportunist organisation.

The Jhapa Movement (*Jhapa Bidroha*) of 1971 is an important part of the explanation for the People's War being waged by the Maoist party, as it had a serious impact on the violent tendencies of the Nepali communist movement. From 1971 to 1996, the predecessor organisations of the Maoist Party and their leaders most vehemently opposed the idea and activities of the Jhapa Movement, which is known for its declaration of armed struggle against the Panchayat system. During those 20 years, the Maoists not only opposed that instance of armed struggle, they also mounted intense criticism of the cadres of that party. But all of a sudden, they started to sing the praises of the Jhapa Movement (which they had cursed for four decades) and to describe themselves as the true successors of that Movement. This sudden about-face of the Maoist Party shows that they are essentially opportunists and this also explains the confusion in their ideas and plans relating to armed struggle. In their own words, 'opportunism resides in their very core'.

The political opportunism of the Maoists is the manifestation of consumer culture and the actual state of Maoist Party cannot be understood without appreciating their consumerism. What everyone should understand is that for the Maoists, theory, politics, policy and programme are nothing but present expediencies. The Maoist Party has not analysed and will not analyse the past, present and the future of anything in order to improve and make more relevant its policies and practice. They have understood history in their own way. The same consumer culture is responsible for their way of using political movements to fulfil their selfish interest. Because of their inconsistency, there are unfathomable gaps between their policies, statements and practice. They are ready to do anything and accept anything for their own benefit. One should not therefore be surprised if they declare themselves, now or in the future, the true representatives of the movement of 1990. Innumerable instances of chaos, confusion and opportunism can be seen in every turn of the armed struggle waged by the Maoist Party.

Mismanagement, opportunism and lack of clarity are seen a good deal in the People's War being conducted by the Maoist party. Because of changes that occur monthly, cadres and followers of the Maoists are forced now to distinguish between Maoism and Maoist thought. Sometimes democratic dictatorship, sometimes multiparty competition, sometimes 'the middle path', the actual path of Maoist thinking represents the most dangerous and sometimes even rightist revisionism. Such distortions and anomalies are to be found in every step of the Maoist struggle, but since they have not made these points clear up until now, a long discussion of it cannot be undertaken.

EXTERNAL CAUSES OF THE ARMED STRUGGLE

While seeking the causes of the armed struggle conducted by the Maoist, it is necessary to distinguish those associated with political developments after the establishment of the multiparty system from those associated with the internal thinking and planning of Maoists. Firstly, then an attempt to list the former.

The first general election was held in the country in 1992. The Maoist Party was able to win 9 seats in the new parliament, with the help of the CPN (UML). The Maoists had conducted the parliamentary struggle fairly well. The armed struggle might have been in their minds, but political violence would have been confined to the pages of history if the democratic process of the country had developed smoothly. But, unfortunately, this did not happen. The Nepali Congress, which had formed the government after winning the majority in the election and had received the accolade of being 'the only democratic party of Nepal' from the western democracies, started to lead the country in the opposite direction. It considered the totalitarian practice of its own party to be the correct approach to 'democracy'. All those who opposed the Nepali Congress became the ultimate enemies of democracy.

There was a naked parade of Nepali Congress power everywhere—a 'white tyranny'. Dozens of people fell victim to the hooliganism of the ruling Party. It became a common occurrence for people to be killed in cold blood and the opposition party cadres to be implicated by means of fabricated cases on trumped-up charges. Within 2 years, the local leaders and workers of the Nepali Congress Party had terrorised the people by lodging false cases against more than 10,000 people, creating havoc. Terms such as pluralism and democracy were confined to the pages of books. People forgot the notorious term 'Mandale' within 1 year. The first term of the government of the Nepali Congress Party was not basically different from the previous Panchayat autocracy.

This was the situation in which local elections took place in 1993. That election was a sheer confrontation between state power and the people. It was a violent clash between state terror and civil society. The Nepali Congress misused that election to excess. It was in fact no election at all. It was an autocratic action taken by the state against the people and the opposition parties. These activities of the ruling party provoked the idea, among some, that it was necessary to fight against the dictatorship of the Nepali Congress. The CPN (UML), which had a widespread mass base, decided to mobilise the people against this state terror but other parties reached the conclusion that they should retreat altogether from the parliamentary process.

The Maoist violence cannot be understood unless this 'background' is understood—these historical political realities that have added fuel to the violent movement of the Maoist Party.

Rolpa, Rukum and other areas, which are now well-known as the cradle of armed struggle, were backward areas from the viewpoint of political awareness, but the Maoist Party had good support there. The ruling Nepali Congress did not have any organisational base in those areas. In the name of expanding its organisation, following the 1990 People's Movement, the Nepali Congress picked up former Panchas and local bullies in those areas among others, and made them local leaders of its party organisation. With their help, the Nepali Congress started to mount a concerted attack on those holding dissenting views. This repression was reminiscent of the repression of the previous partyless Panchayat system. Because of the suppressive state power of the Nepali Congress, the people of those areas were unable to experience any political change. This strengthened the ideas and influence of the Maoist Party. Both the Maoist Party and the people of those areas were compelled to conclude that it was necessary to take up guns against the guns of the Nepali Congress. This created the deepseated opposition that the Maoist Party then spread countrywide in the form of armed struggle.

The Nepali Congress made enemies of the people not only because of its suppressive state power. The people were also disenchanted with the multiparty system, among other things, because of their exaggerated perception about its likely consequences. The Nepali Congress started a misleading and unnecessary propaganda about the 1990 People's Movement. It raised expectations among the people that the problems of food, clothes and shelter would be solved as soon as the multiparty system was established in the country. On the one hand, the Nepali Congress raised expectations (freedom from want, poverty and unemployment) while on the other, it had the audacity to use the 'democracy' of an autocratic state to suppress the very movements that were being built for the realisation of the hopes of the people. This brought a huge disappointment (and both anger and despair) among the people. The difference between 'democracy' and dictatorship became more and more blurred.

A major event, which took place prior to the rise of the Maoist movement, was the Supreme Court decision of 28 August 1995. This event not only replaced the CPN (UML) government, but threatened many aspects of the constitution, including the supremacy of the constitution, the rule of law and the parliamentary system itself. That event weakened the parliamentary system and gave supremacy to the Prime Minister. The court decision also encouraged such dirty games as 'belief–disbelief' 'trust–distrust') and 'party conversion' (crossing the floor of the House) in the everyday business of parliamentary politics. It led to power politics and created instability. This decision effectively transferred the party leadership to dictatorial ex-Panchayat leaders as Surya Bahadur Thapa and Lokendra Bahadur Chanda. This decision also indicated, by bringing about the replacement of the CPN (UML)'s popular government, that good policies are punished in a 'democracy'. This also made it clear that in the 'bourgeois system' (i.e. under capitalism), the reactionary classes do not allow a 'communist' party to implement progressive policies and reforms peacefully. The ultimate result could only be an increasing turn towards violent insurgency and this is exactly what made the Maoist Party take the path of armed struggle.

INTERNAL CAUSES OF THE ARMED STRUGGLE

External factors alone are not sufficient to generate any kind of revolutionary movement or campaign, though there may be good or bad conditions for its conduct. External causes are important, but the final determinant of such a social phenomenon, its rise or fall, are the internal factors. The People's War conducted by the Maoist party cannot be explained by external factors alone. The ultimate determinants of the Maoist insurgency are the theory and practice brought by the Party in a specific context to the issue of revolutionary change and 'progressive action'.

It has already been said that the Maoist Party had no correct Marxist approach—no real vision of Nepali society and of the revolutionary process, its meaning and its significance. Its inability to understand the world, and the changes taking place within Nepal; the dream of revolution and victory based simply on dogma; the lack of understanding of the gist of Marxism had the effect of obscuring the immediate advantages of the progressive movement. The Maoists, entangled in their limited knowledge and in dogma, were encouraged in their turn towards armed struggle by the repressive campaigns of the government against the common people. The Maoist Party was never adequately aware of the ups and downs, progress and setbacks of the revolutionary process. Its opportunism did not even allow it to differentiate between the thrill of victory and the setback of defeat. The victory they had achieved in 1992 was something they had not expected; that was a matter outside the scope of their study. Similarly, the setback that they suffered in 1993 was also beyond their expectation; this was an outcome that they found intolerable. As they had been too buoyant in victory, they became too disappointed in defeat. The two diametrically different results were both beyond their level of consciousness. Because of this, they jumped to the conclusion that they should go underground and launch an armed struggle.

The Maoist leadership has been excessively dogmatic as regards Marxist consciousness, but it also has an overwhelming desire for quick victory—a petty bourgeois vision with the norms, values and ambitions associated with it. Instead of identifying the basis for revolution carefully, it has an assured intolerance and superiority complex. Such non-Marxist concepts and the petty bourgeois attitudes and practices born from such a vision have led it to stand alone, isolated, arrogant and shortsighted in the movement. The Maoists had also been inspired to take to the path of armed struggle because of their failure to understand the fact that reforms were part of a revolution. They have been marginalised in the jungles far away from the mass of the people, for lack of the confidence and courage to make use of the democratic achievements of the People's Movement launched with the widest people's participation and to win the confidence of the people through competition in elections and efforts to persuade them of the correct viewpoint, policies and logic.

The setbacks that the Maoists experienced at the beginning of the 1990s served them ill and carried them nowhere. Their creative consciousness did not grow. They did not know how to overcome their setbacks. The people's multiparty democracy was identified as a failure and the emergence of a democratic political movement was seen as an expression of revisionism. They found themselves caught in a system that they did not accept as new and with which, increasingly, they were not prepared to engage on its terms. Therefore, they decided to make themselves the soldiers of proletarian revolution and became taken up by the theory of armed struggle.

THE DEVELOPMENT OF THE ARMED STRUGGLE

Even before the insurgency began, the campaign conducted by the Maoist Party was mainly a violent movement. The *'Sija'* movement launched by the Maoists in the name of the 'people's war' prior to the beginning of the violent activities was inspired by the concept of armed struggle. But not all the people participating in these activities were committed to unconstitutional and violent ideology. Most of its cadres had the desire to establish their political role by limiting themselves within the constitutional bounds. But the government adopted the policy of repression in total disregard of this, in order to please its own local cadres. The campaign of state terror created a situation for the cadres of the Maoist Party to leave home and to become outlaws. Because of the totalitarian character of the Nepali Congress and its unlawful campaign of repression, the leadership of that Maoist Party encouraged its cadres to abscond instead of advising them to go to court to seek justice. In this way a party that was actively participating in the parliament, also started to make preparations to quit parliament and engage in the protracted armed struggle. In earlier days it had collected funds and when it had enough resources, it plunged in violent actions, collecting domestic weapons. After a long background of armed movement and the preparation of people's struggle, the central committee of the Maoist Party issued an appeal to the people on February 13, 1996 with the slogan, 'Let us move forward on the path of people's war to establish people's power by destroying the reactionary state power'.

At the beginning of the armed struggle, the Maoist Party planned it in terms of three strategic stages, on the basis of the concepts developed by Mao Tse Tung. The first phase was *strategic defence*. In this phase the programme involved organising armed squads, training, attacks on the army and police and the expropriation of collection of weapons, expansion of self-reliance, development of guerilla units, expansion of the revolutionary army, building local government, strengthening the Party building a united front, and developing temporary base areas. Their analysis suggested that until and unless the force of the guerrilla soldiers and the forces of the government reached parity, this phase would continue. The second stage is that of *strategic stalemate*. In this phase, the two parties to the conflict are generally of equal strength. Neither one can effectively defeat the other. The Maoists consider that in the course of a protracted People's War this situation will develop as the war progresses. The third stage is that of *strategic offence*. Reaching this phase depends on making oneself strategically stronger than the enemy and able to take the offensive.

In any war, that stage is relatively short. This stage is often marked by victory or defeat. According to their analysis, the Maoist people's war is advancing through the first stage, namely, the stage of strategic self-defence. In the process of advancing in the basis of the above concept, the Communist Party (Maoist) put forward the slogan, 'Let's consolidate and expand the base areas and local people's government and march towards the formation of the central government!' Similarly, it has put forward the tactical slogan of holding 'an all-party political conference, forming interim government and the drafting of a popular constitution'.

The government failed to pass any significant laws, failed to maintain effective administration and failed to retain the support of the people. The period of the People's War has been a period of unnecessary sacrifice and unwanted turmoil. People did not support the government and the government launched a violent campaign of counter-insurgency. The Maoists, for their part, however, did not truly represent the people's cause, and failed to respect the support they received from the people.

During the long period of the first stage, the country was generally impressed by their high sense of sacrifice. Many citizens expressed respect for them, even while not knowing exactly what they were doing or why. This not only made it impossible for the government to suppress the Maoists but also engendered heightened opposition to it because of its unpopular activities and anti-people repressive campaigns. The government was proved helpless and useless in the face of the effective war manoeuvres of the Maoists. All the campaigns of the government remained a complete failure. The government could neither make laws nor could take administrative action or win over the people.

But, in reality, the period after the initiation of 'the People's War' has been a period of needless sacrifice and an unnecessary torture. In this period, the people did not cooperate with the government; the government took the path of killing and violence. The Maoists, however, failed to understand and respect the roots of the people's support for them. Their attention was focussed only on murder and violence. As time passed, both the government and the Maoists have begun to appear to be the enemies of the people. The government imposed its ideas and plans on the people, and the Maoists took people hostage at gunpoint. By 2001, at the end of a 5 year long journey, marred by meaningless sacrifice, the Maoists and the government stood face to face, whereas the people had been forced to huddle in a corner, full of hatred towards both of them. Towards the end of the 5 years of armed struggle, certainly the government had been shown to be ineffective and the morale of the Maoists was high.

The Maoists had become arrogant from one success in battle after another, but as it expanded militarily, its political focus had become very narrow. In the meantime, the decisions of its Second Congress made it shrink further. The so-called Prachanda Path was the result of and reinforced still further this narrow-mindedness. According to the Maoists, the Prachanda Path was a fundamental principle of the Nepalese revolution and constituted the development of Marxism. This so-called path, in effect, swept away the people's sympathy, which was already declining.

MISTAKEN THEORETICAL (IDEOLOGICAL) CONCEPTS OF THE MAOIST PARTY

The Nepali communist movement as a whole is constantly being developed and extended in the context of struggle against ultra-rightist and ultra-leftist deviations. These cannot be defeated without a deep ideological struggle. The communist movement cannot move ahead unobstructed unless it struggles against such ideas and attitudes. Now, once again, ultra-left deviation has raised its head in the Nepali communist movement. The cause of this deviation is the lack of a real opportunity to form a leftist government after the change of 1990, the dominance of the extreme rightist Nepali Congress government and the failure to pay sufficient attention to the significance and the potential contained in the People's Movement of 1990, all of which have left the country mired in the status quo and a state of backwardness, failing to fulfill the basic needs of the people. The Maoist Party emerged as a new party within the Nepali communist movement and systematically developed to become the ultra-leftist faction. Today, this Party represents a powerful ideological–political deviation, which puts forward the wrong ideology, vision and policies to carry out the social revolution.

The Maoist Party has concluded that the process of socialist world revolution, which started with the October Revolution, has completely finished and has been transformed into revisionism. On the basis of this conclusion, the Maoist Party argues that now there is no socialist country anywhere in the world and that the objective process of socialist construction has ended. Their conclusion paints a sad picture—the inevitability of remaining today under the complete domination of capitalism. This analysis of the Maoist Party carries the world back to the period before 1917, and again the conclusion can be drawn that the world communist movement is obliged to start once again from Lenin. No great effort is required to understand how much such Maoist thinking is romantic, if it ignores the objective reality around it and becomes utopian in its nature.

The Maoist Party is aloof both outwardly and inwardly regarding its objective thinking while using its inner rules in connection with party mobilisation. The Maoists take it for granted that Marxism and Leninism are 'old' and inadequate and cannot provide their guiding principles. They tend to think Maoism to be the supreme form, saying that Marxism and Leninism cannot lead today's revolution. In its political journey, the Maoist Party has undertaken the strange act of the universalisation of the Prachanda Path, rejecting Marxism–Leninism, leaving worldly truth and considering special experience as universal truth, and also considering a few years' experience as universal fact. This latter conclusion is contrary to the tenets of their former Marxism–Leninism. The Maoist Party has taken to the strange practice of ignoring the international experience of the communist movement as material, together with the objective condition of the nation and its proper use as regards to the specific situation. This practice is wrong both ideologically and politically.

THE PROGRAMME OF THE NEPALI REVOLUTION

Not only on the basis of international experience but also on the basis of the Nepali revolution, the attitude of the Maoist Party is unrealistic, proved wrong by international experience and useless from the viewpoint of social emancipation. In the present century, any 'thought', '-ism' or institution is irrelevant if it cannot respect fundamental individual rights. Human rights and respect for others are not only the subject of many declarations, they are the foundation of the expression of an individual's capacity and the basis of the stability of the country's social system. When conscious citizens can actively participate in social processes, the system becomes 'people-oriented' and effective.

Civil rights and duties are neither the product of capitalist ideology nor a 'gift' of capitalism. In reality, the safeguarding of civil rights, therefore, lies in the freedom of the productive forces as has been said by the Marxists for a long time. Because of the lack of understanding, the safeguarding of civil rights, the socialistic system suffered severe reverses in the later half of the past century. We have to understand the fall of Soviet Union and collapse of Cambodia in this context. A state that does not give proper scope for the exercise of human rights, is, in the long run, bound to fall. But these contemporary truths are not audible to the Maoists. They do not realise that the people's rule is the rule of Law—it is the rule of law, and the rule of the majority. They are also not ready to accept the fact that the rule of law is the rule of the people's elected representatives and lastly, they do not realise that this is guaranteed by the framework created by the system of multiparty competition in a democracy.

The basis for the rule of the Maoist Party is ultra-left dictatorship. This party is the symbol of dictatorship because it believes that the individual is subordinate to the gun and that 'gun law' should be the guide to both a citizen's rights and duties. The Maoists are still followers of Stalin in regard to the form of rule. So they understand their so-called New Democratic System as unitary and as involving one party rule, and they dream of applying the same system throughout Nepal. In the analysis of the Maoist Party, democratic features—such as party contests, periodic elections, adult franchise, separation of powers, people's agreement, the mobilisation of the people's will by elected representatives, recall for unsatisfactory representatives—are all characteristics of the capitalistic system. Therefore, they look at them as restrictive and reject their requirements. They do not accept the fact that this interpretation of these democratic characteristics depicts them—the Maoists—not as a democratic force but as a fascist tendency, imposing dictatorship.

They also do not accept the fact that timely changes occurring in the national or international situation can bring about changes in our preconceived notions and that we must go on incorporating timely and responsive elements in our programmes also. In other words, they reject the dynamism accepted by Marxism and rely instead on the foundation created by the norms and values that constitute the 'conventional wisdom' of their programme. They do not pay attention to whether these prefixed norms are appropriate in the present context, or to whether those norms arose in the special circumstances of specific countries or they were universally true. In reality, even if the Maoist Party regards itself as ultrarevolutionary, it does not have the original programme of the Nepali revolution. The Maoists have not studied the class structure of Nepali society, the consciousness of Nepali society, and the class contradictions as they are realised in Nepali society. Whatever they consider their originality, it is based on the blind imitation of the norms and values provided by Mao Tse Tung, more than 60 years ago in China's history.

THE PATH OF THE NEPALI REVOLUTION

The Maoists have no original or genuine analysis of the path of the Nepali revolution as experienced by Nepali society. The path of the revolution of a country follows the concrete realities established by the political, economic, social, cultural, historical, geographical and international situation of that country, and the path of revolution can be determined only by deep study, analysis and synthesis. This is not accepted by the Maoists. The Maoist Party has rejected the rule that the path of revolution differs from nation to nation and that it should be based on the specifics of the very nation concerned—the social consciousness of the country and balance of class forces. The norms and values that underlie the path of social freedom have been rejected now by them as revisionist thought. In the name of being free from revisionism and also in the context of the path of revolution they have adopted only the limited Chinese model of revolution. The theory of the present revolutionary path taken by the Maoist party now was put forward by Chairman Mao, leader of the Chinese Communist Party around 1926. In the period between 1926 and 2002, time has moved on remarkably. The Maoists have closed their eyes to the evolution of social relations in the world and to the changeable condition of the national and international situation. These 'Marxists' reject the methods to be used for progressive social transformation and conclude that from the very beginning, the Nepali revolution should go forward along the path of armed revolution only.

The Maoists have also rejected the history of class struggle in Nepali society. They have not paid the least attention to how Nepali society has developed since the establishment of the Communist Party of Nepal in 1949; how and why the path of revolution changed during the period between the first and the seventh national convention, and how the present communist movement have been coordinated, taking into consideration the agricultural base of Nepal and other such essential characteristics. In the past two decades, the changes that have taken place in Nepali society—in transport and communications, in military technology, in the changing relationship between town and country and many other changes—have not been recognised by the Maoists. Therefore, they are not clear about the path, but they have to carry out their policy in a changing context. Because of this, and out of ignorance, being one-sided and rejecting other forms of struggle, they have emphasised only armed struggle.

THE CLASS ANALYSIS OF POLITICAL FORCES IN NEPALI SOCIETY

The success of the revolution depends on the correct use and deployment of class analysis in the society concerned, and on the identification of the major contradictions. The revolution cannot last long only by talking about revolution a great deal; nor can long-term success be based on victory following some blind and unplanned attack. The Maoists are now at a great disadvantage. They can talk big about revolution, but they are creating a big illusion in the class analysis of various political forces existing in the country. They do not determine the class character of a particular political force on the basis of its theory, policy, programme and practice. They often reach the conclusion on the basis of their subjective desires and wishful thinking.

For lack of a scientific basis, when analysing parties on the basis of their programmes and practice, they put unhelpful labels on the different factions of the Nepali communist movement. As a consequence of what can only be seen as a kind of mental block, they define the CPN (UML)—an established, accepted and democratic party—as a party of reactionary status, and order their guerillas to attack, kill, kidnap, beat, loot and disable the cadres and supporters of the aforesaid and accused party. The Maoist Party does not make a clear distinction between the dictatorial Nepali Congress and the democratic CPN (UML). That is why their attack upon the cadres of CPN (UML) and Mashal is seen by them as equivalent to attacks on the Nepali Congress Party. Not only this, the Maoist Party, which is very violent towards other communists, has adopted an undeclared policy of rejecting the country's sovereignty, impinging on national integrity, forging alliance with all kinds of racial forces and pulling punches on the revivalist forces.

From the very beginning they have talked about the establishment of a republic, undermining the notion of the monarchy on paper and in posters, but in their practice, they have agreed that the king is the biggest patriot. Nor is any

Maoist able to answer the question as to what kind of republic is going to be set up. The relationship between the Maoist Party and other communist factions is extremely bitter, but their relationship with the reactionary *pancha* is friendly and they make themselves safe under their protection and have tried those fighting against their selfishness in so-called people's courts. Over the past 6 years, more than a 100 communist cadres from other parties have been killed or disabled, but the number of conspirators, corrupters and landlords is much smaller. The Maoists are not still able to analyse the class position of the ex-*pancha* party (RPP) or the pro-Indian communal party (Nepal Sadvawana Party). These are parties with respect to which the Maoists are unable to categorise, both with reference to the other communist parties and as regards the kind of policy and practice towards them that is appropriate.

CLASS ANALYSIS AND THE MANAGEMENT OF STRUGGLE

Theoretically, the Maoist Party identifies five classes in the rural areas of Nepali society: landlords, rich peasant, middle peasant, poor peasant and landless farmers or agriculture labourers. But they are not clear with respect to their policy towards those different classes and forces or towards the persons who represent them. They have not still used in practice the fundamental Marxist approach that there should be a real difference in practice regarding 'enemies' and 'friends'. As a result, they have been very hard on members of other groups who have differences of opinion and who cannot agree with their statements, and with the elected representative of other parties (including communist parties) and on middle and even poor farmers and labourers, many of whom have been tortured or killed, whereas their attacks on landlords have been very few. They seem to be committed to petty bourgeois revenge but not to real class struggle.

They are also not clear about two levels of contradiction. There is a great difference between the contradiction between the enemy and the people and the contradictions within the common people in general. The first type of contradiction can be resolved only on the basis of a process of class struggle. But the Maoists are mixing both types of contradiction, declaring their friends to be enemies, and taking revengeful action against them. On the basis of careful observation, however, it would appear that so far the Maoists have not dealt with the contradictions that exist among the mass of the people. On the one hand, they talk of the construction of village people's government and of district people's government and they also try to deal with cases of conflict existing in the village, but the appropriate resolution of contradictions that arise at this level has not been achieved. The decision of the Maoist Party is always in favor of those who lodge their case with the Maoist people's court. The consequence is that the rewards are given to the sycophant and the system merely flatters the Maoists. In many places, they forcefully subject particular categories of persons (including supporters of the CPN/UML and other party cadres) to what is in effect a white tyranny rather than providing justice, favouring some and punishing others in the name of justice while forcing acceptance of injustice by deploying their supporters. This is a petty bourgeois attitude that prevails in the Maoist Party and bears no relationship to Marxist principles.

The Maoist Party has also not distinguished between ideological struggle and class struggle. The class struggle with the reactionary forces is hostile in totality and that can only be resolved by a decisive victory. But ideological struggle is a struggle within the communist movement and this ideological–theoretical struggle should be mainly a friendly struggle. Sometimes, it may become excessively threatening and hostile, but ideological struggle is the struggle of transformation and it should be carried out—and resolved—in a friendly manner, however difficult this may be. The Maoist Party does not understand this. For lack of proper understanding, it has seen the CPN/UML and other parties as enemies in the class struggle; by killing left cadres who maintain their differences with the Maoists, they are painting their petty bourgeois revengeful hands with the blood of fellow communists.

Almost all Nepali intellectuals have drawn the wrong conclusions about the Maoists, as a result of drawing on ideas set out in Maoist documents. This 'study technique' can be misleading. Theory separated from the practice cannot be valid theory. No one can recognise the true Maoists unless their practice, as well as their statements, undertaken in execution of Marxist theory and for the establishment of people's state, is also considered. The Maoists killed Chin Bahadur Rokka in Rukum district in the month of Magh 2056 BS (January/February 2000 AD). He was a poor farmer who owned only 7 Ropanis of sloping land and worked as a mason for his livelihood. He was a member of the Communist Party of which he was a respected and leading personality. The Maoists ordered him to give up his CPN (UML) membership and sent more than a dozen cadres to get him to join the guerrilla army. Chin Bahadur did not respond to the pressure of the Maoists and told them that he would not give up his chosen party. He was killed by the Maoists because he would not abandon his party membership.

In the month of Kartik, 2058 BS (October/November 2001 AD), the Maoists killed Gupta Bahadur Biswakarma. He was a *dalit* (a member of one of the so-called untouchable castes) and also a member of the CPN/UML. The Maoists came to his village for 'tax' collection. He opposed this. He said that 'the people of this village are poor. They are surviving by labouring hard and they cannot pay 10,000 and 20,000 rupees as they have demanded'. The Maoists pressured him to give up his CPN/UML Party membership and join their party. Gupta Bahadur, although owning only 3 Ropanis of sloping land was a B.Sc. graduate and an established teacher. He was extremely logical and active also. It was not strange for the Maoists to attempt to bring him into their party. But he did not obey the command of the Maoists. After that, the Maoists murdered him, chopping him in different parts of his body like chopping faggots with an axe.

There is a village in the area of Mangkha in Sindhupalchowk. The Maoists came to this village, and ordered someone to cook them food, going into the house of a female member of this Tamang community. There was no corn and the female members refused. There was debate for some time, but the females refused to cook for the Maoists. After that, two of the guerrillas raped the daughter-in-law of that house and declared it as 'people's action' (readers will excuse me not giving the name of the village or the name of the woman concerned, out of shame).

A separate book could be written describing such incidents, which fall outside the norms of class struggle and even outside the norms of a People's War. More than 70 per cent of those killed by the Maoists should not have been—they were normal teachers, rural farmers and low-paid civil servants. One quarter of all those killed were political workers and they were killed because they defeated the Maoists in theoretical discussion. The punishment policy of the Maoists recalls that of the fictional Count Dracula or the real dictator, Idi Amin. A man can be killed by shooting or hanging or some other means as an execution; this is regarded as 'the death penalty' by human rights activists. As the Maoists are also opposed to human rights, they see it as legitimate to execute people in this way. But the murders that have been perpetrated are often-heart stricken, wild and medieval in character. The normal extreme punishment of the Maoists is to cut a person's limbs off one by one; clapping and celebrating while killing. In some instances, they have also used the method of killing man by chopping with an axe or slicing with a *khukuri*. The popular political leader of western Nepal Comrade Yadu Gautam was killed by having his throat cut and another cadre from Dolakha, Comrade Ram Bahadur, was killed by hanging. Murder is an extremely reactionary and dirty activity.

THE CHARACTER OF THE MAOIST MOVEMENT

In any given period of time, the issue of determining the character of forces fighting for or against the establishment of a given country has been a matter of dispute and debate. There have also been opportunistic tendencies of depicting them from one angle when they are weak and from another angle when they are found to have gained in strength. To determine their political character is, in fact, a matter of political analysis irrespective of whether they are large or small, weak or strong, pro-establishment or against it. There are three key elements: first is the vision, thought, policy, programme and objectives of the party, organization, forum or forces involved; second, the relationship it has with the common people and nation and third, its activities and practice. The movement led by the Maoist Party should be analysed on this basis.

There is considerable variation in the way in which forces (whether party, movement or other forces) struggling against the state are characterised. Frequently, the governments of powerful states have considered such groupings or movements as the Palestine Liberation Organization, the Irish Revolutionary Army and different liberation movements in Africa as well as movements led by different communist parties in different countries as 'terrorists'. But the characterisation of an organisation or movement has usually been based not so much on universal principles or on a detailed analysis as much as on prejudice and the defence of vested interests. The value of serious theoretical study and analysis has been underestimated. But, it is easy to make a distinction between terrorism and guerrilla insurgency. The organisation or force that has a clear political objective, the direction of a party, a vision, policy, programme and real relationship with the people, that has some public forum and mechanism to draw on the support of some part of the population and that has created a people's army to achieve the declared objective and has based its activities in a certain geographical area, such an organisation, party or movement should be regarded as a rebellious political force and as having taken up armed struggle as guerrilla rebels. But those who are not concerned with the mass of the people, who are organised in gangs, who make ambitious plans for killing in order to advance their own personal interests, attack suddenly, kill and kidnap individuals, sabotage and destroy planes and buses and let off bombs, these fall under the category of terrorist organisations.

Following this distinction, it can definitely be said that the Maoist Party has a political character. But the form of 'people's war' conducted by the Maoist Party is not that of organised guerrilla warfare. For a long time (4 years) in the people's war, there was ambiguity as to its character, because of its dual nature. The Maoists had a party, a programme and long-term and immediate policies. But they did not have a Party character. They were constantly involved in the act of making people's lives more difficult and complicated, because they attacked others without reason, kidnapped people, killed them, and looted banks and financial institutions concerned with people in their day to day work. By studying this complexity, the CPN (UML) decided, for the first time in Bhadra 2054 BS (August/September 1997 AD) that the actual character of the Maoist Party was in fact defined by its ultra-leftist political ideology and terrorist practice.

The Maoist Party maintains an antagonism towards the rest of the communist movement. In its present form, the Maoist movement has in its everyday practice demonstrated its hostility towards the Communist Party and the communist movement.

An analysis of its behaviour reveals this to be systematic. Wrong political thought finally carries over into wrong political decisions and carries the decisionmakers in the wrong direction, to render the party the victim of wrong practice. The movement thus becomes the natural victim of distortion. The distortions seen in the Maoist Party are the evidence of the wrong principles; as a result of the wrong Party direction, problems can be seen in the theory and practice of the Party and in its attitude towards the communist movement as a whole.

Both the thinking and structure of the Maoist Party are anti-people and fascist in nature. There is no system of collective leadership and such a system is not recognised or respected. Maoist thought is actually the petty bourgeois fascist thought of the Prachanda Path, the only guiding principle for the conduct of Party business. Adopting this style of rule is easy but it cannot provide the necessary progressive direction to party rule and the people's forces. Such thinking and style condemn the Party to a cyclone of debate and rebellion. The Party has faced this problem in the past, but the situation is no different today. Since the beginning, this party has been in two minds, which is not surprising, given the lack of arrangements for managing a democratic style of thinking and practice. Reactionary behaviour is appearing with some vigour in the Maoist Party. The supporters of Prachanda have substantial freedom whereas his opponents are under severe constraint in the same Party. The rebellion taking place in the districts, the killing of Ramesh Dhungel, and the death penalty given to Maoists who leave party, reveal the anti-Marxist character of the Party. Not only this, the leaders and cadres have killed not only the cadres of other communist parties, but also their own cadres with whom they may have a difference. Those, who said long live the Prachanda Path received a licence to murder, rape, smuggle, loot and to be corrupt. When the 'Alok* trend'

---

* Alok was one of the senior leaders of the Maoist movement. He was accused by his party of comfort seeking, wonanising and killing of party cadres who were critical towards him. He was arrested and was sent to labour camps for reeducation. He is said to have been killed in the Maoist military operation against the government forces at Gam in Rolpa district.

protected by Prachanda was severely criticised publicly and within the party, Alok was isolated. Eventually, he was accused and Prachanda was acquitted of the charge. Such practices are still going on even after the action against Alok. This proves that Alok did not represent a trend but what he did was only a manifestation of the general character of the Maoists.

Everybody knows that the total income of the Maoists depends on smuggling, forced 'charity' and the looting of banks—these three types of activity are antithetical to the People's War. There is no proper account of where the money collected goes; nobody knows how it is used, whether on individual expenses or institutional corruption. On account of the corruption involved, killing and assault within the Maoist party is common. The best case of this kind was the looting of the Khimti Bank. In this case, the Maoists themselves accepted the fact that individuals from within the Party were involved. Some local cadres had 'deviated from the party' after collecting the money and were publicly exposed while making plans to escape to India, after collecting money in the name of the Maoist party. But the Maoists have also been involved in 'revenge killing' outside the Party. In one example, of 37 cadres of the CPN (UML) murdered by the Maoists, 36 were killed on the basis of personal animosity (and one child was killed unreasonably). In the case of non-party people killed, Maoists always seem to support the landlords, even killing those opposed to the landlords. All of this encourages people to feel that the armed struggle involves not so much a People's Army as a juggernaut.

The lifestyle of the Maoist leadership as regards women in the guerrilla movement further indicates the degree of corruption that exists in the social life of the Maoist Party. Unnatural sexual relationships and sex exploitation, rape and other forms of oppression are revealed by those so abused. The involvement of some of the top leadership in such activities is reported. In a country like Nepal, the manner of the leaders determines the nature of the party. As the individual conduct of those leaders involved in the multiparty system has to undergo criticism, similarly the lifestyle and conduct of the Maoist leadership should be grounds for concern within the communist movement.

Another serious and remarkable aspect of the Maoist Party is the attitude towards the security and safety of the leadership and the sacrifice of the cadres. The Maoist leaders have always stayed within the circle of strict safety. They tend not to be found on the battle field but in Indian cities with good facilities. In the People's War, apart from Suresh Wagle, no high-ranking leaders have 'fallen in battle' during a military encounter and even Suresh Wagle's death has also been denied, as a conspiracy hatched from within the party to suppress differences of opinion. But in this very short period, thousands of Maoist rebels have been killed. The Maoists, in fact, have been raising a harvest of martyrs with a motto of 'Join the queue in the Martyrs line', and the lowest ranking cadres are falling prey to the spree martyrdom. It is one of the characteristics of the Maoist Party that its cadres are pushed into the peoples' war, roused with a sense of sacrifice while its leaders hide in tight security inspired by a high sense of self-protection.

THE IMPACT OF THE ARMED STRUGGLE ON THE GENERAL POPULATION

After the start of the Maoist Party's violent and illegal activities, the first victims of the People's War were local collaborators aligned with the Nepali Congress and local Nepali Congress leaders with close relations with the local administration. The Maoists seized such people, in the name of people's action, and publicly beat, disabled and killed such people. Those who opposed such actions, particularly those in the police and the administration, were given the same kind of punishment. From the very beginning the Maoists applied a technique against the police, which involved seizing and killing them in an ambush when they went to a particular location to investigate an incident after getting information (or disinformation) from the place concerned. Because of this, the police were unable to maintain law and order and have now become very wary of could not reach in the incidental place after getting information and nowadays tend not to go into the villages on the basis of such reports or requests. In this way the Nepal police force, which previously was involved in crime control and keeping the peace and maintaining law and order, has been prevented from continuing this function in the face of Maoist terrorism.

At the beginning of People's War, the police used a technique known as a 'search march' to move into an area where Maoists were thought to be operating. Both groups fought each other, but both also had a policy that included attacking ordinary people by both the groups in a hidden way and in this period there was untold loss of people and wealth. In this period, ordinary people were killed by the police for giving food and shelter to the Maoists; they were also killed by the Maoists for providing food and shelter to the police. Not only this, but each side also used ordinary people as human shields against each other, which was a very cowardly form of behaviour. This created fear and hatred towards both the Maoist and the police. The common people concluded that both the police and the Maoists, because of their behavior, were the real enemies of the people and both relied on the force of the gun.

The war between the Maoists and the police has continued in front of the eyes of terrorised people and in the recent times the victory of the Maoists and shameful defeat of the police have become general across the country. Especially, after the Maoist Party became successful (with major operations including the attack on Dune, the district headquarters of Dolpa, actions in Rukkum and against the armed police base camp at Naumule in Dailekh), the ordinary policemen have effectively become peons for the police officers confined to the safety of the towns. In Nepal today, the police can no longer keep law and order. After the decline of the police, the Maoists have become more aggressive and have been involved widely in abuses of human rights. The hatred and rejection previously directed towards the police have now been redirected towards the Maoist party and now 'the Maoists' has become a word with which to frighten children.

The areas in which peace and security are a major issue are the areas very much under Maoist influence, but where they do not exercise complete control. These areas are developed by them as a war (guerrilla) zone. Now ordinary people are forced to flee if the Maoists are seen from far off and forced to be friendly if they come close. After the removal of the government police stations, people living in those areas have suffered from the chaotic guerrillas of the Maoists. All are forced to pay considerable amounts in 'contributions', to give shelter and to participate in the Maoist programmes as required. In addition to this, people with known opinions hostile to the Maoists have to bear a greater burden than others. People are now in a position where they are obliged to defend the Maoist dictatorship and suppression, but they are very frightened about the possible consequences, including attacks and the mobilisation of the army.

In areas where the Maoists operate but are not in control, law and order is weakly maintained. In these areas, the organisational activities of people with different political views continue. But, time and again, the Maoists intervene in these areas, as does the army, and there are 'people's actions' and 'army actions'. Time and again, the police also are active in these areas so that the areas are not under anyone's complete control and certainly not outside the conflict. In such areas, theft and robbery, looting and rape and murder take place—such things being blamed by the Maoists on the police and the army, and by the army and the police on the Maoists. Dacoits and other criminals operate easily under such lawless conditions. There are also those who undertake criminal activities under the guise of the Maoists or the police; as a result the idea of 'fake Maoists' and 'fake police' has become common. People in these areas have become the victims of the Maoists, the police, the army, as well as looters or dacoits, or whatever they may be.

The areas where there is no direct presence of the Maoists are also affected by terrorism. These areas are regarded as areas of 'reactionary influence' by the Maoist Party. It uses these areas as areas of 'letter terrorism', donation/collection, underground shelter and area of obtaining weapons and other materials. In some of these areas they undertake guerrilla actions, exploding hand grenades or time bombs. On the one hand, the Maoists conduct such activities and on the other hand, in the name of safety, the police force is highly active and mobile in these areas. Ordinary people suffer from constant surveillance, search and inquiry. In fact, even these areas are no exception to the general lack of peace and security.

It cannot be said that the fighting between the Maoist Party and the police has given rise to a clear outcome. Also, to say that the people are the victims of the Maoists, or the police, is not to grasp the root of the problem. The deteriorating political situation has created a widespread situation of social conflict and several types of specific conflict. Not only is there fighting between the Maoists and the police, there is a wider struggle over the last 6 years that has affected the total life of the nation. Initially the impact was felt only in specific areas, but now it has pervaded our entire social existence in a negative fashion.

1. After the start of the armed struggle by the Maoist party, the concept of 'communist' has been widely brandished everywhere—in forest, field, street and parliament. For lack of knowledge, many have regarded it as fine, while others regard it as an insult. On account of this ignorance, there is also confusion about the distinction between dictatorial communism and democratic communism.
2. The armed movement has had a negative impact on agriculture. Many young men have left the villages either to become Maoists in the jungle or to take refuge and find employment in the urban areas. This means that much agricultural land is not farmed and the productive capacity of the land has declined. If this continues, the whole system of agriculture and farming as an occupation will certainly be undermined.
3. Maoist violence has had a negative impact on foreign investment and the tourism industry. Tourists will not come to Nepal because of the news of violence that they read in the newspaper before leaving their own country. Possibly they do not want to visit Nepal, and come only to Kathmandu and Pokhara. The fear will influence our country for a long time. More specifically, over the past few years, Maoist attacks have been targeted at foreign investment offices and projects, and as a result, foreign investment has been discouraged.
4. The regular activities of development and construction are also blocked due to the Maoist terror and governmental suppression. The non-governmental and other associations activated in rural agriculture areas are returning back one after the other for reasons of security. The Maoists are very focused on blocking banking activities and banks in the rural areas. Consequently, agricultural loans are not distributed and the rural areas are deprived of credit. The general effect on investment, production and development has been negative as far as the national economy is concerned.
5. The cultural sector is also influenced due to the violent

activities conducted in the name of the Maoist People's War. The Maoists have tried to change the collective consciousness through the idea that power comes out of the barrel of a gun. Everything is linked to the People's War. The declaration of the People's War itself has become a cultural festival. The mottos of the Maoists and sayings of the Maoists have encouraged 'extreme thought' that is more extreme than the Chinese Cultural Revolution conducted by Mao ever was. The special feature of this 'cultural revolution' is that the Maoists criticise the people's culture but they themselves retain petty bourgeois culture and feudal thinking, which they cannot overcome. Their boycotting of Dashain and Maghi are examples of such misguided cultural revolutionary acts.

6. In much of Nepal, particularly in the middle hills where state power is limited, social life has until very recently been managed through 'traditional' social organisation. This has tended to involve considerable mutual cooperation in daily work and acceptance of long-standing customs and norms. Such forms of 'collective consciousness' and collaborative activity are particularly deeply rooted in those places where there is a strong ethnic cultural influence. These long-standing social practices have been undermined by Maoist intervention. Furthermore, many newer forms of 'civil society', such as community forest-users' groups, *Ama samuha*, farmers' groups and other forms of economic cooperation have come under the control of the Maoist party. At present, in virtually all activities in the rural areas in particular, the gun of the Maoist has become dominant.

The gun is the symbol of the state power and to use the gun for the control of such social activities is a form of dictatorship. It now seems that Maoism in practice in Nepal is a form of dictatorship.

THE PRESENT CRISIS AND THE NEED FOR RESOLUTION

Nepal is today facing a major crisis. The nation is confronted with a complex situation that results from the wrong vision, policy, programme, plan and practice adopted by the Nepali Congress Party, which has largely dominated government and the state since the start of the multiparty, democratic system more than 10 years ago. The crisis of the political, economic, social, cultural, administrative, educational and other sectors has increased and grown deeper and deeper. The nation is caught up in the lack of direction in the economy, the failure of industrial development, the reduction in the rate of growth of national production and the increasing problems in all areas that constitute the backbone of the nation's economic life.

More than half of the population is forced to survive at or below the poverty line. Many people are suffering from the lack of fundamental and necessary requirements such as food, shelter, clothes and security. The educational sector is on the verge of collapse due to 'congressisation', anarchism, groupism and politicisation. Corruption has permeated every sector—high level bureaucrats and ministers are constantly seen to be involved in serious and appalling misdeeds and corrupt activities. The rural population lives in constant insecurity and the very forces that are supposed to provide security are unable to do so, and indeed constitute an additional source of insecurity to ordinary people; at the same time, the police themselves are under threat.

So, Nepal is trapped in a grave crisis. The Maoist movement that started 6 years ago in the guise of a People's War, has grown from a limited insurgency, confined to some districts in the mid-west, to a national rebellion. This is the key political development of the last decade. The violent struggle associated with this conflict has served to deepen the crisis.

A resolution of this crisis requires a coherent and long-term vision and policy, but also immediate decisions. The government of the Nepali Congress has failed to provide either the vision or the concrete policies to solve such a serious problem. The Congress seems to believe that the problem can be solved by violence and suppression. It is looking to the army and the police force to solve the problem. This government is able to provide neither good governance nor peace and security nor development. The government has played no role in the development of a national strategy. The Nepali Congress Party has not even been able to develop its own coherent strategy with regard to the Maoists. The solution to the crisis cannot be sought from this party or government.

But there is danger in inaction and hesitation. If the crisis that faces the country in virtually all economic, social and political dimensions is increased by instability and uncertainty, then the threat to the nation will become even more severe. Therefore, the first and crucial necessity is to analyse the problem first from a political perspective and then to move ahead courageously and strongly to resolve the crisis. This will require a multidimensional approach.

RECOMMENDATIONS FOR A SOLUTION

Any problem should be studied in terms of its size, weight and depth and while trying to identify its solution the process of analysis should move from the circumference to the centre, keeping attention both to the overall structure of the problem and to the complexities of its inner matter. The recommendations outlined below in connection to the crisis in Nepal and the Maoist problem result from an attempt to get to the inner depths, while understanding it also as a more immediate problem requiring urgent decisions.

1. The present multiparty political system should be directed towards and developed for the welfare of the mass of the working people of Nepal, and not for the benefit of a rich and powerful elite of landlords and capitalists. Policy and practice should be focused on bringing benefits to all citizens.
2. There must be a clear commitment in practice—by government, the state and all civil agencies—to the fundamental rights and obligations set out in the constitution, particularly as regards social discrimi-nation.
3. The government must guarantee fair elections and a transparent basis for economic transactions.
4. The state must honour its constitutional duty to allow organisation on the basis of political faith and belief, and the right to mobilise, organise and make people conscious; it should also provide effective support for such developments.
5. The ruling party or parties should respect all parties in opposition, whether large or small.

6. The government should lead and provide a model to all others in respecting the Constitution of the Kingdom, all Acts, Rules and other legislation. The rule of law as the foundation of democracy must be guaranteed by the government first of all. The government's style of flouting laws itself and exhorting opposition parties not to do so will eventually provoke the people to take the path of violent insurgency.
7. The Supreme Court decision of 28 August 1995, should be reviewed. (The government and the court must recognise the danger of encouraging the Maoists and others to seek alternatives to the multiparty system.)
8. The party holding a parliamentary majority must not regard government and state as its own private property. Maximum efforts must be made to achieve consensus on basic issues of long-term national and international interests. There must be a clear political vision for the overall development, transformation and well being of the nation. This must include a programme for the elimination of social, class and cultural differences.
9. There must be both a short-term and a long-term vision of integrated, balanced, coordinated development, paying attention to the means and resources available from the nations own internal resources and those of the world community.
10. The development of the economy of Nepal must be based on the realities of the situation. Effective national development cannot be based only on the models provided by others or run according to the direction of foreign agencies; policy and plans must be developed on the basis of a national vision (goals and strategies).
11. Agriculture is the foundation of the national economy. A far-reaching (revolutionary) land reform is a basic requirement for the progressive transformation of agriculture. It must include the lawful redistribution of land and 'land to the tiller', to provide the basis for a new structure of land tenure and relations within the agricultural community.
12. An agricultural revolution is required in agricultural production, research, distribution and management. The

modernisation of agriculture can be achieved by providing credit, technology, fertiliser, pesticides, market management and necessary infrastructure according to requirements. The development of cooperative and rural industry should also be undertaken in order to strengthen the rural economy and improve living standards.
13. For the development of our economy, there must be a clear programme of national industrialisation. Government must have very clear policy to preserve and develop small and medium industries, and also determine the priorities for big industries (privatisation or state control). The damage caused by blindly implementing a privatisation programme must be recognised.
14. Corruption must be rooted out. Strict laws and surveillance are needed.
15. The government must act to prevent the domination of the national economy by black-marketeers and smugglers.
16. National development strategy must prioritise the reduction of spatial as well as social inequality, giving encouragement to efforts to promote development in remote and disadvantaged regions and areas, to reduce the differences between rich and poor, developed and less-developed regions and areas and between town and country, rich and poor.
17. A special programme should be adopted to provide real assistance to socially disadvantaged classes, castes and communities in different sectors.
18. Special programmes for income generation, employment opportunities and welfare for the poorest must be implemented immediately, with particular reference to the fulfilment of basic needs (food, shelter, clothing and safety).
19. The state must take responsibility for providing a basic welfare framework—in peace and security, education, health, employment and social security—as part of its social contract with the people of Nepal.

Chapter 11

A Radical Reform Agenda for Conflict Resolution in Nepal*

Arjun Karki

INTRODUCTION

Throughout the modern history of Nepal, the people have struggled in various ways against poverty, inequality and injustice in their search for a dignified life. They struggled for a century against Rana autocracy (from 1846 to 1950), for a decade against the inadequacies of the so-called multiparty system (from 1950 to 1959), for three decades against the partyless Panchayat system (from 1960 to 1990) and then, again for a decade, under the current combination of a multiparty system and 'constitutional' monarchy. Despite political changes in 1951, 1960, 1979 and 1990, the form of the state has remained fundamentally the same. Broadly speaking, it represents the interests of the landed gentry and political elites of Nepal. Throughout its history, the role of the state in Nepal has been to maintain internal security, and to appropriate the surplus produced by the peasants, workers and other social classes in the form of taxes to maintain the state apparatus and continued

---

* This paper on which this chapter is based was commissioned from the author by DFID Nepal in April, and produced in May 2002. The views expressed in the paper do not, however, necessarily reflect the opinions of those consulted or DFID Nepal.

A Radical Reform Agenda for Conflict Resolution in Nepal 439

control of the ruling classes (Blaikie et al; 1979, revised 2000, p. 12).

Even after the major political changes of 1990, an aristocracy continues to hold ultimate control of national politics and state affairs. Major landowners and other ruling elites dominate the higher ranks of the police, military, bureaucracy and judiciary in Nepal. This is because this is the class that holds large amount of land, can afford better education (in expensive schools) and nepotistically gain access to political power. The ordinary people of Nepal have never had the opportunity to become *Thalu* or *Thulo Manchhe*. This traditional process of becoming *Thulo Manchhe* or elite has not changed much, even after the restoration of multiparty democracy in 1990 (Dahal, 2000). The land-poor, oppressed and exploited masses are systematically excluded from the fruits of democracy for which they fought for in successive democratic movements. There is a growing realisation among the ordinary people and critical opinion makers that the state has failed to address effectively the question of poverty, injustice and social discrimination in Nepal (Pandey, 1999, p. 1). None of the problems that were supposed to be eradicated by a more accountable government have been addressed significantly.

The political structure that was established as the outcome of the 1990s democratic movement has failed in sharing power and resources among ordinary people in Nepal. The constitution of Nepal 1990 recognises the people of Nepal as the source of sovereign authority and guarantees basic human rights to every citizen of Nepal, consolidation of the adult franchise, a parliamentary system of government, a constitutional monarchy, a multiparty democracy and the rule of law through the establishment of an independent and competent judicial system, maintaining fraternity and the bond of unity among the people of Nepal on the basis of liberty and equality (HMG/N, 1990 p. 1). Most of the provisions made by the new constitution, however, are not actually being practised in the 'real life' of the people of Nepal, especially the most vulnerable people in rural areas. This is because almost the entire upper level of the Nepal political leadership is dominated by the landed classes, who also control the bureaucracy (Mikesell, 1999).

This landed gentry of Nepal not only controls politics and the bureaucracy but also trade, industry, tourism and indeed almost all economic opportunities that exist in Nepal.

There is a widespread perception in Nepal that whole systems are corrupt; the ordinary people have little expectation that the state will ensure equity, justice and sustainable rural livelihoods. Referring to this, one of the leaders of Transparency International in Nepal has stated that 'the state appears incompetent to do anything about combating corruption'; in his opinion, 'the state machinery itself is engulfed by corruption and its important actors are sustaining themselves through alliances with criminal elements of different kinds' (Pandey, 1995, p. 3). It seems that the state in its present form has failed to manage the many class, national and other contradictions within the framework of its existing structures and mechanisms.

Blaikie et al. (1980, revised in 2001, p. 285) argue, on the basis of a re-study of the situation investigated 20 years ago in rural west central Nepal, that the basic structures of the rural political economy of Nepal remain surprisingly unchanged—remarking in particular on the continuing survival of what might be termed a 'middle peasantry' and the vulnerability of a significant proportion of rural households to chronic and acute livelihoods and rights deficits. The extent and intensity of the ongoing Maoist movement, together with the growing frustration among the people in the poorest and most isolated parts of the country, is encouraging landless and land-poor peasants, agricultural workers, *dalits,* people of ethnic minorities, women and other sections of society to join the insurgency as a collective response against the burden of poverty, injustice and marginalisation locally, regionally and nationally. It can certainly be said that a significant proportion of those people who experience the most acute vulnerability in terms of access to land, justice and other rights offered by the 1990 constitution have joined Maoist movement, as they have lost hope of radical change to their lives and livelihoods through mainstream politics in Nepal. It is widely agreed, both within mainstream political parties in Nepal and among foreign observers, that the lack of the essential ingredients of good governance—efficiency, accountability, transparency and the rule of law—in the country have encouraged the poor, oppressed and exploited strata of people to join the Maoists' 'People's War' (Manandhar, 2001).

When the Communist Party of Nepal (Maoist) declared a 'People's War' in Nepal on 13 February 1996, the government did not take it seriously. Some political leaders even ridiculed it as a hoax. In order to muster popular support from the poor, oppressed and marginalised communities of Nepal, the Maoists had issued a set of 40 demands, which laid out various social, political and economic grievances and demands for constitutional and political changes. A cursory study of these demands reveals that most of them could be implemented even within the framework of the present constitution. The government of the day underestimated the Maoists and chose to ignore their demands, which led the nation to the present day impasse.

Contrary to the official assessment of the situation, the Maoists were sufficiently organised and had already expanded the party networks needed to carry out the 'People's War' in Nepal. The spark of insurgency which broke out in the remote mid western hill districts of Rolpa, Rukum and Jajarkot 6 years ago, has now spread all over Nepal. A few political analysts have reckoned this to be the greatest threat to this nation since the 1814–16 war with British India (Rana, 2002). The Maoists unleashed a reign of terror, attacking police stations and military barracks, killing and maiming opposition political leaders and workers of different political parties, robbing innocent villagers and destroying development infrastructures of the country. According to INSEC, 3,671 people had been killed in the name of the 'People's War' as of April 2002.

This chapter is based on a report which was the result of a review of a good number of secondary resources available in the form of books, periodicals, newspapers, research papers and a PhD dissertation. In order to capture the range of diverse opinion in the analysis, a large number of political leaders, members of high-level constitutional bodies, commissions, Human Rights activists etc. were also consulted. This consultation process was immensely helpful in building the analysis, which outlines a radical reform agenda, to achieve genuine and sustained peace, as an instrument for conflict resolution in Nepal. Similarly, the analysis and recommendations presented in this paper are also based on discussions undertaken for other purposes with those involved in the Maoist movement and their ordinary sympathisers in western hills of Nepal.

The analysis and recommendations presented in this chapter are highly influenced by the ideas and feelings expressed by the ordinary people who form the majority of the people of Nepal and who are undeniably attracted to the Maoist insurgency. The experience of other countries shows that widespread movements from below arise only when a large number of ordinary people feel that their livelihoods and basic human rights are at risk under the existing social, economic and political system, particularly when they face severe threats to their livelihoods and feel that there are great discrepancies in rights between the social classes. It is only partly true that 'bread and butter' issues are the essence of lower-class politics and 'resistance' (Scott, 1985). Since the Maoists have been able to overwhelmingly draw their support from the groups of people who are poor and excluded and are discriminated against on the basis of caste, class and ethnicity, and even gender, this chapter argues that until and unless we are able to address effectively the underlying structures and processes that create and perpetuates poverty, injustice and other forms of discriminations in our society, we have little hope of bringing genuine and lasting peace in Nepal.

So, this chapter attempts to analyse the political, social and economic grievances behind the conflict and recommends a radical reform agenda for its resolution. For convenience, it has been divided into three parts. The first part will contain the analyses of the political, social and economic grievances of the people, the second part will deal with the failure of the democratically elected government in addressing the root causes of conflict and the third part will recommend a radical reform agenda which will, it is hoped, contribute to conflict resolution in Nepal, paving way for a genuine and lasting peace.

GRIEVANCES BEHIND THE CONFLICT

Political Grievances

The political system changed in Nepal in 1990 and so too did the leading political figures, but it is widely believed that there has

A Radical Reform Agenda for Conflict Resolution in Nepal 443

been no real change in the style of governance. The people have not experienced any perceptible positive change in their lives. Indeed, negative changes—such as increased corruption, the criminalisation of politics, the politicisation of the state institutions and government bureaucracy, declining agricultural productivity, increased unemployment and price inflation—have made the lives of already politically marginalised and poverty-stricken people more miserable and difficult after the inception of multiparty democracy (Karki, 2001). Under such circumstances, it is not surprising if the socio-economically and culturally marginalised people of the country are willing to accept arms being raised against the state, which has been perceived by ordinary people largely as an instrument of corruption, exploitation and injustice. Following the democracy movement of 1990 and overthrow of the Partyless Panchayat system, people had high hopes of freedom from poverty, injustice and social discrimination. After the inception of multiparty democracy, a number of political parties such as the Nepali Congress, the CPN (UML), the United People's Front and the National Democratic Party came into existence. However, the downtrodden people who had pinned their hopes on the 1990 People's Movement to introduce radical changes in society began to harbour deep discontentment towards the elected governments. Although the government claimed to exercise authority on behalf of the general public, most of its resources were still directed towards the promotion of the interest of the dominant classes, castes and social groups.

Governance

The principal elements of good governance are accountability of civil servants, transparency of decision-making process, predictability of government operations, efficiency in terms of utilisation of government resources and participation of stakeholders and beneficiaries in the development process. In the case of Nepal, however, the consecutive elected governments after 1990 have failed to meet popular expectations with regard to good governance. One of the basic features of good governance is the rule of law, but the experience of the past 12 years has been one of extreme lawlessness, arbitrary rule and violation of people's rights. 'Governance is the exercise of economic, political and administrative authority to manage the country's affairs at all levels. It comprises the mechanisms, processes, and institutions through which citizens and public interest groups articulate their interests, exercise their legal rights, meet their obligation and mediate their differences' (Upadhyaya, 2002) It is widely believed that the problem of governance has arisen in our country due to the failure of the elected representatives to adhere to the norms of democratic culture and the ideals of parliamentary system of government. Kumar argues, 'tragically, the leaders who had a long history of struggle and sacrifice in the past in the struggle for democracy have turned into "Mobutus" under democratic Nepal' (Kumar, 2000). In recent months, a number of foreign 'donors' have also raised the issue of the absence of good governance in Nepal. The 'donors' are openly saying that they are ready to give aid only when there is good governance (Manandhar, 2001). In such a political environment it is only natural that the common people, deprived of democratic governance, are attracted towards the so-called 'People's War'.

Legal and Constitutional Issues

For the first time in the history of Nepal, the 1990 People's Movement formally established the sovereignty of the people. In practice, however, the common people never felt that the sovereign authority rested with them. Furthermore, a large section of the population seems to have felt alienated because of the constitutional declaration that Nepal is a Hindu kingdom. In the same way, a large section of minority ethnic people have taken exception to the content of the national anthem, which glorifies the king and is derogatory to the sovereign people because it describes them as 'subjects'. As the Maoists also share the same view in this regard, almost all the government schools in rural areas and a majority of the private schools in the cities have been forced to drop National Anthem from their daily assembly.

Another point at issue with regard to the constitution is related to the electoral system. The present system of parliamentary election is based on the practice that the party winning majority seats in the parliament forms the government and the party in the minority stays in the opposition. The leader of the parliamentary party of the majority is appointed as Prime Minister by the king. This practice is well within the accepted norms of parliamentary democracy throughout the world. But a section of the Nepalese people is arguing that, in the context of Nepal, this system fails to ensure true representation of popular votes in the government. In the last general election, the Nepali Congress gained only 35 per cent of the votes, but formed the government on constitutional grounds, winning 103 seats out of 205 seats contested. The combined votes of the opposition were 65 per cent of votes cast. Today more and more people are voicing their opinion against this system of representation (see Shah, 2002). This system of representation has created bitter feelings among the people and has made it easier for the Maoists to incite them against the parliamentary system itself.

There is a growing feeling among the critical masses of Nepal that the democratic principle of 'the rule of the majority' should rest on the majority of the voters not on the larger number of seats. The system of considering the majority on the basis of seats in the parliament is unjust as can be seen from the fact that a candidate (Romi Gauchan Thakali) contesting the election from the constituency of a sparsely populated district like Mustang won the seat with 3,891 votes, whereas another candidate (Bam Dev Gautam) contesting election from a densely populated district like Bardiya lost it even after securing 13,247 votes (Election Commission, 1996). Similarly, this electoral system has not given justice to the minority ethnic groups and *dalits* who are not likely to be represented effectively because of their small numbers in any given electorate and the fact that they are scattered in a number of constituencies. The present electoral law provides for 5 per cent of women in the parliament, which is sorely inadequate for a community which forms half of the total voting population (and the legal provision does not mean that 5 per cent women *must be* elected). The existing questionable electoral arrangements and the system of unequal representation is one of the causes of the present day estrangement of the people against the parliamentary system, particularly in rural Nepal from where the Maoists overwhelmingly draw their support.

According to a survey undertaken by PRO PUBLIC, the offices dispensing public services were found to have been involved in the highest degree of corruption. According to the survey, the rate of corruptibility was 21 per cent among civil servants, 20 per cent among MPs and leaders of political parties, 19 per cent among ministers, 18 per cent among the police and 17 per cent among land revenue officials (PRO PUBLIC, 2000). However, the government and the ruling parties not only failed to deal with the cases of corruption sternly, they even rewarded corrupt people with 'election tickets' and appointments to 'lucrative' positions at various levels of government hierarchies. Most people now strongly feel that there is corruption from the prime minister at the top to the janitor at the bottom of the civil administration and from the judges of the Supreme Court down to the summons carrier at the bottom in the judiciary. Worse still, the legal net is so loose that almost every one implicated in the cases of corruption can escape with impunity (Badal, 2002).

The constitution of Nepal 1990 has an anti-corruption clause which stipulates that 'If the Commission for the Investigation of Abuse of Authority (CIAA) finds, upon inquiry or investigation, that a person holding any public office has committed an act which is defined by law as corrupt, it may bring or cause to be brought an action against such person or any other person involved therein in a court with jurisdiction in accordance with law' (HMG/N, 1990) However, corruption at political and administrative level has been rampant in the post-1990 period. No government, formed after the restoration of democracy in 1990, proved able to provide 'clean' administration, nor did they take tangible action against the many cases of corruption. Several ministers, high ranking officials and senior political leaders were found implicated in various corruption cases relating to aircraft leasing deals, the commissioning of contracts and the issuing of licences for business, but none of them was held to account. According to Sushil Pyakurel, member of Human Rights Commission, the government has not only failed to take action against persons found guilty of the violation of human rights or of indulging in corruption, but even rewarded them with promotion. Often, junior civil servants and clerical workers become the scapegoats for such crimes while the real culprit remains unpunished.

The principle of the separation of powers and non-interference in each other's sphere of authority is one of the hallmarks of a democratic system. In Nepal's case, however, constant conflict between the various constitutional bodies has had a debilitating effect on democratic institutions. Following the people's movement, there have been cases of conflict between the King and the Parliament, between the Executive and the Legislature and between the Legislature and the Judiciary. During the initial years, the 'supremacy of parliament' and 'the prerogatives of the Prime Minister' came into open conflict. As a result, the then Prime Minister Girija Prasad Koirala dissolved parliament and recommended the king to declare a fresh parliamentary election, even though his party was still in the majority. Similarly, the king's decision to seek a judicial review of the Citizenship Bill before giving assent to it was viewed by the Nepali Congress, the ruling party, as indicating the intention of the former to go beyond his constitutionally defined functions. A Nepali Congress president even resigned from the post of the Prime Minister after the military refused his orders to launch an assault against the Maoists (the Holeri incident on 12 July 2001 in which the army refused to carry out the government's order to encircle the Maoists), which compelled him to resign.

In the meantime, the much-vaunted independence of judiciary has also come under question. Most of the judges are sons and daughters of big landowners or come from the background of merchant and other ruling elites. They are not only representatives of the upper classes but also are mainly upper castes. Occasionally, they are publicly criticised for their loyalty to mainstream political parties and for taking bribery in delivering justice to the people (see The Kantipur, vernacular daily, 8 November 2001). In the past, the judicial system has mired itself in controversy by going against its own precedents and making controversial decisions. In 1994, the Supreme Court endorsed the decision of one Prime Minister to dissolve the parliament and declare a fresh poll. But it then retracted and declared void the decision of another Prime Minister to dissolve the parliament for a fresh election in 1996. In an interaction with the author of the paper, the head of CIAA said that the present political mess in Nepal started really with that verdict of the Supreme Court.

Economic Grievances

The dire state of the economy has been considered as one of

the prime causes of the spread of violence and insurgency in Nepal. Despite efforts made to uplift the economic status of the people, the pauperisation of Nepali society has been faster in the post-1990 period than even during the rule of the partyless Panchayat system. According to Maoist leader, Babu Ram Bhattarai, 'Nepal has slid to the status of the second poorest country in the world in terms of physical and cultural developments; 71 per cent of its population has fallen below the absolute poverty level; nearly half of the national income is in the hand of the 10 per cent richest people; more than 60 per cent of the population is illiterate, more then 90 per cent of its total population lives in rural areas and 81 per cent of the labour force is engaged in backward agricultural occupations; 10 per cent are fully unemployed and 60 per cent are under-employed or are in disguised employment' (Bhattarai, 1998). The above statistics, compiled by one of the protagonists of the Maoist insurgency, may differ slightly from the official figures, but the actual situation is not very far from the data cited.

'The basic foundation of the Nepalese society is agriculture, and more than 81 per cent of the labour force in Nepal is engaged in this field of production. Similarly, 87.6 per cent of Nepalese live in rural areas and agriculture is the way of life for these people' (Karki, 2001). The above figures are themselves sufficient to prove the importance of agrarian reform as a mechanism to bring about an improvement in the economic life of the nation. The characteristics of Nepalese agrarian production relations can be broadly described as peasant, semi-feudal and capitalist. Since the vast majority of the Nepali people are peasants and own the means of production, such as land, farm animals and farm implements, the peasant form of production relations is important in understanding class relations and the political economy of Nepal. Primarily they are 'owner-cultivators', tenants and tenant-cum-owner cultivators who farm small pieces of land, produce for their own consumption and depend largely on family or exchange labour *(parma)* within their own communities. The landless poor largely depend on agricultural labour, though tenancy and share-cropping may figure in their livelihoods; they work on the farm of large farmers and rich peasants and their surplus labour is appropriated by relatively well-off families.

Since 1940, political forces have raised concern for radical land reform as an instrument of gaining political strength. It has also been widely accepted that livelihood opportunities become limited for rural people without security of land rights. But no major land reform has been attempted following 1964, when late King Mahendra introduced some significant changes in the pattern of land ownership and the ceiling on land holding. That reform, however, was not based on a re-distributive land reform. As a result, the distribution of land is still highly unequal. According to the government statistics, 70 per cent of poor peasants own only around 25 per cent of the land, 25 per cent of middle peasants own around 45 per cent of the land and about 5 per cent of rich peasants own 30 per cent of the land (Bhattarai, 1998). According to Badal, former chairman of the high level Land Reform Commission, the number of landless families is more than 1 million in Nepal. The agenda of land reform has always occupied a prominent place in the economic planning of all the governments established after 1990. But they have failed to implement a redistributive land reform due to the resistance from the feudal elements that have entrenched themselves within the ruling parties. Though the abolition of the *birta* system in 1959 and the introduction of the Land Reform Act 1964 reduced the area of land under big landowners, there are still many large absentee landowners who still covertly hold large areas of land. These landowners are likely to be senior government officials, members of the Rana nobility and other representatives of upper castes whose land claims date back to the Rana period (Karki, 2001). On the other side, the livelihood of the vast majority of the landless and land-poor people is becoming more vulnerable every day. About 300,000 people are entering the pool of unemployment each year (Regmi, 1999) and these unemployed rural youths, land-poor and landless rural people serve as fertile 'seed beds' for the rebel groups to strengthen their power base in Nepalese agrarian relations. Because of lack of land and opportunities for employment, a large number of youths have joined the Maoist insurgency as an option for a better life. This is evident from the statement of a Maoist leader that, '[S] since peasants' interests are very much concerned with the ownership of land, the slogan of land rights could easily motivate them to engage in struggle' (Bhattarai, 1998).

The issue of sustainable development and poverty alleviation has remained a complex—and unsolved—problem in Nepal for a long time. It is more than 45 years since the system of planned development was introduced in the country in 1956. But the process of economic development has affected only 20–25 per cent of the people (Koirala, 2000); that means that 75–80 per cent of the population has *not* been able to benefit from the planned development. Most people consulted for the preparation of this chapter agreed that the gap between rich and poor has been increasing since 1990 and there is growing realisation of concentration of wealth in the hands of a few political elites through misappropriation of public funds.

The idea of a poverty alleviation programme is a challenge to uplift the socio-economic life of the majority living in extreme poverty who are deprived of basic minimum needs. Since the industrial infrastructure is too small to accommodate the growing number of unemployed people, the livelihood opportunities for growing number of jobless people can be created only through radical agrarian reform. The Ninth Plan set poverty alleviation as its major objective and the 58.5 per cent of the total funds to be invested in it was to come as foreign 'aid'. The government is now on the eve of announcing its 10th Five Year Plan with the thrust again towards poverty alleviation. But, economists and members of civil society have already warned that the economy may collapse if it does not take an initiative to reorient its plan to meet the present emergency situation or to suspend the 10th Five Year Plan in favour of an emergency economic plan to address the root causes of conflict (Rana, 2000).

Regional Disparity

In the 1950s, 60 per cent of the total population of the country lived in the hills, 5 per cent in the Kathmandu valley and 35 per cent lived in the *terai*. This clearly indicates that the hill region was the main habitation zone at that time (Bhattarai, 1998). However, by the 1990s, the pattern of distribution of population in different regions had undergone a change and according to the national census of 2001, 49 per cent of people live in the *terai* region, 44 per cent in the hills and 7 per cent in the high hill and mountain regions of Nepal (The Kantipur, 2001). Nepal has been divided into five development regions with a view

A Radical Reform Agenda for Conflict Resolution in Nepal 451

to mitigate regional disparity in development and to allocate resources in accordance with the needs and priorities of the people. But the centralisation of almost all the economic and social services, and financial and commercial activities has defeated the purpose of decentralisation of administration, resources and services. According to Bhattarai (1998), '60 per cent of deposits and 50 per cent of the credits of commercial banks are centred in Kathmandu; one third of internal trade of the country takes place in Kathmandu, 69 per cent of investment in tourism hotels, 60 per cent of motor vehicles in the country and 60 per cent of industries in the country are located in or around Kathmandu. Against this, the rest of the hill regions and most of the rural areas are without basic physical infrastructures such as roads, water, and electricity'. In the same way, the distribution of industries also is not proportional to population distribution and existing human development indices of the districts and the regions. According to Subedi (2002), 70 per cent of large industries and 60 per cent of small industries are located in the *terai*, 80 per cent of the industrial investment is in the *terai* and 90 per cent of industrial employment is also in the *terai*. But rapid urbanisation and massive migration from the hill to the *terai* have also transformed these fertile tracts of land, once known as the granary of the country, into unproductive land, and the landowners are unable to increase productivity and output through more effective cultivation (Subedi, 2002).

A study carried out by ICIMOD (1997) reveals that western hill districts are the most backward and inhabited by the poorest strata of the society, mainly ethnic minorities and the dalits. These very people have been left behind from the process of development because of the regional bias in the central planning of economic development. It is evident from the HMG/N budget for fiscal year 2000–2001 that the budget allocation for Kathmandu, and Morang and Sunsari districts in the eastern *terai* was much larger than for the whole Karnali zone (in the far northwest). It was Rs. 1 billion 441.2 million for Kathmandu, and Rs. 1 billion 90.6 million for Morang. These districts also happen to be the constituencies of the seniormost leaders of the ruling and the opposition parties. In contrast, highly Maoist affected districts such as Achham, Rukum, Rolpa and Jajarkot belong to the districts receiving the least amount of development assistance. The same year, budget allocation for Achham, Rukum, Rolpa and Jajarkot was Rs. 412 million, Rs. 118.9 million, Rs. 108.5 million and Rs. 82.1 million respectively.

In 1970, a Remote Area Development Committee was formed by HMG/N with a view to expedite development activities in remote districts. But it has not achieved anything, except a few minor development projects. According to Hemanta Kharel, member secretary of the Committee, the total budget allocated by the government for the committee in the last 30 years did not even amount to Rs. 400 million. According to another set of statistics, 13 per cent of people live in 'remote districts' but only 5 per cent of the total budget has been allocated for the development of these regions (Ghimire, 2000). This epitomises the level of regional disparity in the centralised development planning of the country. In the context of growing regional discontent, the assurance of the Maoists to provide regional and ethnic autonomy has been attracting more and more people towards them (see Prachanda, 1998).

Class, Caste, Ethnicity and Gender

Arguably, the ongoing Maoist conflict also has a wide social (caste, ethnic and gender) dimension, apart from the aspects of political and economic exclusion of the poor people. In order to understand this problem in its wider perspective, a brief analysis of class, caste, gender and ethnic aspects of the conflict has been attempted in the following paragraphs. There is a consensus among most political analysts and many development experts that the conflict in Nepal is basically a social, economic and cultural issue and is produced and sustained by failed development (Pandey, 1999).

After the introduction of the caste system by the Malla King (Jayasthiti Malla, 1295–1382) and throughout the Rana and Shah regimes in Nepal, so-called untouchable castes and ethnic minorities were excluded from land grants and land rights (Karki, 2001). The general exclusion of the land-poor people from access to land still exists and this has created a deepseated frustration among the vast majority of the rural poor. Today, in agrarian production relations, poverty is shared by land-poor classes, whether landless, or with tiny plots of land. In order to understand the class dimension of social discrimination, it is necessary to understand the alliance of political power and economic elites. Most productive land, wealth and power are concentrated in the hands of a class making up a small percentage of the upper classes (Mikesell, 1999). As a result, the majority, including particularly, low-caste 'untouchables' *(dalits)* and ethnic minorities, work as agricultural labourers, tenants, bonded labourers and other forms of forced labourers in Nepal. The people had expected, after the People's Movement of 1990, that the elected government would implement a radical agrarian reform and make them land owners. But their dream of coming out of the poverty trap through access to land never came true. This frustrated expectation has inspired many land-poor and the landless people to join the Maoist insurgency.

Neupane (2000), a left intellectual, argues that in essence, the structure of Nepali society is one of divisions and conflicts made up of the class division, the ethnic division (other ethnic people against the chauvinism of the *Khasas*), the caste division (so-called untouchables against the ritual purity of the 'high castes') and the division between women and men in the patriarchal system. Hence, there is widespread dissatisfaction, anger and the feeling of revolt among the poor, the ethnic minorities, the *dalits* and women. If this sense of repression and revolt does not find a way out within the existing constitutional arrangement, it is certain to take a non-constitutional path.

In Nepal, the Hindu *Khas* practices have served as the basis of the social and ruling value system of the country. One of the worst arrangements of these practices is the caste system whose archaic form can be seen in the untouchability prevalent in the society. In fact, there are some ideas which equate classes with castes (Berreman in Sharma, 1999, p. 39). The difference is that while a person's class may be changed in accordance with the achievements he or she makes in his or her life, but the caste he or she is born into can never be changed throughout his or her life (Davis in Sharma, 1999). The caste system is a discriminatory social practice and the Hindu *Khas* priesthood has given continuity and respect to this stigmatised practice. In the view of Swami Dayananda, leader of Arya Samaj Movement, 'The caste system is a cancer which is slowly poisoning the life blood of the nation' (Sharma, 1999, p. 34). The Hindus brought this cancer from the

Gangetic plains during the Lichhavi period, but it was institutionalised by feudal kings like Jayasthiti Malla (1360–95), Ram Shah (1605–36) and Prithvi Narayan Shah and by Jung Bahadur Rana. It acquired a status of directive legal principle after Jung Bahadur made it the main basis of the penal code of the nation through the provisions of Muluki Ain (The Civil Code of Nepal) in 1854. This very law made the caste system and untouchability a part of the legal system of the state. Though the Muluki Ain of 1963 has tried to remove this unwholesome practice, it continues in the society even today.

The 'low-caste' *(dalit)* people of Nepal are struggling against higher caste Hindu chauvinism and *Khas* ethnic domination. The struggle of these oppressed people has been effective and fruitful in recent years, but they have not been successful in bringing the Hindu *Khas*-state to atone for its discrimination over the centuries. This is why they are demanding an apology from the state, the Hindu religious authorities and the *Khas* people as well as forms of reservation for oppressed peoples on the basis of the principle of positive discrimination (Neupane, 2001). They have also been consciously and deliberately excluded from the mainstream of society. They lack representation in parliament, appointments in the civil, military and police services; they also lack access to health care, education and other welfare benefits. According to Lawoti (2000), there are glaring disparities in leadership positions in several areas of governance such as the judiciary, executive, legislature, public administration and politics, as well as in the industrial and commercial sectors, and education. For example, there is not a single *dalit* judge, constitutional body head, minister, high ranking bureaucrat, army officer, police officer, member of the House of Representative, national party central committee member, industrial and economic organisational leader and intellectual association. According to some statistics from 1998, Brahmins were 62 per cent literate, whereas only 15 per cent of Chepangs, an indigenous people in the marginal minority, were literate. The same source shows that only 34 per cent of Brahmins but 90 per cent of the indigenous peoples were below the poverty line (Gurung, 1998). The Muluki Ain of 1963 declares untouchability and discrimination against *dalits* a punishable offence, but the law fails to specify the type of punishment. It, therefore, exists but without application. The government has not been able to make legislation effective for the upliftment of the *dalits* in conformity with the spirit of the constitution.

In Nepal, the search for a female identity is a saga of perilous struggle against discrimination, injustice and humiliation. Gender-related issues have found articulation in Nepali society over the last decades, especially after the restoration of multi party democracy. The constitution proclaimed equality between men and women; the empowerment of women has been a universal agenda of political parties. In spite of this, the exploitation of, and discrimination against, women remains intact, keeping half of the country's population away from the mainstream of the social, political and economic opportunities. Many discriminatory laws and acts still weigh heavily upon the women. No special law has been enacted for the uplift of the backward and the *dalit* women, as provided for by the Article 11 of the constitution. The participation of women at the policy level is negligible. The structural framework set up for the development of women in the Ministry for Women, Children and Social Welfare is too narrow and is constrained by inadequate resources and the lack of political will of the government. Despite the existence of punitive legislation against child marriage, unequal marriage and polygamy, these practices still exist. The level of awareness and literacy among women has not increased significantly. Equal shares for women in parental property remain un-established as yet. A Women's Commission has been recently formed, but its authority has been greatly impaired for lack of a constitutional status. The existing patterns of inequality between men and women and the inability of gender-related organisations to address the issues of women effectively in concrete terms explains the presence of a significant number of women among the leaders and guerrilla commanders in the Maoist insurgency. According to one estimate, some 30 per cent of the Maoist activists are women (Tiwari, 1999).

What did the Government Try to Do?

The 1990 People's Movement was an epochal event, which ended the 30-year rule of the autocratic Panchayat system and restored multiparty democracy. It was also a unique opportunity for the agents of change to lead the nation out of poverty, injustice, discrimination and backwardness. During the past decade, consecutive elected governments have tried to initiate the following reform measures:

During the initial years, there was a great degree of enthusiasm among the elected leaders, the majority of whom were political activists who had spent several years in prisons or in clandestine work. These were the years of conflict between the high expectations of the people, for change, and the legal–constitutional obstacles that had been inherited as a legacy from the previous government. The majority of the people wanted sweeping social–political change and were desperate to break out of the poverty trap. In the beginning, the elected government seemed to match public expectations, by taking actions strengthening democratic institutions and empowering the people. The drafting of the democratic constitution was one of the singular achievements of the Interim Government set up immediately after the success of the People's Movement. The Constitution of Nepal 1990, for the first time in the country's history, declared the people to be the sovereign power from which all other powers of the state would emanate. During those years, the elected democratic government also introduced various international human rights instruments in conformity with the spirit of the universal declaration of human rights.

The setting up of a Human Rights Commission and a Commission for the Investigation of the Abuse of Authority (CIAA) were two of the daring steps taken by the new elected government to control corruption. However, the interference of the executive and lack of proper definition of its scope and function has made it a 'toothless tiger' (Upadhyaya, 2002). The National Women's Commission and the National Dalit Commission can also be considered as some of the important initiatives of the democratic governments. They, in fact, constitute important cornerstones for the building of an edifice of democratic governance and for the strengthening of public confidence in governance. But these commissions have been reduced to show pieces. Chairperson of the National Women's Commission, Dr Durga Pokhrel, says that the National Women's Commission has become 'directionless' for lack of relevant legislation defining its status, powers and functions; the appointment of the commission members smacks of political power sharing among the major political parties.

Of all the important steps taken by the elected government, the most important was the formation of the high level Land Reform Commission and the Commission for the Resettlement of the Squatters, during the tenure of the CPN (UML) government. These commissions undertook surveys of the landless people, carried out research on the status of land holding in Nepal and offered practical recommendation for a radical land reform (Badal, 2002). But these recommendations could not be implemented because of resistance from the landlords, lack of vision and commitment of elected leaders to change and the absence of consensus on radical land reform among the parties in the parliament (Badal, 2002). The Deuba government pushed a land reform bill through the 21st session of the parliament and had it endorsed from both the houses of the Parliament. Though it is surely a progressive step taken by the government, it is visibly inadequate: the proposed land ceiling in the bill is too high and still favours the rich peasants. It may succeed in making the land owned by the rich and middle peasants more productive by reducing them to manageable size, but it will not contribute significantly to the land pool to be created for the redistribution of land to the tillers. Another flaw of the bill is its failure to link up to the reform of a broad range of agrarian institutions without which the slogan of land reform will remain no more than a catchword. Land distribution without institutional support will not ensure sustainable land ownership for the people. The example of Bardiya is a painful reminder. There, the government distributed land to the bonded labourers *(Kamaiyas)* but did not pay any attention to the creation of necessary institutional support. As a result, most of the *Kamaiyas* were forced to sell or mortgage their land to landlords and become landless again. The government authorities should see to it that the same mistake is not repeated again.

During the initial years, the outlook of the elected government was promising. But the heyday of democracy was short-lived. Very soon, the leaders of the political parties, although tempered in the fire of revolutionary struggle for three decades, gave in to greed and temptation and paved the way for the alienation of the people from the democratic process.

In 1995, the government, with the assistance of the Asian Development Bank, introduced the Agriculture Perspective

Plan (APP). Its main objectives were to accelerate the growth rate in agriculture through increased factor productivity, to alleviate poverty and significantly improve the standard of living. In effect, the APP's strategy is to accelerate growth through a technology-based green revolution (APPROSC and John Mellor Associates, 1995). The APP has four priority inputs, i.e. irrigation, roads, technology and fertiliser. By these means, the aim is to increase per capita food production in hills and mountains from 219 kg in 1994-95 to 362 kg by 2014-15 and reduce the incidence of poverty from 63 per cent in 1994-95 to 19 per cent in 2014-15. To achieve this, the APP emphasises the dynamic power of the private sector and market forces. The dominant image is that of a rural economy poised for economic growth with a policy focus stressing feeder 'agricultural' roads, chemical fertiliser, shallow tube well irrigation and research into a Prioritised Productivity Package (PPP) of inputs. However, the achievements of the last 7 years suggest that the APP's ambitious and unrealistic plan is not working at all. A recent study carried out by ANZDEC states that APP has largely lost its significance (ANZDEC, 2002).

The APP strategies were highly criticised from the very beginning, but by a few. Cameron (1998) argues that the livelihood challenge in Nepal is immense and there is little evidence that the foundations for advance in the hills economy have been laid as the APP asserts. This is because many people in remote villages are already close to the point of livelihood breakdown. The experience so far suggests that there is no intrinsic mechanism in the APP for ensuring livelihood opportunities to resource-poor peasants and landless people. Since land-poor peasants, landless agricultural workers, *Kamaiyas* and other forms of bonded labourers do not own or often even have access to land, the APP's priority inputs such as irrigation, fertiliser, roads and technology give them nothing. It can be foreseen, therefore, that the APP, if implemented as planned, would rather increase the gap between the rich and the poor and promote the concentration of wealth in the hands of a few landlords and rural elites. Furthermore, the APP also fails to recognise the fact that women are heavily engaged in economic activities, both agricultural and non-agricultural, and does not even consider the extent to which they have power over decisions or over the income associated with those activities. Their role is ignored. Therefore, Cameron argues, the APP fails to grasp the essence of livelihood inequalities in rural Nepal. There is no prioritisation of the livelihoods of vulnerable people by economic, social, geographical or age factors.

The recent study by ANZDEC (cited above) shows that the absence of regular coordination, together with frequent staff changes and the need to attend to immediate priorities, negatively affected the implementation of the APP. It has been observed that each implementing agency continues to work with its own priorities with barely a token acknowledgement of APP objectives; the APP is, consequently, likely to fall far short of its declared goal and objectives. Since the concept paper of Tenth Five Year Plan of HMG/N has also given top priority to the development of agriculture along the lines of the APP, the hope for bringing agrarian change, let alone reform, in the near future is very small (see NPC, 2002). Therefore, peasant movements and other members of civil society argue that a genuine APP needs to be developed, based on the realities of caste, class, ethnic and gender differences prevalent in rural and remote communities. Agriculture development envisioned without grappling with the issue of access to productive resources (such as land) and radical reform of the institutions that directly impinge on the daily life of rural poor cannot bring about the desired changes—reducing the rural poverty, injustice and inequality that systematically exclude the poor from the benefits of any development programme.

Why the Government Failed to Address Public Grievances?

The historic People's Movement of 1990 overthrew the 30-year rule of the autocratic Panchayat system. In the success of the movement, the people of Nepal had seen the dawning of a new golden era in the form of sweeping social–political changes and the enjoyment of a wide spectrum of democratic rights. But they never expected that a political impasse such as the one we are facing today would be waiting for them just 12 years down the road. A retrospective study of the transitional years, however, shows that the objective conditions of what was to happen now existed from the very beginning. The 1990 people's movement was a revolution in the making, which, if not stopped by a triangular compromise (between the Palace, the Nepali Congress and the United Left Front), had the potential of sweeping away every remnant of feudalism leading to a radical transformation of the political economy of Nepal. But unfortunately, the democratic system which was set up after the movement showed too much leniency to the stalwarts of the Panchayat system and left them unpunished. As a result they started to resist the process of democratisation from the very first day of their defeat. Following the restoration of democracy, the 'Mallik Commission' was formed to investigate the excesses committed by officials at the higher echelons of the Panchayat system. The recommendations of the Commission were never implemented. This kind of impunity started the undoing of the democratic government.

The governments of the post-1990 period did not proceed to implement radical socio-economic changes as expected by the people. Successive governments indulged more in reformatory rhetoric than in implementing radical reform programmes capable of touching the lives of the people. The loss of credibility among the people made it difficult for the government to gain confidence. As a result alienation grew between the people and the elected government.

Lack of inter- and intraparty consensus on the major issues of reform was another cause of the failure of the elected government to address the growing discontentment among the people. The elected prime ministers felt the need to pacify their ever-growing intraparty dissension first, rather than to satisfy more general expectations (Kumar, 2000). Similarly, an absence of healthy interrelationship and consensus among the ruling and the opposition parties was also an inhibiting factor in addressing contemporary social, political and economic issues in the way necessary for the consolidation of the parliamentary system of government.

The case for decentralisation arose partly from increasing consensus among 'donors' that the state needed to retreat from many centralised areas of production, regulation and provision (IFAD, 2001). However, this need has never been really felt in the key institutions of government in this country. The centralisation of administration and the tendency of the central authorities and leadership to create loyal supporters rather than a competent and independent bureaucracy have greatly weakened the spirit of decentralisation. The President of the Association of District Development Committees (ADDCN) has stated that the local government bodies, like the District Development Committees, Municipalities and Village Development Committees, have been interfered with by the central authorities. There is no clear definition of the scope and functions of the local government bodies. As the hiring, firing and the promotion of local government employees is done by the ministries, they are not loyal to the elected representatives of local government. The Chief District Officer and the district chief of police are answerable to the home minister and rarely coordinate their activities with the elected District Development Committee. The failure of the government to implement the decentralisation process in full has led to the undermining of the elected local government. The absence of the decentralisation of authority and the practice of keeping handpicked and often incompetent political cadres in the bureaucracy on the basis of nepotism and favouritism, as well as the impermanent nature of appointments owing to frequent changes in the government, have all encouraged corruption. This has increased disaffection among the people.

Last but not the least, the elected governments lacked the will for radical reform and the ruling class did not represent the poor people. The ruling elites came from upper social economic classes, which represented the interest of feudal landlords in the rural areas, the rich peasants and the urban bourgeoisie. Similarly, they represented the higher castes and ethnic groups and were reluctant to introduce radical reforms necessary to abolish inequality in every field of social life. For example, the elected government freed the bonded labourers but showed reluctance to ensure their genuine socio-economic rehabilitation. Instead, the government ordered the military to evict them, burn down their houses and render them homeless. As a result, the majority of the recently 'liberated' *Kamaiyas* have been encouraged to join the Maoist rebellion while the western *terai* regions, such as Banke, Dang, Bardiya, Kailali and Kanchanpur, have been converted into some of the most Maoist-affected areas.

Agenda for Reform

Most conflicts and rebellions are a reaction to the failure of the institutions of interest mediation such as parliament, political parties and the government (Karki, 2001). It is widely agreed among political and social analysts that the present day situation in Nepal would not have arisen if the state had made a timely intervention with appropriate reform measures. A section of the ruling elites took the Maoist insurgency lightly at the beginning and even connived at its growth, hoping that this would contribute to weakening the power base of the mainstream left forces. They may have thought that it could be brought under control with the use of force after the constitutional opposition was made sufficiently weak. This was a grave miscalculation. Even now, the government does not seem to be ready to accept the social-economic dimensions of the conflict. This problem has serious political, economic, social underpinnings and its solution too should be sought by addressing a wide range of social, political, economic and ethnic grievances that are associated with agrarian production relations. In order to bring the Maoist insurgency under control, the following agenda for radical reforms is recommended. For the sake of clarity, I have divided the reform measures into two sections: 1) Agrarian reform and 2) Reform in governance. The agrarian reform will cover the question of redistributive land reform and related institutions. The reform in governance will cover constitutional and judicial issues, corruption, decentralisation, electoral malpractices, social–ethnic discrimination and the issues and concerns of *dalit* and ethnic minorities.

Agrarian Reforms

Nepal is predominantly an agrarian society and more than 90 per cent of people live in the rural areas. This explains why agrarian reform should top the agenda of reform to bring an immediate change in the rights and livelihoods of the people of Nepal. Most of the people involved in the Maoist insurgency come from rural background and have taken to the insurgency, losing all opportunities for the betterment of their lives. Substantial agrarian intervention is likely to wean these people away from the path of violence and terror. From the above discussion, it becomes amply clear that a radical agrarian reform will be the basis of all kinds of socio-economic reforms in the country. As unequal socio-economic and political relations in rural and remote areas of the country have been at the centre of socio-political conflict, radical reform in agrarian production relations

Land Reform

In order to address the inequality in access to land and in the existing agrarian production relations, a radical re-distributive land reform programme should be instituted on the basis of 'land to the tiller'. According to the availability of land and the number of the landless people as projected below, the land ceiling should be fixed at 3 hectares in the *terai*, 5 hectares in the mid-hills, 7 hectares in the high hills and mountains and 1 hectare in Kathmandu Valley. All the cultivable land above these ceilings should be confiscated with compensation. A land pool should be created, comprising the excess public land and the land above the ceilings, to have it redistributed among the landless and the land poor. Land distribution should be supported by building rural-based financial and educational institutions to help the land poor to gain access to the necessary technical support and loans for the modernisation of agriculture, to ensure livelihood opportunities. Irrigation facilities should be expanded to cover the major stretches of cultivable lands. The land distributed to landless people should be placed under the joint ownership of husband and wife. According to Badal, the state could acquire, in this way, more than 3,06,000 hectares of land to be distributed among 1 million landless and land-poor families, if the above land ceiling is strictly enforced. In order to discourage the tendency to keep more land, a progressive tax system (more tax to large holders and less tax to small holders) should be enforced. Similarly, minimum wages should also be fixed and strictly enforced for the safeguard of the livelihoods of various agricultural workers. When distributing the land, the following priorities should be followed: *(i) Kamaiyas* (bonded labourers), *(ii)* landless peasants (agricultural workers), *(iii)* peasants owning less than 0.1 hectares of land *(iv)* peasants owning less than 0.2 hectares of land. Those families whose members hold a job outside agriculture shall not be given priority in distribution of land. In order to make the land reform programme effective, a proper land recording and information system and land use policy should be developed. Similarly, a programme of land consolidation should also be introduced.

Rural Industrialisation and Employment

Rural industrialisation should be given priority and other employment generating enterprises should also be encouraged in the private sector so that gainful employment can be provided for the unemployed in rural areas. In order to encourage agricultural modernisation and mitigate rural unemployment, agro-based rural industries should be promoted. In order to create sustained employment opportunities for young and unemployed people in the rural areas, indigenous resources based poverty alleviation programmes should be implemented, linking them with agrarian reforms. The objective of rural industrialisation should be to reduce pressure on land from the unemployed people by ensuring livelihood opportunities in other rural and agro-based industries. Such industrialisation should be supported by institutions producing skilled manpower for the various agro-based rural industries. This will not only help mitigate rural poverty, it will also slow down the ongoing process of migration of people from the hills to the *terai* and from the rural areas to the urban centres.

Building Rural Institutions

Every social–political system builds certain institutions as its props and pillars. After a change of the system, a great change will be possible only through their reform and rebuilding so as to be able to manage the socio-economic and political conflicts that are bound to emerge within a newly created superstructure. In order to make agrarian reform effective and to create sustainable rural institutions for the resettlement of the landless and the freed *Kamaiyas,* agricultural banks and other financial institutions, irrigation authorities health centres, schools, agricultural research institutes, rural road transportation authorities, and institutions for the distribution of agricultural inputs should be radically reformed in the interest of the oppressed, poor, exploited and socially excluded. The capacities of these rural institutions should be strengthened and their focus should be redirected towards addressing the needs of the landless, *Kamaiyas,* ethnic minorities, *dalits* and women. At present, rural institutions, such as the Agricultural Development Bank, cooperatives and agriculture and livestock service centres, have been working in the interests of

A Radical Reform Agenda for Conflict Resolution in Nepal 465

the rural elites and landed gentry. These institutions should be radically reformed to make them more accountable in the interest of the land-poor and rural agricultural workers.

In order to ensure a comprehensive agrarian reform, an all-powerful Agrarian Reform Commission should be formed under the chairmanship of the deputy prime minister. As the various aspects of reform are linked to more than one ministry, only a commission of this kind will be able to achieve the necessary coordination between the different ministries. The minister for finance, minister for agriculture and land reform, minister for women and social welfare, minister for forests, minister for industry, minister for local development and representatives of peasants' associations, trade unions and NGOs should be the ex-officio members of the commission.

Reform in Governance
Decentralisation

The directive principle of the 1990 constitution states '[I] it shall be the chief responsibility of the state to maintain conditions suitable to the enjoyment of the fruits of democracy through wider participation of the people in the governance of the country by way of *decentralisation* and to promote general welfare by making provisions for the protection and promotion of human rights and maintaining tranquillity and order in the society'. However, despite the introduction of a set of rules and regulations, the president of Association of District Development Committees of Nepal (ADDCN) states that this is not being translated into practice, due to lack of political will in the central government. Experience so far suggests that the concept of decentralisation has been marred by various factors, including lack of devolution of authority both administratively and financially to the local bodies (The Himalayan Times, Monday, 20 May 2002). Therefore, in order to monitor the decentralisation process, the Decentralisation Implementation and Monitoring Committee (DIMC) should be strengthened and empowered in conformity with the spirit of decentralisation as enshrined in the directive principles of the Constitution of the Kingdom of Nepal. Constitutional provisions should be added to ensure a clear division and demarcation of the roles and responsibilities of the central and local governments. The central authorities should abide by the principle of limited governance and choose to keep to itself only essential powers, such as security and foreign relations. The central government should play a facilitating role in terms of local governance. In order to reduce political dispute and interference, the DDC president and Vice President should also be elected by direct franchise and the number of DDC members should be reduced to 11. In order to make the district administration costeffective, functional and viable as an administrative unit, the number of districts should be reduced from 75 to 40. To address the present confusion and misunderstanding between the DDC and the central government in hiring, firing and transferring local government employees, an autonomous body represented by Public Service Commission and DDC officials should be established at the district level.

Reform and Capacity Building of Constitutional Bodies

Constitutional arrangements should be made to strengthen the Commission for the Investigation of Abuse of Authority (CIAA). The commissioners should be appointed from among persons of proven ability and integrity (to be established by background checks) in accordance with the practice of 'public hearing'. The scope of investigation of the CIAA should encompass all the three organs of state. Since the nomination of CDOs and other government administrators as CIAA local representatives is vulnerable to frequent political interference, there is need to increase the CIAA's scope and function, by expanding it to the regional and district levels. A separate wing should be developed under the CIAA to investigate the property of top party leaders, government ministers, high level government bureaucrats, judges, police officers and the chiefs of corporations annually. The government should make provision for necessary resources to be available for the capacity development of the CIAA. The recommendations of the CIAA should be made legally binding on the government.

The Public Service Commission is one of the few institutions that has remained relatively untainted amidst the general degeneration in the values of governance. However, its role has been limited to recommendations for the recruitment of civil servants. As it has little say in promotion, transfer and dismissal of employees, the level of political interference has increased in civil

A Radical Reform Agenda for Conflict Resolution in Nepal 467

service. The practice of direct appointment of employees by ministers in civil service, corporations and state intelligence service has ensured continuity in the culture of favouritism and nepotism. Some of the examples of such acts by the political elites can be found in the recent cases brought to the CIAA regarding the interference of ministers in the appointment of employees in the Agricultural Development Bank and in the Royal Nepal Airlines Corporation (RNAC). In order to ensure a less political, and more impartial and competent bureaucracy, the Public Service Commission should be strengthened and expanded so that it can also play a monitoring role in the promotion, transfer and dismissal of civil servants and police. Special wings should also be developed within the Commission to enable it to take up the responsibility of hiring, firing, transfer and promotion of employees working in state owned corporations and specialised service organisations such as the police and the state intelligence services. The state should allocate the necessary resources to develop its capacity and expand its networks. In order to reduce political interference and eliminate their loyalty to the political elites, the chief and the members of the Public Service Commission should also be appointed through the process of 'public hearing'.

Conflict between constitutional bodies has greatly impaired the image of the parliamentary system of governance. Their conflicts and contradictions have also affected the smooth functioning of the state apparatuses and have resulted in non-coordination among them. In order to solve this problem, an all-powerful arbiter should be created and his or her verdict should be binding to all the constitutional bodies in conflict.

The Judicial Council should be strengthened by enacting a clear and comprehensive set of rules and regulation to govern its functions and scope of authority. The background of judges should be checked through the system of 'public hearing' so that only people with highest competence and moral integrity can be appointed as judges. The promotion and dismissal of judges should be done by Judicial Council in collaboration with the State Affairs Committee of the Parliament. The Judicial Council should also report the functions and performance of the courts to the Parliament through His Majesty the King. The Judicial Council should be responsible for the reward and punishment of the judges in accordance with the Judicial Council Regulation, which is yet to be enacted. There is need for the enactment of a comprehensive Bill to enable the Judicial Council to perform a more responsible role than it is at this moment.

Experiences with the electoral system since 1990 shows that most candidates for the parliamentary election are selected by party bosses and party bureaucrats according to the interests of the party 'sponsors' and thus often are hardly accountable to the people who elected them (Mikesell, 1999). The present system of contesting elections on 'party tickets', on the basis of individual charisma and resources, has not been found truly representative of the peoples' interest. For the majority of citizens, political participation has been limited to casting a vote in the election, whose impact has been diluted by increasing electoral malpractices. In order to correct this, various political parties have offered different recommen-dations. The Nepali Congress is broadly in favour of the present electoral system, but, in order to ensure a free and fair election, it recommends an electoral government under the 15 member council of ministers led by the sitting prime minister. According to the Nepali Congress Party proposal, people outside the ruling parliamentary party may also be included in the electoral government. The CPN (UML) and the Rastriya Prajatantra Party (RPP) are demanding an all-party electoral government. Independent opinion makers, however, believe that an independent government should be formed under the Chief Justice of the Supreme Court consisting of individuals who are not contesting elections and possess high moral integrity and competence.

There are also suggestions that the Prime Minister be elected through direct franchise, to minimise political instability. The Prime Minister, so elected, would choose a cabinet of non-elected citizens of proven ability (mostly technocrats) and integrity (to be established by background checks), each of whom would be confirmed by full parliament. To avoid the ambiguity experienced in the past regarding the dissolution of the House of Representatives, the role and rights of the Prime Minister should be defined clearly. Both CPN (UML) and the Nepali Congress, however, want to establish the dissolution of the House of Representatives as the unrestricted privilege of the Prime Minister. Parties, not individuals, would contest parliamentary seats on the basis of a universal franchise and a proportional representation

A Radical Reform Agenda for Conflict Resolution in Nepal 469

system of election should be introduced. The role of MPs will be to act as law makers and to involve themselves in the monitoring of ministers and heads of the various constitutional bodies through parliamentary proceedings. MPs will not be eligible for executive and cabinet appointment. The electoral constituencies of the country should be redefined on the basis of population distribution, making the electorate approximately the same in terms of numbers in each constituency. The number of the MPs should not exceed 105. In order to capture the ethnic and cultural diversity of the country, the National Assembly should be changed into the House of Nationalities, with provision for representation in proportion to the size of the ethnic population. The number of the members of the House of Nationalities should not exceed 45. These recommendations are worth considering, but are hardly likely to satisfy the Maoists, who do not appear to be satisfied with anything short of a constituent assembly.

Equality to Women, Ethnic Minorities and Dalits

Existing laws that govern the treatment of the minorities are not always implemented, and widespread discriminatory treatment to minorities at the local level has mobilised considerable support for the Maoists. A government policy more carefully devised to avoid caste, religious and ethnic discrimination would decrease inequalities and attract to the mainstream people who may otherwise be swayed by more radical factions. In order to prevent this from happening, there should be a special provision for reservation of seats in the House of Representatives for women and *dalits* ensuring at least 10 per cent representation for women and 5 per cent representation for the *dalits*. Women's right to inheritance to parental property should be ensured through appropriate legislations. Similarly, appropriate legal instruments should be introduced to make it easier to take actions against people discriminating against others by caste, religion or ethnicity and gender.

The contents of the national anthem have been criticised by a large cross-section of the population for glorifying the monarchy and referring to the sovereign people as 'subjects'. It should be amended to capture the multi-ethnic, multi-religious and multi-lingual spirit of the constitution. The constitutional declaration of Nepal as a Hindu kingdom has alienated many non-Hindus and national minorities. This clause, therefore, should be changed and the country should be declared a secular state. Article 6 (1) of the Constitution of Nepal defines the Nepali language as the language of the nation and the official language whereas clause (2) of the same article defines other languages as the national languages of Nepal. All the languages including the Nepali language should be referred to as national languages and Nepali language should be defined as the official language.

Reform in Local Administration

The Chief District Officer, district police in-charge and the district judge are the main pillars of the district administration. Their unfair discharge of duty or complicity with corrupt people seriously compromises their dispensation of justice, administrative service and provision of security to the people. Under the present dispensation, they have been at the beck and call of the central government. Most of these officials are appointed on the basis of their loyalty to the minister concerned or "power centre" rather than on the basis of their expertise, integrity and loyalty to the people and state. In order to control the practice of nepotism, favouritism and corruption at the district level, the appointment, transfer, promotion and dismissal of the Chief District Officers and the chiefs of police should be brought under a separate wing of the Public Service Commission.

Emergency Economic Plan

The economic indicators mentioned earlier show that the economy is today in dire straights. The commitment of the government to meet the security expenses for its anti-Maoist operations has stretched the national economy to the farthest point. The government has brought in a Poverty Reduction Strategy Paper (PRSP) and the 10th Five Year Plan is being finalised. But these do not seem to be more than 'business as usual'. In an extraordinary situation, ordinary economic measures are not likely to save the country from economic bankruptcy. It is therefore necessary to devise an emergency economic programme that could be helpful in addressing the root cause of conflict. Equal weight should be given to development as is being given to security priorities. The emergency economic intervention programme should be oriented towards ensuring dignity, equality and access

A Radical Reform Agenda for Conflict Resolution in Nepal 471

to opportunity for the ethnic minorities, women and *dalits*. In addition to this, it should give priority to employment creation in the rural and remote areas of Nepal and to providing access to quality education for the children of the poor, oppressed, exploited, *dalit* and ethnic minorities. This will surely motivate large numbers of those unemployed youth who chose the violent path in the search for alternate livelihoods to choose economic activities at home and to continue their education for a better future life.

The Role of the International Community

For the last 50 years, the international community has been a part of Nepal's development endeavours. But most development experts admit that Nepal's foreign 'aid' driven development has been a failure. The Maoist leadership states that the general consequences of foreign aid in Nepal are *(1)* failure of poverty alleviation schemes, *(2)* target failures, *(3)* unsustainability of projects, and *(4)* corruption. Similarly, Mikesell (1999) states that most foreign aid in Nepal came in the name of promotion of human rights and democracy, but failed to ensure either. Not only the so-called donors but also the International Financial Institutions such as the World Bank, IMF and Asian Development Bank have been involved in financing numerous development initiatives, ostensibly meant to reduce poverty, but which have failed comprehensively to achieve their declared objectives. Regarding the failure of official development assistance (ODA), Bhattachan (1999) argues that most of these initiatives were in fact dictated by global and national interests and are responsible for major state-led corruption, indebtedness and growing inequalities in Nepal. But this does not mean that the international community cannot do anything. They can, in fact, play a role in building the capacities of the rural institutions that work for the poor. They can provide support in controlling situations that create and perpetuate conflicts in Nepalese agrarian production relations. Their support in generating employment opportunities with a focus on the ordinary people of Nepal could go a long way in ensuring equity, justice and sustainable rural livelihood to bring lasting peace. In order to achieve substantial changes in the exiting agrarian relations, the international community must attach positive conditionality to their aid and loans such as a commitment to redistributive land reform, setting up of rural industries and promoting pro-poor research and technology development and reforming various institutions that could play a significant role in agrarian change. It has been widely admitted that the foreign agencies have put funds largely into areas that were their own priority, instead of gearing their efforts towards meeting indigenous needs and concerns.

Some of the people consulted during the preparation of this chapter raised strong concern over foreign consultants coming to Nepal as part of the international assistance, arguing that this has also contributed to the increase in corruption. Therefore, it has been argued that the international community should give priority to building the capacity of local institutions, so that these institutions can play an instrumental role in prioritising the areas of intervention, laying the emphasis on bringing programmes designed to help the landless class, lower middle class and backward communities. At the same time their assistance should also be subservient to the policy of ethnic integration and be helpful to the micro-economy of rural communities. Similarly, they may also contribute in providing technical and financial assistance in formulating a land use policy, land plotting and land recording and developing land-related information systems.

The international community may also encourage civil society organisations, critical opinion makers, media and academia to work as a pressure group in favour of a genuine agrarian reform, good governance and the effective implementation of the decentralisation policy enshrined in 1990s constitution, and to press for a less political and more accountable, credible, independent bureaucracy and police service. Since most of the issues related to widespread corruption and centralised governance are also associated with the amendment of the constitution of Nepal, this role should be left to the Nepalese civil society, organisations and political parties. All the same, the international community could support civil society's initiatives so that they could make their voice heard by the state authorities. Particularly, their concern to see good governance, anti-corruption measures and a less political and more credible independent bureaucracy and police service could exert very strong moral pressure on the political elite of this country.

Conclusion

After 1990, the democratically elected governments tried to address some of the sensitive issues regarding caste, class and social discrimination. The government instituted the National Human Rights Commission, the National Commission for Women and the National Commission for Dalits. However, none of these commissions formed for addressing the very issues of poverty, injustice and social discriminations were able to do their job properly. Almost all the heads of institutions consulted during this study expressed their frustration regarding the government's reluctance to implement the recommendations made by these bodies and to support them with the resources and expertise needed to carry out their work. In other words, what they said was that despite what-ever rules and regulations were created for the functioning of these bodies, they were in fact constrained by the lack of political will of the leadership of the government. For example, the recommendations of the CIAA and the Nepal Human Rights Commission to the government for taking action against civil servants and other administrative personnel were not implemented by the government. Instead these people enjoyed impunity and the blessing of the senior politicians and ministers. Similarly, some of the accused were actually rewarded by government with promotion to more responsible positions. The other limitations of these bodies are that some of the officials were selected on the basis of their loyalty to one or other political party rather than on the basis of their credibility and integrity. That is why they were often not as assertive as they could have been in taking action against corrupt officials and the political leadership of the country.

Regarding the amendment of the constitution of 1990, there have been several initiatives coming from mainstream political parties. So far, the CPN (UML), the main opposition party of the House of Representatives, the Nepali Congress Party, the ruling party, and the Rastriya Prajatantra Party (RPP) have all come out with their written proposals for amending the constitution of Nepal. Despite obvious differences, more or less all of these recommendations advocate an independent bureaucracy, legal mechanisms for reducing corruptions and 'public or parliamentary hearings' for the appointment of senior government officials. Similarly, these statements also propose the declaration of assets by all political leaders and senior government officials and confiscation of these assets if they fail to produce the source of their earnings. In addition to this, it is also evident from their statements, that there is a consensus among the top three political parties in favour of reducing the number of seats in parliament and the size of the council of ministers. An analysis of these three reform proposals suggests that, if implemented honestly, they would bring about radical changes and improve the present state of political mess and anarchy in Nepal. This would also address the frustrated expectations among the poor, oppressed and exploited masses resulting from widespread corruption and the politicisation of bureaucracy and police service and other state mechanisms. Unfortunately, the government does not seem willing to address the proposals put forward by these major political parties fast enough in face of the urgent needs of the country. Until and unless these proposals are implemented, the ordinary citizens of this country will not believe that the mainstream parties are genuinely committed to these causes.

The reform agenda recommended in the paper might sound sweeping and unconventional. But these are, I believe, the *minimum* preconditions which must be fulfilled if the root causes of the problems are to be addressed and the crisis brought about by the insurgency is to be resolved. The mechanisms for the solution of any problem should always be proportionate to the gravity of the problem. The problems we are grappling with are not ordinary. Therefore the measures we have recommended may not fit within the traditional way of looking at things. In order to bring lasting peace in Nepal, I would like to suggest that the current political crisis and conflict should not only be taken as a *threat* to democracy but also be regarded as an *opportunity* for radical reform to address the root causes of conflict that have created and perpetuated poverty, injustice and social discrimination in this country. These proposals could also be discussed with the Maoists; talks have already been held,* and further talks could be considered.

---

* The first round of talks was held in Godawari on August 30, 2001. The second roux nd was held in Thakurdwara in Bardia district on September 13 and 14, 2001 and the third round of talks was held in Godawari on 23 November, 2002.

PERSONS CONSULTED DURING THE STUDY

Mr Yogendra Nath Ojha, Chairman, Public Service Commission
Mr Surya Nath Upadhaya, Chief Commissioner, Commission for the Investigation of Abuse of Authority
Mr Subash Nembang, President, Public Account Committee, House of Representatives
Mr Keshav Badal, former chairman of Land Reform Commission, HMG/N and chairman of All Nepal Peasant Association
Mr Madhav K. Nepal, Leader of the main opposition party in the House of Representatives and member of the constitution drafting committee in 1990
Ms Durga Shob, Member Secretary, National Dalit Commission – Nepal
Mr Krishana P. Shapkota, President, Association of District Development Committees of Nepal (ADDCN)
Mr Balkrishana Mabuhang, Secretary General, National Federation of Nepalese Nationalities
Mr Gore Bahadur Khapangi, Chairman, Rantria Janajati Party
Mr Gauri Pradhan, Chairman, NGO Federation of Nepal
Mr Prem Dengal, Secretary General, All Nepal Peasant Association
Mr Jaganath Acharya, Former Land Reform Minister, Nepali Congress Party
Dr Durga Pokhrel, Chairperson, National Women's Commission
Mr Shushil Pyakurel, member of National Human Rights Commission

References and Bibliography

Adhikari, S. (2000) Garibi nibaran ra prastut badget, *The Kantipur*, 14 June 2000.
Amnesty International (1997). *Human Rights Violations in the Context of a Maoist 'People's War.'* AI, London.
Amnesty International (1999). *Nepal Human Rights at a Turning Point.* AI, London.
Amnesty International (2002).
ANZDEC (2002). *Nepal agricultural sector performance review,* A Report prepared for the Ministry of Agriculture and Co-operatives, Nepal and Asian Development Bank by ANZDEC Limited, New Zealand, in association with CMS Limited.
APPROSC and John Mellor Associates (1995). *Nepal Agriculture Perspective Plan (1995/96–2014/15),* Kathmandu: HMG/N and Asian Development Bank.
Bhandari, L. (1999). Maoist People's War and government policy: An endless problem. *Dhristi Shaptahik,* Nepali Vernacular Weekly, 23 September 1999.
Bhatarai, B.R. (1998) *Politico-Economic Rationale of People's War in Nepal* (Nepali). Utperak Publications, Kathmandu.
Bhattachan, K.B. (1999). Globalisation and its impacts on Nepalese society and culture, in Dahal, M.K. (Ed.), *Impact of Globalisation in Nepal,* Kathmandu: Nepal Foundation for Advance Studies.
Bhattachan, K.B. (2000). Possible ethnic revolution or insurgency in a predatory unitary hindu state, Nepal. In D. Kumar (ed.) *Domestic Conflict and Crisis of Governability in Nepal,* CNAS, Kathmandu.
Bhattarai, B. (1989) Farmers problems in Nepal—Some theoretical questions. *Jhilko,* Academic Magazine, Aswin, B.S. 2046, Kathmandu, Nepal.
Bhattarai, B.R. (1998). *Rajaniti Arthashstra Ko Aankhi Jhyal Bata* (The Political Economy of Nepal), Kathmandu: Utprerak Prakashan.
Blaikie, M.P., Cameron, J., and Seddon, J.D. (1979, Revised 2000). *The Struggle for Basic Needs in Nepal,* New Delhi: Adroit Publishers.

Blaikie, P., Cameron, J., and Seddon, D. (1980, Revised 2001). *Nepal in Crisis: Growth and Stagnation at the Periphery*, New Delhi: Adroit Publishers.

Cameron, J. (1998). The agriculture perspective plan: The need for debate, *Himalayan Research Bulletin*, Volume XVIII, Number 2.

Carnegie Commission on Preventing Deadly Conflict (1997). *Preventing Deadly Conflict: Final Report*. Washington, DC.

CBS (1998). *Statistical Pocket Book*, Central Bureau of Statistics, Kathmandu, Nepal.

CPN (Maoist) (1995a) Strategy and tactics of armed struggle in Nepal, A document adopted by third plenum of the central committee of the CPN (Maoist) in March 1995, *The Worker*, No. 3, February 1997.

CPN-UML (2002). *CPN UML Statement on the Amendment of Constitution and Socio-economic Reform*, Kathmandu: CPN (UML).

Dahal, D.R. (2000). Nepal's governing elite: Their composition and role in constituting the state, in Kumar, D. (Ed.), *Domestic Conflict and Crisis of Governability in Nepal*, Kathmandu: CNAS Centre for Nepal and Asian Studies.

Dahal, G. (2002). Sushasan, Prashasan and Bikas, *The Himalaya Times*, February 5, 2000.

de Sales, A. (2000). The Kham Magar Country, Nepal: between ethnic claims and Maoism, *European Bulletin of Himalayan Reseach*, Vol. 19.

Dixit, K.M. (2002). Insurgents and innocents: The Nepali army's battle with the maobadi. *Himal South Asian*.

Dreze, J. and Sen, A. (1996). *India: Economic Development and Social Opportunity*. Oxford, Delhi.

Fisher, S., Abdi, D.I., Ludin, J., Smith, R. and Williams S., (2000). *Working with Conflict: Skills and Strategies for Action*. Zed Books, London.

Freire, P. (1996). *Pedagogy of the Oppressed*. Penguin Books, London.

Ghimire, S. (2000). Durgam chhetrako bikas, namama matra simit, *The Deshantar Weekly*, 9 January 2000.

Guevara, C. (1969). *Guerrilla Warfare: A Method*.

Gurung, H. (1998). *Nepal Social Demography and Expressions*, Kathmandu : New Era Books.

Harris, P. and Reilly, B. (eds.) (1998). *Democracy and Deep-Rooted Conflict: Options for Negotiations*. Institute for Democracy and Electoral Assistance, Stockholm.

Harvard School of Public Health (2001). *Conflict prevention initiative, Final report of the Web Conference*, Harvard School of Public Health, 25 January to 1 February 2001, www.preventconflict.org.

HMG/N (1990). *The Constitution of Nepal, 1990*, Kathmandu: HMG/N.

HMG/N, (1990). *The Himalayan Times*, 20 May 2002.

Hoftun, M. (2001). The 1990 Revolution. In M. Hutt (ed.), *Nepal in the Nineties: Versions of the Past, Visions of the Future*. New Delhi, Oxford India Paperbacks.

Hoftun, M., Raeper, W. and Whelpton, J. (1999). *People, Politics and Ideology: Democracy and Social Change in Nepal*. Kathmandu, Mandala Book Point.

IFAD (2001). *Rural poverty report 2001*, Oxford: IFAD.

References and Bibliography

INSEC (1997). *Human Rights Yearbook* (Nepali). Kathmandu.
INSEC (Informal Sector Service Centre) (1996). *Human Rights Yearbook* (Nepali). Kathmandu.
Karki, A. (2001). *The Politics of Poverty and Movements from Below in Nepal*, Ph.D. Thesis, University of East Anglia, School of Development Studies, UK.
Kattel, M.R. (2000). *Sociology of the 'People's War' in Nepal*. Unpublished MA Dissertation, Central Department of Sociology and Anthropology, TU, Kathmandu.
Koirala, P. (2000). Garibsanga Bishweshor Karyanwayan pakshya, *The Himalaya Times*, 11 February 2000.
Kumar, D. (2000). *What Ails Democracy in Nepal, Domestic Conflict and Governability in Nepal*, Kathmandu: CNAS Center for Nepal and Asian Studies.
Lawoti, M. (2000). The unresolved national (jatiya) question, *The Kathmandu Post*, 9 April 2000.
Lenin, V.I. (1962). *The Agrarian Program and Social Democracy in the First Revolution 1905–1907*, collected works, Vol. 13, Foreign Language Publishing House, Moscow. (Originally published 1908).
Maharjan, P.N. (2000). The Maoist insurgency and crisis of governability in Nepal. In D. Kumar (ed.), *Domestic Conflict and Crisis of Governability in Nepal*. Centre for Nepalese and Asian Studies (CNAS), Kathmandu, pp. 163–196.
Manab Adhikar Barsa Pustak (2000). *Nepal, China Southwest Bhada Samjhauta*.
Manandhar, P. (2001). *The Maoist Insurgency, Reform Agenda and Uncertainty*, CIDA, Nepal Programme Review 2001, Canada Cooperation Office, September 25, 2001.
Manav Adhikar *Year Book (2002)*.
Mao Tse Tung (1962). *Analysis of Classes in Chinese Society*, Foreign Language Press, Peking, China.
Mao Tse Tung (1966). *Selecting Military Writings of Mao Tse Tung*, Foreign Language Press, Peking, China.
Mikesell, S.L. (1999). *Class, State and Struggle in Nepal*, New Delhi: Manohar Publications and Distributions.
Mikesell, S.L. (1999). *Class, State and Struggle in Nepal*, New Delhi: Manohar Publications and Distributions.
Muller, J.E. (1988). Democracy, economic development and income inequality', *American Sociological Review*, Vol. 53, Issue 1, Feb.1991, pp. 50–68.
Nepal Election Commission (2056 BS). *House of Representative Election, 2056, Election Results*, Kathmandu: Nepal Election Commission.
Nepal Federation of Nationalities (2001). *Report of the three day Seminar on the World Indigenous People's Day*, organised by Nepal Federation of Nationalities from 7–9 August 2001 in Kathmandu.
Nepal Rastriya Buddhijivi Sangathan Kendriya Samiti (2054 BS, 1997). *Nepalma Janayuddha* (The People's War in Nepal), Nepal Rastroya Budhijivi Sangathan Kendrya Samiti, Kathmandu.

Nepali Congress Party (2002). *A task force report on amendment on the constitution of Nepal 1990,* Kathmandu: Nepali Congress.

Neupane, G. (1999) *Explanation of Social Development: Overview and Analysis of Social Development of Nepal,* Centre for Development Studies, Kathmandu, Nepal.

Neupane, G. (2001) *Transformation of Nepali Society: Background, Environment and Conspiracy,* Centre for Development Studies, Kathmandu, Nepal.

Neupane, G. (2001). *Nepali Shamajko Rupantaran: Pristhabhumi, Paribesh Ra Biuharachana* (Nepal's Societal Transformation: Background, Situation & Strategies). Centre for Development Studies, Kathmandu.

Neupane, G. (2001). *Nepali Shamajko Rupantaran: Pristhabhumi, Paribesh Ra Biuharachana* (Nepal's Societal Transformation: Background, Situation & Strategies, Kathmandu: Centre for Development Studies.

Neupane, T. (2000). Four years of People's War in Nepal (Nepali). *Mahima,* Vernacular Nepali Weekly, February 17, 2000.

Neupane, T. (2000). Four years of people's war in Nepal, *The Mahima,* Vernacular Nepali Weekly, 17 February 2000.

Neupane, T. NPC (2058 BS). *Concept Paper, Tenth Five Year Plan,* Kathmandu: HMG/N.

Nickson, A. (1992). Democratisation and the growth of communism in Nepal: A Preruvian scenario in the making. *Journal of Commonwealth and Comparative Politics,* Vol. 30, No. 3.

NINO (Nepal National Intellectual's Organisation) (ed.) (1997). *Nepalma Janayudha (People's War in Nepal).* Kathmandu. See Nepal Rastriya Buddhijivi...

Onesto, L. (2000). Dispatches: Report from the People's War in Nepal, *Revolutionary Worker,* no. 1014-1036. www.mcs.net/-rwor

Pandey, D.R. (1995). Combating corruption: A nepali perspective, *Paper Presented at the Conference Organised by Transparency International* Milan, Italy, 27–28 March 1995.

Pandey, D.R. (1999). *Nepal's Failed Development: Reflections on the Mission and the Maladies,* Kathmandu: Nepal South Asia Centre.

Philipson, L. (2002). *Conflict in Nepal: Perspectives on the Maoist Movement,* May 2002, A report prepared for the DFID, Kathmandu, Nepal.

Porta , D., Diani, M. (1999). *Social Movements: An Introduction,* Oxford: Blackwell.

Prachanda (1998). Two momentus years of revolutionary transformation, *The Worker,* Vol. 4, No. 4, Kathmandu: CPN (Maoist).

Prachanda (2000). *Problems of the Nepali Revolution, Part 2,* Central Publications Department, Nepal Communist Party (Marxist), Nepal.

Prachanda (2000). Red flag flying on the roof of the world inside the revolution in Nepal, *Revolutionary Worker,* 1043, 20 February 2000 (republished in this collection).

PRO PUBLIC (2000). Dar Nabhayeko Byaktiko Bhar Hunna: Sthai Karmachari Badhi Bhrasta (One cannot rely on a person who has no fear: Permanent employees more corrupt), *Good Governance,* Vol. 3, No. 1, July 2000.

References and Bibliography 481

Rana, M.S.J.B. (2002). *National Security and 10th Plan's Irrelevance*, Institute of Development Studies.
Rastriya Prajatantra Party-RPP (2002). *RPP's Proposal on Amendment of the Constitution of Nepal*, Kathmandu: RPP.
Rawal, B. (1991, 2nd ed.). *Nepalma Samyabadi Andolan: Uddhav Ra Bikash* (Nepali) (The Communist Movement in Nepal: Origin and Development). Pairabi Prakashan, Katmandu.
Regmi, M.C. (1999). *A Study in Nepali History 1768–1846*, Adroit Publishers, Delhi.
Regmi, S. (1999). Garibi nibaran garna nasakine samasys hoina, *The Samachar Patra*, 17 August 1999.
Scott, J.C. (1985). *Weapons of the Weak: Everyday Forms of Peasant Resistance*, New Haven: Yale University Press.
Seddon, D. (1993, 2nd ed.) *Nepal—A State of Poverty*. Vikas Press, New Delhi.
Seddon, D. (2001). Democracy and development in Nepal. In M. Hutt (ed.), *Nepal in the Nineties*. Oxford India Paperbacks, New Delhi.
Sharma, U. (1999). *Caste*, Open University Press: Buckingham & Philadelphia.
Subedi, S. (2002). *The Gorkhapatra*, 30 April 2002.
Thapa, D. (2002). The Maobadi of Nepal. In K.M. Dixit and S. Ramachandaran, (eds.) *State of Nepal*. Himal Books, Kathmandu.
The Constitution of Nepal (1990). Kathmandu: HMG/N, Ministry of Law, Justice and Parliamentary Affairs.
Tiwari, (1999). A note on Maoist People's War in Nepal, *Spotlight*, Vol. 18., No. 29, 19 February 1999.
Upadhya, N.P. (2002). Good governance: Indispensable for development, *The Rising Nepal*, 14 April 2002.
Uprety, P.R. (1992). *Political Awakening in Nepal: The Search for a New Identity*. Commonwealth Publisher, New Delhi.
Vargas, V. (1997). The women's movement in Peru: The early years, in Wieringa, S. (Ed.), *Subversive Women: Women's Movements in Africa, Asia, Latin America and the Caribbean*, New Delhi: Kali for Women.
Verma, A.S. (2001). *Maoist Movement in Nepal* (Nepali). Samakaleen Tisri Duniya, Noida.
Zaman, Z.A. (1973). *Evaluation of Land Reform in Nepal*, Ministry of Land Reforms, His Majesty Government of Nepal, Kathmandu, Nepal.
Zartman, I.W. (1995). Dynamics and constraints in negotiations in internal conflicts. In I.W. Zartman (ed.), *Elusive Peace Negotiating an End to Civil Wars*. The Brookings Institution, Washington.

Journals/News Papers

Deshantar, Vernacular Weekly, 13 July 1997, 19 August 1998, 27 September 1998.
Gorkhapatra, Vernacular Daily, 17 June 2000.
Himal South Asia, Bimonthly, 16 July 2000.
Himalaya Times, 13 February 1998, 16 June 2000.
Janadesh, Vernacular Weekly, 2 May 2000.

Kantipur, Vernacular Daily, 17 August 1999, 3 May 2000, 21 June 2000, 2 August 2000.
The Kantipur, 17 May 2001.
The Kantipur, 8 November 2001.
The Rising Nepal, 18 April 2002.
Mulprabaha, Vernacular Monthly, February 2000, Year 1, Issue 3.
The Worker, Vol. 3, February 1997.
The Revolutionary Worker #1043, 20 February 2000 (http://www.mcs.net/~rwor/a/v21/1040-049/1043/interv.htm).
Samakalin, Vernacular Weekly, 22 May 1997.
Sandhya Times, Vernacular Daily, 31 March 1998.

Web sites and e-mail sites

http://web.amnesty.org/ainsf/countries/
Nepalwatch@yahoogroups.com
www.mcs.net/~rwor/a/v21/1040-049/1043/interv.html
www.satp.org/satporgtp/countries/nepal/docment/papers/nepalese_communist.html
www.satp.org/satporgtp/countries/nepal/terroristoutfits/ndex.html

Index

Achham 451
Adhikari, Man Mohan 9
Adhiya 297, 311
adventuristic 87
agrarian economy 52, 140
Agrarian Reform Commission 464
agrarian reforms 462
agrarian relationships 53
agrarian revolution 53
Agricultural Development Bank 464, 467
Agricultural Perspective Plan (APP) 457
agricultural workers 440
Al Qaida 36
All Nepal Trade Labour Organization 92
All Nepal Women's Association (ANWA) 32, 62, 378, 380-382, 393
(Revolutionary) 170, 386
alliances 53
Ama samuha 433
Ama-Milan-Kendra 178
American Embassy 242
anarchism 434
Andhra Pradesh 89

annihilation 67
anti-terrorist legislation 25
area secretary 98
armed movement 432
armed peasants 406
Armed Police Forces 356
armed rebellion 258
armed struggle 18, 81, 407, 412, 414
  genesis of 406
  impact of, 429
army actions 431
Asian Development Bank 130, 457, 471
assassination 315
Association of District Development Committees (ADDC) 460, 465
Australia 121
Austric peoples 200
autocratic monarchy 171
autocratic panchayat system 455
autocratic state 412

Bahudaliya Janabadi 196
Balanced Development 157
bandh 26, 39, 95
Bangladesh 88, 278

Banke 153
Base Area 26, 307
Bertil Lintner 286
beth-begari 297
Bhaktapur 150, 153
Bharatiya Janata Party 369
Bhattarai, Babu Ram 13, 15, 17, 21, 28, 34, 278, 316, 325, 447
Bhattarai, K.P. 27
Bhichha, Satya Dharma 4
Bihar 89
Bijukchhe, Narayan Man 16
Birendra 36
Birta 310
   system 295
Bolsheviks 164
bomb explosions 406
bourgeois system 327, 412
bread and butter 442
Brest Litovsk Treaty 266
Britain 120
British colonialism 122, 316
British government 44
British imperialism 317, 318
British ministers 44
bureaucracy 442
bureaucratic 321
   capitalists 22, 76, 138, 142, 159

Cambodia, collapse of 418
Canada 121
capitalism 119
   transitional 164
capitalist 392
   class 144
   relations 137
caste 318
   system 453
ceasefire 37, 50, 55-56
Chand, Lokendra Bahadur 25, 412
charity 428
Chaudhary, Dilip 185

chauvinistic 83
Chepang 296
Chief District Officer (CDO) 21, 45, 460
China 12, 230, 248, 291, 310, 346-347, 352
Chinese Communist Party 420
Chinese cultural revolution 79, 305
Chinese model of revolution 420
Chinese revisionism 12
Chitwan 153
citizen's rights 419
civil rights 418
Civil Rights Movement 379
civil society 433
civil war 279
class analysis 291, 421, 422
class context 309
class exploitation 398
class movement 401
class relations 120, 129
class slavery 377
class structure, lack of clarity 310
class struggle 81, 109, 389, 398, 422-423
Cold War 143
Commission for the Investigation of Abuse of Authority (CIAA) 446-447, 456
Communist 12-13
   concept of 432
   manifesto 6
   movement 77, 320, 426
   welfare 397
Communist Party of Nepal (CPN) 9, 13, 16-17, 201, 320, 380, 405, 420
   Fourth Congress 12, 13, 15, 351
   Third Congress 10

Communist Party of Nepal
    (Maoist) 18, 21-22, 28, 50,
    76, 89, 117, 119, 180-181, 183,
    187, 192, 208, 227, 240, 256,
    279, 283, 306, 312, 323, 340,
    346, 351, 389, 407, 415, 426,
    440
Communitst Party of Nepal
    (Marxist) 15-16
    approach of, 413
Communitst Party of Nepal
    (Marxist–Leninist or ML)
    11, 15, 25, 316, 322, 324, 329,
    346-347, 359, 360, 372, 390,
    418
Communitst Party of Nepal
    (Masal) 13, 15, 170
Communitst Party of Nepal
    (Mashal) 13, 15, 208, 325,
    329, 331, 333-335, 342, 346-
    348, 362, 390
Communist Party of Nepal
    (MLM) 16, 77, 79-80, 85-87,
    96, 115, 118, 180, 182, 192, 194,
    197, 210, 228, 247, 270
Communitst Party of Nepal
    (UML) 15-16, 20, 25, 31, 33,
    67, 170, 208, 216, 225, 245,
    253, 298, 316, 332, 339, 361,
    378, 381, 385, 386, 390, 407,
    410-412, 421, 423-424, 443,
    456, 468, 473
Communist Party of Nepal
    (UMLM) 196
Communist Party of Peru (PCP)
    84, 88, 262
comprador 146, 147
Confederation of Communist
    and Maoist Parties of South
    Asia (CCOMPOSA) 32
confiscation of property 75
Conflict Resolution in Nepal
    438
conflict transformation 55

congressisation 434
constituent assembly 30, 33
Constitution of *1991* 408
Constitution of the Kingdom
    436
constitutional monarchy 10
Continuous Revolution 164
corruption 64, 143, 462
CPI 369
CPM 369
crisis and the need for resolution
    433
Cuban State 49
cultural revolution 113, 433
    in China 100

dacoits 431
Dahal, Pushpa Kamal 13
Dailekh 32, 35
dalit 219, 221-222, 388, 424, 440,
    445, 452, 454, 462
Dang 37
Das, Krishna 16
decentralisation 54, 462
decimation 57
Defense Committee 215
Delhi treaty 319
democracy 3, 190, 244, 318, 322,
    410, 412
    intermittent 51
democratic 384, 413, 432
Democratic Party of Nepal 410
democratic political movement
    414
democratic State 51
despotism 51
destruction 57
Deuba, Sher Bahadur 21, 55, 282,
    365, 367, 370, 407
Devi, Kamakchya 379
Dhading 35
Dhami Commission 25
Dhanusha 184
Dhungana, Daman Nath 33

Dhungana, Punya Prabha Devi 381
Dhungel, Ramesh 427
dialectical process 163
dialectical relationship 120
dialectics 364
dialogue 56
dictatorial communism 432
dictatorship 51, 249-250, 323, 412
Dildas, Gyan 4
discrimination 375, 376
disinformation 429
displacement 62
district committee secretary 98
District Development Committee 392, 460-461
Dolakha 35
Dolpa 307, 356-357, 430
Dracula 425
Dutta, Bhim 406

economic insecurity 55
Ekata Kendra 15
Election Commission 445
election tickets 446
electoral malpractices 462
emancipation 87, 377-378
employment 52, 380
encounter killing 57
enemies 50, 59, 422
equal work 398
equality 377-378
   of rights 398
   to Women 469
ethnic minorities and dalits 469
expansionism 144, 151, 374
exploitation 55, 77, 123, 375, 380, 395
exploiters 292

failed development 19
farmers 296
fascist government 65

female education 380
Fernandese, George 373
feudal 83, 321
   exploitation 109
   mode of production 150
   monarchy 169
   ruling class 317
   society 141
   structure 139
feudalism 102, 108, 319, 327
   and imperialism 191
feudalistic landlord 291
food 437
foreign capital 184
foreign debt 122
France 120
free market 141
freedom 377
fundamental rights 358

Gandaki 127
Geneva Convention 41, 394
Germany 120, 126
Ghorahi 37
gift 418
globalisation 139
Gonzalo 89
   thought 346
Gorkha 22, 35, 83, 93, 184, 204, 405
Gorkhali regime 4
Grasp revolution 155
Great Proletarian Cultural Revolution (GPCR) 218
Greece 346
Green Revolution 139
groupism 434
guerrilla 391, 395, 426
   fighters 393
   platoon 104
   squad 104
   war 19, 49, 78, 192, 210, 229, 253
   zone 23, 103-104, 106-107,

203, 205, 212, 229, 233, 248, 430
Gulmi 32, 35
gun law 419
Gurung, Dev 207
Guthi 310

Haliya 296
Haruwa 137
hegemony 121, 126, 141, 144, 377
hidden alliance 315, 321
Hindu kingdom 444
Hinduism 188
HMG/N 446, 451
    Tenth Five Year Plan of 459
human rights 20-21, 45, 56, 244, 418, 425, 441
Human Rights Commission 446, 456
hypocrite 349

ideological struggle 423
ILO 400
imperialism 76, 80, 120-121, 140, 142-143, 144, 148, 151, 190, 319, 327
imperialist-serving state 50
India 278, 346
Indian Army 105
Indian capitalists 127
Indian Congress 369
Indian expansionism 122, 128, 316
Indian National Army (INA) 7
Indo–Nepal treaty 319
industrialisation 145
inequality 145, 304, 376
INGO 149, 170, 184
INSEC 20
Integrated Internal Security and Development Development Programme (IISDP) 37
intellectualism 91
International Communist Movement 346
International Monetary Fund (IMF) 121, 303, 471
Iran 88
Irish Revolutionary Army 425
Italy 121

Jajarkot 22, 24, 31, 35, 50, 91, 101, 105, 184, 204, 307, 441, 451
jana andolan 14, 407
jana jati 66
Japan 120, 126
Jha, Prativa 381
Jhapa 10
    Bidroha 304
    Movement 11, 15, 408
Jhara 297
Joshi, Govinda Raj 29, 356
Juddha Shamsher Rana 378
Judicial Council 468
judicial issues 462
judiciary 454
Jumla-Kalikot 35
Junkers 291
justice 4

Kabre 93
Kalikot 91, 307
Kalikot-Accham-Bajura 35
Kamaiya 53, 137, 296, 457, 461, 463
Kapilvastu 206
Karki 20
Karnali 153, 200
Karnali Regional Liberation Front 28
Kaski 153
Kathmandu 13, 91-92, 101, 106, 150, 153, 243, 278, 330, 379, 432, 451
Kathmandu valley 150, 235
Kavre 184
Khas 188, 454

khukuri 425
kidnapping 400
killing 57
Kilo Sierra II 24-25, 253, 392, 395
King Birendra 12, 408
King Gyanandra 32, 359-360
King Mahendra 9, 11, 448
King Tribhuvan 7, 319
kingship 250
    evolution of 249
Kipat 310
Kipat system 295
Kirat front 29
Koirala, B.P. 7-8
Koirala, G.P. 24-25, 27, 243-244, 252, 254, 284, 361, 371, 447
Koirala, Krishna Prasad 379
Koirala, M.P. 6
Koshi Regional Committee 10
Kosi 127
Kumari, Asta 379
Kumari, Chun 391
Kut 297, 310

Labour Day 382
labour movement 299
labour relations 137, 297
Lal, Pushpa 11
Lalitpur 150, 153
Lama, Nirmal 11, 15-17, 349
Lamjung 32, 35, 206, 394
land distribution 131
land reform 52-53, 139
Land Reform Act 1964 292, 449
land to the tiller 52-53, 158, 169, 436
landlords 75, 91, 101, 134, 293, 295
latent conflict 55
Left Front 15
left parties 57
Left Unity 56

leftist 364, 374, 377, 384, 388
legal 399
legislature 454
Lenin 169, 223, 292, 346, 417
leninism 347, 418
liberalisation 139, 143, 188
liberation movement 405
liberation war 255
Limbus 7
Limbuwan 28
litmus test 255
livelihoods 186, 189
Local Development Officer (LDO) 45
local resistance 67
London Meeting 46
lucrative 446

Madheshi Liberation Front 28
Mafia 389
magarant 28
Magars 19
Mahakali River Integrated Development Project Treaty (MRIDPT) 128, 208
Maharajgunj 354
Majhi National Liberation Front 28
Ma–Le 11-12, 14
Mallik Commission 459
Mandale 410
Mao Tse tung 171, 175, 193, 238, 239, 275, 291, 346-347, 359, 419
    cultural revolution 390
Maoism 10, 97
Maoist 30, 376, 315
    insurgency 448
    leadership 26
    problem 55
    strongholds 52
Maoist attack, victims of 65
Maoist Communist Centre (MCC) 88

Maoist movement 26, 304, 314, 379, 388, 405
  character of 425
  its impact 405
Maoist Party 51, 406, 413, 426, 429
  concepts of 417
marginalisation 19
Maruti–Suzuki (automobiles) 126
Marx, Karl 78, 96, 117, 250
Marxism 97, 377, 418, 420
mass demonstrations 85
mass movement 11
Mass Organisation 170
mass struggle 107
massacre 315-316
Mazumdar, Charu 10, 351
Mehta, Ashok 286
middle classes 295
migration 62
Mikesell 439
Military Commission 23
mobile court 54
modern imperialist 167
monarchy 78, 316, 322, 327, 363
Mukti Sena 6
Muller, Max 304
multinational companies 120, 143
  Bata (shoes) 126
  Brook Bond (tea) 126
  Hero–Honda (motorcycle) 126
  Hindustan Lever (soap) 126
  Hoecht (medicine) 126
  Nestle (coffee, milk products etc.) 126
  Proctor and Gamble (soap, chocolate etc.) 126
multi-party democracy 51
multiparty political system 323, 408
multipartyism 9, 408

Municipalities and Village Development Committees 460
Munims 311

Nari Jagriti 379
Nari Samitee 378
National Anthem 444
National Dalit Commission 456, 473
National Democratic Party 443
National Human Rights Commission (NHRC) 41, 473
National Liberation Front 28
national minorities 469
National People's Movement 14
national surrender 317
nationality 110, 150, 318
National Women's Commission 456, 473
Naxalite movement 79
Nehru, Jawaharlal 8
Nepal 346
  Civil Code of 453
  Constitution of 1990 456
Nepal Human Rights Commission 473
Nepal Janabadi Morcha 13
Nepal Sadbhavana Party 53, 376, 407, 422
Nepal Women's Association 385
Nepal, Madhav Kumar 33, 339, 361
Nepalese Communist movement 224, 408, 417
Nepalese revisionism 224
Nepalese society 55, 273, 295, 404, 413, 419, 420
Nepalese State 50
Nepali Congress Party 6-7, 14, 16-17, 19, 21, 53, 68, 196, 216, 224-225, 243, 253, 319, 323, 325, 328, 352, 365-366, 370,

374, 376, 389-390, 405, 410-411, 414, 417, 434, 443, 447, 459, 468
Nepali people 448
Nepali Revolution 418-420
Nepali security organs 388
Nepali Times 24
Nepali women 383, 404
New Delhi 8, 23
New Democracy 224
New Democratic Revolution 118, 154, 169, 182, 220, 223, 246, 328
New Democratic state 22, 181
New Democratic System 419
Newa Khala 28
NGOs 149, 170, 173, 184, 384, 390, 403
non-Hindus 469
non-Marxist–Leninist 348
non-revolutionary 316
non-violence 57
Northern Ireland 40
nouveaux riches 152
Nuwakot-Rasuwa 32, 35

October Revolution 417
Oli, K.P. 67
oligarchy 51
Operation Kilo Sierra 2 23-24
Operation Romeo 23-24, 202, 392, 395
opportunism, extreme 316
oppressed nationalities 110
oppression 55, 378

Palace Massacre 364
Palestine Liberation Organization 425
Palpa 35
pancha 422
Panchayat autocracy 410
Panchayat System 14, 323, 438
para-military 30

Parbat 35
Parliament 86, 446
parliamentary democracy 407
parliamentary norms 244
parliamentary system 316, 327, 408, 468
parma 448
Parsa 153
patriarchal 166
patrifocal 166
patrilineal 166
patriotic stand 315
Paudel, Vishnu 339
peaceful struggle 86
peasant 101, 102, 189, 440
people's actions 431
People's Army 89, 104, 220, 264
People's Courts 41, 52, 54
people's culture 399
people's government 395
People's Liberation Army 104, 105
People's militia 394
People's movement 323, 407-408, 456
people's power 106
people's revolution 325, 327
people's rights 318
People's War 18, 20, 22, 24, 26, 31, 38, 49, 51, 55, 57, 77, 80, 84, 88, 90, 94, 105, 107, 109, 115-118, 165, 196, 202, 204, 207, 216, 221, 224, 231, 237, 263, 306-307, 310, 321, 342, 358, 368, 373, 325, 389, 393, 396, 407, 412, 424, 426, 440, 444
People's War Group 369
Peoples' Movement 408
Peru 84, 89
petty bourgeois 86, 92, 155
Philippines 84
physical actions 50
Pillage 64

Planned Development 156
Pokhara 13, 432
Polit Bureau 204, 207
politbureau members 86
political 379, 420
 economy 118
 forces in Nepali society 421
 grievances 442
 interference 467
 liberalism 315, 321-323
 movements 405
 oppression 168
 struggle 109
 survival 318
politicisation 434
politics, criminalisation of 442
polygamy 380
poor peasants 132, 166
popular uprisings 3
Poudel, Ram Chandra 29
poverty 19, 51, 55
 alleviation 450
 line 84
Poverty Reduction Strategy Paper (PRSP) 470
power centre 470
Prachanda 16, 27, 33, 38, 211, 257, 259-260, 281, 331, 336, 352, 369, 371, 373, 405, 427
 path 30-31, 259, 276, 337-339, 349, 418, 427
 thought 337
Pradhan, Bhuwanlal 379
Pradhan, Sahana 16
Praja Parishad 5, 405
Prioritised Productivity Package (PPP) 458
privatisation 188
pro-Congress 316
production relations 118, 129
pro-Indian communal party 422
pro-king 349
 political line 315-316

proletarian 92, 114
 revolution 76, 115, 327
proletarians 92
Propaganda Zones 205
public administration 454
Public Security Regulations 33
Public Service Commission 466, 467
Pyuthan 307

radical agenda 52
radical programmes 69
Rai, Ram Prasad 406
Raikar 310
Ram Mandir 369
Ramechap 32, 35, 184, 206
rampant poverty 140
Ramtel, Dil Bahadur 57
Rana 319, 378, 379
Rana autocracy 438
Rana family 51
Rana regime 7
Rana, Chandra Shamsher 378
Rana, Jung Bahadur 4
Rastriya Prajatantra Party (RPP) 17, 53, 196, 216, 225, 376, 407, 422, 468, 473
Rayamaji, Keshar Jung 9
reactionary 119
 classes 129
 influence 431
 organisation 386
 State 22, 190
rebellion 3
Red Army 230
reform 85
Regional Inequality 150
regular courts 54
Remote Area Development Committee 451
remote districts 452
revisionism 114
revisionist group 77
revolt 3, 4, 30

revolution 8, 75, 82, 310, 378, 387
counter 346
revolutionary 19, 77, 85, 87, 119, 155, 436
Revolutionary Communist Party (RCP) 262
Revolutionary Internationalist Movement (RIM) 18, 88, 90, 115, 192, 262, 347
Revolutionary Land Reforms 158
revolutionary
line 113
movement 169
transformation 154, 163
trends 170
worker 27, 77
Right Opportunist Line (ROL) 268
Rokka, Chin Bahadur 423
Rokka, Nimalal 395
Rolpa 19-22, 24, 35, 50, 83, 91, 93, 101, 105-106, 172, 184, 204, 206-207, 218, 307, 360, 391, 394, 411, 441, 451
Royal Army 30
royal coup 9, 10
Royal Family 31
Royal Nepal Airlines Corporation (RNAC) 467
Royal Nepal Army (RNA) 29, 40, 279, 388
Royal Palace 315, 352
Royal Palace massacre 315, 319
Royal Proclamation 9
royalists 327
Rukum 19, 21-22, 24, 27, 31, 35, 50, 76, 83, 91, 93, 101, 105-106, 184, 204, 206, 218, 307, 411, 423, 441, 451
ruling class 140, 317-318
rural agents 98
rural areas of Nepali society 422

rural economy 311
rural industrialisation and employment 463
rural poverty 144
Russia 121, 349

Salyan 22, 31, 35, 91, 101, 105, 307, 393
Samyukta Rastriya Janaandolan 14
Sankhuwasabha 35
satyagraha 13
search march 429
Second National Conference 31, 272
Security Expenses 63
seed beds 449
semi-colonial 80, 122, 154
semi-colonial treaty 124
semi-feudal 22, 119, 138, 142
relations 139
sex 377
sexual exploitation 400
sexual harassment 61, 177
Shah dynasty 317-318, 325
Shah, Rishikesh 362
Shaha, Maya Devi 381
Sharma, Dinesh 29
Sharma, Sita Devi 380
Shrestha, Rabindra 29
Sihanuk 322, 324, 355
Sija campaign 20
Sindhuli 22, 35, 93, 184, 206
Sindhuphalchowk 35, 184
Singh, K.I. 406
Singh, Mangala Devi 379, 381
Singh, Mohan Bikram 11-13, 15, 17, 79, 113, 246, 329, 331, 334, 347-348, 351, 406
Singh, Ram Raja Prasad 406
Siraha 14
slavery 378
social discrimination 51
social ills 53

social justice 3, 55
social oppression 167
social revolution 117
social security 437
social violence 52
social–ethnic discrimination 462
socialist 401
socialist transformation 155
socio-economic reforms 462
sovereignty 318
Soviet Union, fall of 418
Sri Lanka 88, 278, 346
Stalin 251, 346-347
State of Emergency 37, 44, 50, 56
strategic defence 26, 415
strategic offence 415
strategic stalemate 415
struggle 55, 80, 378
study technique 423
Sugauli Treaty 122-124, 317, 318
Supreme Court 446
Suwal, Prayagraj Singh 12

Taliban 36
Tamuwan 28
Tanahun 35
technical education 400
Teej 382
Terai 95, 127, 136, 144, 147, 150-152, 295, 406, 450, 461
Terai National Liberation Front 95
Terathum 35
terrorism 225, 241
Terrorist and Disruptive Activities Ordinance (TADO) 37
terrorists 50-51, 64, 279, 426
Thabang 83
Thakali, Romi Gauchan 445
Thakurani, Dwarika Devi 381
Thalu 439
Thami Liberation Front 28

Thapa, Bhuvan 185
Thapa, Lakhan 4, 405
Thapa, Surya Bahadur 24, 412
Tharu National Liberation Front 28, 95
Thekka 310-311
third world 142
thugs 59
Thulo Manchhe 439
Tibet 8
tourism industry 389
traditional 433
traditional monarchy 352
trafficking 400
tragically 444
transparency 440
Trotskyite 347-348, 360
Tuladhar, Padma Ratna 33
Turkey 84, 88, 346

Udayapur 14
UFPN 21
UK 126
ultra leftist 87, 316
ultra-leftism 181, 196
ultra-leftist political ideology 426
unemployment 51
United Front 308, 327
United Left Front 14, 459
United Nations 397
United People's Front of Nepal (UPFN) 15-17, 19, 183
United Revolutionary People's Council (URPC) 28, 279
Unity Centre 13, 16-17, 19, 170, 201, 208, 339-340, 390
unlawful killings 41
untouchability 168, 376
upper class 143
urban poor 294
USA 120, 126, 130

Vaidya, Niranjan Govinda 17

Village Development Committee (VDC) 97, 172, 392
violence 50

water resources 127
white tyranny 410, 423
women
    community 401-402
    condition of 383
    development of 401
    emancipation of 397, 401
    empowerment of 398, 400-401
    guerrillas 52
    mobilisation of 52-53
    movement of 378, 383, 386, 398-399, 401-404
    participation of 165, 402
    rights of 398
Working Class 141, 144, 312
World Bank 121, 471
world imperialism 126
World War, second 114, 275, 344

Yadav, Ram Brikshya 206
Yog Maya 4